MEDIA,
AUDIENCE,
AND
SOCIAL
STRUCTURE

CONTRIBUTORS

JEFFREY C. ALEXANDER

JAMES R. BENIGER

VICTORIA BILLINGS

JOEL M. CANTOR

ITHIEL de SOLA POOL

DON A. DILLMAN

PHYLLIS ENDRENY

EDWARD L. FINK

HERMAN GRAY

JOEL W. GRUBE

PETER L. HIRSCHBURG

ROBERT KAPSIS

PHILIP LAMY

GLADYS ENGEL LANG

KURT LANG

JACK LEVIN

THELMA McCORMACK

KATHRYN MONTGOMERY

W. RUSSELL NEUMAN

JAMES J. PARKER

DENISE H. PAZ

ANDREA L. PRESS

MELISSA RAPP

JOHN P. ROBINSON

MILTON ROKEACH

KARL ERIK ROSENGREN

MICHAEL SCHUDSON

JOHN L. SEWART

ELEANOR SINGER

YASEMIN SOYSAL

ANN SWIDLER

D. GARTH TAYLOR

RALPH H. TURNER

CHARLES R. WRIGHT

MEDIA, AUDIENCE, AND SOCIAL STRUCTURE

edited by

Sandra J. Ball-Rokeach
Muriel G. Cantor

SAGE PUBLICATIONS
The Publishers of Professional Social Science
Newbury Park Beverly Hills   London   New Delhi

For information address:

SAGE Publications, Inc.
275 South Beverly Drive
Beverly Hills, California 90212

SAGE Publications Inc.
2111 West Hillcrest Drive
Newbury Park
California 91320

SAGE Publications Ltd.
28 Banner Street
London EC1Y 8QE
England

SAGE PUBLICATIONS India Pvt. Ltd.
M-32 Market
Greater Kailash I
New Delhi 110 048 India

Printed in the United States of America

Library of Congress Cataloging-in-Publication Data

Main entry under title:

Media, audience, and social structure.

   Bibliography: p.
   Includes index.
     1. Communication—Social aspects—United States—
Congresses. 2. Mass media—United States—Congresses.
I. Ball-Rokeach, Sandra. II. Cantor, Muriel G.
HM258.M372   1986   302.2   85-27871
ISBN 0-8039-2581-6
ISBN 0-8039-2582-4 (pbk.)

FIRST PRINTING

mhh
6-29-89

CONTENTS

Dedicated to Mendel and Joel
and to our parents

ACKNOWLEDGMENTS

WE WOULD LIKE to express appreciation for the good work of the organizers of the sessions held at the 1984 meetings of the American Sociological Association, from which we have selected many of the papers for this volume. All of the sessions from which papers were selected for this book, including those involving the coeditors, are listed below. All of these papers have been revised for publication herein.

- J. Michael Armer, Organizer and Presider, Social Change/Technology session (paper by James R. Beniger)
- S. J. Ball-Rokeach, Organizer and Presider, Thematic session, Media Linkages of the Social Fabric (papers by Karl Erik Rosengren and Jeffery Alexander)
- Muriel G. Cantor, Organizer and Presider, The Production of Popular Culture session 1 (papers by Robert Kapsis, John L. Sewart, Herman Gray, and Philip Lamy and Jack Levin)
- Lynda M. Glennon, Presider, and Muriel G. Cantor, Organizer, The Sociology of Popular Culture session 2 (papers by John P. Robinson and Edward L. Fink, James J. Parker, and Victoria Billings)
- Gerald Marwell, Organizer, Section on Collective Behavior and Social Movements Roundtable (paper by Peter L. Hirschburg, Don A. Dillman, and S. J. Ball-Rokeach)
- Eleanor Singer, Organizer and Presider, Mass Media session (paper by W. Russell Neuman and Ithiel de Sola Pool)
- Charles R. Wright, Do the Media Matter? New Contributions from Social Psychology, session for the Section on Social Psychology (papers by Ralph H. Turner and Denise Heller Paz, S. J. Ball-Rokeach, Milton Rokeach, Joel W. Grube, and Gladys Engel Lang and Kurt Lang)
- James Wright, Organizer and Presider, Public Opinion session (paper by D. Garth Taylor)
- Barbara Rosenblum, Organizer, Sociology of Art, session 1 (paper by Ann Swidler) and session 2 (paper by Andrea Press)

Monica Seff has been enormously helpful and good-humored in the tedious process of reference verification, as have Meryl Anne Klein, Adam Schaffer, and Joan Kraft in proofing and indexing. Rita Koontz and Susan Miller of the Social Research Center at Washington State University have been a constant help in the many clerical details involved in putting this work together. The students enrolled in Ball-Rokeach's spring 1984 seminar, Media Systems and Effects, critiqued several of the papers and provided insightful suggestions for revision.

INTRODUCTION
The Media and the Social Fabric

THE CHAPTERS IN THIS VOLUME, most of which have never been published elsewhere, are among the best examples of recent sociological work on the mass media. Taken as a whole, they show that the study of mass media and mass communications thrives and is an important contributor to social science research. Not only has the drastic famine in American mass communications research ended (see Gans, 1972), but the field has broadened in scope since the 1930s and 1940s. Then research focused on only the content or the audience, ignoring the broader theoretical questions such as how media contribute to social integration and social change and how content is created and controlled both in the United States and in other parts of the world. This book shows that in the past few decades steady progress has been made toward developing an integrated sociology of mass communication. Several kinds of essays are thereby provided: one set to illustrate the complex relationships that can exist among the political, cultural, and economic contexts in which content is produced and distributed; another examining the role of audiences as part of the larger media system; and still another that examines not only how people depend upon and use the media to obtain information and entertainment, but also how audiences are both affected by and find meaning in media content. Although varying in methodological and theoretical orientation, all the researchers and scholars in the pages that follow adhere to the sociological perspective (see the chapter by Michael Schudson in this volume).

This introductory essay presents our framework as background for the articles provided in the collection. By *mass media* we mean a system that is constituted by the configuration of organizations and institutions producing and distributing cultural products that are theoretically available to entire populations in given societies at approximately the same time. We also mean a system that is embedded in the rest of society in such a way that it both affects and is affected by the political, economic, and all the other social systems that constitute a society. The mass media system, with its special information and communication resources, is embedded in virtually every corner of societal life, whether it be conflict, change, control, or social integration.

Mass here means that the audience of consumers of cultural products is relatively large and undifferentiated by both occupation and class. In other words, the audience desired is demographically heterogeneous. Being "mass," it is conceptualized as also anonymous to the communicators and, often, to each other. The members of the audience share dependencies upon the resources of the media system for informational and symbolic products that they need to attain personal goals, such as social and self-understanding, orientation to effective action and interaction, or solitary and social play.

The media studied in this book include television, radio, film, the live theater, and print, especially newspapers and magazines. Although the distribution of mass media in the twentieth century has been changed radically by advances in technology, technology alone does not define mass from more individual or personalized media. For example, telephone calls, home movies, and home video are available because of advances in technology, but receivers (audience) are addressed as individuals or as specific constellations of relatively small numbers of people who share tastes, interests, or personal goals. The mass media differ from other kinds of media in other important ways as well; mass media content is typically produced in complex organizational settings. Moreover, their contents are not only produced differently from other forms of symbolic content (textbooks, for example), but they are transmitted to and received differently by audiences.

Mass communications refers to the interactive processes and structures through which content is not only produced, but also transmitted and received. The study of these processes and structures forms the foundation for a social science of the mass media. Our definition of mass communication is broader than that presented in most texts because media production and transmission are included along with audience feedback, pressure group activity, and even the larger social context. Mass communication therefore includes complex relations among large sets of interacting variables only crudely categorized by terms such as *media, audience,* and *society* (Ball-Rokeach & DeFleur, 1976).

BACKGROUND

In the chapter following our introduction, Charles Wright provides a detailed statement of the historical background and development of sociological media inquiry. For purposes of this introduction, however, we draw attention only to certain themes of that historical development that have influenced how we have organized this volume.

Early media studies focused primarily on the power of the media (then press, radio, and movies) to influence opinions and behaviors. Most researchers in the 1930s and 1940s used either an experimental social psychological approach or applied Harold Lasswell's (1948) more political issue: "who says what to whom through which medium with what effects." Both exemplified the one-directional "hypodermic needle" approach that, however, resulted in studies giving contradictory findings about media power. In the early 1940s Paul Lazarsfeld (and his students and colleagues, for example, Bernard Berelson, Elihu Katz, Robert Merton, and Herta Herzog) reported studies that forced sociologists to reconsider the role media play in the lives of their audiences. By conceptualizing the "audience" as individuals and members of society connected to families, work organizations, and communities, the idea that media exert powerful one-directional influence came under attack.

The empirical conclusions from these studies were best summarized in Joseph Klapper's (1960) work, *The Effects of Mass Communication*. In capsule form, the conclusions were as follows: Mass society and critical theorists such as those from the Frankfurt school (Horkheimer & Adorno, 1944) or C. Wright Mills (1951, 1956) were wrong in attributing enormous sociopolitical power to the mass media; the evidence from the research by Lazarsfeld and his students, especially *The People's Choice* (Lazarsfeld, Berelson, & Gaudet, 1944) and *Personal Influence* (Katz & Lazarsfeld, 1955), demonstrated that the sociopolitical effects of the media are weak; the processes of selective exposure, selective perception, and interpersonal influence equip audiences and their interpersonal networks with the "power" to determine what will become both short-term and long-term media effects. Klapper's review of research showed that rather than changing political opinions and basic values, the media tended to reinforce existing and commonly held points of view. Klapper extended his conclusions to claim that the media system is relatively impotent as an influence on both values and behavior when compared to that of family, peers, and other social influences.

Although Klapper's position became widely accepted by social scientists in the United States, it was not long before a dispute arose about his views as well. It should be noted that both Klapper and Lazarsfeld were employees of the Columbia Broadcasting Company (CBS) and, although they conceptualized the audience sociologically, they accepted the content itself uncritically as a given, as though it had no origins in creative and organizational settings. For whatever the reason, almost all of the research carried out during the heyday of mass media studies in the United States (the 1930s, 1940s, and early 1950s) focused on the effects of content without recognition that content was created within a social system.

Media effects, moreover, were narrowly conceived as reversals of attitude or behavioral conversions mostly with regard to voting preferences and behavior. Cumulative long-term effects that went beyond the time frame of a campaign were rarely addressed, nor were effects upon social processes, such as conflict, integration, and change. In a sense, the failure to recognize that content is created within a social system reflected a larger myopia; namely, the failure to recognize that the media's importance lay at least as much in effects upon culture and society as it did in conversion effects upon individuals. In her contribution to this volume, Thelma McCormack draws particular attention to how American media studies lost their original "vision" of understanding how and when the media act as a force for or against social change. It is possible, for example, that the media during the 1930s and 1940s were more powerful than usually recognized. Most media of the time were created by people holding similar fundamental views and political opinions as the majority of the audience, and during a time of crisis (the Depression), the media succeeded in reinforcing the status quo and contributed to the maintenance of the system in the United States. Although there were few studies to verify the media's power, it is commonly believed that Hitler's and Roosevelt's causes were enhanced by their ability to communicate through radio. In Germany the result was revolutionary change, and in the United States the changes were through the legislative system. Thus, when the focus of attention shifts from the individual to political and social processes holding societies together or radically changing them, it is not at all clear that the media system could be called "impotent" even in the pretelevision era of the 1930s and 1940s.

Because media research did not then take into consideration the interactive nature of the mass communication process with the necessity for studying decision making, audiences, and "effects" as integral parts of the media system, it soon became clear, even to the Lazarsfeld group, that the state of media research had become stagnant (Berelson, 1959; Lazarsfeld, 1963). With the exception of several sociological studies on "gatekeepers" in media organizations (in particular by Breed and McPhee), it was not until the late 1960s that researchers changed their focus. In the United States, John Riley and Matilda Riley (1959) and Herbert Gans (1966) offered structural and interactional models to study mass communication. In England as well, sociologists helped set the new direction for a more integrated and comprehensive approach. The English scholar, Raymond Williams (1975), for example, recognized that the study of mass media (television in particular) presented just another form of cultural study and showed how a neo-Marxist approach could be used as a base for theory as well as ideology. Also in England, Philip Elliot (1972) and Jay Blumler (1969) began to look at the social contexts in which communications actually operated and that influence media content. With these seminal writings and the theory and research that followed (such as the work of Ball-Rokeach, Cantor, Gans, Gerbner, Gitlin, Gurevitch, Hirsch, Katz, Engel Lang, Lang, Larsen, McCormack, Schudson, Tuchman, and Wright), the study of both mass media and mass communications again flourished.

SOCIAL STRUCTURE AND MEDIA SYSTEMS

Examination of the media in different societies shows that their structure, contents, and audiences differ according to their cultural, legal, and economic features. The media system plays very different societal roles, because its relations to the political, economic, and other social systems vary markedly, say, from advanced capitalist bureaucracies such as the United States, to emerging socialist Third World states, to communist bureaucratic states such as the USSR. Thus, before the content is even created, there are political, economic, and social realities that set the stage for the nature of media content. To understand why the media produce the content they do and the cultural, societal, and personal consequences of consuming media products, one must first understand these structural relations between the media and the other social systems that constitute a society. What, for example, is the relationship of the media to the political, military, and economic systems of a society? One must also understand cultural realities, such as traditions, values, and rules that may influence the creation of media content. Both the structural position of the media in a society and their cultural context can be expected to vary from society to society and within historical time.

Although understanding such differences between societies is fundamental to understanding any particular media system and its mass communication products, one must also understand the organizational structure of the media in a particular country. Mass media everywhere do share one characteristic: They are organized. All mass communicators, whether as government or commercial employees, work in formal, complex, bureaucratic structures with extensive divisions of labor. Everywhere mass media exist (and now they are worldwide), the power to decide what is broadcast or distributed ultimately rests with very few people who usually occupy formal roles in bureaucratic structures. These "communicators" are the most concrete controllers of media information resources—creating, gathering, processing, and disseminating—resources that have become fundamental to the conduct of societal, cultural, organizational, and personal life.

Thus, in addition to structural and cultural aspects of a society that affect the nature of media products, one must bring a sociology of organizations to bear in the analysis of mass communications. What, for example, is the media's legal and financial structure, and what is the division of labor? We cannot rely solely on an industrial model in seeking to answer such questions, because we also recognize that regardless of the rigidity of the bureaucracy and the way work is allocated, the production of media content remains a creative act. However, without understanding how content is controlled (selected and created), by whom, under what conditions, it is not possible to understand what messages finally reach audiences, no matter how creative those messages may be.

For example, in the free enterprise system as it exists in the United States, those who control the means of communication (for example, newspapers, radio stations, television stations) and the means of distribution (such as networks and distributors) must depend on advertisers and other sources of financial support (such as financiers and international trade agents) as well as the creators. To make matters even more complex, they must also depend upon the judicial, regulatory, and legislative agencies to continue to provide a situation that is conducive to their production process. Power over what is shown rests finally with those who own or finance the media, rather than with the individual creators. Actors, for example, are powerless to choose the roles they play and then how to interpret them. Stars may exert somewhat more control, but actors usually do not become stars unless they are in agreement with those in control (Cantor, 1980).

One reason power rests with the controllers rather than the creators is that there are more people able to create content than there are jobs available. Unless journalists, actors, writers, or other creators satisfy the producers, editors, or officials, they are replaced. In those parts of the world where the government is in charge, power is concentrated even more in the bureaucracy. Research carried out in the past decade or so also shows that the degree of bureaucratic control varies according to the medium and even within the same medium. For example, some media organizations are run more democratically than others and in some there is more conflict between managers (editors, producers, directors) and the "workers." Yet the degree of conflict between controllers and creators should not be overdrawn. Usually there is general agreement within an editorial staff or on a set because both the creative people and the decision makers subscribe to the same basic values and norms. As Gaye Tuchman (1978) has pointed out, the ideas of professionalism are shared widely among reporters and editors. News therefore represents a fundamental belief consensus. Struggles that arise over content are negotiated within the framework of this belief consensus. Television entertainment also represents a negotiated struggle within the confines of a constructed value and belief consensus whereby dissidents are excluded.

Only media workers, "communicators," who ascribe to the values and beliefs of those who control the organization are likely to hold or to be offered elite positions within those organizations. Once holding positions within media organizations, "communicators," especially in large market areas, often acquire prestige and high status. Thus, those recruited for positions both in the managerial and creative roles are likely to be far above their audiences in income and social status, and if they also become celebrities or famous, they also might become role models or set standards of behavior (and morals) for part or all of the population. The culture of the working and middle classes may thus be affected by these men (mostly) and those few women who are willing to suppress their own values if necessary (and usually it is not necessary) to create content within the constraints imposed by organizations.

By studying media organizations one can also learn much about the society fostering those organizations. In the United States, media organizations are likely to be part of larger conglomerates where profit making is the most important goal. The media organization then is to be comprehended fully only when we learn who controls it.

In addition to conglomerates that may own media and nonmedia organizations (for example, RCA owns NBC and many nonmedia businesses, and Coca-Cola owns Columbia Pictures and other media-producing and distributing companies), we also have to trace out the numerous connections between media organizations and political, educational, scientific, religious, citizen, and other organizations that affect media policies and practices.

THE AUDIENCE AND SOCIAL STRUCTURE

As should be clear from the above paragraphs, the study of media organizations is essential for understanding how the media operate as links to the larger social system. Probably the most visible linkage the media provide is to the audience. Just as the media share certain organizational realities in which they produce content, so do media audiences share certain social and personal realities concerned with understanding, acting effectively in, and engaging in private and social play. The media system is intricately involved in all of these aspects of the life of its audience. The media, moreover, link audiences and all the various publics within an audience to most, if not all, the institutions they must deal with, willingly or unwillingly, over the life course. Whether we like it or not, most of us must at one time or another deal with family, political, economic, educational, health, military, religious, legal, and other institutions. For many of these dealings, we come to depend upon the media system for the information we need to understand and to act effectively, whether it be decisions or problems associated with marriage, health, voting, career, child care, employment, or any of the other facets of everyday life. We also share a dependency upon the media system when it comes to the underrated dimension of play. Play is a vital component of human life; it not only serves to reduce tension and help us manage stress, it also is a major source of socialization and, equally important, individual and collective enrichment.

Thus, from our point of view, the media audience is not to be understood as mere consumers who passively accept anything that the media offer, but as active individuals and members of social groupings who consume media products in the context of their personal and social goals. In modern societies, that means quite a lot. Because the media system plays such an important role in society, linking the audience to all its various institutions, it is necessarily the case that the media will play important social and personal roles in individual and collective life.

It is not enough, then, to understand how content decisions are made. We must also understand what audiences or publics are served by media content and what difference it makes. It must always be remembered that media organizations provide symbolic content to audiences. Mass communicators who control the production of media content often try to justify the selection of stories and formats by claiming that they are merely providing products just as any other entrepreneur does, and through ratings and sales they know what the consumers (the audiences) want. As businesspeople, the communicators justify their decisions by claiming they are only conduits for audience desires. Yet most research shows that the audiences' input remains indirect and obscure. In other words, audiences have widespread dependencies upon media content but little direct or systematic role in determining content.

This does not mean that the audiences' role is always unimportant. The conditions and the ways in which audiences can and do play a part in content formation have just recently been considered by social scientists (Billings, this volume; Cantor, 1980; Cantor & Cantor, this volume; Gitlin, 1983; Montgomery, this volume). Probably the most common ways in which such audience participation occurs is either by media organizations creating their own visions (with or without research) of the content preferences of certain publics within the larger audience or by the actual formation of publics within the larger audience who come together as interest groups to have their say in some aspect of media content. Examples of such interest groups vary widely, from the public relations activities of corporations seeking to protect their interests, to social movements seeking to draw public attention to their issues, to less organized publics who express their allegiance as fans or annoyance as protestors of specific types of media content.

Publics who actively try to affect media content are not equal. The media audience, like the media themselves, is connected to the larger social structure. The media system's connections to that structure empower it, but there is much greater variability in the degree of power of individual and collective members of the audience. Some have greater access to the media due to their higher class or status as, for example, economic and political elites. As most recently argued by Paletz and Entman (1981), the opportunity for media access and the ability to control some aspect of media content translates to political power. Power holders, for example, may be sheltered from public accountability, and scrutiny of particular events and decisions can be withheld by the media. Indeed, virtually all individuals or groups seeking to maintain or to acquire power in modern societies must concern themselves with media relations wherein they seek to get their message into the flow of media content or to avoid undesirable media coverage. While many individuals and groups may not like their dependency on the media, they are forced to face the fact that the media system is vital for information and communication. The media system links virtually all major parts of the society to one another, and is thus involved in virtually every major process of conflict, change, integration, and control that power seekers, communities, states, and whole societies must face.

ORGANIZATION OF THE BOOK

This introduction and the chapters that follow should alert students that the study of mass media and mass communication requires the recognition that communicator, audience, and content must be studied within the society in which they exist; all three intertwine into a media system that exists within the web of social relations that constitutes a society. It is no longer proper to investigate the influence of the media on individuals and groups or on society and social process without recognizing that both the media and their audiences make up a system, interacting on each other within the dynamics of the social structure. The complex, interrelated series of questions that we have tried to identify here calls for a more integrated sociology of mass communication.

We have taken our conception of the multifaceted questions that should orient media inquiry as a guide to our organization of the chapters contributed to this volume. Not all of the questions that we have posed in this introduction are covered, and some are covered better than others. To a large extent, the strengths and weaknesses in this regard reflect the strengths and weaknesses of the field. We begin with three chapters from distinguished media scholars who describe and reflect upon the historical and theoretical foundations of media inquiry (Part I). We then turn to the question of the media and process, both the large societal processes of control, adaptation, and integration, and the community process of anticipating and coping with natural disasters (Part II). The next set of chapters reflects our view that media content and effects cannot be explained fully without an understanding of both the media as organizations and their audiences as indirect or direct participants in the media production process. These chapters concern either the question of how and why media organizations operate as they do or the question of media relationships to interest groups and specialized audiences (Part III). In Part IV, attention turns to the most frequently asked media effects question, How do we conceptualize and measure the effects of media coverage or of media content on public opinion processes and on political beliefs and behavior? The last set of contributed chapters (Part V) brings us to one of the most diverse and active areas of inquiry, analysis of media content. Both the traditional quantitative and the more recent forms of qualitative content analysis are represented. In our concluding remarks to this volume, we examine how the contributed chapters, taken as whole, point us to the future of sociological analysis of the mass media and mass communication.

PART I

SOCIOLOGICAL INQUIRY INTO THE MEDIA AND MASS COMMUNICATIONS: HISTORICAL AND THEORETICAL ORIGINS

THE THREE CHAPTERS that follow all deal, albeit in different ways, with the historical foundations of contemporary mass media and mass communication theory and research. The authors—Charles R. Wright, Thelma McCormack, and Michael Schudson—were invited by the editors to write their chapters especially for this volume. Each of them has made a substantial contribution to mass media studies and, thus, is in a good position to take a holistic look at the present state of the art and how it is or should be grounded in classical sociological perspectives and issues. These scholars' judgments and recommendations reflect their differing theoretical points of view and their differing substantive interests.

Chapter 1

MASS COMMUNICATION REDISCOVERED
Its Past and Future in American Sociology

Charles R. Wright

THIS BOOK DEMONSTRATES, through the various chapters presented, the importance of a sociological approach to the study of the mass media. It also suggests the need to take mass communication into account in addressing major sociological topics of social order and social change. The editors' introduction aptly captures these interdependent themes: the media and the social fabric.

What could be more central to sociology than the study of matters affecting social order and social change, social processes and social institutions—the social fabric, so to speak? How surprising it must be to the reader, then, to discover that one purpose of this book is to demonstrate a *resurgence* of American sociological interest and inquiry into the nature of mass communication and its role in society.

Resurgence implies a revival marked by a swell of motion and momentum—a new wave of interest and research activity. On my optimistic days I see that happening. But here, to err on the modest side of optimism, I shall speak not of a resurgence but of a rediscovery. Contemporary sociologists and other communications researchers are reviving their interest in studying mass communication and the mass media from a sociological perspective. It is important, if anything approximating a resurgence is to occur, that today's students and tomorrow's researchers be reassured of the importance, legitimacy, and relevance of the sociological study of mass communication. Therefore, in this essay I will demonstrate American sociology's historical stake in this field and briefly discuss what I regard as some promising directions in sociological research on mass communication.

SOCIOLOGICAL INTEREST
IN MASS COMMUNICATION

Sociology in America, since its very first years as a new and untested academic discipline, has recognized the significance of mass communication in analyses of contemporary society. This recognition has been expressed in sociological theory and research more explicitly during some periods of our academic history than others. Consider one introductory sociology textbook. The authors present what they label an organic view of society: that society is made up of interdependent parts and that it functions through social processes that cannot be explained fully in terms of the individual characteristics, psychology, and behavior of its members. Society is real and is, if you will, a system. The textbook contains chapters on such familiar sociological topics as population, the family, and social aggregates. There is also a chapter devoted to the communicating apparatus or, more colorfully, the "social nervous system."

"A communicating system," the authors state, "penetrates the whole social organism ... ramifying throughout society to its minutest subdivisions, and, as a whole bringing into more or less complete psychical contact all these parts of the organism." (The source of the following quotations is given below.)

Ideas, expressed through any of a great variety of symbols (oral, written, gestural, and so on) are preserved and transported by the media of communication, including the press, books, and other technical devices. But—and here is a sociological rejection of sheer technological interpretation—"In connection with all these technical devices for preserving and transporting symbols, we find *functional arrangements of persons and property into social organs.*" The authors then describe and analyze these social institutions for mass communication, arguing, among other points, that the various communicating channels in a society are arranged and coordinated so that, eventually, "the many communicating channels are combined into a great system."

Following this general description and theoretical analysis of communication systems, the authors present a specific account of the structure of the press, including, later on, a critique of newspapers for falling "far short of normal service, (1) in reporting fact, (2) in giving direction to public opinion, and (3) in the form and contents of information communicated."

Nothing seems unfamiliar or startling here. The text clearly relates communication in general and the mass media in particular to the society and, if you will, to the "social fabric." It also places the study of mass communication squarely in the mainstream of sociology.

What is remarkable is the publication date. These excerpts are not taken from the latest American introductory textbook in sociology but from the *first*! It was written by Albion W. Small, head of the first department of sociology in America (at the University of Chicago) and his coauthor, George C. Vincent. It was published in 1894! Hence my point that American sociologists have had an interest and a stake in the study of the mass media ever since sociology became recognized as a discipline here (Small & Vincent, 1894).

This was no passing fancy. America's sociological interest in mass communication was evident throughout the early and mid-twentieth century and (as this book testifies) persists today. A few examples will illustrate its continuing presence in the sociological enterprise, without attempting here to present a full and systematic accounting or history of the field.

We do not wish to make too much today of Small's early description of the role of mass communication in the social order. His work was in the tradition of large-scale sociological theories of society and did not directly contribute to specialized research on mass communication. Nevertheless, Small was supportive of a scientific, research orientation for the new field of sociology, and his administration at Chicago created a receptive climate for future empirical sociological studies. These studies included pioneering sociological research on the press by Robert E. Park, who joined the Chicago department in 1914, and by his students. Among Park's most familiar contributions to the sociology of mass communication are his essay on the natural history of the newspaper and his study, *The Immigrant Press and Its Control* (1922). His students' works include the well-known study, *News and the Human Interest Story,* by Helen MacGill Hughes (1940).

Other sociology students at Chicago at the time, whether directed by Park or others, worked on communication topics that sound fully modern today. Among these are doctoral dissertations concerning the influence of newspapers upon the growth of crime and other antisocial activity, in 1910; the relation of the newspaper to the political development of Japan, in 1919; religious journalism, in 1920; the Negro Press, in 1922; and a sociological study of news, in 1931. (For details about the early Chicago school, see Robert E.L. Faris, 1967.) Chicago's later sociological contributions to the study of mass communication include, to mention but a few, Herbert Blumer and Philip M. Hauser's work for the Payne Fund Studies on Motion Pictures and

Youth, in the 1930s (1933); Leo Bogart's studies of television (1956) and of newspaper readers (1981); Eliot Freidson's work on audiences (1953); Morris Janowitz's study of the community press (1952); Gladys Lang and Kurt Lang's research on television and politics in the 1950s and later (1968); and a sociological "portrait" of American journalists by John W. Johnstone, Edward J. Slawski, and William W. Bowman (1976). The National Opinion Research Center (NORC) at the University of Chicago also played an important role in contributing to studies of mass communication. This included fieldwork on national surveys of Americans' communication behavior, the Johnstone survey, and early content analyses of television programs, by Donald Horton and others (1951).

Early sociological recognition of the importance of mass communication systems was not limited to the Chicago school. At Columbia University, Franklin Henry Giddings gave it attention, for example, in his monumental work, *The Principles of Sociology* (1916). Giddings, like Small, was more theoretician than empirical researcher. Yet he too was dedicated to establishing sociology as an academic discipline and was supportive of an empirical approach through statistical research. One of his best-known students, William Fielding Ogburn (later on the faculty at Columbia and then Chicago), soon established himself in empirical research, contributing, among other accomplishments, studies of the impact of new communication technology on society and social change.

Others associated with Columbia's sociology department during the first decades of the twentieth century also recognized the importance of mass communication in their works, either while at Columbia or subsequently. Robert S. Lynd and Helen Merrell Lynd's now classic study, *Middletown* (1929), for example, devotes a chapter to the topic of "getting information" in Middletown, describing how newspapers present the news. Lynd and Lynd note that "Middletown's dependence upon [the press or] some such artificial diffusion of information grows as the city grows." In this and in their follow-up study, *Middletown in Transition* (1937), they relate this development to their sociological concern over the possibility of an inadequately informed citizenry and the consequences for public opinion and politics in a democracy. The mass media, thus, are regarded as relevant to matters of social structure, power, and the political process.

I have mentioned Ogburn's work, which included a study (with S. C. Gilfillan) of the social effects of the telephone, telegraph, and radio broadcasting for the President's Research Committee on Social Trends (1933). This presidential committee's published report also contained a study of the agencies of communication by two other former Columbians, Malcolm M. Wiley (then at the University of Minnesota) and Stuart A. Rice (then at the University of Pennsylvania). Wiley and Rice's chapter (1933) associates the mass media with matters of social change and social control. "Impressive as technological changes have been in other fields," they assert, "there is no more striking example than in communications of how they operate to instigate social change, modifying the material environment, creating new and perplexing problems of adjustment and changing manners and morals."

Mass communications, Wiley and Rice propose, "may be studied either in terms of the symbols which are transmitted or the agencies facilitating transmission." The authors review trends in transportation systems, point-to-point communication (postal service, telegraph, cable and wireless, and the telephone). Then they turn to what they label the "agencies of mass impression," namely, newspapers and periodicals, motion pictures, and radio. These mass media are the agencies "through which large numbers of individuals may simultaneously receive the same communications and be correspondingly influenced." This, in turn, affects public opinion. "It is as agencies of control that the [mass media] raise problems of social importance," they point out, thus remarking the media's relevance to the study of social control, a topic of long-standing sociological importance and interest.

The major thrust establishing a continuing interest at Columbia, however, started with the communications studies of Paul F. Lazarsfeld and Robert K. Merton in the 1940s and 1950s. Lazarsfeld's work in communications (alone or with others) includes, among other studies, the following: *Radio and the Printed Page* (1940) and other collections of studies by Columbia's Office of Radio Research (later the Bureau of Applied Social Research), such as *Radio Research 1941* (1942), *Radio Research 1942-1943* (Lazarsfeld and Stanton, 1944), and *Communication Research 1948-1949* (Lazarsfeld & Stanton, 1949); *The People Look at Radio* (Lazarsfeld & Field, 1946) and *Radio Listening in America* (Lazarsfeld and Kendall, 1948); voting studies, including *The People's Choice* (Lazarsfeld, Berelson, & Gaudet, 1944) and *Voting* (Berelson, Lazarsfeld, & McPhee, 1954); and *Personal Influence* (Katz & Lazarsfeld, 1955).

From the start Lazarsfeld presented research on mass communication in the context of its relevance for social problems and for matters of sociological and social psychological interest. The introduction to *Radio and the Printed Page* (1940), for example, notes that, since it is no longer possible to make major decisions in local town meetings, the future of democracy depends upon whether we can find new ways for the formation and expression of public will without impairing our democratic form of government. ... It becomes of increasingly grave importance, then, how the existing media of communication are used and misused, and what can and cannot be done with their help is a most vital topic for social investigation.

The People's Choice was originally described as a study of the effects of radio and the printed page in the presidential campaign of 1940. Its social and sociological significance were clearly foreshadowed in these remarks from *Radio and the Printed Page*.

In his preface to the second edition of *The People's Choice* (1948), Lazarsfeld offers the study as an example of a kind of sociological research that would help bridge the gap between large-scale, unmanageable sociological questions and manageable but less satisfying descriptive research. He labels it "dynamic social research." In effect, this orientation links much of Lazarsfeld's social psychological communication research to underlying questions about stability and change in people's opinions and behavior and their significance for sociological matters such as public opinion, social order, and social change.

Robert K. Merton also provided an important theoretical, empirical, and scholarly legitimacy to sociological interest in mass communication at that time in Columbia's history. Merton's interests focused on the sociology of mass communication, such as his classic study of the Kate Smith war bond radio marathon, *Mass Persuasion* (1946); his theoretical analysis (with Lazarsfeld) of the relation between mass communication and organized social action (1948); his study of patterns of influence and communication behavior (local and cosmopolitan influence) as they relate to social structure (1949); and his theoretical essays on mass communication and the sociology of knowledge (1949), which he likens to "two species of that genus of research which is concerned with the interplay between social structure and communication."

In the 1950s a third student of public opinion and mass communication, Herbert H. Hyman, joined the Columbia department. Hyman, long associated with NORC, added to the interest in studying the social psychological and sociological implications of mass communication. His research linked the study of mass communication to questions about socialization and public opinion, among other topics. Examples can be found in his classic study of political socialization (1959) and in his attention to the roles of both mass communication and face-to-face communication in matters of public opinion and social change (1961, 1967).

In the 1960s Lazarsfeld and Merton's primary research interests moved to areas other than mass communication. But Columbia's recognition of the relevance of mass communication for sociological studies of social structure and processes continued. It is reflected, for example, in the publications of other sociologists now or formerly on its faculty, or their students. These are far too many for complete citation in this brief overview. Among them are works by Allen H. Barton (1973), Robert T. Bower (1973, 1985), Warren Breed (1955), Lewis Coser (1975), W. Phillips Davison (1965, 1976), Herbert Gans (1979), Elihu Katz (1955, 1977), Patricia Kendall (1949), Joseph Klapper (1960), Rolf Meyersohn (1958), Ronald Milavsky (1982), William Robinson (1942), Bernard Roshco (1975), Eleanor Singer (1985), and Charles R. Wright (1959, 1960, 1975, 1985). In various writings each of these authors has related mass communication to matters of social structure, social order, social change, social control, or socialization.

The Chicago and Columbia departments were not the only ones to pay attention to mass communication in their formative years. The theoretical work of Charles Horton Cooley, at the University of Michigan, is an important example. In his classic work, *Social Organization: A Study of the Larger Mind* (1909), Cooley devotes several chapters to consideration of the possible social consequences of modern communication (that is, mass communication). He relates it, on the one hand, to the enlargement of citizens' knowledge about empathy for the larger world beyond the local community and, on the other hand, to potential pathologies of superficiality and strain for society and its members.

As another example, Edward Alsworth Ross (long associated with the University of Wisconsin) is remembered for his sociological works on social control and social processes. But he also was mindful of the relevance and potential importance of mass communication to these processes. Ross regarded the mass media as facilitating human intercourse. We draw our example from one of his later works (1940), but it serves: "The improvements in means of communication occurring in our time constitute the greatest progress man has ever made in eliminating distance as a barrier to the meeting of minds. In a few years, perhaps, one will be able to call up on 'long distance' almost anyone on the globe ... *and see him while talking with him.*" An overly optimistic statement, perhaps, but nonetheless it recognizes the importance of modern communication to our social processes.

Considerable attention was given to mass communication at the University of Washington, too, especially during the period following World War II. With the presence of such faculty members as Robert E.L. Faris, George A. Lundberg, and Stuart C. Dodd, the Washington department provided an encouraging intellectual atmosphere. A number of the sociology students of that time, or their students, have contributed to the sociology of mass communication. Among them are Sandra Ball-Rokeach (1969, 1976, 1982, 1984, 1985), William R. Catton, Jr. (1969), Melvin DeFleur (1958, 1982), Richard J. Hill (1964), and Otto N. Larsen (1954, 1958).

These examples, and others that could be supplied, illustrate sociology's long-standing interest in mass communication research. I have argued, therefore, that the current renewed interest in mass media study by American sociologists may aptly be labeled the *rediscovery* of a field nearly lost. This leaves unanswered the questions, In what sense was it nearly lost and why? These are discussed briefly below.

THE COMMUNICATION RESEARCH MINE: WAS SOCIOLOGY'S VEIN ABANDONED?

One contemporary explanation offered for the alleged drop in sociological interest in mass communication during the 1960s and 1970s is that scholars were discouraged by the lack of mass communication "effects" found by Lazarsfeld and others of the Columbia School in the 1940s and 1950s. The belief is that Lazarsfeld and others "found" that the mass media had no effects on people's beliefs and behavior (particularly voting behavior) and that therefore the mass media are either unimportant or less important than other social factors. I have yet to find the conclusion in Lazarsfeld's research that mass communication (or the mass media) is either socially or sociologically unimportant. Nor does the research show that mass communication has "no effect." The interpretation of relatively weak media effects applies mainly to certain specific instances under study and addresses very limited meanings of "effects" (such as converting Democrats into Republicans, or vice versa, during election campaigns). Perhaps the impression of no effects comes from efforts to summarize or simplify more complex arguments concerning direct and indirect influences given more fully in the text. Be that as it may, I think Sandra Ball-Rokeach (1986) is correct in noting that the *belief* that this is what the Columbia studies showed became widespread in certain academic circles among sociologists and students of mass communication in the 1970s. The belief that research showed that the media had "no effects" and were relatively unimportant matters, it may be assumed, turned some scholars and their students away from the study of mass communication as a specialty within sociology.

I would also like to suggest some other possible explanations for what happened to the field. One is that television nearly killed it. The rapid growth of television in America from the late 1950s to the present set the stage for public concern about television's "effects." Mostly these were conceived of as harmful effects on individual viewers, with bad consequences for society. Aggression, violence, crime, delinquency, sexual promiscuity, to mention but a few, these were the kinds of things people worried about. This is nothing new; similar public concerns had been raised about radio, motion pictures, and the press, and these concerns sometimes stimulated research on these topics: The Payne Foundation Studies for motion pictures and the Rockefeller Foundation studies of radio effects are examples. Most of these studies, ambitious and pioneering though they were, were relatively modest compared to the flood of demands for research that came from political and social groups wanting to know about the impact of television.

Who was to do this research? Sociologists might have taken the lead—and some did. But in the 1960s the ranks of empirically trained sociologists in communications were thin compared with the larger number of available and skilled psychologists and communication researchers with degrees in communications. At that time some of the latter also shared, by virtue of their training and interests, an individualistic, psychological orientation toward mass communication. There was a good "fit" between the public's conceptions of mass media's effects and the paradigms favored by many psychologically oriented researchers. Initially this was often a modified stimulus-response view of the communication process and later a specification, as, for example, in terms of cognitive development or child development. In time, the focus of most funded mass communication research became the kinds of "effects" that fit these conceptions. Usually they had the added advantage of appearing to be suitable for scientific study through experimental methods, mainly within the laboratory or classroom.

Such formulations contribute much to our understanding of human communications under certain conditions. But they often neglect the social contexts and social nature of communication, including mass communication. Narrowing the focus of communications research to effects on individuals and treating mass communication as yet another form of personal stimulus, this research lacked relevance for precisely those topics central to sociological interest. It seemed remote from sociological concerns about mass communication's relationship to social structure, the social order, social control, social change, and socialization. Sociologists lost some of their interest in the direction the field was taking.

I suspect that the social demands for immediate research on the suspected "evil" effects of television temporarily swamped the field. Sociologists were easily outnumbered in the process, and, as a result, sociological paradigms did not prevail. I suspect too that the topic of mass communication lost some of its appeal for new generations of sociological students who were not in a position to see its relevance to larger sociological matters. But now, it is hoped, this is changing. The study of mass communication and the mass media is again an interest of sociologists, including established scholars and students. In this revival do some research directions seem more promising than others? Are there some useful guides for the new student?

FUTURE DIRECTIONS:
BUILDING ON THE SOCIOLOGICAL HERITAGE

The need for more knowledge about mass communication is so great and the topic so complex that it would be foolish to advocate its study solely in sociological terms. That is not my purpose here. We need many approaches to the subject. It is apparent from the preceding discussion, however, that one important approach is sociological.

In these brief concluding remarks I suggest a few directions sociological research can take that, in my judgment, seem promising. One general guide for the future, it seems to me, is to recapture some of the fruitful paths of the past. One needs to go further, of course, and should not fear to explore uncharted areas.

I see promise in current efforts to reestablish the importance of mass communication for the social system. A good example is Sandra Ball-Rokeach's work (1976, 1984, 1985) on media dependency, on the conditions and social processes leading to greater or lesser interdependence of the mass media and other social institutions. There is interest, too, in studying the consequences of this interdependence. One promising direction of this research is the attempt to unravel changes and differences in institutional interdependence over time and among societies. Another interesting direction is the effort to examine how the dependence of individuals on the mass media for news, information, and other gratifications varies with changing social conditions (periods of social stability and change). These are clearly sociological questions.

A second area that seems promising is the study of the influence of mass communication and the mass media on social processes. A good example is Lang and Lang's continuing research on the influence television has had on the political processes in America. One important direction for sociological research in this area is to study the possible long-term "effects" of mass communication in ethnic group assimilation, in the socialization of children and adults, and in politics. These are good prospects for research and take a long-term perspective. Recently a conference on research strategies for studying the long-term effects of the mass media was sponsored by the University of Washington's School of Communication (Kurt Lang, Director), at Lake Wilderness, Washington, 1985.

A third promising area for research is the analysis of mass media as social institutions and social organizations, considering the production, distribution, and exhibition of mass-communicated news and information. One good example is Muriel Cantor's continuing research (1971, 1980, 1985) on television production and distribution. A fruitful approach in this area is the application of concepts from the sociology of organizations and the sociology of work to the analysis of the production of mass-communicated entertainment and news. Sociological concepts such as reference groups, lines of authority and responsibility, occupational statuses and roles, status sets and role sets can be usefully and instructively applied to the study of mass media organizations. Additional progress in this area, as has been suggested by Josephine Holz and me elsewhere (1979), can come from the comparative treatment of mass communication institutions and other social institutions, such as those encountered in government, health care, education, manufacturing, and the like. That is, there is much to be gained from considering both how mass media are similar to and how they differ from other organizational arrangements in society.

It seems important to consider, as far as possible, mass communication in the context of the total communications resources of a society. This means studying how mass media fit into the combinations of interpersonal communication, personal experience, and mass-communicated news and entertainment. These studies address social psychological questions concerning how people come to know about and interpret their social and physical environment. A good example is Ralph Turner's research (1980, in press, and his chapter with Denise

Paz, this volume) on how Southern Californians make sense of the complex mixture of information about earthquake predictions from the mass media, rumor, and private experience. One sociologically interesting feature of this area of research is the attempt to discover and specify how people's reliance on combinations of sources of information and guidance relates to their positions in the social structure. Another consideration is the social consequences of differential communication experience in terms of quality of life (including their chances for survival).

Finally, in the sociology of mass communication, as in all areas, comparative research is welcome and needed. This includes historical and other kinds of comparisons over time, comparisons between societies, between communications media, and, as mentioned, between mass media and other social institutions.

There are other promising areas of research in addition to those discussed above. Indeed, this volume contains many good examples of exciting research that are worthy of further study and discussion. This means there is much work to be done. I share, along with the coeditors and other authors in this volume, the conviction that this work can benefit from a sociological perspective. The study of mass communication and the mass media is an important part of sociology. We invite the reader to join us in the current revival of this challenging field of investigation.

Chapter 2

REFLECTIONS ON THE LOST VISION
OF COMMUNICATION THEORY

Thelma McCormack

NOT LONG AGO, toward the end of World War II and in the early part of the 1950s, there was a vision that communications theory would unify all of human knowledge. This daring and innovative idea, put forth most brilliantly and persuasively by Norbert Wiener, began to fade almost before it was attempted. Few persons had the breadth of knowledge Wiener had to carry out the enterprise, and those who, like Karl Deutsch, tried to prepare their own disciplines (political science) for the transformation by recasting them into the language of communication soon discovered that the old ambiguities and conceptual impasses still remained. There were, then, no immediate or middle-range payoffs for the effort, and, eventually, the yearning for the unification of knowledge was itself set aside—at least temporarily—as scholars returned once more to their more parochial and limited intellectual compartments.

Today, there is very little left to Wiener's grand aspiration, which, in retrospect, looks more and more eccentric. And even within our narrower and separate disciplines there is almost nothing to remind us that communication was once regarded as the master key, the common element in all of the physical, natural, and social sciences, as well as the link between the sciences and the humanities. Communication has become a course among courses, a patchwork of courses scattered throughout a university curriculum, and taught often by people whose intellectual deficiencies are embarrassing. It is an area of knowledge often overlooked in textbooks. At worst, it is a service course; at best, a specialization that can claim no privileged entitlement to scarce university resources.

Yet the need to unify knowledge remains, and so does the problematic nature of communication in our modern life. Indeed, both have become, if anything, more acute, but we seem to lack the imagination, the collective will, and the confidence to do anything more than acknowledge our debt to those thinkers who elevated communications from a wartime strategic interest to a transcending and preeminent branch of knowledge.

Despite the rise and fall of Wiener's vision of a unified knowledge, some of its influence remains. One of these legacies is the belief that the laws that govern interpersonal communications are applicable to mediated large-scale systems of communication. If we can understand how small face-to-face groups or social networks send and receive messages, if we can isolate the types of distortion that occur in an interview, we can build a body of knowledge from which we can generalize to all forms of communication. The only difference between the school orchestra playing for parents and a digital recording played on a quadrophonic acoustical system to an unseen audience of thousands whose musical appreciation ranges from amateur to connoisseur is scale. Otherwise, they are governed by the same principles: Someone is playing; someone is listening.

If this proposition is correct, it should work both ways. Our cumulative knowledge about the mass media of communication should apply equally well to interpersonal communication; we too should be able to generalize from our analyses of television, newspapers, movies, and radio to the small group, the family, personal friendship networks, and other primary group relationships. But that assertion is seldom made; rather it is assumed that if we can track communication in small networks and through the labyrinths of larger ones, we are on the way to understanding how the big broadcast networks serve modern societies.

Ultimately, we may be able to develop abstract propositions that apply to both mediated and unmediated communication, but for now we must insist that, until proved otherwise, they are different. The starting and ending point for us is history, a social context that shapes us and the media we create. There may be intriguing parallels between the telephone conversations of friends and a phone-in radio show, between gossiping and reporting. But there are major analytic differences when communication is (a) mass produced (b) by an occupational group, (c) using a technology, (d) working within a large-scale organization with its own internal division of labor, (e) but that is also constrained by laws, influenced by a political culture, and (f) has a future determined by the changing tastes, shifting interests, and extent of leisure among consumers. Each of these contextual variables must be considered. To decontextualize our subject matter for the sake of some universal that may be quite trivial is to miss not only its political significance, but our own as well in choosing to study it.

Specifically, our discipline begins in that turbulent period in the late fifteenth and sixteenth centuries, when European agrarian feudalism was crumbling, and the modern forms of urban life, a money economy—mercantilism, later capitalism—and the bourgeois state were emerging. The Reformation and the Counter-Reformation were the first of modern revolutions that, though not the result of the new print media, would have been impossible without them. From Martin Luther's hymns, to eighteenth-century political tracts, to the clandestine films made in Latin America today by dissident groups, the media have always been part of great social and political changes. They have had more than influence; they have had power.

Yet, ironically, our academic literature emphasizes only one side. We are better able to explain social order than social change, social reproduction than social innovation, equilibrium than disequilibrium. It is this state of affairs that I regard as the current crisis in communications theory. Our lost vision is not the dream of a unified knowledge, but the more modest expectation that we have something to say about freedom and social change.

SOCIETAL MODELS

Our inability to comment professionally on issues such as civil liberties, freedom, and democratic institutions is recent, and the result of a shift from traditional political science to political sociology. In the older framework, political philosophers wrote about the necessity of a free press and the political factors that would attempt to subvert it. They never doubted that when these problems were removed or mitigated—as they could be—the system would work much as its eighteenth-century founders and nineteenth-century exponents thought it would. Thomas Jefferson was still the commanding figure in the background; John Stuart Mill, in the foreground.

But the limitations of this way of thinking were becoming more and more evident. It was an eighteenth-century concept of human nature in the age of Freud, a nineteenth-century concept of a marketplace in a twentieth-century world of media monopolies. With respect to the media, there was a tendency to judge them in static terms: democratic media equals good, totalitarian bad; competitive media good, monopolistic bad; objectivity good, partisanship bad; laissez-faire media good, government-controlled media bad. These judgments threw no light on how the media functioned in the social world. New typologies were needed and a different set of indicators was called for.

Political sociology brought a perspective that was at once both less individualistic and less mind-centered. It emphasized political socialization and political cultures. Although media institutions were analyzed and their performance monitored, it was the processes of communication—persuasion and influence—that became the focus of research interest. Thus, in the process of socialization, the media could either politicize or depoliticize people, and political cultures could be placed on a scale ranging from highly political to apolitical. Terms such as the *fourth estate* disappeared from the new vocabulary as the political press itself seemed to disappear, whereas the entertainment media were viewed as potentially and indirectly political. Debates about the First Amendment gave way to attitudinal studies of political tolerance and intolerance, attitudes that in turn were extensions of a larger social or personality configuration.

The intellectual achievements of this behavioral perspective are many, and, if nothing more, it demonstrated the narrowness of the older normative model. In addition, it opened the way to bring contemporary psychology and sociology into discussions of the citizen and the state. But in this new intellectual space we failed to notice that the various societal models were, in different ways, conservative. By redefining problems, political sociology often dissolved them or hived them off. And this structured how we studied the media. Any graduate student, on the Right or Left, will readily describe the functions of the media as social control, the legitimation of class values, or contributing to systems maintenance, terms that presuppose either no change or a regressive change. But he or she has no concepts for understanding how the media can themselves constitute a revolutionary force.

It may help, then, to look very briefly at the dominant societal models and to examine how our present communication literature can be located within them.

CULTURAL

The cultural model is essentially a Durkheimian model in which the normative integration of a society is endangered from within by anomie and alienation. Symbolic systems such as religion and political rhetoric help to create a collective consciousness, an identity that reinforces the normative integration. Much of our research on the media and the formation of national identity in ex-colonial countries is based on the premise that the media can bring together disparate regional or cultural groups, can raise a level of group consciousness through a distinctive use of language and cultural symbolism that is exclusive to it.

The basic unit of study is the symbol, which may be anything from political imagery to art forms. The test of the media, then, is not accuracy or objectivity, but credibility. As Durkheim himself pointed out, we never have enough information. However, the symbols are codes that reflect deeper meaning in much the same way as dreams are projections of the unconscious. For Durkheim, the reality behind totemic figures was society itself, and the peculiar logic of many rituals was a social logic. In any event, a large part of our literature is the analysis of symbolic content either in relation to the universal imperatives of social organization, as Durkheim thought, or in terms of a more transient social structure, as Mannheim and other sociologists of knowledge held.

The cultural model assumes that we are symbol creators, that we think with our imaginations and fantasy, but what we are seeking, above all, is meaning, a set of meanings that can be shared with others to form social bonds. The contribution of symbolic interaction studies belong here, as do the various studies of the media and collective behavior, including, of course, the rituals of political conventions, political campaigns, and electoral behavior.

But meaning is not just created; it uses existing meanings embedded in tradition. The past, then, never vanishes; it is layered over so that what often seems like the new will continue to reach and touch a very wide group of people. In this way, the persistence and continuity of culture are ensured. When changes do occur, they are slow and selective, avoiding any normative conflict that could weaken the social cohesion. Many of our studies, then, on the media and socialization or on diffusion would be derived from this cultural model.

To summarize, the cultural model is a conservative one: in part, because of its emphasis on normative integration; in part, because of its emphasis on cultural continuity; and, in part, because it sociologizes the political.

CYBERNETIC

In this model a society is defined as an open, adapting system in which communication is a form of information processing directed toward problem solving and advance planning. It assumes there is a consensus with respect to end values, but what endangers the system is not the lack of normative integration, not alienation or indifference. It is error: either misinformation or incomplete information. There are many ways this can occur. The lines of communication, themselves, may be responsible; they can be too long, too complex, or too noisy, like a bad telephone connection. But administration itself may be responsible, by creating distrust and secrecy. Improvement, then, can be made by tightening up the systems of communication and the way messages are sent; it can also be made by changing authority structures. Many of our contemporary studies of media organizations are applications of organizational theory to news-gathering and editorial activity.

In the systems model, the citizen is a member of a team. But, like other members of the team, the individual seeks to reduce ambiguity and vagueness, not because these are emotionally intolerable, but because they increase the probability of error. Nothing is more desirable than correct, checked, and up-to-date information for the planner, and the same is true for the citizen whose knowledge of the world is unreliable and/or dated.

Although the cybernetic-systems model has no concept of dissent, it does have a concept of censorship. The right to know belongs to the system, not individuals, but a compelling case can be made against censorship based on the interference it creates in the larger information pool from which we draw. To the extent, then, that we do studies of media bias based on information (the amount, the selectivity, the reliability), we are working within this model. It is sometimes regarded as a more liberal model than the cultural one because it regards traditional knowledge as a possible source of ignorance that leads to improper analysis in a cognitive process. Yet, it is a model without a value system that could create strains within the social structure. For the same reason, it is seen as an expanding model that can be used for analyzing world systems despite national diversity.

CONFLICT

The third model is a conflict model of society that assumes deep irreconcilable cleavages within the social structure. Under these conditions, genuine normative integration would be impossible and would result only in a synthetic, superficial gloss. Similarly, more and better information would not close the gap, and, indeed, might polarize the parties still further. In short, structural inequality based on class, race, or gender is not a subjective misunderstanding or lack of goodwill; it deals with distributive injustice and the struggle between the disadvantaged and the advantaged.

In contrast with the two previous models, the unit of study here is ideology. Whether it is imagery or information is of little importance because all forms of symbolic expression can be seen as a challenge to an existing power structure or a justification of it. Our new cultural studies of hegemony and theories of dependency fall within this model, as do many of the older studies based on Marxist analysis of the class bias in everything from comic strips to science.

The test, then, of a system of communication is which group it is serving: the "haves" or the "have-nots." And the media become, in effect, an arm of social movements on the Right or on the Left. From the point of view of the Left, the function of media analysis is to demystify the claims of the elites, to expose the way in which their claims rest on social prejudice and self-fulfilling prophecies, and, at the same time, to dislodge the liberal myth that we can reduce social inequality through orderly, incremental, legislative change. The Right is equally critical of the liberal myth, but it attempts to mobilize support for a more regulated morality and a less regulated economy.

In general, the sympathies of scholars doing media research have been with the disadvantaged, and this has resulted in an imbalance in the research alluded to earlier. We have all become experts in demonstrating how those in power use knowledge and culture to defuse any dissident group, to devalue social groups (women and visible minorities), and to idealize models of society and persons that benefit them. And the more research we do of this sort, the more we convince ourselves of this reality and preclude consideration of other models. Thus, the conflict is transferred into the groves of academe as well. But, in any event, the conflict model has resulted, by default, in being conservative insofar as it has failed to offer any counter models that would focus on the success of social change.

CONCLUSION

The three models discussed—cultural, cybernetic, and conflict—are intended to illustrate the way in which our various discrete studies fall within a societal model, although the hypotheses used may derive from other sources. Most people who do media research are unaware of their place within these models and of the theoretical consequences that follow. Yet, this should be the point of departure for any kind of sociological understanding of the media and of what we are doing when we study communication. It is the difference between an analysis of society based on communication theory and an analysis of communication based on social theory.

At the same time, I want to raise the question of whether the three models are now exhausted; or, more generally, whether the perspective of political sociology has gone as far as it can, and the time has come to examine it more critically. To return, however, to the earlier normative analysis of politics as if our political institutions were autonomous and as if our political behavior were separate from our life histories would be counterproductive.

A different model would be more political than societal, in the sense that it recognizes that political activity is a distinctive way of behaving and is recognized as such by the actors involved. Similarly, political media can be judged only in terms of political media, not in terms of broad entertainment and audience pleasure; they form their own subculture and they are perceived as political by those either in power or seeking it. A new model, then, begins with an understanding of the political process and the role of social movements.

From the point of view of a left-wing social movement, the rightwing media are not merely influential or persuasive; they are powerful. Conversely, from the perspective of a right-wing movement, the left-wing media, however small and tacky, however badly mimeographed and coffee-stained, carry more weight than the *New York Times*. In other words, when the media are analyzed in terms of power, we generate a new set of propositions about the media.

Here the term *power* is not measured by the impact the media have on their audiences, but by the impact they have on both other media and other institutions. Similarly, the power the other media and other elite groups have over the political media should constitute a significant part of the analysis. Neither "effects" studies nor "uses and gratifications" studies will reveal very much about how the managers of financial institutions, the directors of medical foundations, the executives of insurance companies, or the heads of labor organizations perceive a new monthly magazine that speaks for environmentalists. They may all respond in the same way, or they may be divided; they may react in a lukewarm way, or overreact. All of these and other responses are possible permutations in a model that starts from a concept of power.

The precedent for this model was studies conducted of the underground press during World War II. The power these media had far exceeded the number of persons who saw or read the material. Those papers (and broadcasts) were regarded as subversive by Occupation forces, regardless of how few people had any contact with them. The same dynamics are involved in a less dramatic situation when an elected school board censors a high school newspaper critical of nuclear installations. No one is more astonished than the student editor, and no group is more quickly politicized than the students working on the paper. More empirical studies are needed of this kind of event to develop a base for further theorizing.

To summarize, what I have suggested here is that the lost vision of communications studies is our failure to concentrate our thinking on social movements and social change, which are the testing grounds, if not the "killing fields," of democratic freedoms. I have placed a large part of the responsibility here on the influence that political sociology has had on the study of politics and communication. I would not, however, like to leave the impression that this period in our development has not been one of enrichment. Nor should the major scholars in this field be blamed because we have reached a period in our social history that is intensely political yet lacking a theory of politics and the media. The focal point should be on those periods in history, past and present, where changes are taking place, and where we can look at the various insurgent social movements and the way they use and are used by the media. Otherwise, it seems to me, we are doomed to go on documenting the impossibility of social change until we ourselves may come to believe it.

Chapter 3

THE MENU OF MEDIA RESEARCH

Michael Schudson

THERE IS NO LONGER A FAMINE in mass media research. Now the question is, How nourishing is the feast? From 1972 to 1985, media sociology has developed in three directions. It has been neo-Weberian, with an emphasis on the concepts of organization, profession or occupation, production, and market; neo-Marxist, with attention to the concepts of hegemony and ideology; and neo-Durkheimian, with a focus on concepts of ritual and culture. There has been a tendency for each approach to take up a different aspect of the role of media in society. The neo-Weberians examine the producers of culture, the neo-Marxists the symbolic content of culture, and the neo-Durkheimians the public reception of culture.

This, of course, is very crude, and certainly some of the best work has mixed different theoretical approaches and jointly attended to production of culture, the cultural objects themselves, and their reception. But if some simplification can be pardoned, I want to address these three approaches separately, discussing some of the strengths and difficulties of each.

NEO-WEBERIAN APPROACH: ORGANIZATION, PROFESSION, PRODUCTION, AND MARKET

The "production of culture" perspective in the study of media emphasizes the ways that organizations, seeking power and profit, operating within competitive markets, and organized as bureaucracies, create cultural forms. Although this makes use of some of the greatest strengths of sociological analysis, it is a surprisingly novel angle on the study of the media. Early sociological studies of the media—such as Robert Park's essays on news, Helen MacGill Hughes's study of the human interest story, or the Payne Fund studies of the movies—focused almost exclusively on media content and not on how that content came to be. Media sociology of the 1940s and 1950s was most commonly social psychological in orientation. Even the early studies of media organizations, the "gatekeeper" studies, focused on an individual within an organization and how that person sifted and selected stories to be printed in a newspaper. The organizational constraints remained in the background.

As a result, the production of culture studies since 1970—of print and television news, country music, Hollywood, and the record industry—added a genuinely new element to the sociological account of the media. In a more symbolic interactionist vein, but one also stressing that culture is *produced,* Gaye Tuchman (on the news media) and Howard Becker (on "art worlds") maintain a focus on the social construction of meaning. Indeed, the turn of other sociologists toward studying the organizations that produce culture confirmed what symbolic interactionists had been saying for a long time—that the meanings we live by are social constructions. What the production of culture studies added was to *locate* this "social construction" in specific institutions and to emphasize that some institutional actors have much more power to construct meaning than others.

It is hard to imagine a sociology of the media today without the work of Gaye Tuchman, Muriel Cantor, Herb Gans, Paul Hirsch, Richard Peterson, David Altheide, Edward Epstein, Leon Sigal, Walter Powell, Lewis Coser, Charles Kadushin, Paul DiMaggio, and many others who have sensitized us to the organizational component of cultural creation. This is not to say that the neo-Weberian approach is by itself sufficient. There are two respects in which this approach can run into trouble.

First, if you treat a media organization the same way you treat any other organization, there is a danger of missing the special significance of the media. To see the newspaper or the television news as a "product" is not just to be hardheaded and realistic ("The media are businesses, after all."); it is to choose a particular metaphor. The news, for instance, *is* a product, yes. It is *like* other products, such as soap, toothpaste, and automobiles. But it is also unlike them. Unlike toothpaste, the news has direct bearing on politics. Unlike automobiles, the news is negotiated daily between government officials and privately employed, young, literate, overworked, and undereducated semiprofessionals. Most important of all, the news is a central symbolic resource and cultural focal point. There is a danger, one to which even recent papers on the media succumb, of incorporating the media so fully into the sociology of organizations as to lead the poor reader to forget what, after all, we wanted to discover about the distinctive properties of the media.

The second danger, of course, is that an exclusive emphasis on the production of culture may, though it need not, overlook the significance of the cultural product itself and the way it is received by the public. Organizational approaches can be imperialistic and give the impression that they tell the whole story. They don't.

NEO-MARXIST APPROACH: HEGEMONY AND IDEOLOGY

There is nothing new about studying the content of the media itself as a text. Nothing is more old-fashioned. Within sociology, the Marxist tradition has been the richest tradition of content analysis, especially well represented by the Frankfurt School critics.

There have been new approaches to content analysis in the past decade, especially a new emphasis on analyzing visual material (very gracefully managed in Erving Goffman's *Gender Advertisements,* 1979), and a new attention to formal methods of analysis and structuralist or semiotic models.

But most important in stimulating neo-Marxist analysis of media content has been a redefinition of the power of the media, not as entirely derivative of the power of other social institutions, nor entirely and unproblematically successful in generating false consciousness. The media are now treated by most neo-Marxists as "hegemonic," persuasive rather than coercive, and vital rather than supplementary to ruling-class power. In Gramsci's view, the cultural apparatus of a society is vitally important. Power flows not just from the barrel of a gun; the maintenance of power in society requires the tacit consent of the people who are ruled. This, of course, is music to the ears of any social scientist, Marxist or otherwise, committed to studying the media. It offers a theoretical justification for looking at precisely the institutions one was fascinated by anyway.

Further, a Gramscian view of hegemony holds that the media often operate rather subtly, not by pounding propaganda into people's heads but by creating a commonsense understanding of the world. The media provide not thoughts but a background for thinking that makes it possible for ruling groups to win genuine consent without using brute force. (This perspective bears some resemblance to the familiar "agenda-setting" view of the power of the media, but it is a good deal broader and less mechanical.)

The idea of hegemony is consistent with a view that common sense is constantly renegotiated. This, too, is appealing as a way of understanding how the media attain power in liberal societies in which there are obvious limits on their power and there is obvious evidence that they do not always present a uniform point of view. (There is all too little attention in media sociology to the role of media in nonliberal societies.)

Discussion of "hegemony," in my view, has been altogether too abstract and sometimes turns "hegemony" right back into a synonym for the absolute power of ruling groups to control the consciousness of all citizens. The concept is much more interesting and flexible than that. The writings of Todd Gitlin provide a good account of what can be done with the concept of hegemony, in part because Gitlin works to combine what I call the neo-Weberian with a neo-Marxist perspective. What he did in *The Whole World Is Watching* (1980) has not been matched by any other full-scale study that I know of—he examined not just media content but also its direct and documentable impact on a particular social movement. In other words, he paid attention to how media messages were received and interpreted by a specific population.

NEO-DURKHEIMIAN APPROACH: RITUAL AND CULTURE

The neo-Durkheimian position is the least well known and least well developed in media sociology, although it is nicely represented in this volume's chapter by Jeffrey Alexander. The neo-Durkheimian position holds that the experience of audiences with the mass media provides people a sense of connection to the collective whole that few other institutions today can rival. This is not to say that the media express the collective will. Nor is it to say that "we get the cultural fare we deserve." The neo-Durkheimians do not locate a collective will in every presidential address or television sitcom. On the contrary, they imply that most media fare has little or nothing to do with moments of collective transcendence. Like Durkheim himself, the neo-Durkheimians look especially at certain rare occasions of heightened attention, what Katz calls the "high holidays" of the mass media. Some media moments, uniting a nation or even many nations (the televising of the Olympics, for instance), transcend the everyday. These events are set off from most other media programs—they tend to be broadcast live, for one thing. People's experience of these events is set off: People gather around in groups, watch "religiously," talk about what they watch, and have a sense that they are experiencing something special. These media events, in a word, have an "aura" about them that few phenomena in the media do.

If this is the main emphasis in the neo-Durkheimian perspective, there is also a neo-Durkheimian tilt to the sociologists who have become interested in studying genre and formula in fictional and non-fictional settings. Although Swidler, Rapp, and Soysal (this volume) attend to the social constraints on generic forms, they also pay homage to formulas themselves as cultural resources. Different cultures have different formulas and genres with differing sorts of resonance. The trouble here is in unpacking the generic forms. They are *not* universal or timeless structures. They are *not* first principles, though they must be understood, as in the Swidler et al. chapter, as forceful constraints on the production and creation of meaning at any given moment. But genres shift and change, as I have shown in the case of the news story that moved less than a century ago from a chronological format to an inverted pyramid format. Literary and rhetorical styles that were well established in early nineteenth-century America have now passed into near oblivion, although a social analyst of 1850 would have rightly taken them to be cultural resources and format constraints of enormous power and considerable age.

The strength of neo-Durkheimian work on genres is to show that cultural forms are real constraints on social action. The weakness, as with Durkheim himself, is a tendency to leap to ahistorical generalization and to take genres as givens, rather than as historical crystallizations with an archaeology of their own.

I should conclude, naturally, that the best work will take advantage of the gains of the neo-Weberians, the neo-Marxists, and the neo-Durkheimians all. Perhaps. Some of the best work, however, will be more in one vein than in another, inspired by one work or one teacher rather than another, fighting with and fighting off one intellectual demon rather than an anthology of them. That is how traditions tend to work. And I do not see any immediate synthesis or reconciliation of various perspectives in the offing—or, in my view, a need for it.

I see a need for something else. I see a need for hard work, especially the hard work of cross-national comparative studies, of which we have remarkably few sophisticated examples. I see also a need for sociological research on the media grounded in an understanding of social and political processes. The study of the media is full of apocalyptic and deterministic sloganeering (the medium is the message, the TV is the modern god, the personal computer will democratize access to information, advertising creates our values). This is easy to fall into, if for no other reason than that the media pay us more attention when we provide them crisp and striking aphorisms rather than truth. But the sociological task is to understand the media, not to serve them. There is a lot of nourishment in media sociology today, but more than a little junk food, too. We should be able to recognize the difference.

PART II

MEDIA AND SOCIAL PROCESS

THE EMPHASIS upon the media's persuasion powers characteristic of earlier eras has given way to a view of the media as an information system that controls scarce and prized information resources essential to the social organization, productivity, and welfare of modern societies. In a sense the past is repeating itself, as this contemporary way of looking at the media and mass communication is quite consistent with the views of pre-1940 theorists and researchers (see the chapters presented in Part I). The analysis of the media as an information system is, of course, also indicative of the fact that our society has become an "information society."

One of the major social process problems that any modern bureaucratic society must address is how we effectively control the process of production and all the social relationships that revolve around this economic base of our society. In his chapter, "The Information Society: Technological and Economic Origins," James Beniger treats the media system as part and parcel of a larger system of social control. He argues that the origins of the information society are rooted in the Industrial Revolution and its continued expansion to the present day. Once-sufficient control technologies (such as bureaucracy) have had to be supplemented with computer-based telecommunications media and other control technologies. W. Russell Neuman and Ithiel de Sola Pool have directed their attention to another potential "problem" of the information society—information overload in "The Flow of Communications into the Home." They seek to test the frequently asserted notion that individuals in modern society exhibit the psychological distress of information bombardment. Their findings provide sound reason to question the validity of such claims and a basis for admiration of human adaptability as well. Another remarkably complex "problem" of social process in modern societies is how we hold the whole thing together, or how we effectively link our social structure to our culture. Karl Erik Rosengren addresses this problem in his chapter, "Linking Culture and Other Societal Systems." He pays particular attention to the linkage role of the mass media system.

The two remaining chapters in this section—those by Ralph Turner and Denise Paz and by Peter Hirschburg, Don Dillman, and Sandra Ball-Rokeach—address a more concrete question of social process: How do people and communities come to understand, plan for, and cope with the prospect of an earthquake or the reality of a volcanic eruption, respectively? With the media having become the primary emergency alert system in our society, it is not surprising to find that both of these chapters emphasize the role of the mass media in community adaptation to potential or real crises.

Chapter 4

THE INFORMATION SOCIETY
Technological and Economic Origins

James R. Beniger

WE LIVE TODAY in an Information Society. Unlike every other society we know, after some 50,000 years of human history, the contemporary United States, Canada, Western Europe, and Japan no longer depend primarily upon hunting and gathering, agriculture, or the processing of matter and energy to produce valued commodities. In only the past few years, the industrial economies of these countries have given way to information societies, so named because the bulk of their labor force engages in informational activities such as systems analysis and computer programming, while the wealth thus generated comes increasingly from informational goods such as microprocessors and from informational services such as data processing. The processing of matter and energy, it would seem, has begun to be eclipsed by the processing of information.

How can this be? It seems counterintuitive that an intangible such as information might provide the basis for a major national economy in the same way as, say, wheat, coal, steel, or automobiles. Certainly some attempt at explanation would appear to be in order. And yet, despite scores of technical and popular books and articles documenting the advent of the information society, no one seems even to have raised—much less answered—what seems to be the most obvious question: Why information? Among the great multitude of things that human beings value, why should information, embracing both goods and services, come to dominate the world's largest and most advanced economies?

In attempting to answer this question, we immediately confront the problem that information is not just another economic commodity. Unlike other commodities, information can be sold as often as demand allows, without ever being consumed—in the final sense—or lost to its seller. Unlike other commodities, information can be more valuable to give away than to receive, as demonstrated, for example, by the growing role of advertising in modern economies. Information even lacks a physical existence of its own, separate from other commodities, so that it cannot be stored, processed, or exchanged except through the organization and movement of otherwise extraneous matter and energy—microwaves, say, or paper and ink. Indeed, considering the conceptual difficulties surrounding information, it would seem unlikely to become visible at all as an economic commodity, much less to be singled out as the most recent indicator of advanced economic development.

Even if we did manage to account for the importance of information in modern economies, however, we would immediately confront a second question: Why now? Because information plays an important role in all human societies, we must ask why it has only recently emerged as a distinct commodity, one that as yet dominates only a half dozen national economies, and those in only the last few years. Material culture has also been crucial throughout human history and yet capital did not displace land as an economic base until the Industrial Revolution. To what comparable technological and economic "revolution" might we attribute the similar displacement of the capital base by information, or the eclipse of the industrial by the information society?

My answer is what I call the "Control Revolution," a complex of rapid changes in the technological and economic arrangements by which information is collected, stored, processed, and communicated and through which formal or programmed decisions might effect societal control. From its origins in the last decades of the nineteenth century, the Control Revolution continues to this day, accelerated most recently by the development of microprocessing technologies. In terms of the magnitude and pervasiveness of its impact upon society, intellectual and cultural no less than material, the Control Revolution already appears to be as important to the history of this century as the Industrial Revolution was to the last. Just as the Industrial Revolution marked a historical discontinuity in the ability to harness energy, the Control Revolution marks a similarly dramatic leap in our ability to exploit information.

But the questions remain: Why the new centrality of information and why now? No study of technological innovation or economic history can possibly hope to answer such questions, no more so than, say, the history of organic evolution might explain the importance of information to all living things. In both cases, the reasons that information plays a crucial role will not be found in historical particulars, but rather in the nature of all living systems—ultimately in the relation between information and control. Life itself implies purposive activity and hence control. Control, in turn, depends upon information and activities involving information: information processing, programming, decision, and communication. Were this not the case, we could not begin to explain society's growing preoccupation with microprocessors and computers, technologies that cannot perform work in the physical sense, nor create any wholly new information, but merely transform inputs from one form to another. Would such seemingly modest technologies be likely to evoke our entire era, already known popularly as the "computer age," were information processing, programmed decision, communication, and control not somehow central to the information society?

The purposive nature of all living systems suggests an answer to our first question, *Why information?* All economic activity is by definition purposive, after all, and hence requires control to maintain its various processes to achieve its goals. Because control depends upon information and informational activities, however, these will enter the market—as both goods and services—in direct relationship to an economy's demand for control. But if control is in fact crucial to *all* living systems, why did the economic demand for control—in the form of informational goods and services—increase so sharply in the late nineteenth century, thereby consolidating the Control Revolution and the eventual rise of the information society? Economic activity might indeed depend upon control, and control upon information, but why do these relationships seem so much more important now than, say, a century ago? Could the information society have preceded the Industrial Revolution?

Such questions of timing become easier to answer if we consider that national economies, again like living organisms, constitute concrete open processing systems engaged in the continuous extraction, reorganization, and distribution of environmental inputs to final consumption. So long as the energy used to process and move these material throughputs does not much exceed that of human labor, individual workers in the system might also provide the information processing required for its control. Until the last century, in fact, even the largest and most developed national economies still ran at such a human pace, with processing speeds enhanced only slightly by draft animals and wind and water power, and system control increased correspondingly by modest bureaucratic structures.

Once these factors—energy consumption, processing and transportation speeds, and the information requirements for control—are seen to be interrelated, the Industrial Revolution takes on new meaning. By far its greatest impact, from the new perspective, was to speed up a society's entire material processing system, thereby precipitating what I call a *crisis of control,* a period in which innovations in information-processing and communication technologies lagged behind those of energy and its application to manufacturing and transportation. With the rapid increase in bureaucratic control, however, and a spate of innovations in industrial organization, telecommunications, and the mass media, the technological and economic response to the crisis—the Control Revolution—had begun to remake societies throughout the world by the turn of the century.

Though just now emerging, the information society has not resulted from recent changes, but rather from increases in the speed of material processing—traceable to the steam engine—that had begun more than a century ago. Similarly, microprocessing and computing technology, contrary to currently fashionable opinion, is not a new force only recently unleashed upon an unprepared society, but merely the most recent installment in the continuing development of the Control Revolution. This explains why so many of the computer's major components have been anticipated, both by visionaries and by practical innovators, since the first signs of a control crisis in the early nineteenth century. If the Control Revolution did come in response to the Industrial Revolution, however, why does it show no sign of abating more than a century later? Two forces seem to sustain its development. First, energy utilization, processing speeds, and control technologies have continued to coevolve in a positive spiral, advances in any one factor causing—or at least enabling—improvements in the other two. Second, additional energy has increased not only the speed of material processing and transportation but their volume and reliability as well. This, in turn, has further increased both the demand for control and the returns on new applications of information technology. Increases in the volume of production, for example, have brought additional advantages to increased consumption, which manufacturers have sought to control using the information technologies of market research and mass advertising. Similarly, increased reliability of production and distribution flows has increased the economic returns on informational activities such as planning, scheduling, and forecasting.

SOCIETAL TRANSFORMATIONS

One tragedy of the human condition is that each of us lives and dies with little hint of even the most profound transformations of our society and our species that play themselves out—in some small part—through our own existence. When the earliest *Homo sapiens* encountered *Homo erectus*, or whatever species had served as our immediate forebear, it is unlikely that the two saw in their differences a major turning point in the development of our race. If they did, this knowledge did not survive to be recorded, at least not in the ancient writings now extant. Indeed, some 50,000 years passed before Darwin and Wallace managed to rediscover the secret—proof enough of the difficulty in grasping even the most essential dynamics of our lives and our society.

This conclusion holds for even that most significant of modern societal transformations, the so-called Industrial Revolution. Although it is generally conceded to have begun by mid-eighteenth century, at least in England, the idea of its revolutionary impact does not appear until the 1830s in pioneering histories such as those of Wade (1833) and Blanqui (1837). Widespread acceptance by historians that the Industrial Revolution constituted a major transformation of society did not come until Arnold Toynbee, Sr., popularized the term in a series of public lectures in 1881 (Toynbee, 1884/1920). This was well over a century after the changes he described had first begun to gain momentum in his native England and at least a generation after the more important ones are now generally considered to have run their course. Few before Toynbee had begun to reflect upon the profound transformation that signaled the end, after some 10,000 years, of predominantly agricultural society.

Two explanations of this chronic inability to grasp even the most essential dynamics of an age come readily to mind. First, important transformations of society rarely result from single, discrete events, despite the best efforts of later historians to associate the changes with such events. Human society seems rather to evolve largely through changes so gradual as to be all but imperceptible, at least compared to the generational cycles of the individuals through whose lives they unfold. Second, contemporaries of major societal transformations are frequently distracted by events and trends more dramatic in immediate impact but less lasting in significance. Few who lived through the early 1940s were unaware that the world was at war, for example, but the much less noticed scientific and technological by-products of the conflict are more likely to lend their names to the era, whether it comes to be remembered as the nuclear age, the computer age, or the space age.

THE CONTROL REVOLUTION

Few turn-of-the-century observers understood even isolated aspects of the great societal transformation—what I shall call the "Control Revolution"—then gathering momentum in the United States, England, France, and Germany. Notable among those who did was Max Weber (1864-1920), the German sociologist and political economist, who directed social analysis to the most important control technology of his age: bureaucracy. Although bureaucracy had developed several times independently in ancient civilizations, Weber was the first to see it as the critical new machinery—new, at least, in its generality and pervasiveness—for control of the societal forces unleashed by the Industrial Revolution. For a half century after Weber's initial analysis, bureaucracy continued to reign as the single most important technology of the Control Revolution. After World War II, however, generalized control began to shift slowly to computer technology. If social change has seemed to accelerate in recent years as argued, for example, by Toffler (1971), this has been due in large part to a spate of new information-processing, communication, and control technologies such as the computer—most notably, the microprocessors that have proliferated since the early 1970s. Such technologies are more properly seen, however, not as causes but as consequences of societal change, natural extensions of the Control Revolution already in progress for more than a century.

Revolution, a term borrowed from astronomy, first appeared in political discourse in seventeenth-century England, where it described the restoration of a previous form of government. Not until the French Revolution did the word acquire its currently popular and opposite meaning, that of abrupt and often violent change. As used here in *Control Revolution*, the term is intended to have both of these opposite connotations. Beginning most noticeably in the United States in the late nineteenth century, the Control Revolution was certainly a dramatic if not abrupt discontinuity in technological advance. Indeed, even the word *revolution* seems barely adequate to describe an age that brought—within the span of a single lifetime—virtually all of the basic communication technologies still in use a century later: photography and telegraphy (1830s), rotary power printing (1840s), the typewriter (1860s), transatlantic cable (1866), telephone (1876), motion pictures (1894), wireless telegraphy (1895), magnetic tape recording (1899), radio (1906), and television (1923).

Along with these rapid changes in mass media and telecommunications technologies, however, the Control Revolution also represented the beginning of a restoration—though with increasing centralization—of the economic and political control lost at more local levels of society during the Industrial Revolution. Before this time, control of government and markets had depended upon personal relationships and face-to-face interactions; now control came to be reestablished by means of bureaucratic organization, the new infrastructures of transportation and telecommunications, and systemwide communication via the new mass media. By both of the opposite definitions of *revolution,* therefore, the new societal transformations—rapid innovation in information and control technology, to regain control of functions once contained at much lower and more diffuse levels of society—constituted a true revolution in societal control.

Here the word *control* represents its most general definition: purposive influence toward a predetermined goal. *Control* encompasses the entire range from absolute control to the weakest and most probabilistic form, that is, any purposive influence on behavior, however slight. Economists say that television advertising serves to *control* specific demand, for example, and political scientists say that direct mail campaigns can help to *control* issue voting, even though only a small fraction of the intended audience may be influenced in either case.

Inseparable from the concept of control are the twin activities of information processing and reciprocal communication. Information processing is essential to all purposive activity, which is by definition goal directed and must therefore involve the continual comparison of current states to future goals, a basic problem of information processing. Simultaneous with the comparison of inputs to goals, two-way interaction between controller and controlled must also occur, not only to communicate influence from the former to the latter, but also to communicate back the results of this action (hence the term *feedback* for this reciprocal flow of information back to the controller). So central is communication to the process of control that the two have become the joint subject of the modern science of cybernetics, defined by one of its founders as "the entire field of control and communication theory, whether in machine or in the animal" (Wiener, 1948, p. 11). Because information processing and communication are inseparable components of the control function, a society's ability to maintain control at all levels (from interpersonal to international relations) will be directly proportional to the development of its information technologies. Here the term *technology* is intended not in the narrow sense of practical or applied science, but in the more general sense of any intentional extension of a natural process, that is, of the processing of matter, energy, and information that characterizes all living systems. *Respiration* refers to a wholly natural life function, for example, and is therefore not a technology; the human ability to breathe under water, by contrast, implies some technological extension. Similarly, voting is one general technology for achieving collective decisions in the control of social aggregates.

Each new technological innovation extends the processes that sustain life, thereby increasing the need for control and hence for improved control technology. This explains why technology appears autonomously to beget technology (Winner, 1977), and why, as argued here, innovations in matter and energy processing create the need for further innovation in information-processing and communication technologies. The nineteenth-century revolution in information technology was predicated upon, if not directly caused by, social changes associated with earlier innovations. Just as the commercial revolution depended upon capital and labor freed by advanced agriculture, for example, and the Industrial Revolution presupposed a commercial system for capital allocations and the distribution of goods, the most recent technological revolution developed in response to problems arising out of advanced industrialization—an ever-mounting crisis of control.

CRISIS OF CONTROL

The later Industrial Revolution constituted, in effect, a consolidation of earlier technological revolutions and the resulting transformations of society. Especially during the late nineteenth and early twentieth centuries, industrialization extended to progressively earlier technological revolutions: manufacturing, energy production, transportation, agriculture—the last a transformation of what had once been seen as the extreme opposite of industrial production. In each area industrialization meant heavy infusions of capital for the exploitation of fossil fuels, wage labor, and machine technology, and resulted in larger and more complex systems, systems characterized by increasing differentiation and interdependence at all levels.

One of the earliest and most astute observers of this phenomenon was Emile Durkheim (1858-1917), the great French sociologist who examined many of its social ramifications in his *Division of Labor in Society* (1893/1935). As Durkheim noted, industrialization tends to break down the barriers to transportation and communication that isolate local markets (what he called the "segmental" type), thereby extending distribution of goods and services to national and even global markets (the "organized" type). This, in turn, disrupts the market equilibrium under which production is regulated by means of direct communication between producer and consumer:

> Insofar as the segmental type is strongly marked, there are nearly as many economic markets as there are different segments. Consequently, each of them is very limited. Producers, being near consumers, can easily reckon the extent of the needs to be satisfied. Equilibrium is established without any trouble and production regulates itself. On the contrary, as the organized type develops, the fusion of different segments draws the markets together into one which embraces almost all society.... The result is that each industry produces for consumers spread over the whole surface of the country or even of the entire world. Contact is then no longer sufficient. The producer can no longer embrace the market in a glance, nor even in thought. He can no longer see limits, since it is, so to speak, limitless. Accordingly, production becomes unbridled and unregulated. It can only trust to chance.... From this come the crises which periodically disturb economic functions. (Durkheim, 1893/1935, pp. 369-370)

What Durkheim describes here is nothing less than a crisis of control at the most aggregate level of a national system, a level that had little practical relevance before the mass production and distribution of factory goods. Resolution of the crisis demanded new means of communication to control an economy shifting from local, segmented markets to high levels of organization—what might be seen as the growing "systemness" of society. This capacity to communicate and process information is just one component of what structural-functionalists following Durkheim have called the problem of *integration,* the growing need for coordination of functions that accompanies differentiation and specialization in any system.

Increasingly confounding the need for integration of the structural division of labor were the corresponding increases in commodity flows through the system, flows driven by steam-powered factory production and mass distribution via national rail networks. Never before had the processing of material flows threatened to exceed in both volume and speed the capacity of technology to contain them. For centuries, most goods had moved with the speed of draft animals down roadway and canal, weather permitting. This was the infrastructure, controlled by small organizations of only a few hierarchical levels, that supported even national economies. Suddenly, thanks to the harnessing of steam power, goods could be moved at the full speed of industrial production, night and day and under virtually any conditions, not only from town to town but across entire continents and around the world. To do this, however, required an increasingly complex system of manufacturers and distributors, central and branch offices, transportation lines and terminals, containers and cars. Even the logistics of nineteenth-century armies, then the most difficult problem in processing and control, came to be dwarfed in complexity by the material economy just emerging as Durkheim worked on his famous study.

What Durkheim described as a crisis of control on the societal level, he also managed to relate to the level of individual psychology. Here he found a more personal but directly related problem, what he called "anomie," the breakdown of norms governing individual and group behavior. Anomie is an "abnormal" and even "pathological" result, according to Durkheim (1893/1935, p. 353). As Durkheim argued, anomie results not from the structural division of labor into what he called distinct societal "organs," but rather from the breakdown in communication among these increasingly isolated sectors, so that individuals employed in them lose sight of the larger purpose of their separate efforts. Like the problem of economic integration, anomie also resulted, in Durkheim's view, from inadequate means of communication. Both problems were thus manifestations, at opposite extremes of aggregation, of the nineteenth-century control crisis. Unlike Durkheim's analysis, which was largely confined to the extremes of individual and society, this chapter will concentrate on intervening levels, especially on technology and its role in the processing of matter, energy, and information—what might be called "material economy" (as opposed to the abstracted ones that seem to captivate most modern economists).

RATIONALIZATION OF BUREAUCRACY

Bureaucracy has served as the generalized means to control any large social system—in most institutional areas and in most cultures—since the emergence of such systems by about 3000 B.C. Because of the venerable history and pervasiveness of bureaucracy, historians have tended to overlook its role in the late nineteenth century as a major new control technology. Nevertheless, bureaucratic administration did not begin to achieve anything approximating its modern form until the late Industrial Revolution. As late as the 1830s, for example, the Bank of the United States, then the nation's largest and most complex institution, with 22 branch offices and profits 50 times those of the largest mercantile house, was managed by just three people: Nicholas Biddle and two assistants (Redlich, 1951/1968, pp. 113-124). In 1831, President Andrew Jackson and 665 other civilians ran all three branches of the federal government in Washington, D.C., an increase of 63 employees over the previous 10 years. The Post Office Department, for example, had been administered for 30 years as the personal domain of two brothers, Albert and Phineas Bradley (Pred, 1973, chap. 3). Fifty years later, in the aftermath of rapid industrialization, Washington's bureaucracy included some 13,000 civilian employees, more than double the total—already swelled by the American Civil War—only 10 years earlier (U.S. Bureau of the Census, 1975, p. 1103).

Further evidence that bureaucracy developed in response to the Industrial Revolution is the timing of concern about bureaucratization as a pressing social problem. The word *bureaucracy* did not even appear in English until the early nineteenth century, yet within a generation it became a major topic of political and philosophical discussion. As early as 1837, for example, John Stuart Mill wrote of a "vast network of administrative tyranny . . . that system of *bureaucracy,* which leaves no free agent in all France, except the man at Paris who pulls the wires" (Burchfield, 1972, p. 391); a decade later Mill (1848, p. 529) warned more generally of the "inexpediency of concentrating in a dominant bureaucracy . . . all power of organized action . . . in the community."

That bureaucracy is in essence a control technology was first established by Weber, most notably in his *Economy and Society* (1922/1968). Weber included among the defining characteristics of bureaucracy several important aspects of any control system: impersonal orientation of structure to the information that it processes, therefore usually identified as "cases," with a predetermined, formal set of rules governing all decisions and responses. Any tendency to humanize the bureaucratic "machinery," Weber argued, will be minimized through clear-cut division of labor and definition of responsibilities, hierarchical authority, and specialized decision and communication functions. The stability and permanence of bureaucracy, he noted, are assured through regular promotion of career employees based on objective criteria such as seniority.

Weber identified another related control technology, what he called "rationalization." Although the term has a variety of meanings, most definitions are subsumed by one essential idea: Control can be increased, not only by increasing the capability to process information, but also by decreasing the amount of information to be processed. In Weber's day, the former approach to control was realized through bureaucratization, and today increasingly through computerization; the latter approach was then realized through rationalization, what computer scientists now call "preprocessing." Rationalization must therefore be seen, following Weber, as a complement to bureaucratization, and may be defined as the destruction or ignoring of information in order to facilitate its processing. This might at first seem a contradiction, considering that the proliferation of "paperwork" is usually associated with a *growth* in information to be processed, not with its reduction. Imagine how much more processing would be required, however, if each new case were recorded in an unstructured way, including every nuance and in full detail, rather than by checking boxes or filling blanks, or in some other way reducing the burdens of the bureaucratic system to the limited range of formal, objective, and impersonal information required by standardized forms.

Equally important to the rationalization of industrial society, at the most macro level, were the division of North America into five standardized time zones in 1883 and the establishment the following year of the Greenwich meridian and international date line, which organized world time into 24 zones. What was formerly a problem of information overload and hence control for railroads and other organizations that sustained the local system was solved by simply ignoring much of the information, namely, that solar time is different at each node of a transportation or communication system. A more convincing demonstration of the power of rationalization or preprocessing as a control technology would be difficult to imagine.

CHRONOLOGY OF INNOVATION

Table 4.1 presents selected innovations in information processing, communication, and control for the period 1837-1899, from the invention of the telegraph to the turn of the century. These years cover roughly the period from the crisis of control in the railroads, in the early 1840s, to the resolution of the crisis in the area of economic activity that it last reached—control of consumption—in the 1890s. Table 4.1 presents a selective sampling of 50 of the innovations in information technology that constituted the nineteenth-century Control Revolution, at least in the United States. This list of innovations reveals a steady development of organizational, information-processing, and communication technology over at least the decades of the 1850s through 1880s, a period that lags industrialization by perhaps 10 to 20 years. Remarkable is the sharp periodization of the listing: Virtually all of the innovations in control through the 1860s can be found in transportation and distribution; about two-thirds of that in the 1870s and later come in production or consumption. Similarly, more than three-quarters of the 20-odd listings for distribution come before 1870, nearly all of the 20 for production and consumption come after this date. Only the dozen innovations in the control of transportation seem to be distributed evenly over the entire period.

No less remarkable is the similar periodization in the development of information-processing, communication, and control technologies. Each of the major sectors of the economy tended to exploit a particular area of information technology: Transportation concentrated on the development of bureaucratic organization; production on the organization of material processing, including preprocessing, division of labor, and functional specialization; distribution concentrated on telecommunications; marketing on mass media. These relationships account for the patterns in nineteenth-century control technology, evident in Table 4.1, that parallel those for the economic sectors.

Most bureaucratic innovation arose in response to the crisis of control in the railroads; by the late 1860s, the large wholesale houses had fully exploited this form of control. Innovation in telecommunications, including the telegraph, postal reforms, and the telephone, followed the movement of the crisis of control to distribution. Innovation in organizational technology and preprocessing, including the shop-order system of accounts, routing slips, rate-fixing departments, cost control, uniform accounting procedures, factory timekeepers, and specialized factory clerks, followed the movement of the control crisis into the production sector in the 1870s. Most innovations in mass control, including full-page newspaper advertising, a trademark law, print patents, corporate publicity departments, consumer packaging, and million-dollar advertising campaigns, came after the late 1870s, with the advent of continuous-processing machinery and the resulting crisis in control of consumption.

TABLE 4.1
Selected Innovations in Information Processing, Communication, and Control of Production, Distribution, and Consumption, 1837-1899

Years	Innovations
1837	Telegraph demonstrated, patented
1842	Internal organizational structure in business (Western Railroad) carefully defined
1844	Congress appropriates funds for telegraph linking Washington and Baltimore; messages transmitted
1847	Telegraph used commercially
1851	Telegraph used by railroad (Erie)
	First-class mail rates reduced from 5 to 3 cents an ounce up to 300 miles carried, from 10 to 5 cents for up to 3,000 miles
1852	Post Office makes widespread use of postage stamps
1853	Through bill of lading introduced
1854	Hierarchical system of information gathering, processing, and telegraphic communication instituted to control a trunk-line railroad (Erie) from the superintendent's office
early 1850s	Commodity exchanges opened; standardized methods adopted for sorting, grading, weighing, inspecting
1855	Registered mail authorized, system put into operation
	First-class mail rates reduced, for second time, from 5 to 3 cents an ounce for up to 3,000 miles carried
1857	Weighing scale for use on railroad tracks introduced
	Business (Pennsylvania Railroad) enunciates line-and-staff concept: line managers direct workers in basic functions of organization, others (staff executives) set standards
1858	Transatlantic telegraph cable links America and Europe, service terminates after two weeks
late 1850s	Railroads come to employ more accountants and auditors than any government, federal or state
	"To arrive" or futures contracts, futures markets appear
1862	Federal government issues paper money, makes it legal tender
1863	Manual block signal system introduced in railroads
	Free home delivery of mail begins in 49 largest cities
1864	Railroad postal service begins using special mail car
	Postal money order system established to insure transfer of funds
1865	Premiums (lighographed pictures) given for coupons on manufactured product (Babbitt Soap)
1866	Telegraph service resumes between America and Europe
	"Big Three" telegraph companies merge in single nationwide multi-unit company (Western Union), first in United States
1867	Railroad cars standardized
	Automatic electric block signal system introduced in railroads
	Telegraph ticker installed inside brokerage house
1869	Book (Rowell (1869) published for advertisers listing all U.S. newspapers with accurate estimates of circulation

TABLE 4.1 Continued

Years	Innovations
late 1860s	Modern bureaucracy—organization structure with a half dozen or more operating departments controlled by a hierarchy of salaried managers—emerges in large wholesale houses Traveling salesmen employed
1870	First federal trademark law passed, 121 registered
1874	Interlocking signal and switching machine, controlled from a central location, installed by railroad (New York Central) Label patents authorized, first goes to a breakfast hominy label Labor union labels attached to products (cigars)
1875	U.S. plant (Carnegie's Edgar Thomson Steel Works) explicitly designed to facilitate throughputs "Open contract" makes advertising firm sole agent for advertiser
mid-1870's	Shop-order system of accounts—based on routing slips—developed for control of material flows through factories
1876	Telephone demonstrated, patented
1878	Commercial telephone switchboards and exchanges established, public directories issued
1879	Full-page newspaper advertising introduced
1881	Second federal trademark law passed
1883	Uniform standard time adopted by United States on initiation of American Railway Association
1884	Factory (Midvale Steel) incorporates rate-fixing department Long-distance telephone service begins
1885	Book (Metcalfe 1885) published on cost control of factories Post Office establishes special delivery service
1886	Railroad track gauges standardized
1887	Interstate Commerce Act sets up uniform accounting procedures for railroads, imposes control by Interstate Commerce Commission Time recorders ("autograph" type) introduced in factories
1888	Employee time recorder (paper tape) introduced
1889	National publicity stunt used to promote commercial product (Quaker Oats)
1891	Trading stamps redeemable for premiums introduced
1893	Railroad Safety Appliance Act requires trains to have standard automatic couplers, air brakes Print patent introduced, first to H. J. Heinz for five words in shape of pickle
early 1890s	Car accountant offices—to monitor the location and mileage of cars on railroads—supplant fast-freight and express companies
1897	Company (General Electric) creates bureau to publicize itself, broader developments in its industry
1898	Rural free delivery of mail (RFD) systematized by Post Office
1899	Use of product differentiation, consumer packaging, million-dollar advertising campaign to establish new consumer product (Nabisco's Uneeda Biscuit) nationally
1890s	Timekeepers and specialized clerks, first "staff" employees in many factories, introduced to fill out shop orders and routing slips

THE INFORMATION SOCIETY

One major result of the Control Revolution, in response to the nineteenth-century crisis of control, has been the emergence of the so-called information society. The idea dates from the late 1950s and the pioneering work of an economist, Fritz Machlup, who first measured that sector of the U.S. economy associated with what he called "the production and distribution of knowledge" (Machlup, 1962). Under this classification, Machlup grouped 30 industries into five major categories: education, research and development, communications media, information machines (such as computers), and information services (finance, insurance, real estate, and so on). He then estimated, from national accounts data for 1958 (the most recent year available), that the information sector accounted for 29% of gross national product (GNP) and 31% of the labor force. He also estimated that between 1947 and 1958, the information sector had expanded at a compound growth rate double that of GNP. In sum, it appeared that the United States was rapidly becoming an information society. Over the intervening 20 years, several other analyses have substantiated and updated the original estimates of Machlup (1980, pp. xxvi-xxviii). By far the most ambitious effort to date has been the innovative work of Marc Uri Porat for the Office of Telecommunications in the U.S. Department of Commerce (1977). In 1967, according to Porat, "information activities" (defined differently from those of Machlup) accounted for 46.2% of GNP—25.1% in a "primary information" sector (which produces information goods and services as final output) and 21.1% in a "secondary information" sector (the bureaucracies of noninformation enterprise).

The impact of the emerging information society is perhaps best captured by trends in labor force composition. Table 4.2 shows the relative sizes of four sectors of the civilian labor force: agriculture, industry, service, and information (1800-1980). As can be seen in Table 4.2, the United States began overwhelmingly in agriculture, the location of roughly 90% of the labor force at the end of the eighteenth century. The majority of U.S. labor continued to work in agriculture until about 1850, and this remained the largest single sector until the first decade of the twentieth century. Rapidly emerging, meanwhile, was a new industrial sector, one that continuously employed at least a quarter of U.S. workers between the 1840s and 1970s, reaching a peak of about 40% during World War II. Today, just 40 years later, the industrial sector is close to half that percentage and declining steadily— it might well fall below 15% in the next decade. Meanwhile, the information sector approaches half of today's U.S. labor force.

TABLE 4.2

U.S. Experienced Civilian Labor Force by Four Sectors, 1800-1980

Year	Agricultural	Industrial	Service	Information	Total Labor Force (in millions)
		Sector's Percentage of Total			
1800	87.2	1.4	11.3	0.2	1.5
1810	81.0	6.5	12.2	0.3	2.2
1820	73.0	16.0	10.7	0.4	3.0
1830	69.7	17.6	12.2	0.4	3.7
1840	58.8	24.4	12.7	4.1	5.2
1850	49.5	33.8	12.5	4.2	7.4
1860	40.6	37.0	16.6	5.8	8.3
1870	47.0	32.0	16.2	4.8	12.5
1880	43.7	25.2	24.6	6.5	17.4
1890	37.2	28.1	22.3	12.4	22.8
1900	35.3	26.8	25.1	12.8	29.2
1910	31.1	36.3	17.7	14.9	39.8
1920	32.5	32.0	17.8	17.7	45.3
1930	20.4	35.3	19.8	24.5	51.1
1940	15.4	37.2	22.5	24.9	53.6
1950	11.9	38.3	19.0	30.8	57.8
1960	6.0	34.8	17.2	42.0	67.8
1970	3.1	28.6	21.9	46.4	80.1
1980	2.1	22.5	28.8	46.6	95.8

NOTE: Data for 1800-1850 are estimated from Lebergott (1964), with missing data interpolated using Fabricant (1949); data for 1860-1970 are taken directly from Porat (1977); data for 1980 are based on U.S. Bureau of Labor Statistics projections (Bell, 1979, p. 185).

At least in the timing of this new sector's rise and development, the data in Table 4.2 are compatible with the hypothesis that the information society emerged in response to the nineteenth-century crisis of control. When the first railroads were built in the early 1830s the information sector employed considerably less than 1% of the U.S. labor force; by the end of the decade it employed more than 4%. Not until the rapid bureaucratization of the 1870s and 1880s, the period that marked the consolidation of control, did the percentage employed in the information sector more than double to about one-eighth of the civilian work force. With the exception of these two great discontinuities, one at the advent of railroads and the crisis of control in the 1830s, the other at the consolidation of control in the 1870s and especially in the 1880s, the information sector has grown steadily but modestly over the past two centuries.

Temporal correlation alone, of course, does not prove causation. With the exception of the two discontinuities, however, growth in the information sector has tended to be most rapid in periods of economic upturn, most notably in the postwar booms of the 1920s and 1950s, as can be seen in Table 4.2. Significantly, the two periods of discontinuity were punctuated by economic depressions, the first by the Panic of 1837, the second by financial crisis in Europe and the Panic of 1873. In other words, the technological origins of both the control crisis and the consolidation of control occurred in periods when the information sector would not have been expected on other economic grounds to have expanded rapidly if at all. There is therefore no reason to reject the hypothesis that the information society developed as a result of the crisis of control created by railroads and other steam-powered transportation in the 1840s.

A wholly new stage in the development of the information society has begun to emerge, since the early 1970s, from the continuing proliferation of microprocessing technology. Most important in social implications has been the progressive convergence of all information technologies—mass media, telecommunications, and computing—in a single infrastructure of control at the most macro level. A 1978 report commissioned by the president of France, an instant best-seller in that country and abroad, likened the growing interconnection of information-processing, communication, and control technologies throughout the world to an alteration in "the entire nervous system of social organization" (Nora & Minc, 1978, p. 3). The same report introduced the neologism "telematics" for this most recent stage of the information society. Crucial to telematics—the convergence of information-processing and communications technologies—is increasing digitalization: coding into discontinuous values, usually two-valued or binary. Because most modern computers process digital information, the progressive digitalization of mass media and telecommunications content begins to blur earlier distinctions between the communication of information and its processing, as well as between people and machines.

Digitalization makes communication no less difficult from person to person than from person to machine, machine to machine, and even machine to person. Also blurred are the distinctions among information types: numbers, words, pictures, and sounds, and eventually tastes, odors, and possibly even sensations—all might one day be stored, processed, and communicated in the same digital form. In this way, digitalization promises to transform currently diverse forms of information into a *generalized medium* for processing and exchange by the social system, much as, centuries ago, the institution of common currencies and exchange rates began to transform local markets into a single world economy. We might therefore expect the implications of digitalization to be as profound, for macrosociology, as the institution of money was for macroeconomists. Indeed, digitalized electronic systems have already begun to replace money itself in many informational functions.

SOCIETAL DYNAMICS RECONSIDERED

Despite the chronic historical myopia that characterizes the human condition, as documented in an opening section of this chapter, it is unlikely that the more astute observers of our era would fail to glimpse, however dimly, even a single aspect of its essential social dynamic. For this reason, the ability of a conceptual framework to subsume social changes noted by previous observers might be taken as one criterion for judging any claim to portray a more fundamental societal transformation. The progress of industrialization into the nineteenth century, with the resulting crisis of control, the technological and economic response that constituted the Control Revolution, and the continuing development of the information society, including the telematic stage just now emerging—together these factors account for virtually all the societal changes noted by contemporary observers. Indeed, the various transformations they identify can be subsumed readily by major implications of the Control Revolution: the growing importance of information technology, as in Richta's (1969) scientific-technological revolution or Brzezinski's (1970) technetronic era; the parallel growth of an information economy (Machlup, 1962, 1980; Porat, 1977) and its growing control by business and the state (Galbraith, 1967); the organizational basis of this control (Boulding, 1953; Whyte, 1956) and its implications for social structure, whether a meritocracy (Young, 1958/1961) or a new social class (Djilas, 1957; Gouldner, 1979); the centrality of information processing and communication, as in McLuhan's (1964) global village, Phillips's (1975) communication age or C. R. Evans's (1979) micro millennium; the information basis of postindustrial society (Bell, 1973; Touraine, 1971); and the growing importance of information and knowledge in modern culture (Mead, 1970).

In short, particular attention to the material aspects of information processing, communication, and control will make possible the synthesis of a large proportion of the literature on contemporary social change. Despite the Control Revolution's importance for understanding contemporary society, especially the continuing impact of computers and microprocessors, the most useful lesson applies to our understanding of social life more generally. The rise of the information society itself, more than even the parallel development of formal information theory, has exposed the centrality of information processing, communication, and control of all aspects of human society and social behavior. It is to these fundamental informational concepts, I believe, that we social scientists might hope to reduce our proliferating but still largely unsystematic knowledge of social structure and process.

Chapter 5

THE FLOW OF COMMUNICATIONS
INTO THE HOME

**W. Russell Neuman
Ithiel de Sola Pool**

CONSIDER THE MILLION YEARS of human presence on the earth. For the first 900,000 years, the period in which our basic physiology and mental capacity came to take its current form, the typical human experienced only an occasional grunt or gesture in a normal day. It was not until 100,000 years ago that primitive speech began to take form. At this point, the mind was required to store and process an occasional utterance or perhaps a brief narrative story or two in an average day. At about 3500 B.C. writing was invented. Now ideas and events could be captured fully and passed on to succeeding generations.

If human existence on earth were compressed into 24 hours, the emergence of writing would come at 8 minutes before midnight, Gutenberg's popularization of movable type and mass printing at 46 seconds before midnight, and finally the telephone, radio, and television all within 8 seconds of midnight. Given that speech and writing are such recent inventions, it would seem that the human mind would be working at close to capacity in processing the information from conversations with friends and family members and an occasional few paragraphs of text. How could it be possible to process the barrage of images and language brought to us by high-speed printing and the electronic media? The television set throws forth 3,600 images a minute per channel. Radio on average generates just under 100 words per minute, totaling between 3,000 and 5,000 words broadcast by radio each minute of each day in the typical market. The average daily newspaper contains 150,000 words and several thousand graphic images. Magazines and books add to the flow of information on a similar scale. In historical perspective, it is clearly an information explosion. Is there evidence that the audience is stunned and numbed by information overload?

Psychological experiments show that in some circumstances high demand for information processing can induce tension and anxiety. Military studies indicate that information overload sustained at extreme levels over long periods of time can induce a psychological passivity and a withdrawal syndrome. Other studies of problem-solving exercises demonstrate that the human mind has a functional limit of about seven factors that it can process simultaneously. There are indeed clear and distinct limits to human information-processing capacity.

But we believe that research on experimentally induced information overload is an inappropriate model for understanding the flow of communications into the home. Military and industrial psychologists have, quite appropriately, studied stress on air traffic controllers, battlefield commanders, and business executives. These working professionals are under constant pressure to evaluate multiple streams of information and make critical decisions, bearing at times on matters of life and death. Educational psychologists study how pressures on achievement-oriented students can lead to debilitating test anxiety. But such environments are profoundly dissimilar to the casual monitoring of communications that characterizes mass media exposure in the home.

How well do our primitive and feeble brains respond to the greatly expanded flow of mass communications? They do quite well, thank you. The human psyche is remarkably adaptive and resilient. Media audiences have developed considerable skill in organizing, filtering, and skimming information and maintaining a partial attentiveness to the flow of broadcast and print information. Most people do not feel bombarded or overloaded by the expanded array of available mass media. On the contrary, for the most part they seek out more media exposure and respond enthusiastically to the expanded choices available. People *choose* to turn on the radio for several hours and the television set for two to four hours each day. In the United States, 97% of cars are equipped with radios because the market demands it. People routinely listen to radio and increasingly to television in the kitchen as meals are prepared and consumed. Clock radios are likely to be the first thing heard in the morning, Johnny Carson the last thing heard before a weary viewer drifts off to sleep. This is, indeed, voluntary behavior, surely a puzzling phenomenon to those who equate exposure to the mass media as a form of Chinese water torture.

If a crudely formulated hypothesis of psychological information overload represents more myth than reality in the free-choice situation of mass media exposure, how are we to interpret and understand the very real growth of information flow into the home? We have been working on an alternative formulation. We call it the Equilibrium Model.

The premise of the model is that there are indeed finite limits to individual information-processing capacity and appetite for media exposure. We posit that the central equilibrium of media exposure is a decline in attentiveness to each medium as the number of media to which one is exposed goes up.

This equilibrium can be seen at both individual and aggregate levels. At the individual level, in a household where the television is on 10 hours a day, the average attentiveness per unit time is likely to be lower than in the household in which it is on only 2 hours a day. In the former case, the TV set is often used as a secondary activity while other activities such as cooking, cleaning, and talking are taking place in the room. In the latter case, TV viewing is, for the most part, a primary, single-attention activity of prime-time viewing. Or, also at the individual level, one might expect the amount of time spent with a given magazine to be greater in a household subscribing to two to four magazines compared to a household subscribing to over a dozen.

At the aggregate level we note that since the full penetration into the American home of television in the early 1960s, there has been a slow but steady rise in exposure levels from five to seven hours of viewing time per household per day. But a closer analysis of the data reveals that most of this growth represents expanded viewing at the fringe times (early morning, early evening, late evening), not in the high-attentiveness prime-time viewing period.

Figure 5.1 outlines the basic dynamics of the Equilibrium Model. A central premise is the concept of a continuum of media attentiveness. Ordinarily, we tend to think of media exposure as dichotomous—either one has read a book or not, either one has seen a television program or not. And this dichotomous notion of media exposure has become an accepted convention measuring audience size in the communications industry. Advertisers, producers, and audiences alike have become comfortable with the traditional measures of circulation, box office, and Nielsen ratings. But as numerous more detailed research studies uniformly document, there is in reality a continuous sliding scale of attentiveness. Some print media are read carefully from cover to cover, some partially read, some skimmed, in some cases just picture captions are read, and frequently periodicals are never even opened. There are, of course, parallel continua for attentiveness in radio, television, and other media.

The analysis that follows is based on a model of countervailing pressures for attention and time, and the corresponding competition for a share of the individual's limited entertainment/information budget. The data allow us to document some intriguing trade-offs among competing media over the last two decades and we hope for some informed projections into the future.

AN OVERVIEW OF THE
COMMUNICATIONS FLOW FINDINGS

We have compiled data on trends in the circulation and use of the mass media and a number of point-to-point media in the United States for the period 1960 to 1980.[1] We tracked the amount of information supplied, the amount consumed, and corresponding cost data. The basic unit of measurement is the number of words transmitted and actually received in the home through each medium each year.

The data here provide a plentiful resource for those concerned about "information overload." The average American, by our estimates, is exposed to 61,556 words from the mass media each day. Most of that (87%) comes from radio and television. That works out to just under 4,000 words per waking hour, about 60 words per waking minute per person per day. This represents a growth of 151% from 1960 to 1980.

The critical issue for the Equilibrium Model is the comparison of supply and consumption. Yes, indeed, media consumption has grown, but the supply has grown considerably faster. In 1960, the mass media supplied about 3 million words per capita per day. Our measure of supply simply includes all of the unwatched available channels and unread newspapers, magazines, and books delivered to the home.[2] By 1980, words supplied had grown to almost 11 million, a growth of 367%!

The modesty of growth in consumption compared with supply for this period attests to the steepening gradient of resistance to new media. Each item of information produced faces a more competitive market and, on average, a smaller and less attentive audience. The ratio of words consumed to words supplied by 1980 had fallen to less

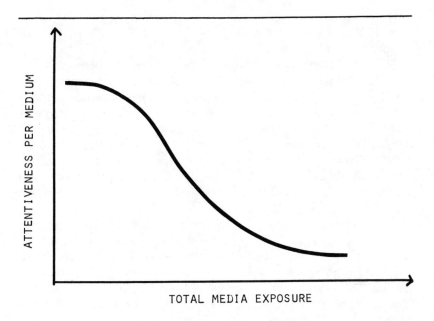

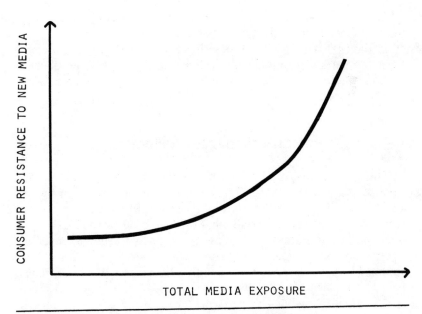

Figure 5.1   The Equilibrium Model: Theoretically Derived Curves

than half the level in 1960. The ratio has fallen in each of the mass media we have studied.

By 1960, television had reached near universal penetration of American homes and was already an undisputedly dominant force in advertising economics and in share of the average American's leisure time. The radio and motion pictures industries had already completed fundamental adjustment to the competition of television during the 1950s. Thus, the only "new" industry through this period was the belated discovery of the market for cable and pay television in urban and suburban markets in the 1970s. For the most part, then, these figures represent the steady state battle of attrition and growth of the major mass media in the United States.

The pattern of winners and losers is quite clear. The electronic media have been gaining and this gain has been achieved at the expense of the print media, especially newspapers. The pattern of media exposure is not directly reflected in the profitability of the various media, especially advertising-supported media, through this period. The newspaper industry, for example, in competition with other media for advertising support over the past two decades has done very well. But in time, these patterns of use are likely to affect industry economics in this decade, especially with the introduction of videotex, teletext, and a variety of new home video media. Figure 5.2 summarizes these basic findings.

In the next section we will describe our methodology for deriving these estimates of communication flow into the home. The following section will review the data in detail for two exemplary media, television and cable.

METHODS OF MEASUREMENT

The methodology that allows us to make such estimates was first developed at the Ministry of Post and Telecommunications in Japan.[3] The key decision was to translate all flows of information into units of words.[4] This required ascertainment of the typical word rate for each medium. An important distinction, as we have noted, was made between words supplied and words consumed. Our definition of a word supplied is that it is available at people's homes so that all they would have to do to hear or read it would be to choose to do so, at most turning a switch or opening to a particular page. Thus, the number of words supplied by television would grow not only if broadcasters broadcast more words, but also if the number of receivable stations

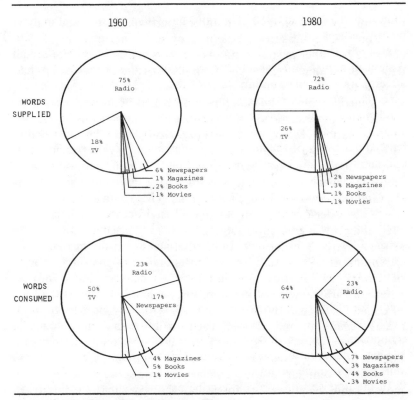

Figure 5.2   Overview of Communication Flows

increased (for example by cable importing additional signals) so that
the listener had more alternatives at hand, or if second sets came into
the home so different members of the family could choose different
stations at once. The data from which the supply time series were calculated were thus primarily data on the activity of information industries, and did not take account of the behavior of the audience
members in choosing what to attend to.

On the other hand, words consumed are those that the members of
the population actually heard or read. The basic data from which such
estimates are derived are behavioral surveys, such as time-budget
studies. Such data are generally collected by particular media industries in audience studies and present some problems of com-
parability. No doubt, many of the statements we now make will have
to be revised in the light of new, fuller, and better-adapted time series
and behavioral measures. The present results share many of the infir-

mities of any work with index numbers, particularly new and unexercised ones. The measures are derived by secondary analysis of data collected for other purposes, and not always consistently. Nor are all data reported annually, so some interpolations and extrapolations had to be used.

In general, users of the data reported here, as of any index number, should give more credence to trends than to comparisons across different situations. Many operational decisions go into the construction of any index number, and these apply differently in different situations. Thus, comparing specific production or consumption indexes across media at one point in time is likely to be less valid than comparing rates of growth or decline across time. These data are appropriate for the broader questions of the overall environments, media trade-offs, and growth gradients, but not for more focused questions, such as the advertising efficiencies of alternative advertising media.

An important omission for an understanding of the full character of communication flow was interpersonal conversation. Unfortunately, we are unaware of any appropriate data. Another is the level of communications flow in various work settings, especially from internal memoranda and reports.[5] The available data do include media exposure at work, such as reading the newspaper on a coffee break, but not internally generated, work-related communication.

Table 5.1 summarizes the formulae and data sources used for computing communications flow for each of the major mass media. Recall that we defined *words supplied* as "made available in the home." All the person need do is turn on a set and select a channel, or select a print medium to read. Accordingly, the basic formula for computing words supplied for broadcasting is the number of broadcasting stations receivable by the average listener times the number of minutes broadcast per day times the number of receiving sets per capita times the word rate per minute. The growth in television broadcasting over the last two decades reflects growth on each of these variables except word rate. The expansion of FM broadcasting and the multiplication of the number of radios in the home resulted in a similar growth pattern for radio. Both the television spectrum (VHF and UHF) and the radio broadcast spectrum (AM and FM) are now at the saturation point in the larger and middle-sized market areas. Further growth is still possible, however, because of cable and new technological developments that allow for more efficient use of existing spectrum, such as Low Power Television (LPTV) in television and Subcarrier Digital Transmission (SCA, teletext) in radio and television and higher frequency broadcasting, such as the FCC's new allocations for Multichannel-MDS and Direct Broadcast Satellites.

TABLE 5.1
Estimating Communications Flow

Medium	Words Supplied					Words Consumed	
Television/cable	(6.62) Number of broadcasting stations per average market (1, 2)	(922) Number of minutes broadcast per station per day (3)	(1.45) Number of receiving sets per household (4)	(153) Words per minute (5)		(196) Minutes exposed per day (6, 11)	(153) Words per minute (5)
Radio	(16.9) Number of broadcasting stations per average market (3)	(992) Number of minutes broadcast per station per day (3)	(5) Number of receiving sets per household (4)	(60) Words per minute (5)		(162) Minutes exposed per day (6, 12)	(68) Words per minute (5)
Newspapers	(1.2) Circulation per household (1, 7)	(150,000) Words per issue (5)				(18.3) Minutes exposed per day (11)	(240) Average reading speed (13)
Books	(22.9) Book sales per household (8)	(100,000) Words per book (5)				(18.3) Minutes exposed per day (11)	(240) Average reading speed (13)
Magazines	(24.7) Circulation per household (9)	(45,000) Words per issue (5)				(6.4) Minutes exposed per day (11)	(240) Average reading speed (13)
Motion pictures	(18.5) Number of theatrical screens per average market (14)	(2.7) Showings per screen (10)	(620) Seats per screen (1)	(135) Minutes per movie (10)	(110) Words per minute (5)	(2.5) Minutes exposed per day (14, 15)	(100) Words per minute (5)

SOURCES: (1) Sterling and Haight (1970); (2) Broadcasting/Cable Yearbook; (3) Standards Rates and Data Service; (4) Television Factbook; (5) MIT Research Program on Communications Policy: sampled estimates from *Boston Market* (Spring 1980) for broadcast media and movies, sampled and pooled estimates (1960, 1965, 1970, 1975) for print media; (6) A.C. Nielsen; (7) Ayer Director of Publications; (8) U.S. Bureau of the Census; (9) Magazine Publishers Association; (10) National Association of Theater Owners; (11) Robinson (1977, 1980), Szalai (1972); (12) Radio Advertising Bureau; (13) Sandborn Associates; (14) Motion Picture Association of America; (15) Predicasts, Inc.

The formulae for the print media is a simple function of the circulation per capita times the size of an average issue in words. So growth and decline in the supply of print media in this chapter will be a direct function of circulation and issue size.

The measures for theatrical motion picture supply are a bit more problematic. One element of noncomparability is that, by definition, theatrical motion pictures are not seen in the home. They are included here because they are an important element of leisure mass communication behavior. We selected a measure of supply based on the number of theatrical showings times the average number of seats per screen times the average number of words per movie. These calculations seemed to generate the most comparable ratios of supplied to consumed content. Movies, of course, ultimately represent an important component of network and pay television communication flow and contribute to those indices as well as theatrical exhibition. Home video, through both direct sales and rental of video recordings to the home, represents an increasingly important distribution channel but entails too small a share of aggregate viewing time up through 1980 to warrant inclusion in this time series.

The measures of consumption are all a simple function of average number of minutes of exposure per medium per day per person times rate of words per minute broadcast or read. We are very much at the mercy of the available data here. Because of the nature of broadcast advertising economics, A. C. Nielsen and the other broadcast research services provide detailed time-series exposure data. In print the basic audited measure is circulation rather than time exposed, so we have relied on academic time-budget studies and interpolated for yearly growth and decline estimates. The estimate for declining newspaper exposure is especially controversial and likely to be subject to further field research. There seems to be fairly extensive evidence that daily newspaper reading has declined, especially among the young, but the data are incomplete.

The sources for each element of the formulae for each of the media are listed in Table 5.1. Further detail can be found in de Sola Pool, Inose, Takasaki, and Hurwitz (1984).

ANALYSIS OF TELEVISION AND CABLE

Television is by far the dominant American mass medium. Even at the beginning of our time series in 1960, when television had been available for only a little more than a decade, it was already responsible for 50% of the communications flow consumed in the home. By

1980, that share of the communications flow had grown to 64%. These proportions are measured in words. The dominance of television would be even more overwhelming if the measure included graphic communication or was based on time spent with the media.

Figure 5.3 outlines the data for supply and consumption of television and cable programming. Supply in Figure 5.3 is indicated by the solid line and is measured against the metric on the vertical axis on the left-hand side of the figure. In the case of television, the metric is millions of words supplied per capita per day. Media consumption is indicated by the dashed line and is drawn against the metric on the right-hand vertical axis, in this case measured in thousands of words consumed per capita per day. The inclusion of both words supplied and words consumed on a single graph may be disconcerting at first because of the very different scales involved. The ratio of mass media words supplied to words consumed is, roughly speaking, about 100 to 1. That will be reflected (with a few exceptions) in the left-hand and right-hand scales in these figures. The advantage of this format, however, is that the graphs allow for a comparison of supply and consumption and illustrate in most cases the growing disjuncture between the two.

The supply of television grew a phenomenal 536% over this 20-year period. That works out to an annualized per capita growth rate of 8.8%. The growth rate in the first decade was actually somewhat faster, 9.4% compared to 7.4% for the most recent decade. The growth rate of television supply may well return to the 10% range in the 1980s, as a result of the steep growth curve for cable television, with its ability to multiply the number of available channels for subscribing households by a factor of from three to six.

The growth from 1960 to 1980 reflects a combination of factors, including the growth of both VHF and UHF broadcasting, the expansion of multiset households (approximately 50% of American households had multiple sets by 1980) and at the tail end of the curve, the expansion of cable television. Cable television occupies an increasingly large portion of viewer time and the trade-off between cable-delivered versus broadcast services will continue to be the subject of research in this vein. But in the present analysis of broad trends of communications flow, we combined cable and broadcast viewing into a single indicator, because cable-originated programming, including pay television, occupied only 2% of the communications flow by 1980.

Television viewing has also expanded dramatically in the last two decades. Total growth in viewing is 192% for an annualized growth rate of 3.3%. That rate holds steady for most of this period. But the

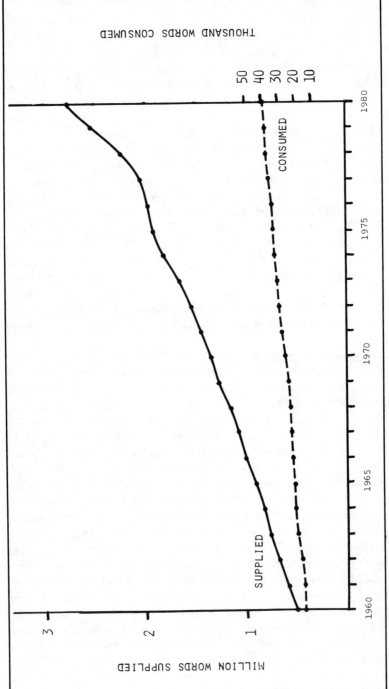

THOUSAND WORDS CONSUMED

MILLION WORDS SUPPLIED

SUPPLIED

CONSUMED

Figure 5.3 Television/Cable

decline of growth in consumption predicted by the Equilibrium Model does show up in the last two years, when the growth rate falls to 2.4% per year. The growth in time spent in front of the television set may well continue for a number of years, especially with the expansion of video games, home video, and videotex-type media. But television, narrowly defined as viewing over-the-air network broadcasting, will fall as a percentage of total media exposure.

CONCLUSION

In a related essay on the fragmentation of the mass audience, Neuman (1982) reported on the growth and decline of various media over the past century. The point was made that as new media emerge, the old ones adjust and specialize in various ways in order to survive. One of the most clear-cut examples of this is the competition between radio and television. In the 1930s and 1940s, situation comedy and adventure programming in prime time on radio dominated the attention of the American public. Families would gather in the living room and literally stare at the radio as Jack Benny and other national celebrities performed. That prime-time, high-attention function was taken over by television during the 1950s. People no longer sit around and stare at their radios. In fact, the great bulk of radio listening takes place while other activities are being undertaken. Indeed, it is hard to imagine an audience member simply sitting, listening to the radio. The special advantage of this music-oriented medium is its pleasant accompaniment to other activities.

This pattern of increasing inattentiveness and partial attentiveness is the hallmark of the Equilibrium Model. Radios are cheap and omnipresent. Because of low production costs, radio stations are in plentiful supply. But the persistence of radio against competition generates costs of a different sort—the lower attentiveness of audience members. Where once families gathered around their radios and hung on every word, the medium now provides background music and features "easy listening" and "fewer interruptions."

Because our measures of media exposure in the above graphs are simple units of time of exposure multiplied by word rates, we have, if anything, underestimated the increasing gaps between supply and consumption. Attentiveness per unit time is not independently measured. This is not accidental. In most cases, the data are collected by the industries themselves, which, for competitive reasons, prefer to measure exposure in ways that maximize their apparent audiences.

The expansion of television viewing in the last decade has been primarily at the margins, that is, early and late evening rather than prime time. Similar to radio, viewing in these time periods often accompanies other activities. Careful experimental research indicates that the viewer's eyes remain on the set only 65% of the time while the viewer is in the room. One-third of the time, viewers are engaged in other activities while viewing. These proportions are likely to increase. Some audience members, for example, use MTV, the rock music cable channel, as the functional equivalent of radio. It is simply turned on and left on as background music, with the audience member paying attention only when a particular favorite comes on, much as they would turn up the radio for a favorite song.

Are people reading less of the magazines they subscribe to? Probably. But the data available thus far are frustratingly incomplete. The success of the *People* magazine format in which much of the readership restricts itself to skimming by reading picture captions, may well become increasingly dominant. The picture of the gentleman in the smoking jacket attentively reading his magazine in his study is more a phenomenon of the advertising trade press than of American media behavior.

In the final reckoning, motion pictures and books will be directly determined by market demand. If people have less available time they will buy fewer books and go to the movies less often. In the case of newspapers, magazines, radio, and television—the less expensive habitual media—the economic basis is different. They are advertiser supported.

Here the critical element will be the ability of research to relate audience attentiveness to advertising effectiveness. With the established media somewhat insecure about their place in the electronic future, each industry will for a time stick close to its traditional estimates of audience size, calculated in circulation and units of time. Each will keep its measures of advertising effectiveness and advertising efficiency basically incomparable with other media, again for fear of possible competitive disadvantage. The motion picture industry will continue to measure its progress in box office dollars rather than admissions, so that rising ticket prices can mask dips in attendance. The television networks will increasingly promote themselves in terms of audience size rather than audience share per unit time to downplay the inroads of independent broadcasters, cable, and pay cable. Even the advertising industry, with its strong ties to existing media, will be cautious about proposing any new metrics of media exposure.

But we predict that ultimately three factors will coalesce to force change in media audience measurement. The first is the fact that we are getting close to the inflection point on the equilibrium curve. The reservoir of available time and reduction of attentiveness that has allowed expansion of mass media thus far is near exhaustion. The growth of new media will increasingly lead to a direct and proportionate loss of audience for existing media.

The second factor is that because of the increasing prevalence of electronic delivery and display, what once were perceived by producers and audience members alike as unique media become competing media.

The third factor is that electronic forms of audience measurement will also grow. Nielsen's metered sample will ultimately monitor videodisc, videotape, videotex, teletext, and video games as well as television.

It remains to be seen whether coordinated cross-media audience measurement will emerge before the technology forces the issue. Furthermore, and perhaps more important, it remains to be seen whether an independent measure of audience attention will become an industry standard. Television Audience Assessment in Boston is perfecting a diary/questionnaire approach. Roger Percy in Seattle, as well as both Arbitron and Nielsen, has experimented with mixed electronic and questionnaire methodologies. Burke Marketing in Cincinnati has developed an approach based on day-after recall of commercial messages. None has tried to apply its techniques to multiple media.

The Equilibrium Model leads to a prediction that ultimately a shakeout will occur across the mass media. It may emerge gradually or as a sudden economic crisis. Our candidate for the leading indicator of a crisis in media economics would be a weakness in demand in the next few years for network television advertising as the spring advertising season opens. Television is the dominant medium and its advertising is aggressively priced. It is a likely bellwether. We feel that if research on communications flow and audience attentiveness is well publicized and the major players encourage intermedia competition now, rather than put it off, the corresponding economic adjustments will be more gradual and less likely to lead to a shakeout crisis.

We began this chapter with a critique of psychologistic interpretations of information overload. Does it make sense to argue that the increasing flow of mass-mediated communication will leave the unsuspecting audience member stunned and numb? After reviewing the research, we concluded that because of the way media are casually monitored in the home setting it is indeed an unlikely result. Then we took a long hard look at the increasing ratio of media supply to consumption. Our final conclusion is that if there are to be victims of communications explosion they are more likely to be found within the media industries rather than within the audience.

NOTES

1. This analysis is drawn from the data collected by the Communications Flow Census Project directed by Ithiel de Sola Pool with support from the Markle Foundation. Research associates on the project include Sophia Wong, G. Richard Fryling, Roger Hurwitz, and Gavan Duffy. The initial report from this project was published by Professor Pool under the title "Tracking the Flow of Information" in the August 12, 1983, volume of *Science*. The full report, *Communications Flows: A Census in the United States and Japan,* includes complete data tables and extensive comparisons to parallel Japanese data and has been published by Tokyo University Press, and in the United States by North Holland Press. This particular report is part of a series from the Future of the Mass Audience Project for which W. Russell Neuman is principal investigator.

2. We will use the phrase "delivered to the home" or some variant throughout this report as an informal descriptor of leisure-time mass-communications behavior. It is true, of course, that people listen a great deal to radio in the car, watch television at a neighbor's home, and read a newspaper on the train or on a coffee break at work. We will simply include these behaviors (insofar as current data collection techniques permit) within our definition of leisure media exposure "in the home."

3. See Tomita (1975). The Japanese study was done under the direction of Professor Hiroshi Inose of Tokyo University and Mr. Nozomu Takasaki of the Research Institute of Telecommunications and Economics.

4. The Japanese attempted to include measures of the flow of graphic communication as well as words, and used the concept of the information bit derived from classic communication theory as the central metric. Television versus magazines, radio versus books, confronts us with a classic issue of apples and oranges. Each uses a very different mix of graphic, textual, and audio communication and no single metric could possibly do justice to each. The unit of the word was selected by the MIT research team as the optimal first cut at comparative measurement. We have not included estimates of graphic communication in these data.

5. We are, however, currently analyzing new sources of time-series data on informative flow in the office setting and hope ultimately to integrate those findings into the current data set.

Chapter 6

LINKING CULTURE AND OTHER SOCIETAL SYSTEMS

Karl Erik Rosengren

THE CULTURE OF HUMAN SOCIETY is a set of abstract, human-made patterns of and for behavior, action, and artifacts (Tylor, 1958; Kroeber & Kluckhohm, 1952; Kroeber & Parsons, 1958; Vermeersch, 1977). Culture is acquired and transmitted by means of meaningful symbols. As a system, culture may be conceptualized in terms of structure and process. As process, culture manifests itself as regularities in behavior and actions of groups and aggregates of individuals. As structure, it must be conceptualized as supraindividual, abstract wholes of ideas, beliefs, and values.

Both as structure and as process, the system of culture is related to other societal systems—economy and polity, for example. Within a given society, four types of such relations are possible (Rosengren, 1981. Table 6.1 orders these four types in a typology. It is a typology of relations between culture and other societal systems, but it is also a typology of theories concerning these relationships. For centuries, heated debates have raged along the axis, materialism/idealism. Gradually, however, scientific and scholarly discussions have moved to the ideologically less inflammable but perhaps more realistic axis, interdependency/autonomy (Bell, 1976; Bunge, 1981; Harris, 1980; Lumsden & Wilson, 1981).

The whole of society can be interpreted and explicated in terms of each of the main societal systems—in political, economic, religious, scientific, artistic terms. Yet the system of culture—society's basic ideas, values, and beliefs about and for itself and the world at large—is more central to all other societal systems than is any other system. Culture is close to them all, although the "distance" between the rest of the systems varies from case to case.

Figure 6.1 presents a typology of these mutually interacting societal systems, visualizing their relationships in terms of a circumplex (Guttman, 1954; Katz et al., 1973; Shepard, 1978; Lumsden & Wilson, 1981). The circumplex locates the subsystems in this two-dimensional space in a way that suggests their closest "neighbors" in society. Boundary lines between subsystems, the "spokes of the wheel," have been made undulating to indicate that the location of each subsystem is not completely unequivocal. Yet it seems fairly reasonable that the neighbors of economy, for example, are polity and technology, or that scholarship falls between literature and science. The substantive subsystems in Figure 6.1 are mapped in terms of their manifest or recognized functions along a two-dimensional functional typology—instrumental/expressive and normative/cognitive. For example, economy and technology have a primarily instrumental orientation, whereas their neighbors—polity and science—are more normative and cognitive, respectively. Art and literature, on the other hand, are primarily expressively oriented; their neighbors—religion and scholarship—are more normative and cognitive, respectively. In combination, the two functional dimensions represent the four ultimate values of "truth, utility, beauty, and righteousness or holiness" on which are built the fundamental institutions of society (for example, science, economy, art, and religion, respectively). This typology of values is similar to several other Weberian or Parsonian typologies, particularly the one presented by Namenwirth and Bibbee (1976).

At the center of the circumplex—"the hub of the wheel"—we find culture. Culture is both cognitively and normatively oriented, both expressive and instrumental. Culture, then, unites and relates the subsystems one to the other. The two boundary circles of the hub il-

TABLE 6.1

Four Types of Relations Between Culture and Other Societal Systems

| | | Other Societal Systems Influence Culture? | |
		YES	NO
Culture Influences Other Societal Systems?	YES	Interdependence	Idealism
	NO	Materialism	Autonomy

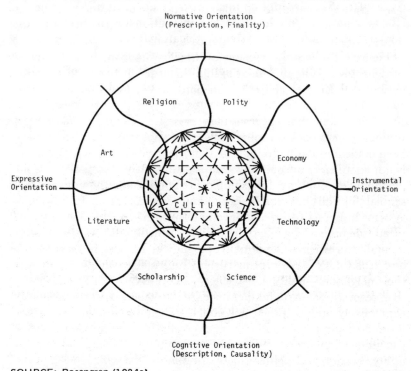

Figure 6.1 **The Great Wheel of Culture in Society**

SOURCE: Rosengren (1984a).

lustrate the fact that there are specific cultures, such as political or scientific cultures, as well as a more general culture that is more or less common to the whole of society. The dashed network within the hub relating the various subsystems to each other tells us something about the complexity of the overall system and of the immense communication and coordinating functions fulfilled by culture.

Because culture is seen as a system of symbols standing for ideas, beliefs, and values, the study of culture is necessarily a study of symbols and symbol systems. We cannot, however, neglect culture's concrete manifestations, material objects (artifacts) and social action. To capture these manifestations, we would have to add a third dimension to the wheel, making it a cylinder or a cone that would include three levels: symbols, objects, and actions. It is characteristic of systems of symbols, objects, and actions alike that they are produced, maintained, and developed within the framework of institutions. But in the case of culture broadly defined, there is no institutional structure. Rather, culture falls back on the institutional structures of other systems, especially those systems' educational and socializing agents. Socialization, then, mediates between culture as structure and culture as process; it is the linkage among the three dimensions of the social fabric that we have identified: symbol, object, and action.

SOCIALIZATION

The theme of socialization covers the twin stories of growing and staying human. Three fields of discussion may be discerned: the content, the process, and the agents of socialization.

When discussing the content of socialization, a distinction is often made between "primary socialization," or the learning and teaching of cultures at large that are not tied to specific roles or statuses, and "secondary socialization," or the learning and teaching of specific social roles and statuses (Berger & Luckman, 1967). Primary socialization takes place mainly in the central regions of the wheel of culture, whereas secondary socialization usually takes place in the various peripheral sectors of the wheel. In a given society, the content of socialization may thus be characterized as more or less central/peripheral, more or less expressive/instrumental, more or less cognitive/normative.

There are always two parties involved in the socialization process—society and the individual. But differences occur among the major socialization theories with respect to how the individual and how the society should be characterized (Burrell & Morgan, 1979; McCron, 1976; Rosengren, 1983a). The individual may be seen as a largely passive object of socialization by society through agents such as the family, the school, or the mass media. Or the individual may be seen as a more or less active subject taking part in and affecting the process of socialization. Society may be seen from either a conflict or a consensus perspective. It may be necessary for some analytical purposes to choose one of these views of the individual and of society over the other. But in reality, all individuals are both active subjects and passive objects and all societies are characterized by both conflict and consensus (Thunberg et al., 1982). These may sound like bland platitudes, but the fruitfulness of this way of proceeding is especially evident when considering the socialization role of the mass media. Mass media may, for example, be regarded as contributors to consensus in a conflict-based society. In relation to the mass media, the individual stands out both as a passive object and as an active subject.

In modern complex societies, we have at least eight large groups of socializing agents: family, peer groups, work groups, churches, legal agencies, schools, organizations (such as trade unions), and mass media. The knowledge, norms, and skills mediated by the mass media cover the whole range of culture—from concrete, specific, implicit, lived culture to abstract, general, explicit and formalized culture; from bland mainstream culture to subcultures of bitter conflict. The mass media of the modern society are thus able to take over large parts of the socialization carried out both in informal groups (for instance, peer and work groups) and formal organizations (such as schools and trade unions). A number of scholars have observed that the mass media have indeed taken over socialization functions formerly fulfilled by the family, the churches, and the schools (Ball-Rokeach, 1985; Gerbner, 1984; Noble, 1975; Postman, 1979). Of course, the role played by any socializing agent varies not only between societies and over historical time but also over the life span of the individual (Rubin, 1985). Adolescence is one of the most dramatic periods of flux in this respect. It is when TV consumption rapidly falls from extremely high to low rates, being replaced by transistor and taperecorded music (Johnsson-Smaragdi, 1983; Roe, 1983). This radical change in media habits reflects a larger shift in agents of socialization, away from home and parents to peers and peer groups.

In the interplay between various socializing agencies, the mass media have usually been regarded as a disturbing factor, inappropriately imposed on the more important and legitimate socialization processes taking place in family or at school. Excessive media use has been seen as eroding morals, debasing beauty, destroying knowledge, and preventing much useful work; in other words, working against the ultimate values of the wheel of culture—righteousness, beauty, truth, and utility. But mass media use is not independent of other socializing agents. It may, for example, be affected by the shortcomings or even failures of other socializing agents—school, for instance, or the family (Roe, 1983). There is interaction not only between the individual and socializing agents, then, but also among the socializing agents themselves (for instance, the notion of structural dependency; Ball-Rokeach, 1985). It is within the parameters of such double interactions that we are all being continuously socialized, and that the media function as linkages in the social fabric.

Two important and general characteristics of interactions between the individual and socializing agents are the various resources of the individual in the socialization process, and the degree of control exerted by the socializing agents. Combined, these two characteristics yield the four general types of socialization presented in Table 6.2. For

TABLE 6.2

Four Types of Socialization

		Control Exercised by Socializing Agent	
		High	Low
Individual's Resources	Rich	Consensual Socialization [1] (strivers, conformists, careerists, early adopters)	Pluralistic Socialization [2] (revellers, rebels, bohemians, innovators)
	Poor	Protective Socialization [3] (loners, pedants, petty officials, late adopters)	Laissez-Faire Socialization [4] (losers, lumpers, dropouts, laggards)

each type of socialization, there is an outcome presented in the form of a personality type. These socialization (Chaffee et al., 1973) and personality types are ideal types that are seldom or never manifested empirically in their pure form. This typology may be employed to characterize the content, the process, and the agents of socialization. In the case of media socialization agents, this line of thinking would lead us to media system dependency theory as developed by Ball-Rokeach (Ball-Rokeach, 1985; Ball-Rokeach & DeFleur, 1976; Ball-Rokeach, Rokeach, & Grube, 1984; DeFleur & Ball-Rokeach, 1982). If, for example, individuals' resources are poor in the sense that their environments do not provide them with stable and reliable alternative socialization resources, then they are more likely to come to depend upon the media as a socializing agent than are individuals with rich socialization resources. As such, media system dependency may be conceptualized as an independent variable—a configuration of individual, positional, and structural characteristics (Ball-Rokeach, 1985; Thunberg et al., 1982) leading to more or less intensive and extensive mass media use—or as dependent variable, the effects and consequences of such media use (Ball-Rokeach, Rokeach, & Grube, 1984; Rosengren & Windahl, 1972, 1977; Rubin & Windahl, 1982; Windahl et al., 1984). Both as dependent and independent variable, media system dependency would be lowest in cell 2 of the typology presented above, highest in cell 3, with cells 1 and 4 coming in between.

DEVELOPING CULTURAL INDICATORS

Mass media function as linkages for culture and other societal systems in two ways: (1) they help to transform abstract patterns of ideas, values, and beliefs into patterns of action and artifacts—"vertical linkages," and (2) they help culture in acting as a generalized mediator between different systems of society, relating them to one another—"horizontal linkages." Horizontal and vertical linkages may be related to dependency theory. Individual media system dependency (Ball-Rokeach, 1985) represents a special case of vertical linkages. Structural dependency represents a special case of horizontal linkages. To explain and understand both linkages, we need reliable and valid measures tapping relevant aspects of both culture and other societal systems.

The systematic, scholarly study of culture has proceeded at least since the romantic era in the late eighteenth century and early nineteenth century, but not until the 1930s did Sorokin (1937-1941) launch a main attempt to measure culture and cultural change in a way comparable to the way other large societal systems were being measured. At about the same time, Ogburn (1933) took on the task of developing measurements of *Recent Social Trends* (I-II) by building societal indicators. From this period, three types of societal indicators emerged: economic, social, and cultural. Economic indicators tap societal characteristics pertaining to the production and accumulation of goods. Social indicators tap societal characteristics pertaining to the distribution and consumption of goods (and ills) in society. Cultural indicators tap societal characteristics pertaining to continuity and change—the structure of ideas, beliefs, and values serving to maintain and reproduce society as a whole and its various subsystems, but also serving change and innovation in society.

Although Sorokin, Ogburn, and others (for instance, Lasswell & Namenwirth, 1968; Stone et al., 1966) had pioneered the study of cultural indicators, Gerbner (1969) was the first to introduce the term "cultural indicator" in the late 1960s. Gerbner has maintained a regular monitoring activity of American television, developing and applying a number of cultural indicators, the most widespread of which has become the "violence profile" (Gerbner et al., 1980). These efforts have been widely discussed and criticized (Gerbner et al., 1981a; Hirsch, 1980; Hughes, 1980), but they have also been replicated in other parts of the world (Melischek, Rosengren, & Stappers, 1984).

Yet another interesting research tradition with clear implications for cultural indicators research was initiated by David McClelland and the group around him, whose achievement, affiliation, and power motives seem to pervade different cultures differently, varying over time within cultures (McClelland, 1961, 1975; McClelland et al., 1953).

Also, Rokeach's measurements of terminal and instrumental values as distributed in populations and expressed in ideological texts are relevant to cultural indicators research (E. Block, 1984; Rankin & Grube, 1980; Rokeach, 1973, 1974, 1979; Rous & Lee, 1978). Inglehart's measurements of materialistic and postmaterialistic value constellations have been pursued since the late 1960s and clearly tap important cultural characteristics (Inglehart, 1977, 1984, 1985). Two other attempts to measure different aspects of culture are being made in Hungary and Sweden. The Hungarian efforts (Hankiss et al., 1984) build on survey material and relate to Rokeach's "value survey" (1982). Rokeachan values are central also to the Swedish efforts based on content analysis of dailies and weeklies and including other perspectives as well (Andren, 1984; E. Block, 1984; P. Block, 1984; Goldmann, 1984; Nowak, 1984; Rosengren, 1983b, 1984a).

Three methodological types of cultural indicators roughly correspond to three major research traditions in social research and the humanities: content analysis, survey research, and secondary analysis of statistical, mostly behavioral data. Researchers' use of these various types of cultural indicators will gradually make the many-faceted nature of culture increasingly clear, and in the process the concept of culture will be theoretically refined. Equally important, the relationship between objective and subjective indicators of societal life should become clearer because culture is the prime mediator or link between them (Rosengren, 1985).

HORIZONTAL AND VERTICAL
MEDIA LINKAGES

As previously indicated, horizontal media linkages concern the ways in which the media act to link the various subsystems of society. In order to study such horizontal linkages, cultural indicators should be related to economic and social indicators. In addition to external influences upon society, there are four theoretically possible relations between society's subsystems that were identified in Table 6.1 as interdependence, idealism, materialism, and autonomy. In order to disentangle which of these relations apply in any one society, it is necessary to examine economic, social, and cultural indicators within the same study.

Societal change—economic, social, and cultural—takes place on a time scale ranging from millennia over centuries and decades to years or parts of years. "It would be strange indeed, if the relations between culture and social structure were to be the same under those very different (temporal) circumstances'' (Carlsson et al., 1981). It would seem reasonable to assume, for instance, that the more extended the time scale, the more basic the driving force behind the change. In the very short run, a few years and less, one might expect autonomy, and in the perspectives of decades, one might expect interdependence. At present, we have only fragmentary evidence that may be applied to try to answer such basic questions about the nature of the horizontal linkages within society. However, pioneering work by Namenwirth (1973), Namenwirth and Bibbee (1976), Weber (1981, 1984), Klingemann, Mohler, and Weber (1982), Barr (1979), Kleinknecht (1981), and others holds promise for producing the evidence required to answer such basic questions (Rosengren, 1984a). Only when such evidence is available will we be able to answer the more specific question of how the media act to link societal subsystems.

The study of media linkages between the system (macro) and the individual (micro) levels—vertical linkages—comes to the fore in two different connections. Within each societal subsystem, media link the symbolic level to the levels of actions and artifacts (objects). The relations between the various subsystems can be studied at the macro level alone—for instance, at the symbolic level. But when we approach the problem of the mechanisms relating the systems to each other, it is unavoidable to include the micro level, for culture is a macro phenomenon internalized in flesh-and-blood human beings.

In contrast to the lack of research on horizontal media linkages, the vertical relationships between the media and the individual have been studied a great deal. Two dominant approaches are effects research and uses and gratifications research (Blumler & Katz, 1974; Palmgreen, Wenner, & Rosengren, 1985). More specific research traditions in the area are diffusion of news research (Quarles et al., 1983; Rosengren, 1973), agenda-setting research (McCombs & Shaw, 1972; McCombs & Weaver, 1985), "spiral of silence" research (Noelle-Neuman, 1974, 1979, 1983; Taylor, 1982, 1985), and cultivation research (Gerbner, 1969, 1984). Each of these approaches and traditions may be seen as relevant to specific parts and aspects of the study of the mass media forming vertical linkages in the social fabric. All of them represent specific cases of media socialization.

Gerbner's cultivation research deals with individuals' values and cognitions as influenced by their differential contacts with society's culture as transferred by television. As such, this research tradition is one of the most relevant to the question of vertical linkages of the social fabric created by the mass media. Systematic, yearly measure-

ments of the content of television drama establish the main characteristics of the "TV world"—the picture of people, society, and the
world at large offered by television. These are employed as cultural indicators and are linked to the process of cultivation by comparing
heavy and light TV viewers in terms of their conceptions of themselves, the surrounding society, and the world at large. A major vertical linkage question is, Are those people steeped in the "TV world"
more inclined to regard themselves and their environment in a way
reminiscent of that "TV world" than are people less immersed in that
"TV world?" The main answer to this question offered by Gerbner
and his associates is yes, television does shape in significant ways the
conceptions and attitudes of various groups of viewers (Gerbner,
1984; Gross, 1984; Morgan, 1984; Rothschild, 1984; Signorielli,
1984). The type of socialization process studied by Gerbner's group—
cultivation—represents a special case of enculturation, enculturation
by television. That TV's influence is felt with differential strength in
different social groupings and within different social strata has
become increasingly evident and emphasized within the Gerbner
group (for instance, Rothschild, 1984).

Gerbner's approach adds new impetus to effects research, being
part of the more general movement away from specific short-term effects toward more general and long-term effects. It also has been applied to many of the sectors of the wheel of culture presented in Figure
6.1. The types of content examined include conceptions of violence in
society (Gerbner et al., 1980), tolerance and intolerance toward blacks
and gays (Gross, 1984), beliefs about older people (Gerbner et al.,
1980), political attitudes (Gerbner, 1984), role socialization resulting
in differential job aspirations (Hedinsson, 1981; Hedinsson & Windahl, 1984; Morgan, 1980), and health and medicine (Gerbner et al.,
1981b).

Cultivation analysis has been harshly criticized (Hirsch, 1980;
Hughes, 1980), but it has also stimulated many replication attempts in
and out of the U.S. context, attempts that have produced mixed results (Bouwman, 1984; Hawkins & Pingree, 1984; Hedinsson & Windahl, 1984; Wober, 1984). Gerbner's approach, nonetheless, represents a major, viable innovation in the resesarch trying to map media
linkages of the social fabric by carrying out a two-pronged analysis
that contains both micro analysis (the cultivation study) and macro
analysis (the cultural indicators study) within the same framework. Its
weak spots are the representativeness of the media content analyzed in
the cultural indicator part of the program, and the techniques of
measurement and analysis used in the cultivation part. In addition, the

variables dominating in the program tend to tap opinions and beliefs more than values and value orientations so central to the concept of culture.

Taking a long view on the role of media as vertical linkages in the social fabric, it is clear that the confluence of socialization research, mass communication research, and value research should not be postponed. In the long run, the role of socialization and its various aspects—content, process, agents—can be neglected in this field of research only at the risk of never fully grasping the role of media as vertical linkages in the social fabric. For a beginning, already well-known measures of the various aspects of media use (amount of consumption, type of media content preferred, dependency relations with different media and different types of media content, circumstances of consumption) could be included in cultural indicators research through simultaneous administration of survey studies. Conversely, value batteries such as those created by Rokeach and Inglehart could be included in some routine measurements of media consumption.

CONCLUSION: INTEGRATING THE STUDY OF HORIZONTAL AND VERTICAL LINKAGES

The development, application, and integration of individually oriented and system-oriented cultural indicators based on content analysis, survey research, and secondary analysis of behavioral and other relevant data is a demanding task in its own right, made especially fascinating when undertaken in productive interaction with relevant parts of socialization research. If pursued by a number of research groups in different countries, it will result in increased understanding of culture as structure and culture as process, culture as patterns of ideas and values, and as patterns of actions and artifacts. The role of the media as linkages among the various levels and manifestations of culture will stand out more clearly. In order to assess the nature of the relations between culture and other societal systems, we must go even further, beyond cultural indicators to include economic indicators, objective social indicators, and subjective social indicators, as well as more specific indicators tapping conditions in various societal subsystems such as political or scientific indicators.

Real stepping-stones for such an integrated research enterprise are already offered by cultural indicators research, such as that of Inglehart and Rokeach. Inglehart's repeated measurements of materialism and postmaterialism in various populations could be formally related to

(1) other cultural indicators based on content analysis of mass media content and on secondary analysis of behavioral statistics,

(2) economic indicators tapping growth and stagnation in the economy,

(3) objective social indicators tapping the use of the resources put at the disposal of society by the economic subsystem,

(4) subjective social indicators tapping the perception and evaluation of those resources by various subgroups in the population,

(5) measures of media use and media dependency in the same subgroups of the population.

Rokeachan measures of the values of freedom and equality could be formally related to equality and freedom in society as tapped by objective social indicators measuring bias and skewness in the distribution of economic and social resources. A good starting point for such studies would be the series of cultural indicators collected within the framework of the Swedish Cultural Indicators Research Program by Eva Block in her study of political values as manifested in representative samples of Swedish newspaper editorials from 1945 to 1975. Other studies in the same program offer similar opportunities for other values and other subsystems of society (P. Block, 1984; Goldmann, 1984; Nowak, 1984; Rosengren, 1984b).

But sooner or later, new and independent studies must be launched, building on integrated data collections of system-oriented and individual-oriented cultural indicators. Such studies will be very demanding in terms of resources. But they will present some answers to the questions discussed in this chapter. That is, they will offer a much deeper understanding than our present one of the role played by the mass media as horizontal and vertical linkages in the social fabric, linkages between culture as structure and culture as process, between culture and other societal systems.

Chapter 7

THE MASS MEDIA IN
EARTHQUAKE WARNING

Ralph H. Turner
Denise H. Paz

WITH MEMORIES OF DESTRUCTION by the 1971 San Fernando-Sylmar earthquake and two years of occasional reports on the newly developing science of earthquake prediction still fresh, southern Californians were bombarded in 1976 by an unprecedented flood of earthquake news. On February 13, the U.S. Geological Survey reported that a vast area along the San Andreas fault nearest to Los Angeles was uplifted, in a pattern that had often preceded earthquakes in the past. This region of the fault had been "locked" for over a century, since the last Richter magnitude 8 + quake, against the continuous lengthwise movement of the entire fault. Two months later, James Whitcomb of prestigious California Institute of Technology publicly advanced the "hypothesis" that, on other bases, Los Angeles was due for a destructive quake within one year. And in late November, Henry Minturn, falsely claiming to have qualifications as a seismologist and offering affidavits to verify a string of previously successful predictions, was featured by local and national television in forecasting an earthquake for Los Angeles on December 20. Meantime, more people were killed in more great earthquakes around the world in that same year (1976) than in any other year in the century.

As the keystone in a study of community response to the earthquake threat, we systematically monitored local media coverage of earthquake topics in 1976, 1977, and 1978; conducted a field survey of 1,500 adult residents in Los Angeles County in early 1977; and carried out five additional telephone surveys in 1977 and 1978, and in January 1979 immediately after a moderate but nondestructive earthquake struck in the metropolis.[1] In this chapter we shall summarize some of the findings on public reliance on different media sources for different kinds of earthquake information, applicability of the two-step flow hypothesis, individual differences in media usage, and relations between media coverage and the ebb and flow of rumor.

USE OF MEDIA SOURCES

In light of the rapid succession of newsworthy items throughout 1976, it is hardly surprising that nearly everyone had heard something about earthquakes, and that as many as 43% felt that there would probably be a damaging earthquake locally within a year. To identify the leading information sources we asked, "During the past year have you heard about earthquakes or earthquake predictions or earthquake preparedness from *any* of the following sources?" Items included in the checklist are given in Figure 7.1, with the addition of "people" and "organizations" that were sometimes volunteered in response to a concluding probe for other sources. The saturation levels for television news, newspapers, and radio are striking, as is the use of multiple sources. Nearly half the respondents learned about earthquakes from five or more of the sources, nearly two-thirds used four or more sources, and only 1 person in 14 heard about earthquakes from just a single source.

It is of interest that the treatments in greater depth, characteristic of television specials and magazine articles, reached substantial segments of the population. The high rate for movies undoubtedly refers mostly to the movie *Earthquake,* which was being shown at that time and may have been an important source of prevalent misconceptions. A series of professionally written and acted television spots, prepared by the California Office of Emergency Services, had disappointing impact as compared to regular news broadcasts. Similarly, the carefully crafted pamphlets on earthquake safety mailed to all residents as enclosures to their telephone bills were remembered by relatively few.

The relative *importance* of media sources, as distinct from prevalence, was tapped by a different sequence of questions. Respondents were asked to describe any "predictions, statements or warnings about earthquakes in Southern California heard in the past year or so." Up to five answers were listed, and for each the respondent was asked, "Do you remember what your *chief source of information*

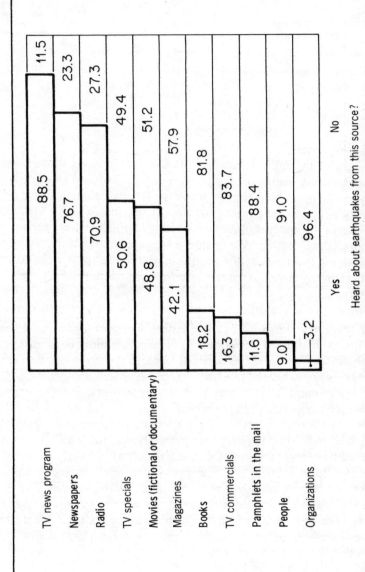

Figure 7.1 Sources of Information about Earthquakes, Earthquake Predictions, and Earthquake Preparedness

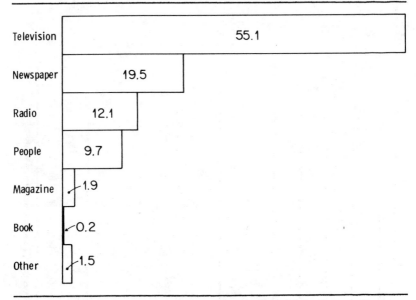

Figure 7.2 Chief Source of Information about Earthquake Predictions, Forecasts, and Cautions

about this prediction was?'' The question was open-ended, and the results are summarized in Figure 7.2. Figure 7.2 cannot be compared directly with Figure 7.1 because the topic was narrowed, because percentages are based on 1,788 *reports* rather than 1,450 *people,* and because the volunteered answers could not be broken down into exactly the same categories as the checklist.

The three primary sources and their order remain the same. But the differences in relative importance are greatly accentuated. Television is named by nearly three times as many people as newspapers and by more than four times as many as radio. "People" sources assume greater importance than before, surpassing newspapers and books. Although not many respondents think of their family, friends, and associates as sources of information on earthquakes, many of those who do are inclined to accept people as their *chief source* of information.

AFFINITIES

Do people learn about different kinds of announcements from different media sources? To answer this question we grouped announcements people mentioned into scientific, general (or vague), pseudoscientific, and prophetic. In addition, we looked separately at the Minturn pseudoscientific forecast for a quake in Los Angeles on December 20, 1976 and at the forecast that California would break off and fall into the Pacific Ocean because of the wide recognition they received. The results appear in Table 7.1.

When we look at the four inclusive types of announcement and the two best-known specific forecasts separately, the disproportionate reliance on television applies in every instance. Likewise, newspapers always remain far behind, but in second place. Nevertheless we can still observe some *affinities* between particular media and types of announcements. There is some affinity between television and general announcements. Relatively more of the people who mentioned rather vague and general earthquake forecasts credited them to television. Perhaps television commands a low level of attention for detail, or specializes in very brief news items, or perhaps it is just that more people are exposed for longer periods to television. In contrast, there is an affinity between scientific announcements and newspapers and magazines. The reporting of scientific announcements is facilitated by the provision for longer items in newspapers and magazines, and people who are interested in science are probably more motivated to make the effort to read extended accounts.

Radio and people as sources show affinity with pseudoscientific announcements. The affinity also shows separately for both the Minturn and "breakoff" forecasts. It is quite in accordance with theories of rumor that pseudoscientific beliefs should be spread disproportionately by word of mouth whereas the printed word is prominent in the spread of scientific information. Radio "call-in" and "talk" shows may contribute to the spread of rumors by airing them and by being especially responsive to timely public preoccupations, even while program moderators attempt to discredit them.

Prophetic announcements, although credited principally to the leading media, show a distinct affinity with books and with "other" and "don't know" as the source. One interpretation of this affinity is that the worlds of secular and religious prophecy have their own networks and media for communicating among those who are interested in prophecy. To a greater extent than is true for the other types of announcement, they supplement the standard media with their own books and magazines and perhaps tracts and meetings. At the same time, they are significant runners-up to scientific announcements in newspapers and magazines, in which they are often covered in special departments.

TABLE 7.1

Chief Source of Information by Type of Earthquake
Prediction, Forecast, or Caution

| Type of Medium | Inclusive Types of Announcement | | | | Specific Announcements | |
	Scientific	General	Pseudo-scientific	Prophetic	Minturn	California Breakoff
Television	47.1	58.3	51.3	43.7	54.9	37.4
Newspapers	27.5	14.1	18.5	23.6	17.9	22.0
Radio	10.1	11.4	13.6	5.6	13.4	11.4
People	6.2	8.8	11.1	7.6	9.7	15.4
Magazines	22.2	1.5	1.3	5.6	1.0	4.1
Books	0	0	.3	.7	.2	.8
Other, Don't know	6.9	5.9	3.9	13.2	2.9	8.9
Total	100.0	100.0	100.0	100.0	100.0	100.0
Announcements	276	660	708	144	619	123

We also have a separate record of people's chief source of information about the Southern California uplift. The pattern of information sources is almost identical to that for all scientific announcements and equally different from the pattern for general, pseudoscientific, and prophetic announcements.

CREDIBILITY OF SOURCES

Not all announcements are taken equally seriously. For each "prediction, statement, or warning" people remembered, we asked how seriously they took the announcement. The presumed scientific or nonscientific character of the announcement and the communication source are the most important variables we uncovered to explain these differences. In general, scientific announcements are more often taken seriously than prophetic and pseudoscientific announcements, even though they are usually thought to refer to earthquakes of lesser intensities. The most striking finding about source and credibility is that magazines and books are much more credible than any of the other sources. Perhaps prophetic announcements would have been taken less seriously if they were not disproportionately reported in books and magazines.

Differences among the other sources are not striking. Television and newspapers are about equally credible, coming next after magazines and books. Radio falls below television and newspapers, having about half the credibility of magazines and books. Although the difference is slight, people have the least credibility as sources of information.

CHANGING MEDIA USE

An important concern of our investigation was the effect of an extended period of waiting for a vaguely forecasted disaster in the unspecified but presumably imminent future. The battery of questions about earthquake announcements was repeated for fresh samples of respondents at five-month intervals throughout 1977 and 1978. The information contained in Figure 7.2 (for February 1977) is graphed cumulatively in Figure 7.3, with comparable information for each of the four subsequent surveys. By comparing the relative area of each medium over time, the reader can easily see how reliance on particular media changed.

The steady decline in reliance on television after early 1977 is remarkable. The drop from 52.7% to 33.6% at the end of 1978 is highly significant and approximates a linear trend line quite closely ($F = 72.03; 1, 3df; p = .01$). In sharp contrast, principal reliance on newspapers almost doubles (18.7% to 36.7%) during the same period. This relationship is also highly significant and the increase is loosely described by a linear trend line ($F = 29.48; 1,3 df; p = .05$). Although television was cited more than two and a half times as often as newspapers at the beginning of the study period, newspapers were cited slightly more often than television by the end of the period.

Although the changes are more erratic and are not statistically significant, the general trend for radio is similar to the trend for television, and the general trend for books and magazines (not graphed separately) is similar to that for newspapers. Hence the observed changes might be described as a shift away from the airways to the printed word as prime sources of information about future earthquake prospects.

An explanation can be found in elaborating the idea of affinities between particular media and types of content. Perhaps the effect of repeated attention to the same topic leads people to seek more detailed and profound information. Having heard repeatedly that we are overdue for a severe earthquake, people are attentive only to new and elaborated information about the earthquake threat. The printed word can more easily convey such elaborations than television and radio with their brief announcements incorporated in daily news broadcasts.

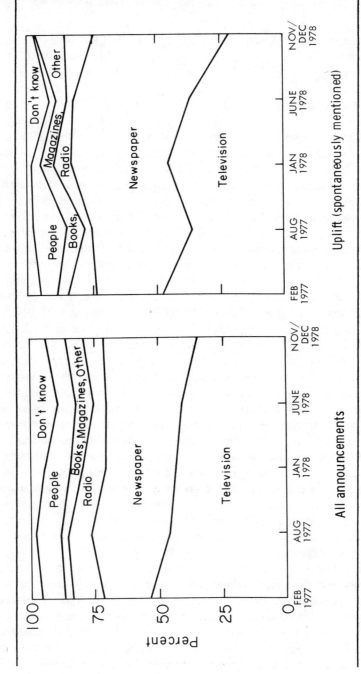

Figure 7.3 Chief Source of Information on Earthquake Predictions, Forecasts, and Cautions

Some of the change in media prominence might have been the consequence of changing types of announcements. Accordingly we have graphed separately, for comparison, the sources given for information about the uplift (Figure 7.3), when the uplift is mentioned as one of the "predictions, statements, or warnings about earthquakes" people have heard. The downward trend for television, although less linear, is magnified (from 46.6% to 22.2%). Starting from a higher level, the use of newspapers increases by the same proportion as before, from 26.0% to 51.9%.

Comparing the sources for information about the uplift and about all earthquake announcements suggests two observations. First, the shift from television to newspapers cannot be explained primarily by the greater salience of the uplift. Second, a disproportionate amount of the shift is by people who are sufficiently tuned in to the scientific basis for concern about earthquake warnings. Thus, increased relative salience of the uplift and increased reliance on the print media combine to suggest a pattern of awareness and communication that, although less intense than at the start of our investigation, is less frivolous and more securely harnessed to reality.

COMMUNICATION STYLES

Although a combination of media use and discussion is the normal communication pattern, individual *communication styles* differ. We distinguished three sets of respondents. First are those who relied exclusively on the media without engaging in discussion of earthquake topics. The number who rely exclusively on discussion is too small for separate analysis. But we can combine those few with all respondents who mention family members, friends, co-workers, or other discussion partners as the chief source of information about one or more earthquake predictions, near predictions, or forecasts. The result of this sorting process is to separate respondents who identify the media as their chief source of information and use informal discussion to sift and extend their understanding from respondents who place greater than customary reliance on informal discussion as an authoritative source of information.

Two-thirds of our respondents use interpersonal discussion to supplement the mass media, confirming the applicability of the two-step or multistep flow model in which the first step is media exposure and the second step is interpersonal discussion of media messages. About a quarter of the respondents rely exclusively on the mass media and are therefore not exposed to the important effects of interpersonal discussion. A relatively small fraction (9%) of the respondents are willing to accept interpersonal discussion as a primary source of information about earthquakes.[2] The low reliance on interpersonal discussion in spite of high rates of participation in such discussion is consistent with Ball-Rokeach's (1985) elaboration of media dependency theory. The media system as a whole is structurally located to serve as our primary disaster and emergency alert system, creating individual dependency for most of our respondents. On the other hand, such infrequent primary reliance on interpersonal discussion seems anomalous in light of the high credibility accorded unusual animal behavior and personal intuition as earthquake signs—most likely disseminated through interpersonal discussion (Turner et al., in press, chapter 10).

Three sets of variables will serve to illustrate the significance of this trichotomy of communication styles. First, what effect has experience with earthquakes on communication style? Two measures of experience were used and compared. The first was simply the number of earthquakes experienced personally, from none to five or more. The second measure was the extent of physical injury and property damage experienced personally or vicariously in an earthquake. Damage and injury to the respondent and to close personal associates were combined on the assumption that vicarious experience within one's primary group has the same effect as personal experience. Associations between the two measures of earthquake experience and communication style are presented in Table 7.2.

Respondents with little or no earthquake experience are found disproportionately among those who rely excessively on interpersonal discussion. There seems to be a naive reliance on interpersonal sources and probably a hypersusceptibility to rumor among the inexperienced that is rare among people who have experienced three or more earthquakes. The effect of personal and vicarious experience of earthquake damage is just as clear and dramatic, but on the tendency to supplement media information with clarifying interpersonal discussion rather than relying exclusively on media reports.

These two relationships suggest something about the differing effects of quantity and quality of earthquake experience. The very fact of experiencing earthquakes, without in most cases experiencing personal loss, reduces naive susceptibility to rumor and to accepting neighborhood and office talk as truth. But the more personal experience of an earthquake's fury motivates individuals to seek clarification and evaluation of what they hear or read in the media through discussion with friends, family members, and work associates.

TABLE 7.2
Patterns of Communication Use by Earthquake Experience and Awareness

Experience and Awareness Variables	Exclusively Media	Discussion Supplements Media	Disproportionate Reliance on Discussion	Total %	Total Number
Earthquakes experienced					
None	31.4%	54.8%	13.7%	99.9	299
One	22.6	69.1	8.4	100.1	740
Two	21.0	71.2	7.7	99.9	271
Three or more	28.7	69.4	1.9	100.0	108
Personal and vicarious earthquake loss					
None	30.5	61.4	8.2	100.1	709
Little	23.8	66.9	9.3	100.0	354
Moderate	14.9	75.1	10.0	100.0	221
Extensive	13.4	76.5	10.1	100.0	149
Awareness of uplift					
Not heard	52.4	33.2	58.6		
Heard, not understood	16.4	16.5	14.8		
Heard and understood	16.4	19.4	10.2		
Heard, understood, and relevant	14.7	30.9	16.4		
Total percentage	99.9	100.0	100.0		
Total number	353	952	128		
Awareness of endangered groups					
None	47.3	30.0	41.7		
One	21.1	26.0	26.8		
Two	14.0	20.8	18.9		
Three or more	17.6	23.2	12.6		
Total percentage	100.0	100.0	100.0		
Total number	336	937	127		

But what is the effect of communication style on level of awareness of earthquake hazard? Again, two indexes were used. As a simple hazard awareness indicator, we measured awareness of the so-called Southern California uplift or Palmdale Bulge. By combining answers to a series of questions, we could classify each of our respondents as not having heard of the bulge, having heard of the bulge but not understanding its possible connection with earthquakes, having heard and understood the connection but not anticipating damage where the respondent lived, and, finally, having heard, understood, and grasped the personal relevance of the bulge. As an index of *social* awareness we asked if some groups of people were in greater danger than others from an earthquake and who they were. The high-risk groups mentioned most often included people living in old, unreinforced masonry buildings, people living near an earthquake fault, the elderly, the poor, the disabled, and people in institutions. The index was the number of groups volunteered, from none to eight. In this case results are similar for the two variables. People who rely on the media as their chief information source but filter media information through interpersonal discussion show greater awareness than either those who rely exclusively on the media or those who rely disproportionately on interpersonal discussion. They are more likely to have heard, understood, and appreciated the personal relevance of the uplift as a potential earthquake precursor, and they are more often broadly aware that not everyone is equally at risk from an earthquake.

A third set of variables includes fear and concern about the prospect of an earthquake based on a three-item index, belief in the probability of a damaging earthquake within the next year, and an index of personal and household earthquake preparedness based on a checklist of 16 commonly recommended measures. Respondents who rely solely on the media expressed less fear and concern, were less likely to have expected a damaging earthquake within a year, and had taken fewer of the recommended measures for personal and household earthquake preparedness. The difference between respondents who used discussion to supplement the media and those who relied disproportionately on discussion were not substantial. Interpersonal discussion, whether alone or coupled with primary reliance on the media, seems crucial in making the earthquake threat real. There is a difference in *quality* of awareness, suggesting that interpersonal discussion brings the message to life, with attendant effects in arousing fear, instilling the conviction that there *will* be an earthquake, and stimulating people to do something about it.[3]

Parenthetically, we have assumed that communication style is cause and both awareness and quality of awareness are effects because that seems more plausible than the opposite assumption. But the reader should be warned that this is an assumption rather than a finding from our investigation.

LOCAL EXPERTS IN
EARTHQUAKE INFORMATION DIFFUSION

In attempting to understand the communication process, we asked whether the counterpart to opinion leaders in political communication operated in mass communication about earthquake hazard. Each person interviewed was asked, "Including yourself, is there *anyone* in your circle of friends who seems most knowledgeable about earthquakes or earthquake prediction?" If the answer was yes, the respondent was asked, "Who is that?" A total of 257 respondents, or 17.8% of the entire sample, could identify a local expert. When we separate the 36 respondents who named themselves from the rest, 15.2% of the sample knew someone among their circle of friends they regarded as expert. About half of the local experts were identified as friends, about a third as relatives and members of the immediate household, and about one-eighth as work associates. The overwhelming majority of respondents said they had no one in their social circle to whom they could turn for expert counsel on earthquakes and earthquake predictions. Thus, although discussion plays an important part in earthquake communication, it is primarily a sifting process among peers. If reliance on opinion leaders has been essential to the crystallization of public opinion on political matters, the dearth of local experts could be a serious impediment to the crystallization of viewpoints concerning the earthquake threat and could help to account for the absence of any real public opinion on earthquake preparedness.

As we look for personal characteristics that distinguish our local experts from other people, it is important to remember that the experts are strictly self-designated. Conversely, when the respondent identifies someone as a local expert, we cannot say whether the designated individual would make a corresponding self-designation. And in neither case can we tell whether there is truly expert knowledge involved, or whether the attribution is without objective justification.

To facilitate analysis we have labeled the three groups of respondents as follows: *local experts* (self-designated); *associates*—individuals who identified someone in their circle other than themselves as "most knowledgeable"; *peers*—individuals who could identify no one in their circle as "most knowledgeable." The statistical method of stepwise discriminant function analysis was used to determine which characteristics from a battery of 26 distinguished among local experts, associates, and peers. We selected 10 variables by the procedure.

The local experts have more education and are more often male, unmarried, and not working than either associates or peers. The experts are more likely to say that they have gleaned information about earthquakes from books. And they endorse a more favorable set of attitudes toward science and scientists. The use of books, the higher level of education, and the more favorable attitude toward science suggest an intellectual orientation that sets the self-designated local experts apart from others. The fact that they are more often male and have more education but are not distinguished by their occupations suggests that a traditional *status* element may also have entered into these self-conceptions.

Experts and associates together are distinguished from peers on the basis of three communication variables. They are more likely to have gleaned information about earthquakes from television specials, to have discussed the "possibility of an earthquake happening in Southern California" with someone, and to have attended a meeting dealing with earthquakes and earthquake preparedness. The associates also stand apart from both the experts and the peers in three interesting respects. Although they resemble the experts in having discussed the earthquake prospect, their discussions encompass a wider range of partners. Although they resemble experts in having attended meetings, they have attended more meetings. In addition, associates are distinguished from both experts and peers in being able to identify a larger number of groups of people who are especially at risk because of the earthquake threat. Thus, the associates play a more substantial part in the process of interpersonal communication on the earthquake threat, and they are more sensitive to the *social* implications of the situation. In some sense the associates, who may have sought out local experts, are more socially aware and exhibit a more responsible concern for fostering communication than either the experts or the peers.

Efforts to apply the classic theory of opinion leadership in the diffusion of mass communication leads us to identify a more complex *expert-associate system,* in which both local experts and associates are distinguished from peers and play special roles in the dissemination of earthquake awareness. The experts and their associates may constitute a social circle within which opinions are sifted, issues defined, and some consensus reached. As Kadushin (1966) and Merton (1968) have suggested for other realms of opinion, informal social circles composed of experts and people who take a special interest in earthquake problems may form a crucial bridge from the media to the general public.

There is support here also for Van den Ban's (1962) proposal that opinion leadership forms a hierarchy rather than a mere dichotomy. The wide involvement of the associates in informal networks suggests that they may serve as opinion leaders for people outside of these informal social circles, even though they neither see themselves nor are seen by others as experts. The information and viewpoints exchanged between experts and associates may eventually be disseminated, via the associates, to many of the less interested peers. Because there is less social distance and more informal communication between them and the peers, associates may constitute the crucial link between book-reading local experts and the general public. Their less intellectual orientation to earthquakes and their more egalitarian contact with the general public allows them to appreciate more fully the potential human implications of the earthquake threat and to convey this understanding to others. The associates' greater awareness of specially endangered groups seems to reflect the distinctive nature of their bridging role.

RUMOR AND THE MEDIA

We conclude our discussion with examination of the hypothesis that rumor flourishes to fill voids in more authoritative information, especially from the mass media. Major rumor flurries in October and November 1976 occurred when media coverage of earthquake threat declined after extensive attention to the uplift and the Whitcomb (Caltech) forecast, but earthquake preparedness television "spots" and pamphlets enclosed with telephone bills caused many people to suppose there were developments about which they were not being told.

The moderate earthquake of New Year's Day 1969 provided an opportunity for further test of this hypothesis. Our telephone survey of 509 residents, completed soon after the quake, demonstrated that many people were thinking about the relationship of this quake to the major earthquake anticipated on the basis of the uplift and other precursory signs. Many people had heard that the New Year's Day quake could be one more sign that "the big one" was imminent, that

TABLE 7.3
Source of Information About Southern California
Uplift and the New Year's Day Earthquake

Information Source	Chief Source Concerning Uplift	Interpretations of the New Year's Day Earthquake		
		No Bigger Quake Soon	Big Quake Coming Soon	Makes No Difference
Detailed Percentages				
Media	84.0	10.8	5.3	5.5
Books and magazines	3.7	—	—	0.5
Authorities	—	2.7	—	2.2
Family and relatives	2.1	8.1	2.6	6.6
Friends and neighbors	3.7	37.9	31.6	35.2
Coworkers and classmates	1.7	16.2	36.8	28.0
Don't know, others	4.8	24.3	23.7	22.0
Total	100.0	100.0	100.0	100.0
(Total number)	(294)	(37)	(182)	(38)
Summary Percentages				
Media, publications, authorities	87.7	13.5	5.3	8.2
Lay people	7.5	62.2	71.0	69.8
Don't know, others	4.8	24.3	23.7	22.0

this quake released some of the accumulating strain and thereby lessened the imminent prospect of a big one, or that this quake bore no relationship to the anticipated great quake. But scientists were reluctant to discuss these questions publicly, about which they were themselves so unsure. Hence the media generally ignored these issues in their coverage throughout January, under the misconception that ignoring public preoccupations discourages rumor.

In our survey we asked people if they had heard any of these interpretations and from what sources. Later in the interview we asked the usual questions about awareness of the uplift and chief source of information, which we report for comparison. True to the pattern in our previous interviews, 88% named the media or magazines and books as their chief sources of information about the uplift (Table 7.3). Only 7.5% named friends, relatives, or co-workers.

When we asked where people had heard interpretations of the New Year's Day earthquake, the answers were quite different. On the average, fewer than 10% named the media, books and magazines, or an authoritative source. Even with a sizable group unable to remember the source, over two-thirds named laypeople as their source. The most frequent answers were friends and co-workers. The significance of the small quake for the future had been the topic of widespread discussion at work and among friends. Without guidance from authoritative sources, relayed through the media, people turned to friends and co-workers for their interpretations.

Consistent with these findings, the investigators personally heard rumors about supposed earthquake forecasts during the month of January. In light of a widespread disposition to interpret the New Year's Day earthquake as the harbinger of a major disaster, and media disregard of this topic, there is little wonder that people were unusually susceptible to such rumors.

NOTES

1. A complete report of findings from this research will be found in Turner et al. (1986).

2. Only 18 people of the 1,450 who constitute the entire sample are omitted from this analysis, either because they neither heard about earthquakes from the media nor discussed earthquake topics informally, or because they supplied incomplete information and could not be classified. One way or another, nearly everyone heard about earthquakes.

3. Our conclusion that interpersonal discussion makes a threat more real, enhancing both fear and adaptive response, says nothing about whether the media present balanced or overdramatized accounts of the earthquake threat. However, Goltz (1984) has recently called into question the common belief that the media perpetuate disaster-response myths on the basis of a content analysis of reports on four major earthquakes by two leading Los Angeles newspapers. In addition, our content analysis of earthquake warning stories in six Los Angeles newspapers revealed a prevalent pattern in which opening statements of alarm were followed closely by calming reassurances (Turner et al., in press, chapter 2).

Chapter 8

MEDIA SYSTEM DEPENDENCY THEORY
Responses to the Eruption of Mount St. Helens

Peter L. Hirschburg
Don A. Dillman
Sandra J. Ball-Rokeach

WHEN WASHINGTON STATE'S Mount St. Helens volcano exploded in May 1980, affected populations were faced with an event that few living Americans have ever experienced, an event for which most could not have had even indirect knowledge upon which to base predictions or to organize reactions. If people knew anything of volcanos, it was probably of the bubbling Hawaiian kind, dissimilar to Mount St. Helens, which exploded like a nuclear bomb. It was not just the average citizen who lacked a frame of reference to interpret the Mount St. Helens explosion; it was also official agencies that were unable to provide information about what to do and what to expect. Few could have known or anticipated that day could become night, as a black cloud of ash moved dramatically over the whole of eastern Washington State. Nor could people comprehend that this cloud would deposit up to several inches of ash in areas hundreds of miles from the volcano site. Once the ash fell, no one "knew" what impact it might have. It was not at all similar to any other ash in their experience, as it contained both a fluffy top layer that swelled up into the air with the slightest disturbance, and a heavy layer that turned to a cement-like texture when dampened. Was it harmful to breathe? Would it damage homes, cars, crops, or other property? And how do you get rid of it? These were questions for which no one seemed to have an answer (Dillman, 1980).

The uniqueness of the Mount St. Helens event provided an opportunity to examine information-seeking activities under a rare condition of intense and pervasive ambiguity (Ball-Rokeach, 1973) in which past experience was of no help in defining or assessing the situation. We thus set about to conduct research to find out if people conformed to their normal patterns of information-seeking activity under this ambiguous condition.

MEDIA SYSTEM DEPENDENCY THEORY

Ball-Rokeach and DeFleur (1976) point to ambiguity as one of the key conditions under which affected persons should be highly dependent upon media information resources. Ambiguity is a problem of either insufficient information to define a situation or insufficient information to select one definition of a situation as opposed to another (Ball-Rokeach, 1973). Media system dependency is defined as a relation in which the attainment of goals is contingent upon the resources of the media system. The two major types of media system dependency (Ball-Rokeach, Rokeach, & Grube, 1984) implicated by this event were understanding dependencies (for instance, "What is happening and what does it mean?") and orientation dependencies ("What actions should I take and how can I interact with family, friends, and community?"). The third type of individual media system dependency, play, also became relevant as "normal" life was suspended and people had to find ways to entertain themselves and to cope with the stress of ambiguity while stuck at home. But this dependency became more relevant after the initial period of ambiguity resolution.

In any instance in which ambiguity is experienced and interpersonal networks lack information or expertise needed to resolve ambiguity, the media system becomes the major alternative information source. This is due to the media's structural position as an information system in our society. In this case the media are structurally located to act as a liaison among the average citizen and their community disaster agencies and relevant experts. But the media do not or cannot always provide the information service required to resolve the experience of ambiguity. Thus, incomplete or contradictory media information may exacerbate the ambiguity problem. For the first few days, the information coming from the media was conflicting (such as wear a wet mask or wear a dry mask, the ash will damage plant life or the ash will not damage plant life). Nonetheless, people will keep looking to the media for ambiguity-alleviating information because ambiguity is a problem that demands solution and because most people lack direct access to superior alternative information resources. The Mount St. Helens volcano was an extreme example of pervasive ambiguity giving rise to media system dependency. Even when people learned that Mount St. Helens had blown up, what that meant in terms of consequences for the person and the community was entirely unknown. Under the logic of media system dependency theory, conditions of high ambiguity should disrupt normal patterns of information seeking. We should observe a diminution of the effects of social category differences (such as education) and individual differences (such as attitudes) on not only which media forms are used (for instance, print versus electronic) but also in the relative use of media versus interpersonal resources. People sharing the same novel event also share the same communications environs that, in this case, the electronic media could reasonably be expected to dominate the information-seeking activities of people, despite social category and individual differences. The electronic media would be selected by "information consumers" (Ball-Rokeach, 1985) because of their information advantages, such as their speed of transmission, their mode of transmission (which was not subject to the vagaries of ashfall-disrupted transportation and delivery systems), and, most important, their structural connectedness to the best available "expert" information sources. Therefore, the media we examine in this research are two of the major electronic forms: radio and television.

The logic of media system dependency theory suggests the following hypotheses about people's information-seeking activities to resolve ambiguity-based problems of understanding and orientation in the case of the Mount St. Helens volcano:

(1) The mass media will be the primary information system employed by persons seeking to resolve ambiguity.
(2) When media information is insufficient to resolve ambiguity, people will nonetheless continue to look to the media for ambiguity-resolving information.
(3) People sharing the same ambiguity experience will exhibit similar patterns of media use, despite social categories and individual differences.

METHODS

Between June 18 and July 22, 1980, telephone interviews were conducted with a sample of 1,494 eastern Washington households in which we ascertained when and how individuals learned of the May 18 eruption and what it meant. The sample included all Washington State counties east of the Cascade Mountains (the range in which Mount St. Helens is located) and was systematically drawn from telephone directories in proportion to the population of each county. Although the sample included households outside the areas of significant volcanic fallout, it was decided that the whole of eastern Washington should be included, as virtually all areas received some degree of detectable ashfall. Moreover, the disruption of communication and transportation (low visibility during the ashfall and engine damage afterward) meant that even residents of areas receiving very small amounts of ash were in some way affected by the event.

The "total design method" (Dillman, 1978) was employed for purposes of data collection. This method has been demonstrated to produce quality results with a high rate of response. From the original sample, 1,157 households were contacted (77.4%). Interviews were completed with 1,023 respondents (68.5% of the original sample and 88.4% of the contacted households). The interview process was terminated when Mount St. Helens erupted once again. This subsequent eruption produced ashfall in some of the sample areas, such that respondents could have confused the more recent eruption with the original eruption in responding to questions.

The present analysis is limited to that portion of the survey that dealt with information-seeking activities on or several days after the original May 18 Sunday eruption. Respondents were asked whether they used the following media and interpersonal sources in their attempts to determine what was happening on May 18 and what impact it might have: radio, television, local relative, distant relative, local friend, and distant friend. For the days following eruption day, respondents were asked about their use of radio, TV, relatives, friends, and neighbors. Newspapers were not included because the eruption occurred after the Sunday edition was published, and the ashfall prohibited normal delivery of newspapers for several days thereafter.

The diffusion literature suggests a number of relevant factors that we examined as possible correlates of information-seeking activities, including age, sex, education, rural/urban residence, income, learning locale, distance from home, and distance from the event (Adams, 1981; Adams et al., 1969; Bogart, 1950, 1981, 1984; Bonjean et al., 1965; Budd et al., 1966; Burgoon, 1980; Deutschmann & Danielson, 1960; Greenberg, 1964; Hill & Bonjean, 1964; Larsen & Hill, 1954; Medalia & Larsen, 1958; Mendelsohn, 1964; Mulder, 1980; Schwartz,

1973; Sheatsley & Feldman, 1964; Spitzer & Spitzer, 1965; Stevenson, 1980; Turner & Paz, 1985). For the purposes of this analysis, the eruption and the ashfall are treated as separate events. Because persons experiencing these novel events are known to have been unable to obtain definitive information on their meaning and their implications in the first days of these events, we assume that our respondents were in a state of ambiguity (Dillman, 1980).

FINDINGS

As shown in Table 8.1, the mass media were by far the most frequently utilized information sources on the day of the eruption—Sunday, May 18. Both radio and television were employed by over 80% of the population. Of the interpersonal information sources, distant relatives were most commonly employed. Respondents may have been trying to discover what the impact was in areas other than their own. In any case, the media were predominant as information sources on eruption day, despite the fact that most respondents originally learned from interpersonal sources that an eruption had occurred (Hirschburg & Dillman, 1983). In the days following the eruption, information-seeking activity generally increased, most notably in the use of interpersonal sources (Table 8.1). Increases in the use of interpersonal sources may reflect the inadequacies of information provided by the media. Nonetheless, use of media sources remained at very high levels, suggesting a continued dependency and expectation that, sooner or later, definitive information would be forthcoming from the media.

Overall, then, hypotheses 1 and 2 are confirmed by our findings. Respondents experiencing the ambiguity of the Mount St. Helens volcano sought information from media sources primarily (hypothesis 1), even when those resources did not immediately resolve their ambiguity (hypothesis 2). Test of hypothesis 3 requires us to examine the extent to which respondents representing different social categories differed in their utilization of media and interpersonal information sources. We assume that social category differences are associated with different patterns of information seeking under normal conditions (DeFleur & Ball-Rokeach, 1982), but these differences diminish when there is a shared experience of ambiguity. The experience of ambiguity could be expected to become more homogeneous as respondents went from first knowledge of the eruption to several days after the eruption when definitive information on the consequences of the ashfall and

TABLE 8.1
Percentage of Population Utilizing
a Particular Information Source

Source	Sunday	Beyond
Radio	81.8	86.6
TV	85.4	89.1
Local relative	11.5	36.7
Distant relative	13.5	(36.7)*
Local friend	13.0	44.7
Distant friend	3.9	(44.7)*
Neighbor	NA	45.4

*Data on information seeking beyond Sunday did not discriminate between local and distant contacts. The same value thus appears in both categories.

the likelihood of subsequent eruptions was still not available from official channels. Thus, if our hypothesis is valid, we could anticipate that social categories and individual differences would make less difference in the pattern of information seeking in the days after the eruption than on eruption day.

SOCIAL CATEGORIES

Age: Although the number of significant X^2 (p < .05) differences among age groups in their use of different information sources increases from the day of the eruption (Table 8.2) to several days after the eruption (Table 8.3), no clear pattern of differences emerges. For example, no significant difference was found among age groups in their radio use on the day of the eruption. In the days following the eruption, the majority of all age groups reported radio use, those over the age of 69 using it the least (77.9%) and those in the 40-49 age group using it the most (90.7%). These age differences, although significant, cannot be interpreted as a consistent or linear function of age.

Sex: No significant sex differences were found either on the day of the eruption or in the days following for any of the media or the interpersonal information sources considered (Tables 8.2 and 8.3).

Education: Only the reported use of television produced significant differences among educational groups on the day of the eruption (Table 8.2), but these differences were not linear. All educational groups reported high use of television, ranging from 72% for the "grade school or less" group to 89% for "high school graduates." In the days after the eruption, the only significant difference among

TABLE 8.2
Chi-Square Levels for Sunday Information-Seeking Activity

Characteristic	Radio	TV	Local Relative	Distant Relative	Local Friend	Distant Friend
Age	.6235	.0448*	.9143	.4330	.0732	.0481*
Sex	.6374	.9514	.1082	.8661	.1094	.5637
Education	.1185	.0263*	.0634	.8636	.6499	.8353
Rural/urban	.0098*	.0136*	.4053	.4539	.0441*	.4053
Income	.4432	.0852	.4231	.5264	.3261	.0488*
Learn. locale	.8179	.0032*	.7106	.4618	.8562	.5711
Dist. event						
Volcano	.0028*	.0480*	.2691	.0149*	.9547	.3964
Ashfall	.0001*	.0011*	.0063*	.1922	.2874	.1882

*Significant at .05.

TABLE 8.3
Chi-Square Levels for Subsequent Information-Seeking Activity

Characteristic	Radio	TV	Neighbors	Relatives	Friends
Age	.0217*	.1316	.1087	.0047*	.0001*
Sex	.5721	.9259	.7363	.2224	.5788
Education	.2606	.5134	.2673	.2354	.0162*
Rural/urban	.0197*	.2066	.8556	.5690	.2990
Income	.6192	.5490	.0860	.0633	.1026
Learn. locale	.9883	.0143*	.6506	.4286	.2628
Dist. event					
Volcano	.0023*	.9190	.0102*	.3553	.5217
Ashfall	.7041	.9787	.9468	.6776	.1702

*Significant at .05.

educational groups was in their use of friends as an information source (Table 8.3). Such use increased with degree of education, going from 34.6% for the grade school or less group to 63.2% for the group with some graduate training. Those respondents with the highest degree of education—a graduate degree—however, depart from this trend: Only 32.8% reported use of friends as an information source subsequent to eruption day.

Rural/Urban Residence: On the day of the eruption, significant differences between rural (population fewer than 2,500) and urban residents were observed in their use of radio, television, and local friends (Table 8.2). These differences, although statistically significant, are not large: 83% and 76% of urban and rural residents, respectively, employed radio; 84% and 91% of urban and rural residents employed TV, respectively; and only 14% and 9% of urban and rural residents employed local friends, respectively. These differences, nonetheless, speak to the overwhelming use of media as opposed to interpersonal information resources on eruption day. In the days after the eruption, the only remaining significant difference (Table 8.3) was in radio use, with a slight tendency on the part of urban residents (N = 799) to use radio more—87.9% versus 81.6% for the 202 rural residents (X^2 = 5.44, d.f. = 1, p = .02).

Learning Locale: Being at home or away when hearing of the volcano had little impact on subsequent information-seeking patterns. Although significant differences are observed for television use on both the day of the eruption and several days thereafter, these differences are small in magnitude. For example, 91.2% of those at home (N = 569) used TV in the days after the eruption compared to 86.3% of those who were away (N = 432) at the time of the eruption (X^2 = 6.00, d.f. = 1, p = .01).

Distance from the Event: We examined the effect of distance from the volcano and distance from areas of ashfall. Whereas Table 8.2 reveals several statistically significant differences for the distance variables, these differences are not linear and are therefore extremely difficult to interpret. Perhaps the most substantively interesting finding is that the number of significant differences on the distance variables reduces as we move from the day of the eruption (Table 8.2) to several days thereafter (Table 8.3), particularly on the distance from the ashfall variable. In the present case, distance variables may be misleading, as the more crucial variable determining the level of volcano damage was whether an area was in the path of the volcano as determined by wind direction.

DISCUSSION

Hypothesis 1, that the media would be the primary information source employed by persons experiencing the ambiguity attendant to the Mount St. Helens volcano, is clearly supported by our findings. Although both interpersonal and media sources were employed, the media were the dominant information source. Hypothesis 2, that the media would remain the dominant information source despite the absence of ambiguity-resolving information coming from the media, was also supported by the findings. Our interpretation of this finding is simply that people know that the media system is in a far better structural position eventually to obtain ambiguity-resolving information than are their interpersonal networks.

The homogenization of information-seeking practices predicted in hypothesis 3 was also supported by our findings. Contrary to the typical situation in which people of different social categories exhibit somewhat different media use patterns, we found few substantively meaningful social category differences in that the electronic media were dominant generally throughout the population. Some differences were observed in which type of electronic media form was employed, but these differences tended to be either small in magnitude or nonlinear. Neither did we find differences of note among social categories in their relative use of interpersonal versus mass media information sources. Again, there were a few differences in which type of interpersonal source was employed, but these differences were difficult to interpret. Finally, differences between individuals vis-à-vis where they were when they learned of the eruption of the distance between Mount St. Helens and their residence made no discernible or consistent difference in their information-seeking behavior.

Thus, the experience of the eruption of Mount St. Helens would appear to have been an almost pure case of pervasive ambiguity, ambiguity that became a shared intense experience. Under such a condition, the structural centrality of the media system becomes eminently clear. It is the primary information system upon which people of all social categories depend to attain their goals of understanding and orientation. Under these ambiguity conditions, the social environs were not immediately interpretable and were inherently threatening. Although the Mount St. Helens event is an extreme case, we see it as an example of a more general process of modern societies undergoing rapid social change.

Rapid social change produces the same kind of social environs, albeit less intense and focused. Thus, the volcanic environmental change of Mount St. Helens caught people without an established social reality that they could employ to understand and to act. In the same way, rapid social change catches people without an established social reality to define and interpret events going on around them. In the rapid social change case, we would also expect to find the media system dominant in people's searches for information to make the world interpretable and, therefore, less threatening. The major obvious differences between rapid social change processes and the Mount St. Helens event are the discreteness, uniqueness, and uniform salience of the volcano experience as contrasted to the ubiquity, long duration, and varying levels of personal salience of social change processes. We suggest, however, that the interpretability and level of threat of the social environs may be arrayed on a continuum ranging from low in the case of stable societies to moderate in cases of societies undergoing rapid social change, and, finally, to high in such cases as those represented by Mount St. Helens. Viewed in this way, what we have learned about people's information-seeking behavior in the case of Mount St. Helens may be regarded as relevant for understanding the importance and dominance of the media system under the condition of an ambiguous social environment.

PART III

MEDIA ORGANIZATIONS AND THEIR AUDIENCES

THE CHAPTERS IN THIS SECTION (with the exception of Robinson and Fink) revolve around a common theme, connecting content with both the form and the organizational settings in which content is created. In different ways each shows how important the social organization of production is to the content produced. Each chapter emphasizes the importance of the "system" in which various content are created, and each makes an important contribution to understanding the complexity of the media system in the United States, a system that includes the audience and their connections to content and to the organizations responsible for its creation.

The key tasks of sociological analysis of media content and its effects are to specify how content is created, how it changes through time, and how content relates to the social and economic conditions under which it is created. The chapters included here address these important issues in some detail. Herman Gray alerts us to the complexities of broadcasting, showing that alternative systems exist along with the dominant ones. Examining some of the social and economic realities of community radio, he suggests that organization at all levels—national, state, and particularly local—strongly influences what the public has available through radio. James Parker and Robert Kapsis examine the film industry and relate the organization of product to the messages transmitted through commercial films. Parker shows that as the Hollywood film industry and the larger society changed, so did the content of crime films. Kathryn Montgomery and Muriel and Joel Cantor consider television in different ways—how the form and organization of the medium constrain the creator and how its audiences contribute to what we are able to see. Each of these chapters shows that the creative process is embedded in the social structure, and each either explicitly or implicitly emphasizes the collective nature of the creative process. The "audience," as part of this collective process, includes different publics or groups than the term usually implies. Montgomery examines how pressure groups influence creators, and Cantor and Cantor consider ratings and more active viewers (those who write letters and stop actors on the street). Both agree that the audience is not entirely powerless but also not the most powerful in deciding on what we see and hear. Victoria Billings, in her examination of nineteenth-century theater, asks this question: How can an audience directly cause artistic innovation? In answering that question historically, she attributes even more power to the audience than others do, but she too shows how the industrialization of culture limits the ability of the audience to innovate in the theater.

John Sewart's article is an ambitious attempt to use qualitative data from newspapers and other accounts to document a connection between capitalism and the "way the game is played." He too emphasizes television, showing how its commercial nature has influenced the rules of sport, making some sports less challenging for the players but often more exciting for the viewers. However, Sewart, along with others, emphasizes the interactional nature between the audience and the cultural product, insisting (as do others) that it is not possible for entrepreneurs or any other group to impose their will completely on the audience.

The only chapter in this section that does not consider how content is related to the social organization of production is John Robinson and Edward Fink's report of a survey of audience musical tastes. These researchers find that audiences for music are stratified into subgroups or taste segments. Such research is valuable for several reasons. It helps to dispel myths about mass audiences of undifferentiated taste and mass culture, and it can generate more in-depth studies of the system in which music is produced.

Chapter 9

SOCIAL CONSTRAINTS AND THE PRODUCTION OF AN ALTERNATIVE MEDIUM
The Case of Community Radio

Herman Gray

THE AIM OF THIS CHAPTER is to specify and empirically describe
some of the significant variables that shape and constrain the activities
of community (noncommercial) radio broadcasters. The focus is on
the social, economic, political, and organizational contexts in which
these broadcasters operate. In particular, this chapter examines how
regulation, market structure, economic conditions, organizational
structure, and ideology influence community broadcasters and their
programs.

The primary data come from interviews, observations, and participation in community radio stations (KAZU, KUBO, and KUSP)
located in the Monterey Bay area in Northern California. Interview
material was also collected at the 1983 and 1984 Annual National
Federation of Community Broadcasters (NFCB) conferences in Santa
Cruz, California and Washington, D.C.[1]

The Monterey Bay area is an ideal place to study community radio
because it is home to five noncommercial stations, as well as a diverse
mix of commercial stations. Stations in this area illustrate the differences between commercial and noncommercial radio and the variations among community broadcasters in the same market area. KAZU
is a small community station located in Pacific Grove, California. In
1983, when the interviews were conducted, the station manager described it as being in a state of transition. The station's history is punctuated with varying stretches of inactivity, uneven programming, and

financial crisis. Until 1983, the 8-year-old station did not experience any development or growth in its funding, organization, or programming. The station operated with a budget—$40,000 a year; 80% of its income was generated from direct listener appeal. The station operates with 1 full-time and 2 part-time paid staff along with 60 volunteers.

KUBO is a minority owned and operated station in Salinas, California. In 1983 the station had been on the air for three years. Its bilingual programming is aimed primarily at Chicano and Mexican farm workers and youth. The station offers a mix of public affairs, music, and news. It broadcasts from a large, modern studio that also serves as a training facility. In 1983 a paid staff of 6 along with 85 volunteers operated the station. Eight months later (August 1984), due to a financial crisis, the paid staff had been reduced to three people who were being paid on an irregular basis.

KUSP is the flagship community station in the market. The station was 12 years old in 1984, and it operated with a paid staff of 7, over 150 volunteers, and a budget of $200,000 annually. The programming schedule is eclectic; the station offers music, news, and public affairs. Throughout its history, KUSP has shown a consistent pattern of growth in programming, budget, and staff.

REGULATION AND POLICY

Noncommercial or, as it is more commonly called, public broadcasting in the United States is not a single system. Rather, public ratio and television stations are a confederation of various types of licenses, each organized somewhat differently. These types are

(1) *community licensees* (the subject of this chapter), those stations that are licensed to independent nonprofit corporations or foundations;

(2) *university licensees*, stations that are licensed to state colleges and universities, private colleges and universities, or other institutions of higher education;

(3) *local authority licensees*, stations that are licensed to local administrative units, including city governments, school boards, and local library systems; and

(4) *state licensees*, those licensed to state government agencies, commissions, and boards of education.

Noncommercial radio has existed alongside commercial radio since the 1920s, when radio became a mass medium. However, it was not until 1967, when the Public Broadcasting Act (as an amendment to the

1934 Communication Act) was passed, that public radio as we know it was established (Barnouw, 1978). Although the primary purpose of the Public Broadcasting Act was to support and regulate public television, it also included provisions for public radio as well (Avery & Pepper, 1980; Barnouw, 1978). The act provided for the establishment of a quasi-government agency, the Corporation for Public Broadcasting (CPB), to oversee public broadcasting. Under certain conditions, CPB provides financial support for local programming, and it also has direct responsibility for National Public Radio (NPR), which was established to link member stations into a program-sharing network.

In 1975 a small, loosely organized group of community broadcasters formed the National Federation of Community Broadcasters (NFCB) outside of the administrative and funding boundaries of NPR and CPB. The formation of NFCB was significant for public radio. Because CPB and NPR formally affiliates with those stations that represent primarily educational and middle-class interests, a significant segment of noncommercial broadcasters had no organizational affiliation—in particular, stations representing minorities and the less economically advantaged. Thus, NFCB provides an organizational base for stations that might otherwise be excluded.

In comparison with commercial broadcasting in the United States, public broadcasting is small. Fewer people are employed in public broadcasting and resources for programming are more limited. Within each type of licensee, there are stations that vary according to resources and size of the market they serve (NFCB, 1981). The major features that distinguish noncommercial from commercial radio are the former's nonprofit status and its inability to sell air time to advertisers for profit. These features are supported by law and custom. When operating costs (and profits) at commercial stations are generated from selling advertisements, community stations must cover operating costs through patron underwriting, direct appeals to listeners who subscribe at specified rates, gifts, federal grants, private and corporate support, and special events (for instance, dances, auctions, concerts, raffles, and sales).

Community stations are generally disadvantaged in comparison to the other kinds of noncommercial licensees because they often lack tax or institutional support. Noncommercial broadcasters, if they qualify, are eligible to receive public financing from the United States government, either directly to the stations in the form of grants for specific projects or indirectly through support from CPB, from state and local governments, from grants from private corporations and foundations, and from contributions and subscriptions from viewers and listeners. However, not all public stations are treated equally. For example, just two of three stations examined here, KUSP and KUBO, qualify for support from CPB. To qualify for such support, a station must conform to strict requirements in the areas of staff size, budgets, administration, and governance. Also, since 1967, federal policy has shifted. The Reagan administration has reduced federal involvement in local broadcasting, and at the state and local level, policy for community radio remains mixed and uneven. Different states have different levels of support for community broadcasting.

For example, in 1984 Alaska led the nation in the share of the budget allocated to noncommercial broadcasting. In contrast, California was forty-fourth in the allocation of financial resources. The California 1982-1983 statewide budget cuts had diminished the existing low support for noncommercial broadcasting, and because of the nature of the system, community radio, with its lack of institutional support, suffered more than other public-type licensees. The cuts resulted in the elimination of major training, administrative, and program services for public broadcasting and were felt directly by stations and organizations providing services to disadvantaged and minority audiences.

The shift from federal to state and local support exacerbated already serious funding problems. In addition to competing with each other, community stations must also compete with other nonprofit organizations for funds from local governments that give community radio a low priority, especially during a time when these governments have commitments to balanced budgets, tax ceilings, programs of fiscal austerity, and increased demands on resources.

Regulations at the federal level designed to preserve and protect noncommercial radio have produced a variety of structural consequences. These regulations have contributed to variations in the kinds of stations operating (in terms of size, budgets, and programming) and structural competition among community stations. For example, by limiting community stations to a specific range (between 88 and 90 mhz), the FCC has produced a form of structural competition among noncommercial radio stations. Also from the point of view of programming, funding, and audience development, such close proximity places stations with similar programming, ideology, and goals in direct competition with each other. Although the policy protects noncommercial broadcasters from direct competition with commercial stations, it has subsequently created competition among the noncommercial stations.[2] Federal policy also affects community broadcasters in the area of ownership. Because they are nonprofit organizations, community broadcasters are subject to policies that regulate their legal, administrative, and financial activities. These guidelines stipulate the boundaries of permissible activities—especially in the areas of fund raising, contributions, and tax benefits—and are often translated into ambiguous rules specifying how money can be generated and used in the name of noncommercial radio.

ECONOMIC AND MARKETING CONCERNS

The two major factors that affect the economic circumstances in which community stations operate are direct reliance on audience as a major source of funding and the availability of alternative sources of funding, such as the federal government and private corporations. A significant proportion of economic support (45% in 1981) comes from direct listener appeals (Rubinstein, 1983). This strategy assumes a level of financial stability in the station's market. Moreover, reliance on direct listener support assumes a high level of listener loyalty and familiarity with the notion of community radio. Familiarity in this case means that listeners have commitment to a station, program, or programmer that motivates them not just to listen but to subscribe as well. These appeals run the risk of turning away a greater number of listeners than it attracts. First-time listeners are often difficult to attract because of this method of fund raising. Nevertheless, because direct listener support is such an important source of funding, community stations and the NFCB staff have raised it to the level of a science.[3]

Stations serving poor and minority communities face additional financial burdens, and therefore many of them rely heavily on financial support from other sources, especially the federal government. As KUBO's financial crisis illustrates, stations that rely heavily on federal and state funds are in a vulnerable position. The situation is a virtual "catch 22" for minority-owned or rural stations that serve economically depressed audiences or geographic regions with low population density. Whether stations complement federal support with grants from private corporations or rely completely on audience subscriptions, many operate in a state of perpetual economic uncertainty. This differential access to stable funding sources represents a structural source of inequality among community stations. It is one of the consequences of an inconsistent federal policy in the establishment, operation, and funding of public stations.

When there is a change in policy, those stations that receive most of their funding from the government have their operations affected. Those stations able to balance federal support with strong local resources are still affected but to a much smaller degree. Such stations are often better able to replace and absorb financial losses incurred through budget cuts and changes in policy than are stations located in poorer areas or those that maintain greater reliance on state funding.

The presence of other stations (commercial, other public licensees) in the market also directly affect the community broadcaster's funding strategy. For example, along with KUSP, KAZU, and KUBO, the Monterey Bay area market also supports a college station (partially funded through listeners and patrons), a high school station, and several commercial operations. The signals of community stations from the adjacent markets (San Jose and San Francisco) are also received in sections of the Monterey area. The presence of these nearby stations (especially community) is significant in terms of programming and funding because they attract listeners, patrons, and grants from the Monterey area, forcing local stations into a more competitive position.

The development of KUBO and KUSP illustrates just how the policy and composition of the market shapes the economic response of a station. KUSP's first four years were spent essentially as a small organization that relied primarily on direct listener support for funding. Significantly, these pre-NFCB years were a time when policy for community radio was nonexistent. In its formative years the station very much resembled the current stage of development of KAZU. Almost from the beginning, KUSP's dominant appeal has been to a professional middle-class audience. By programming consistent offerings of classical, jazz, and world music, the station established its place with this segment of the audience.

With growth and expansion also came the necessity to locate other sources of funding, especially from the public sector and private corporations. The station's subsequent use of public and private funds (through NFCB membership and CPB qualification) helped to supplement the reliance on direct listener appeals and local patrons. Its strategy has been to build on rather than replace the original source of funding.

The period of expansion was also characterized by the station's relative dominance (among community stations) in terms of programming, access to patrons, and listeners. It was dominance, however, achieved not so much through monopoly as through its presence as the first major noncommercial station in the area and the absence of major competitors in the noncommercial sector. KAZU remained limited in operation. KUSP was thus able to develop and expand in a relatively open and noncompetitive environment; its major obstacle was not so much other stations as the very novelty of the concept of community radio.

KUBO's ability to enter and enjoy stability in the market benefited from the existence of NFCB, CPB, and Western Bilingual Radio. KUBO quickly developed organizationally and financially through the financial support of CPB and other state agencies. Because CPB represented a significant source of funding during the station's formative years, the station began as a major programming force among commercial and noncommercial stations in the market.

KUBO's initial appeal was to a rural poor and working class, often mobile (migrant) Hispanic audience. Curiously, the station also attracted a predominantly white professional middle-class audience with its broadcast of the popular news program *All Things Considered* from National Public Radio. This initial reliance on listeners remains essential to the station's long-term survival in its community. However, because the station began with a stable source of external support, it did not have to depend on the audience and local patrons to the same degree as did either KUSP or KAZU. This circumstance has allowed the station to develop a strong programming presence and establish a rapport with its host community. In spite of this strong presence, the constant threat of economic insecurity remains.

Both KUSP and KUBO entered the market and developed through very different routes and under different circumstances. The differences in their careers explains each station's relationship to and use of funding resources as well as how and why each station came to depend on the various funding strategies they each have.

Although in noncommercial radio those who "pay the piper" do not necessarily "call the tune," its "requests" are carefully considered.[4] This indirect impact on programming and operation is most apparent in the areas of gifts, grants, and patron support. Stations that use patrons must compete with both other noncommercial as well as commercial stations for their support. Along with direct listener appeals, patron support is the area perhaps most affected by competition from other community broadcasters in the same market.

The latitude for control of the relationship between community broadcasters and patrons is much greater for noncommercial than commercial broadcasters. It is, however, a relationship that must be carefully managed. In the area of grants, for example, noncommercial stations often have to conform to stipulations and requirements of the granting agency that, as in the case of CPB, specify criteria such as staff size, budgets, and organizations.

Some community stations—the members of the Pacifica Foundation, for example—have elected to forego patron underwriting and pursue specific grants because the constraints attached to such funding often violate the political values of the members.[5] KPFA's 30-year presence in the large urban market of the San Francisco Bay area makes its decision to rely on gifts and direct audience appeals a rational and practical response. A station such as KAZU or KUSP that serves a smaller area might find it difficult to survive at its current operating level on this criterion.[6] At KUSP popular programs (and those that generate substantial financial support) are scheduled for maximum exposure. During a recent scheduling change, the station's block classical programming was switched from morning to evening.[7] This change was partially stimulated by the need for a general programming change because there had not been one in the station's 11-year history; it was also prompted by the competition from other noncommercial and commercial stations with similar programming. Nevertheless, this major programming change could be made because the staff recognized the presence of listener *loyalty* and a financial base of community support for the station.

The influence of economic factors on the operation and products of community stations is clearly different from those at commercial stations. Although the influences are expressed in different forms and combinations than at commercial stations, they nevertheless shape the activity and products of noncommercial stations.

ORGANIZATION AND IDEOLOGY

The organization in which cultural producers also work directly shapes its products and the ability of producers to accomplish their goals (Hirsch, 1978). To be effective community broadcasters, they must successfully manage their internal and external environments by maintaining access to essential resources—funding, personnel, programs—and providing some means of coordinating and processing these resources. The organization and management of these resources are shaped by the characteristics of the market environment (economic competition), internal values (ideology), and organizational division of labor. The major organizational division of labor is between the management (staff) and operation (volunteers) of a station. This organization of personnel into volunteers and paid positions, staff and operations, is maintained through the structure of the station (open participation, emphasis on contributions, and ability rather than professional expertise) and ideologically through the members' collective commitment to political, cultural, or organizational ideals (such as alternative culture, liberal politics, and participatory organization).

Community broadcasters sometimes operate with a mixed organizational structure depending on their market situation, size, and ideology. The smaller stations rely primarily on volunteers and are organized according to collectivist principles (Rothschild-Whitt, 1979). Explicit ideological values usually form the basis for generating loyalty and participation from volunteers. The larger stations operate with a mixture of bureaucratic and collective approaches. A small, paid managerial staff administers a core of volunteers organized according to collectivist values.

At KUSP, for example, a paid staff of 7 manage the day-to-day operation of the station, while over 150 volunteers provide essential support services—clerical helpers, telephone answerers for fundraising events, producers, and air staff.[8] Although the paid staff manages the daily operation of the station, the reliance on volunteers for programming and other essential responsibilities means that the staff to a large extent must share the values, ideologies, and judgments of volunteers.

At KUSP ideology and organization are created and sustained through its nonprofit structure. Each volunteer who has contributed "a minimum of six hours of labor per month for four consecutive months is a voting member of the stations' major decision-making body" (bylaws of the Paraphysical Foundation, KUSP, Santa Cruz). Membership entitles volunteers to vote on policy concerning the station's direction and operation. Members of the station's governing board of directors are selected from this group, as are members of various station committees.[9]

People who participate in cultural organizations such as community radio are guided by values and beliefs that give meaning and direction to their activity. These values and definitions form the basis for identification, recruitment, and socialization of members. They also shape the terms in which members of the organization cooperate and collaborate to accomplish their work. These definitions, values, and explanations form the basis for the "ideology" of cultural organizations, be it a record company, publishing house, art collective, or radio station (Becker, 1982; Gray, 1983; Sanders, 1982). At KUSP these ideologies do not exist as codified rules and procedures. To the extent that they are formally articulated they appear in the constitution, but even here the organization's value system is not expressed completely. The organization's ideology is expressed as bits and pieces of shared understandings and practices that unite, guide, and legitimate the activities of the members. The ideology of this and similar organizations provides members with a source of identity and meaning, thereby "wrapping" activities into a set of understood and transferable explanations, definitions, and objectives.

Community broadcasters often hold a different, possibly an alternative, definition of their programming and activities in comparison to other forms of radio, especially commercial radio. This sense of difference is expressed in the *programming approach and content*: the preference for programming based on a notion of tastes rather than popularity; the use of eclectic cultural programs and program blocks; *audiences*—such as minority groups, nontraditional groups (such as bilingual), and a range of taste cultures; *personnel*—for example, programmers are selected based on availability, knowledge, and community membership rather than popularity or professional qualification; and *politics,* usually a liberal left perspective fused with an explicit attempt to address in detail social, controversial, and political issues.[10] These seemingly diffuse elements play a major role in shaping the membership, organization, activity, and programming at community stations.

Dissimilar to commercial radio, in which advertising time along with popularity of programming is considered in the selection and presentation of programs, community radio programming is also a function of individual personnel, expertise, availability, and audience "need." Programmers, moreover, are valued for reasons that go beyond technical expertise or professional broadcast experience. Knowledge of music, community membership, and access to resources may all account for the presence of a given program or the role of a volunteer.

This combination of ideology and organizational structure provides members of the community radio station with an explicit investment in the station. Organizationally, this investment generates the necessary commitment, participation, and supply of personnel required to maintain the operation. For example, the decision to change programming at KUSP was subject to long and exhausting discussions and debates at all levels of the organization—committee, staff, board, and foundation. Ideologically, such investment sustains the belief in and adherence to the values and goals of the organization.

COMMENTARY AND CONCLUSION

The cases presented here suggest that structural and interactional conditions have pushed and pulled community broadcasters in different directions. Broadcasters such as KUSP and KUBO have moved in the direction of institutionalization. The demand of financial stability and organizational efficiency required by CPB has meant, for example, greater reliance on bureaucratic management and sound fiscal policy. Although the ideal of a broad base of participation has remained and has been realized to some degree, it has not been without costs. For some broadcasters the requirements for new audiences, management of internal organization, and stable bases of economic support have resulted in the emergence of a different definition of these stations' organizations and programs.

The institutional responses represent major adjustments to external environments and the internal constraints facing these broadcasters. These adjustments and stages, however, are only meaningful in the context of the shifting historical pressures and imperatives facing community broadcasters. In this sense, we might see the current stage of community broadcasting as a crucial stage in the overall direction and development of the medium in the wider context of American broadcasting. The same constraints that have pushed community broadcasters toward institutionalization (that is, federal policy and regulation, funding, and organization) also enables them to remain different in significant respects from their commercial and other noncommercial counterparts. The major areas of difference are in the broad base of participation, the range of programming offered, and the forms of social organization that these stations use to organize their activities.

Community radio derives its alternate character from its operations in a commercially dominated system. This circumstance, along with the external and internal constraints already identified, shape the range and content of the programming generated by these stations. Given the impact of policy, organization, and funding requirements on community stations, the programming areas in which an alternative posture is expressed most explicitly occur in the areas of information sharing, public affairs, and cultural programming.

The major strength of community broadcasting is its local focus. With its emphasis on bilingual audiences, KUBO, for example, is a major source of information and programming on a range of issues. The station provides information on topics such as citizenship requirements for immigrants, unionization, health, and nutrition that might otherwise be bypassed by other media. WVSP, in Warrington, NC, is the major source of cultural and information programming for rural Blacks in northeastern North Carolina. Its coverage of a local hospital struggle and the labor struggles of workers at J. P. Stevens established the station as an important source of information for its audience (Adler, 1981). More recently, WVSP served as a major organization and information center for the local campaign to stop Polychlorinated Biphenyl (PCB) dumping in Warren County.

Many of the broadcasters in community radio continue to provide coverage of local social and political issues such as school board meetings, city council meetings, and other public forums. The reemergence and popularity of "newstalk" radio in the commercial sector has taken some of the edge off of community radio's widespread use of the popular "call-in" format. Nevertheless, this format remains an important feature of public affairs programming among community broadcasters.

Community stations also operate as training and programming outlets for various segments of the population, especially minorities, youth, and senior citizens. The absence of specific commercial imperatives means that programs created by and aimed at these segments of the audience will not be jeopardized by the pressure to put on more popular and profitable programming. Thus, although structural imperatives, especially economic, continue to influence the operation and programming of these stations, their specific response has allowed them to continue to remain relatively open and accessible.

In the area of aesthetics and cultural programming, the response of community broadcasters to external and internal constraints has also made it possible for them to play a vital role in the presentation of music and arts programming that would otherwise remain off the air because it is often risky, unpopular, and incompatible with the conventional formats of commercial radio. In this respect, public radio remains the primary medium for broadcasting music not usually played on commercial radio such as jazz, western, classical, ethnic and twentieth-century experimental music, as well as radio drama and feature documentaries.

As we have seen, the broader context in which community broadcasters operate conditions both the nature and the range of their specific organizations and programming. As community radio matures and is able to compete more vigorously with other forms of mass media—cable, commercial, and public—what will be its role in the contemporary media system? In a media system characterized by mass production and distribution, increasing corporate concentration and monopoly, community radio will remain an important local means of spreading information, providing access, and creating a sense of community based on shared participation. The specific form and range of these responses will, however, continue to change with the constraints faced by community broadcasters.

NOTES

1. The National Federation of Community Broadcaster's membership is made up of community broadcasters located throughout the United States. Its functions include lobbying and providing information about the availability of funds, policy, and regulatory changes. Not all community broadcasters belong to the organization (Mullally, 1980, p. 189).

2. Competition is not the only relationship among these stations. There is some degree of cooperation as well. On occasion, they cooperate and complement each other in the areas of programming and information sharing, and, although discussed, not yet in fund raising.

3. By constantly appealing for money by interrrupting regular programming, broadcasters increase the risk of losing potential listeners and subscribers. During one particularly difficult and slow fund-raising period at KUSP, the on-the-air staff had to compete with the World Series, weather, other community stations (some of whom were having fund raisers), commercial stations, and the fact that the country was in the midst of a major economic recession.

4. Not quite the same as advertising, patron underwriting allows commercial businesses to donate money to stations in exchange for an acknowledgment that its business is a supporter of the station. With the move toward deregulation, FCC rules governing the patron underwriting have been relaxed. For example, a patron's name can be mentioned more frequently. Although deregulation has made patron underwriting a more viable and attractive source of financial support for noncommercial stations, some community broadcasters fear that this move also makes noncommercial radio more like commercial radio.

5. The Pacifica Foundation has stations in Berkeley, California; Houston, Texas; Washington, D.C.; Los Angeles, California; and New York City.

6. KUBO has a similar policy. It will not accept grants or gifts from companies on the American Federation of Labor and Congress of Industrial Organizations (AFL-CIO) boycott list or firms involved in unresolved labor disputes. Again, part of its abil-

ity to take this position rests with its CPB support and its acceptance in the community (interview with KUBO station manager).

7. Among the programs that were not moved by the rescheduling were both the Sunday morning classical show and the Friday evening reggae program. The reggae program did lose one hour of its four-hour time slot.

8. The 7 paid staff positions at KUSP are station manager, program director, news director, production director, special events coordination, development director, and public relations director.

9. The station operates with a constitution; the bylaws are created and amended through ratification by the organization's membership.

10. This particular ideological character among community broadcasters is explained in part by the historical circumstances in which community radio developed.

Chapter 10

THE ORGANIZATIONAL ENVIRONMENT OF THE MOTION PICTURE SECTOR

James J. Parker

THE CENSORSHIP OF CRIMINAL CHARACTERS

A major transformation of the American motion picture criminal character was from the slum-bred racketeer-gangster of the 1930s to the inherent psychopath of the 1940s.[1] These content changes reflected changing relations among organizations of the film industry (including major studios and independent producers), private and public institutions that seek to regulate the industry, and domestic and foreign markets.

In the 1940s with America at war, propaganda agencies of the federal government replaced the Catholic Church as the dominant regulator of American film content. The Church in the 1930s had feared the criminal character was an exemplar for emulation by the domestic audience. The 1930s criminal was shown as a faceless bureaucrat-businessman to make him unenticing to American youth and thus less likely to be imitated. In the 1940s, however, the suggested association of

AUTHOR'S NOTE: Preparation of this chapter was supported in part by funds from the National Institute of Mental Health (#5 T32 MH15123-07) in the form of a postdoctoral fellowship in the Department of Sociology, Yale University. The analyses and conclusions do not necessarily reflect the views of the above organizations. My work on cultural production has benefited from the comments and suggestions of Robert Denberg, Robert Hanson, Ray Cuzzort, Bruce Kawin, Edward Rose, Grant Johnson, Albert J. Reiss, Jr., Paul DiMaggio, Kai Ericson, and Muriel Cantor.

gangsters with ordinary businessmen and American slums weakened the legitimacy of American capitalism. The federal government now feared he was a poor exemplar for representation to foreign audiences. The psychopathic criminal became suitable because he was properly distanced from the group life of America. Alien and atypical, born rather than bred bad, he was no land's man. Nonrepresentative of America, he was the perfect scapegoat for the characterization of crime (see Figure 10.1). Changes in crime film characters and formulas, then, are discussed below in the context of changes in an environment of organizations.

THE ORGANIZATIONAL ENVIRONMENT
OF THE MOTION PICTURE SECTOR

Motion picture content (such as psychopathic characters) and thematic formulas (such as murder mysteries) are products of a "negotiated struggle" (Cantor, 1980, p. 117) among organizations of a motion picture "sector" (Scott & Meyer, 1983) over what is to be shown to target audiences or markets. We can delineate this motion picture sector as a set of functionally related organizations (firms, trade associations, church groups, and government agencies) interacting for motion picture production, distribution, and exhibition, including the regulation of each of these phases by private and public institutions. This sector, furthermore, may be readily separated into three spheres: the film industry, institutional regulators, and a market or audience for which films are created.

The film industry is composed of corporate firms and trade associations. Firms are of two types. Major corporations, which control a large part of the market, generally produce, distribute, and exhibit their own films. Independents are smaller companies that limit themselves to only one or two of these functions.

Regulating institutions try to make media content conform with their ideal social order. The Catholic Church was the private organization most involved in regulating films during the 1930s and 1940s. Public organizations most active were state censorship boards and federal propaganda agencies.

The third sphere, the audience or market, represents the critical juncture in the negotiated struggle between industry and institutions. Industry firms guess how markets might respond to their latest story. Institutional guardians guess how their constituents might be affected by that proposed film. Film formulas and character types, then, are

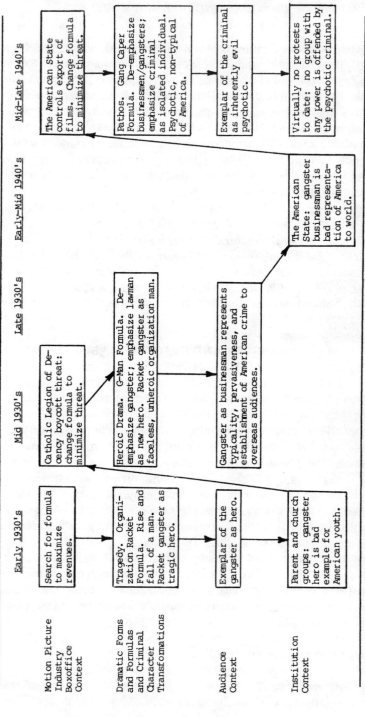

Figure 10.1 American Crime Formulas and Criminal Character Transformation, 1930-1950, within the Production Context of Industry, Audience, and Institutions

the products of negotiation between industry and institutions. Once devised, they become standard versions used again and again. Representing safe bets for industry firms, they are optimum versions satisfying two likelihoods: that they will meet with the same institutional approval as their prototype, and that they will repeat the prototype's marketplace success.

On one hand, the industry tries to deliver to target markets what it believes they want. On the other hand, the industry must legitimate itself to powerful institutions, each seeking to present audiences their group's vision of a proper social order.

Ultimately, there exists what C. Wright Mills (1963, p. 409) has called a "cultural apparatus," an "overlap of culture and authority," a "tacit cooperation of cultural workmen and authorities of ruling institutions." Who exercises greatest control—whether it be filmmaking artists, motion picture firms, or regulating institutions—is difficult to determine. What is clear, however, is their negotiated struggle and eventual convergence on specific crime film formulas and content.

INDUSTRY AND INSTITUTIONS
THROUGH THE 1930s

THE EARLY YEARS OF FEDERAL AND STATE REGULATION

After the turn of the century, many municipalities and states instituted local censorship boards to stem the glorification of crime and sex on the nation's screens. Pennsylvania in 1911 was the first state to enact such legislation. Several states and municipalities followed with codes that borrowed heavily from the Pennsylvania code; others developed their own (McClure, 1971, p. 136).

Until World War II, the federal government was largely inactive in the control of films, the chief exception being censorship during World War I (Creel, 1972; Mock & Larson, 1968). If there was not much federal censorship before 1942, there were certainly many calls for it. From 1915 to 1940, approximately 60 congressional bills sought to gain some government control over motion picture production (McClure, 1971, p. 135). All were largely ineffective.

THE FILM INDUSTRY IN THE 1930s

Major Firms. The film industry in the late 1930s nearly qualifies as a classical oligopoly in which the top four firms control 80% of the market. Five companies—Fox, Loew's (MGM), Paramount, RKO, and Warner—known collectively as the "big five" or "the majors"—earned 70% of all domestic film rental receipts for 1935-1939. Three additional majors—Columbia, United Artists, and Universal—earned an additional 25%. These "big eight" also accounted for 95% of all large budget ("A") films (U.S. Department of Justice, 1940, p. 33).

Independents. Independent producers and distributors earned the little remaining revenues and produced few big-budget productions. The domain of "indies" was small budget ("B") films that they produced in great number (34% of all American feature films, 1935-1939, were made by indies) (U.S. Department of Justice, 1940; U.S. Senate, 1942, p. 28). Many were crime or action films.

Independent producers were rarely their own masters. The majors controlled the domestic market through ownership of the theater chains. The films of each major were given greater playing time at the most profitable first-run downtown theaters. Independents generally had only a means of producing films but no means of distribution (film exchanges) or exhibition (theaters). Thus, their films were often confined to the less profitable second-run houses in nonurban areas. Indies, then, were economically discouraged from making large-budget films that, for them, would probably be unprofitable (Conant, 1960, pp. 36-37, 112-113; Whitney, 1958). It is important to bear in mind that although smaller budgets allowed independents some freedom to take content risks that the majors could not take with large-budget films, this relative freedom was always constrained by the majors as well as by indies' own desire to maximize their markets and revenues.

Trade Associations. Firms band together in trade associations to drive out competition, to lessen interfirm conflict, and to cope with the external threats that each firm individually would have had to face. The Motion Picture Producers' and Distributors' Association of America, Inc. (MPPDA), formed in 1922, was the industry's most powerful trade association, performing functions such as public relations, legal matters, and approval of film content. The Production Code Administration (PCA) of MPPDA, formed about 1930, served this latter function, passing judgment, for example, on portrayals of sex and crime.

The Roman Catholic Church. Although several church and parent groups organized in the 1930s to fight characterizations of violence and sex, none was as effective as the Roman Catholic Church's Legion of Decency. Organized in 1934, its pledge was read aloud by the priest in Catholic mass one Sunday each year and, repeating after him, sworn to by the laity. That first pledge read in part, "I shall do all that I can to arouse public opinion against the portrayal [in moving pictures] of vice as a normal condition of affairs, and against depicting criminals of any class as heroes and heroines, presenting their filthy philosophy of life as something acceptable to decent men and women" (Facey, 1974, p. 144).

Of all censorship groups, the legion wielded the largest box office threat. The Production Code, in fact, had been commissioned in 1930 by MPPDA president Will Hays and by a devout Catholic layman. It was written by a Catholic priest, Father Lord (Lord, 1946; McClure, 1971, pp. 143-148).

THE GANGSTER AS TRAGIC HERO: INTERNAL REGULATION OF CONTENT

After the flurry of interest that surrounded early gangster "talkies" such as *Little Caesar* (1930) and *Public Enemy* (1931), concern grew among Catholics, state boards, and the U.S. Department of Justice that American youth might emulate glorified gangster characters and so take to a life of crime. The title of Robert Warshow's famous essay 1948), "The Gangster as Tragic Hero," neatly describes the early 1930s gangster portrayal.

There were two strategies for dealing with the threatened Catholic boycott of theaters or other external threats to industry profitability. These were internal control over exhibition, thus limiting the type of film that would be publicly displayed, and internal control of film content. The industry tried both means to substitute internal for external regulation.

Control of the means of regulation also is an effective way for larger firms to maintain their market dominance over smaller firms (Hirsch, 1975). A $25,000 penalty sanction by the MPPDA in 1934, to be levied on theaters showing films not approved by the PCA, gave the "big eight" the leverage to bar independently produced films from their theaters. Because an indie had to procure a PCA seal on its film to show it in "big eight" theaters, MPPDA members—the majors and the larger indies—could refuse them bookings and so limit a film's distribution. Additionally, the PCA could suggest deletions to a film, making its seal contingent upon cuts that might make it unlikely to be booked by exhibitors. A federal government report in 1941 noted that "few complaints have been made by independent producers regarding the activities of the Production Code Administration," yet "there remains a definite question whether such control of the business of potential or prospective competitors can properly be lodged in the hands of an interested industry group" (U.S. Senate, 1941, p. 66).

Cuts to a finished film could damage the plot structure and affect its marketability; in addition, required changes were costly. One film, circa 1928, was reportedly made acceptable to a local censorship board at the cost of $28,000 (Federal Council of Churches, 1931, p. 126). This was half the production cost of an entire silent film, one-tenth the cost of the average sound film (Conant, 1960, p. 29).

Internal content control was also used by the industry to regulate the regulators. Editing a film for one market did not necessarily make it acceptable elsewhere. The Production Code, then, was a strategy to satisfy any regional censorship statute by offering conservatively drawn guidelines. The safest bet when content was potentially inflaming to varying public sensibilities or institutional watchdogs—as were the tragic gangster films—was to begin production with formulaic story content that had already been found generically suitable for all tastes (Best, 1981, pp. 613-614). By incorporating institutionally acceptable content in the early, preproduction phases of story generation and scriptwriting, a filmmaker might avoid more expensive production and postproduction costs. As the tragic gangster formula continued to draw protests, a new crime formula was planned.

In an effort to control the communication media that it felt had created folk heroes of Depression bank robbers such as John Dillinger and Pretty Boy Floyd, the Department of Justice organized a Crime Conference at the end of 1934. In his address (U.S. Department of Justice, 1936, p. 9) former secretary of state Henry L. Stimson compared the "sordid Dillingers and Baby Face Nelsons" to "our Daniel Boones and Davy Crocketts," saying,

> It is not unnatural for the boys of a country which has recently lost its frontier to be excited and stimulated by tales of danger and thrilling adventure. But it is certainly not right for such a spirit to be fanned up artificially by the engines of a sensational press ... by the movies and by the other modern instruments of mob excitement (Applause).

Media representatives, including three delegates from MPPDA, promised greater cooperation in the future (MPPDA, 1935, p. 27). The MPPDA secretary made two promises: that motion pictures "shall not contribute to the making of crime and criminals or to the undermining of character," and that films would portray "the best and most scientific methods of crime suppression by police and other law enforcement agencies'' (U.S. Department of Justice, 1936, p. 121).

THE G-MAN FORMULA

These pressures from Catholics and the Department of Justice led to a new formula that changed the gangster from a heroically exciting to a boring character. At the urging of the Production Code office, the gangster was made into a faceless organization bureaucrat—a blander racketeer than the tragic hero he replaced—and pushed into the background as an antagonist (Martin, 1937, pp. 132-134). The industry compensated for this loss of dramatic interest by supplanting the gangster with a new protagonist to spur audience excitement. The G-man (government agent) formula was born in 1935. In films such as *G-men* (1935), which was produced immediately after the Crime Conference, the federal agent succeeded the gangster as hero-protagonist, and audience excitement continued to reign as the bullets of G-men replaced those of criminals.

Some gangster films of the later 1930s, such as *Dead End* (1937) and *Angels with Dirty Faces* (1938), went so far as to slyly denounce emulation as a cause of delinquency. Because the screen criminal had been blamed as an exemplar for actual delinquents, these films labored to show the metaphoric rejection of the criminal by the delinquent character. Furthermore, these films suggested it was American social problems such as poverty and slum housing that were the real causes of crime (Parker, 1984).

FROM SOCIAL PROBLEM TO MENTAL PROBLEM

A consequence of the federal government's burrowing into the industry in the 1940s was the proliferation of psychopathic characters in the American film. To save the face of a nation the madman was enlisted. He represented no one but himself. The cause of this madness was rarely discussed, but when it was, it was blamed on individual sickness, single-event trauma, or heredity. Suddenly missing from those films was any notion of social responsibility for his problem. In short, the 1930s American filmmaker had attempted to show that American social problems (and *not* movies) caused individual criminals (who gravitated to organized mobs). Delinquency and crime were portrayed as rooted in slum crowding (*Dead End*, 1937); ill housing

(*One Third of a Nation,* 1939); poverty (*Wild Boys of the Road,* 1933); organized crime (*G-men,* 1935); brutal institutions (*Crime School,* 1938); and dishonest government officials (*Great Guy,* 1936). In the 1940s social causality would be turned about face so that the individual with his inherent mental problem was shown to be the root cause of social problems such as crime. If before it was group problems that were blamed for personal problems ("You can take the boy out of Brooklyn but you can't take Brooklyn out of the boy"), by the mid-1940s the peculiar problems of one individual were blamed for group problems ("One rotten apple spoils the barrel"). Key to this change was the American government's "overseas information program."

THE WARS YEARS

THE FILM INDUSTRY IN THE EARLY 1940s

War brought a boom market. Annual admissions income (in constant 1972 dollars) went from less than $2.5 billion for any year in the 1930s to almost $4.5 billion in 1946 (Parker, 1983, p. 711). War brought fewer films but longer play-dates (Balio, 1976, p. 226). The homefront audience was ready to pay to see almost anything, and so films ran for longer periods in one area. Domestic revenues thus were high throughout the war.

The freezing of many foreign (especially European) markets during the war was met by greater distribution to Latin America (Parker, 1983, pp. 692-700, 850-851). Foreign market revenues for the majors, like domestic revenues, also appear to have increased during that time (*Moody's* 1942, p. 900, 1943, p. 918, 1947, p. 1,579; Warners, 1958).

Independent producers also profited from the war. Their revenue increases, however, were largely from the domestic market (*Moody's,* 1943, p. 946, 1953, p. 677) as foreign distribution of independent productions was more constrained by federal censorship than that of the majors. With increasing domestic revenues and new wartime tax breaks for independents, however, their number quickly grew (Balio, 1976, p. 226). In 1939 there were about 10 independent production companies. By 1945 there were 40 (Conant, 1960, pp. 112-113). The Production Code Administration continued to monitor film content (for about 98% of all American releases).

CRIME FILMS IN WORLD WAR II:
AXING LAWLESSNESS

Professional organizations throughout the 1930s had urged the Production Code office to make screen villains out of characters who were not representative of their groups (Gerbner & Tannenbaum, 1962, p. 211). Lawyers, for example, felt that the Hollywood "shyster" was giving them a bad name. With the world at war, concern with group reputation grew to epidemic proportions. It became the task of American federal agencies to see that America, *in toto,* would not be defaced and defamed. In short, this meant that the villain would be an unemployed representative of no social group whatsoever (Weaver, 1943).

During the 1940s, despite the freezing of many foreign markets, the American film industry continued to earn 30% to 40% of all its revenues from the foreign market (*Film Daily Yearbook,* 1945, p. 41, 1946, p. 43, 1947, p. 49, 1948, p. 59, 1949, p. 65, 1950, p. 71). Thus, it was vulnerable to export control, and the American state had an opportunity to come between the industry and its path to that world market. The state also had a reason. That reason was propaganda—or, as it was known, "the Government's overseas information program." There was a need during the war for America to counteract Axis propaganda. American films were shown to enemy or neutral country audiences to discredit the United States. Especially troublesome were "pictures involving the lawless element of the United States" because "they tended to impress the people of foreign countries that we were a nation of gangsters, bootleggers, black marketers, and so on. The depiction of juvenile delinquency, crooked mayors, and cowboys who took the law into their own hands were particularly frowned upon" (U.S. Office of Censorship, 1946, p. 159).

Two federal agencies were especially prominent in this wartime effort: the Office of War Information (OWI) and the Office of Censorship (OC). OWI's chief function was to coordinate the government's information program to allies and neutrals outside America as well as to home-front civilians. Their Bureau of Motion Pictures performed content analyses of scripts and finished films, and their agents met daily with Hollywood producers, directors, and writers (Koppes & Black, 1977). In 1942 they issued a *Government Information Manual for the Motion Picture Industry* (U.S. Office of War Information, 1942), a sort of government "production code" to guide the making of pictures. OWI's primary sanction was selection and deselection of films to occupied (liberated) territories such as North Africa (Parker,

1983, pp. 959-1,002). Secondarily, however, they could advise the Office of Censorship on the "suitability" of films for all foreign viewing.

Censorship had export authority for the remaining world markets. The primary market they controlled was England, which contributed half of the industry's foreign revenues (Parker, 1983, pp. 848-900). An estimated 1,170 American films, or 86% of all those released from May 1942 to August 1945, were previewed by the Office of War Information. A similar percentage also had been reviewed in one or more screenplay stages. An estimated one-third (32%) of all American-produced feature films released to American theaters during this period had had "problems" in screenplay or film versions that were "corrected" in order to be acceptable to OWI. Another third (20%-35%) of all feature films released by Hollywood encountered no resistance from OWI, having been produced to conform fully with OWI objectives (U.S. Office of War Information, 1944, 1945c).

A decision to retain troublesome content meant that the film would probably encounter federal resistance when submitted for export. At least 50 gangster-crime-juvenile delinquency films were denied export licenses by the Office of Censorship during the war. This was about one-third of the approximately 150 feature films disapproved for export. About 30 more were westerns, banned because they, too, portrayed American lawlessness. In sum, for all (4,492) U.S. feature film productions first released in the period 1932-1945, 2.3% were denied export licenses by the Office of Censorship during the war (U.S. Office of Censorship, 1943, 1944, 1945a, 1945b).

Some crime films denied export were produced before the war—for example, organization racketeer films such as *Scarface* (1932) and *Manhattan Melodrama* (1934), corrupt politician films such as *Great Guy* (1936), and juvenile delinquency films such as *Dead End* (1937) and *Crime School* (1938). Yet others were organized crime or delinquency films made during the war, such as *Roxie Hart* (1942), *Truck Busters* (1943), *Youth on Trial* (1944) and *Crime, Inc.* (1945). Almost all those made during the war that were disapproved for export were small-budget films that could be made with greater content risks without committing financial suicide if later restricted from the foreign market.

Of those films produced and first released during the peak censorship period, 1943-1945, a much greater percentage of independent releases than of major studio releases were denied export licenses: 5% to 2%, respectively (*Film Daily Yearbook,* 1952, p. 125; U.S. Office of Censorship, 1943, 1944, 1945a, 1945b). Furthermore, indies were more likely to produce crime films that were disapproved by the OC. More than 2.5% of independents' domestic releases for 1943-1945 were crime films that were disapproved, compared to fewer than 1% of the majors' releases. This was partly due to the more sensational nature of most small-budget films, made for the lower bill of double features or for juvenile matinee audiences. Partly it was due to the production systems of smaller studios that had fewer controls than those afforded the majors with their large story departments. Likely too, however, was a bias in the Office of Censorship similar to the one often stated by OWI film reviewers, that these films—of poorer quality and cost (that is, of shabby "production values")—generally offered poor representations of America.

MURDEROUS MADMEN FILMS OF THE 1940s

The Film Noir and No Land's Man

Other crime genres—notably the *film noir* murder mystery—emerged during the war and flourished during the postwar period by incorporating portrayals of villainy that were "suitable" for the "Government's overseas information program." These dark movies of the 1940s have been called *films noir* because of the gloom and shadow world that pervades their style or tone (Schrader, 1972). Many of the psychopathic gangster films and almost all of the "psychological" films, including the murder mystery and suspense thriller formulas, are *films noir*. These were likely made in great abundance partly because of the high number of psychiatric casualties of war and the concurrent rise in popularity of psychiatry (Deutsch, 1948; Maisel, 1946; Menninger, 1948; Parker, 1983, pp. 163-173, 395-399).

The relations among these new attitudes and the new cycle of films cannot be easily proven; the growing collaboration over psychological films between the American industry and federal agencies can be. For example, in 1945 an OWI reviewer found that the screenplay for *The Two Mrs. Carrolls* (1947) "suggests nothing contrary to the Government's Overseas Information Program" because the story's main villain, an American, "is presented as a psychopathic individual, in no way representative of his nationality" (U.S. Office of War Information, 1945a). This was no isolated example. From mid-1943 there was continuous federal pressure to dissociate the villain from all groups by portraying him as a psychopath. An OWI report in September 1944, for example, suggests OWI's role in pressuring for psychopathic villains and the industry's general compliance. For all screenplays seen by OWI during the preceding year, 19 "overseas problems" were found by OWI that showed "unsympathetic or unreal characters made typical of whole groups or nations." Of these 14 were corrected at OWI's request (U.S. Office of War Information, 1944).

OWI's favoring of psychopathic criminal characters did not mark the origin of the psychological character. Nevertheless, OWI pressure in the form of daily "advice" and "suggestions" fueled the shift to this new crime character. The trend quickly spread in the 1940s, with themes such as the gothic novel formula, the *Jane Eyre* story of a woman marrying a wealthy but strange man who might be insane and/or driving her insane (for example, *Gaslight,* 1944, and *Dragonwyck,* 1946); or the murder marriage formula, in which a man and a woman are engaged to marry, or married, with one spouse plotting or threatening to murder the other (for example, *Spellbound,* 1945, and *The Two Mrs. Carrolls,* 1947).

Warner Brothers production records show the move to this new crime character. The percentage of all Warner films that were gangster films dropped sharply, from 9% of their releases for the 1937-1943 precensorship period to 3% in the 1944-1950 censorship period. For those same periods mystery stories fell only slightly from 13% to 11%. Furthermore, production funds were increasingly funneled into mysteries rather than gangster films. The average cost of a gangster film was greater than the average cost of a mystery in both precensorship years for which figures are available, 1940-1941 and 1941-1942. It was about the same in the transitional year 1942-1943 and was less for the seven censorship years, 1943-1944 through 1949-1950. In addition, there was greater growth of the mystery film budget than gangster budget. Mystery film costs increased 675% from the 1939-1943 period to the 1944-1950 period, gangster films only 177% (Warners, 1950, 1958). Therefore, after export restrictions were imposed by federal agencies in late 1942, major studios were less likely to allocate large amounts of funds for films that might be restrained from reaching foreign markets. Studios often decided in advance whether to make films on a "domestic" or an "overseas" budget (U.S. Office of War Information, 1945b), and it appears that the mystery story had least censorship risk for the large foreign budget.

Film Formulas: Quality Control and Industrial Standards

The industry internalized the censorship threat from the federal government by adopting new production standards as well as new report categories. First, the PCA loosened the code in 1944 in order to allow murder mysteries freer rein (Parker, 1983, pp. 488-506). In that same year they also formally recognized the psychological film by creating new PCA coding categories of "psychological mystery" and "murder mystery" (Hays, 1945). Second and more subtly, though more important, was the 1946 change in a Production Code regulation from "The history, institutions, prominent people and citizenry of *other* nations shall be represented fairly" to "The history, institutions, prominent people and citizenry of *all* nations shall be represented fairly" (original emphases). As MPA executive Francis Harmon noted, this change was made by the Production Code Administration in order to demonstrate to a now awakened State Department that the film industry appreciated its new "social responsibility" to "seeing to it that America was represented fairly on the screens of the world" (U.S. House, 1947, p. 2567).

These were more than gestures of compliance. From a mere handful before the war, by 1947 more than 7% of Hollywood's annual releases were psychological films. Many more contained psychopathic characters (Cogley, 1972, p. 284). These continued to be made in large numbers throughout 1948-1949, although exhibitors had been complaining for almost two years that the public was fed up with these films and would consume no more (Parker, 1983, pp. 550-553).

Psychological film production dwindled by 1950, as formulas turned to anticommunist melodramas and psychological westerns, clearly dated in the past, safely pointing to inherently troubled outlaws rather than to lawless communities.

THE ORGANIZATIONAL ENVIRONMENT AND THE NEW GANGSTER FILM IN POSTWAR AMERICA

THE FILM INDUSTRY

The American film industry in the late 1940s continued to earn a fair proportion of its revenue in foreign markets. At this time only 1 out of 10 Hollywood films was profitable if domestic revenue alone was considered. By contrast, almost half of all films made in 1940 had been profitable without foreign revenues (*Film Daily Yearbook,* 1949, p. 65; Johnston, 1949). Estimated revenue from the foreign market had grown from about 35% of all Hollywood's earnings in 1939 to almost 50% by the mid-1950s (*Film Daily Yearbook,* 1945-1957; Huettig, 1944, p. 70).

The wartime boom in foreign revenues was fueled in 1945-1947 when frozen markets reopened. By 1948, however, many countries had imposed restrictive import laws, such as import quotas or limitations on the screen time allotted for nonnative productions in order to protect their own film industries. Foreign revenues plummeted (Guback, 1969; Parker, 1983, pp. 1006-1008; U.S. House, 1947, pp. 2558-2560, 2568-2572; Warners, 1946, 1958).

THE MOTION PICTURE SECTOR IN POSTWAR AMERICA

After the war, OWI and OC were terminated. The overseas information functions of OWI, however, were transferred to the Department of State in 1945-1946. Export restrictions, except for occupied countries, were dropped. The Department of State, however, became increasingly disturbed about the uncontrolled flood of U.S. films in the foreign market that portrayed America unfavorably. Many of these were low-budget crime films from indies, whose number had swelled from 40 in 1945 to 100 in 1947 (Wasko, 1982, p. 107). The majors, too, were worried because each day brought new foreign import restrictions. This meant that increased competition from independents on the supply side met a decreased number of available slots on the demand side. To make matters worse for the majors, some countries even favored the generally poorer-quality, low-budget indie productions because they were less of a threat to their own film industries (U.S. Department of State, 1948a). A shrinking foreign market for the majors seemed assured unless something was done.

By the late 1940s, the Department of State was working vigorously to help the American majors with international trade negotiations (U.S. Department of State, 1946; 1948b). That bargaining had become a major international concern, first, because of the cash-poor situation in many countries of the postwar world and, second, because of the growing desire of many countries to restrict imports in order to reestablish their local film industries, which had been crushed or restrained by war (U.S. House, 1947, pp. 2584-2588). By working almost exclusively with the majors' new foreign trade association, the Motion Picture Export Association (MPEA), the State Department favored major film companies at the expense of the independents' foreign market position (Parker, 1983, pp. 1003-1045). This strengthening of the majors' monopoly power at American independents' expense was likely a violation of the Webb-Pomerene Act, an antitrust loophole that allowed American companies limited monopoly power. This limited oligopoly was allowed provided it did not restrain the international trade power of other American firms. A Justice Department investigation of possible Webb-Pomerene violation by the majors might have uncovered State Department complicity. This investigation, however, was curtailed at the request of the State Department (U.S. Department of State, 1947; Wright, 1984). Many of the independently produced federal agent films of this period (discussed below), then, may be understood as futile attempts to woo State Department aid in international trade negotiations.[2]

THE POSTWAR GANG PSYCHOPATH
AND THE FEDERAL GOVERNMENT

The organization gangster had largely disappeared from films during the war, especially from large-budget films, but the gangster character was not obsolete. Rather, he was remade. An advertisement for *Federal Man* (1949) symbolically captures the essence of the late 1940s government-guided gangster film. In that ad, the G-man figure is foregrounded as protagonist while the psychopathic criminal is backgrounded as antagonist. A caption screams: "Mastermind of the T-Men vs. the twisted brains of the underworld!" Gone is the large established organization of gangsters, replaced by the fringe gang and the fringe criminal. The gangster now operated with a gang of misfits, brought together for a makeshift crime caper.

American crime films of the late 1940s often featured the federal agent, especially FBI agents, Treasury Department agents, and Department of State operatives. They were shown stopping criminals through intelligent use of their vast and sophisticated crime-breaking technologies (such as fingerprint files, police radio networks, electronic tracking devices, and photographic enlargements). Best known of this formula is Warners' large-budget film, *White Heat* (1949), featuring a criminal with an unresolved Oedipal complex, a man who hated women and had spells when he felt as if a white buzz saw was splitting his head. He was pitted against the "T-Man," armed with all the technology and craft that law-abiding men could devise.

CONCLUSIONS

Motion picture form and content has been rendered meaningful within the context of organizations in an environment marked by a struggle for existence and dominance, with organizations fighting not only for economic resources but for legitimacy as well. When and where what film form and content will appear are determined by markets, by organizations representing institutions, by industry firms and trade associations, and by the relative power of all within this motion picture sector.

Each institutional regulator used different means to control crime film formulas and characters for their target audience. The Church threatened to boycott domestic exhibition; the federal government managed distribution to foreign markets. Both control of exhibition and distribution brought production compliance with desired content changes. Content was modified in ways that legitimated filmmakers to institutions that guarded access to domestic and foreign markets. The organization racketeer satisfied Church demands that crime not be made heroic to domestic audiences. The psychopathic criminal satisfied federal demands for a criminal who did not represent America unfavorably abroad.

Major studios that already dominated markets had the extended resources and power necessary to internalize the external threats that regulators posed to their control. Independent film producers largely had to adopt forms set by the major studios. Content was modified by the trade association of the majors, the Motion Picture Association's Production Code Administration. Overlap of institutional censors with major studios and their powerful associations created the machinery that made coercion of independents possible.

Finally, the film industry's merging with traditional guardians of social norms and values, the church and state, can be understood as "informal cooptation" (Selznick, 1984, pp. 14-15) of institutions by industry or, similarly, as the rise of industrial culture and the rationalization of the institutional framework (Habermas, 1960, pp. 91-122). Conversely, this merging may be seen as coercive compliance of industry by institutions (DiMaggio & Powell, 1983, pp. 150-151). What is quite clear, however, is Mills's notion of an "overlap of culture and authority" (1963, p. 409). All these views root cultural changes (that is, changes in film content) in the organizational environment of a sector that produces, regulates, and consumes it rather than simply attributing changes to an amorphous *zeitgeist,* and a populace that gets what it wants in a marketplace of culture.

NOTES

1. This chapter is a much-abbreviated version of my doctoral thesis (Parker, 1983). I began by viewing and taking extensive notes on several hundred films of the 1930s and

1940s. This comprised about 100 crime and juvenile delinquency films (predominantly of the gangster genre), 60 murder melodramas (of the suspense-thriller genre), and 20 psychological melodramas (mystery genre). I am using "crime film" here to include all of these genres.

My hermeneutics grounded my understanding of what constituted portrayals of crime in documented understandings of persons working for film companies or institutions within the motion picture sector. Trade journals, such as *Variety, Motion Picture Herald*, the *Hollywood Reporter*, and *Screenwriter*, were examined. Archives of federal agencies and censor boards were combed. Individual studio and film industry archives were less frequently consulted. For a full discussion of my interpretive method, see Parker (1983).

2. The decline of the "B" movie, of course, was due to many factors, most prominent among them being the birth of television. The direction and extent of Department of State involvement with the majors and independents is left for a future project.

Chapter 11

HOLLYWOOD FILMMAKING AND AUDIENCE IMAGE

Robert Kapsis

THIS CHAPTER IS PART of a broader research agenda examining how film projects develop as they pass through the complex interorganizational network of production companies, movie studios, distributors, mass media gatekeepers, and movie theaters that mediate between filmmaker and consumers. As part of that larger project, the focus in this chapter is on how the future audience is identified by the artistic and financial decision makers at different phases of the production process, and how changing and sometimes conflicting images of the target audience and other reference groups influence the content of a film. The information and analysis were drawn from indepth information collected in a field study on the preproduction, shooting, and postproduction of a recent Hollywood genre film, *Halloween II.*

RATIONALE

Scholars have employed several different frameworks to characterize how content decisions are made for media arts: assembly line, entrepreneurial, product image, art world, reference group, and audience-image conflict (see Ryan & Peterson, 1982, and Peterson, 1979, for concise descriptions of these models). Audience conflict, reference group, and art world models, although not necessarily mutually exclusive, are particularly useful when applied to the production of an individual film. Each will be discussed briefly below.

Although Herbert Gans (1957) developed the audience conflict approach almost 30 years ago, it still can be productively applied to enhance understanding of contemporary mainstream Hollywood filmmaking (Jarvie, 1970; Jowett & Linton, 1980). According to this view, collaborative film production characteristically involves interpersonal conflict among movie producers, directors, script writers, and studio executives over what the audience will like or accept. Gans's approach is to document how the future audience is identified by artistic and financial decision makers at different phases of the production process and to show how changing and often conflicting images of the audience influence the content of a film. Gans (1957) writes,

> The making of a picture itself can be viewed as a decision-making process. As each creator applies his audience image in the decisions that have to be made, he is "representing" some of the publics who will eventually see the movie. The completed picture is a combination of the decisions made by its creators, and also a compromise or perhaps more correctly, a "negotiated synthesis," of their individual audience images. However, this synthesis takes place within a power structure, and the final decisions are often made by studio executives who point the compromise in a direction that seems to assure the largest box office. (p. 318)

To illustrate this model, Gans describes the making of the film, *The Red Badge of Courage*—a nongenre film directed by John Huston and produced by MGM in the early 1950s. (Gans relies upon Lillian Ross's 1952 account of the production of the movie.) Differences in audience images between the creators and financial decision makers involved in this film were unusually extreme. Director Huston envisioned an art film that would appeal to a highbrow audience. Having finished shooting the film, Huston left to go to work on another film. The producer of *The Red Badge of Courage*, Gottfried Reinhardt, tried to preserve Huston's original vision but lost the fight to the higher-ups at MGM who argued for a film that would appeal to a more middlebrow audience.

Selecting a nongenre film to illustrate his points may have led Gans to exaggerate the amount of conflict inherent in making Hollywood feature films. Nonetheless, as I will show in this chapter, the audience conflict model is relevant to mainstream Hollywood genre films. Even when filmmakers and studio chiefs agree on the demographic characteristics of a film's target audience, differences of opinion will arise over how this audience will respond emotionally and cognitively to different aspects of the film. Moreover, filmmakers' and studio executives' perceptions of how audiences will respond to a genre film in production are influenced by how other films in the genre are currently doing in the marketplace. For example, when the climate for such a film deteriorates while it is still in production, financial decision makers will frequently attempt to alter the film's content in order to make it more in touch with the times.

A second model to be evaluated—the reference group approach—is a refinement of the audience conflict model. The reference group conception distinguishes between primary audiences (readers, viewers, listeners) and secondary audiences (those in control of the medium, such as other filmmakers). In a study of how TV producers select materials for their programs, Muriel Cantor (1971) found that, overall, the secondary audience was a more important factor in influencing a producer's decision regarding content than his image of the primary audience (see also Cantor, 1980).

The third approach to decision making to be examined is Howard Becker's "art world" framework, which is the most comprehensive sociological picture to date of how works of art are produced. Artists create their work, Becker (1982) says, "at least in part, by anticipating how other people will respond, emotionally and cognitively to what they do" (p. 200). According to Becker, artists tʑ   ᵤ account not only the existing dispositions of the primary audience (to borrow Cantor's term), but also "the way other members of the art world will react to what they decide" (1982, p. 202; see also Goldman, 1983; Rosenblum and Karen, 1979). As Becker astutely observes, "It is easiest to uncover the dialogue with the art world which underlies the semiautomatic operations of experienced practitioners by watching those for whom none of it is automatic because they are still learning" (p. 208). For example, the novice film director's ability to solve common problems with maximum efficiency may reflect a failure to incorporate the imagined reactions of relevant others, such as the producer, the cinematographer, or the film editor into his or her decisions (Mukerji, 1977).

To assess the relative applicability of audience conflict, reference group, and art world models to decision making in Hollywood feature filmmaking, I will examine the making of the 1981 horror-suspense film, *Halloween II*. For my purposes, tracing the metamorphosis of *Halloween II* is appropriate for two reasons. First, it is a genre film, making it more representative of Hollywood feature filmmaking than the art film discussed by Gans.[1] Second, *Halloween II* is a sequel to a recent commercial hit. Since the release of the film in 1981, Hollywood has stepped up its production of sequels. Thus, to examine *Halloween II* is to highlight the production process of a type of

American film that is quite common today and should remain a major Hollywood staple in the years to come.

THE DATA

Detailed information was collected on the preproduction, filming, postproduction, and marketing of *Halloween II.*[2] The film was produced by Debra Hill and John Carpenter, directed by Rick Rosenthal, and distributed by Universal Studios. In February 1981, two months before actual filming began, I met with Debra Hill, who agreed to make available to my west coast research team information on the development, production, and marketing of the film. The team consisted of two former students of mine at Queens College. Mindy Pomer, who had initiated the contact with Hill, headed the team and was assisted by Gregg Simon. During the period in which *Halloween II* was made, both were enrolled in graduate sociology programs on the west coast. As a first step, we examined the original shooting script and kept a record of all subsequent revisions of it. Starting in April 1981, at least one of us was on the set every day during the film's six-week shooting schedule, resulting in the gathering of several hundred pages of field notes. During postproduction, we interviewed members of the cast and crew (including the on-line producer, director, and cinematographer) in order to gain an understanding of the various factors—artistic and otherwise—that influenced the content of the film (e.g., changes in the way the potential audience is perceived). Executives from Universal Studios involved in the marketing and advertising of the film were also interviewed, as were executives from Pickwick, Maslansky, and Konigsberg (PMK), the public relations firm handling publicity for the film. To set *Halloween II* within a broader context, we also interviewed artistic and financial decision makers involved in other horror-suspense projects during the period *Halloween II* was in production.

THE SETTING

Any critical analysis of decision making in the creation of a genre film must begin with an understanding of the genre and the production system at roughly the time during which the individual genre film in question was in production.

In the mid-1970s, two of the top-grossing films were *The Exorcist* (1973) and *The Omen* (1976), both big-budget, major studio horror films. These films spawned a number of sequels and imitations, none of which made much impact on the public. By the fall of 1978, few people, it seemed, were interested in seeing horror films. Then came John Carpenter's low-budget film, *Halloween,* about an energetic killer of teenage baby-sitters. The film became the most profitable independent feature ever made, and its director enjoyed the blessing of the critics, some of whom had originally passed off *Halloween* as just another low-budget horror film. In the wake of *Halloween* came an invasion of movies so similar in style and content that a new subgenre emerged. Films such as *Prom Night, Friday the 13th, Terror Train,* and *Friday the 13th, Part II* stole *Halloween*'s plot (psychotic killer terrorizes teenage baby-sitter/prom queen/camp counselor), and upped the violence quotient. Characteristic of this horror subgenre was successively more graphic depictions of violence, blood, and gore. The "knife-kill" film (so called by science fiction writer, Harlan Ellison) had been born.

The boom in low-budget horror films continued well into spring 1980, when plans to make a sequel to *Halloween* got under way. The 1980 boom in horror provoked a backlash on a number of fronts. Many film critics (e.g., Ebert, 1981; Farber, 1981) complained of both the explicit and exploitive violence of these films, as well as of their rampant misogyny (the victims often were independent young women who, the films implied, were asking for it). Also during this period, newspapers and magazines became increasingly reluctant to publish certain types of movie ads, especially those containing explicit violence or depicting women in danger.[3] An additional assault against horror films came from the Classification and Rating Administration (CARA) of the Motion Picture Association of America, that assigns the ratings to theatrical films. Richard D. Heffner, chairman of CARA, admitted to me in 1981 that since the arrival of the knife-kill films three years earlier, his office had gotten tougher on violence. Some movies, said Heffner, that received an R rating three years ago would be X-rated today. By fall 1981, when *Halloween II* was about to be released, the media backlash against horror films had reached its zenith (for a more detailed account of this backlash see Kapsis, 1982).

Moreover, by this time the market had become saturated with horror, and production of knife-kill movies fell off. Marketing executives concentrated on "positioning" the films that were already finished, releasing them when national and regional markets were not already glutted with horror films. On the eve of *Halloween II*'s theatrical release, most studio executives were pessimistic about the short-term commercial future of the low-budget horror film.

PREPRODUCTION:
THE EMERGING GAME PLAN

The challenge of *Halloween II* was to make a film that would end the knife-kill cycle but would not be as bloody as recent films in the genre. The game plan was to create a thriller or suspense film rather than simply a horror film. Director Rick Rosenthal says he was hired for *Halloween II* because of his work on a short called *The Toyer,* which "was not a horror film but a psychological thriller. There was no blood in it, no killing in it." Rosenthal adds, "I felt the way to do *Halloween II* was to be as suspenseful as possible, to be off-beat and oblique. That was my game plan." Line producer Debra Hill concurred that the premise of the sequel, as with the original, was to build fear and suspense rather than repulse the audience with graphic displays of blood and guts. At the same time, the filmmakers recognized that because of recent developments in the horror genre, the sequel would have to be more graphic and violent than the original. "In the case of *Halloween II,*" said Rosenthal, "some of the audience is built in, but if the film doesn't rise to the level of their expectations, you are going to be in trouble." Rosenthal's plan was to make a film that had a "sufficient number of 'got to see scenes'" to generate "good word-of-mouth" for the film. Indeed, the original Carpenter and Hill script was most compatible with this strategy, calling for no less than a dozen grisly killings.

Before a script for *Halloween II* could be written, Hill and Carpenter had to choose between basically two approaches that the script could take. The first was to write a conventional sequel, set several years later, with Laurie Strode (Jamie Lee Curtis) in college and Dr. Loomis (Donald Pleasence) using her as bait to attract the killer (known as The Shape), still at large. This idea was under serious consideration, but Hill and Carpenter eventually rejected it because they felt that audiences would find this updating of the story highly implausible. As Hill put it, "How could The Shape hold down a job with that mask on?" Instead Hill and Carpenter decided to do a continuation that would pick up at the precise point when the original ended.

Although director Rosenthal was not actively involved in the drafting of the script, he offered Hill and Carpenter some preliminary advice concerning certain problems he believed were inherent in any continuation of a horror or suspense film that might make it more difficult for *Halloween II* to be as frightening or suspenseful as its predecessor. In an interview with us, Rosenthal read the following from some preproduction notes he had prepared, which reflect how images of the target audience shaped early discussions of the film:

> It seems to me that one of the principal early pleasures an audience has is the anticipation, and then the revelation of "the boogeyman." Is there a way we can deliver this, even though the audience has already seen him and knows who he is? Can we create a sequel people can go to even though they haven't seen the first *Halloween*? Can we introduce new characters without stopping the flow of the story? We need the characters, because there are only three who survive from *Halloween*. Can we start on the high note we've agreed upon, and still find a way to find a lull, so that we can slowly start building [the suspense] again, to give the film peaks and valleys, or will we be forced to try and sustain that high for the entire film?

The script of *Halloween II* went through four revisions, and the final script was completed just before filming began. The early script changes are interesting in that they provide preliminary support for Howard Becker's assertion that "art worlds, rather than artists, make works of art" (1982, p. 198)—a reasonable assertion in view of "the multiple choices made throughout the life of a work by the many different people who cooperate in its making" (1982, p. 194). A diversity of individuals and exigencies altered the script of *Halloween II*. Consider a few examples. The final script contained fewer and shorter dream sequences than the first draft because director Rosenthal persuaded Hill and Carpenter that the original scenes "didn't fit" and would seem to the audience as "parts of another movie." Dropped altogether was a scene in which the Jamie Lee Curtis character finds a body with hypodermic needles through its head. "You could say that I was a driving force behind that decision," affirms Ms. Curtis, whose concern throughout the film that her character do more than find bodies and scream reflects her desire to act in more serious films. Other changes in the script were motivated solely by nonartistic factors that further illustrate how an art world shapes the art produced. Becker (1982) writes, "what is available and the ease with which it is available enter into the thinking of artists as they plan their work and into their actions as they carry out those plans in the real world"

(p. 92). For example, an opening scene, in which two young boys hear six gunshots while trick-or-treating, was cut, not because the filmmakers themselves did not like it but because California child labor laws prohibit children from working as actors late at night while school is in session. Scheduling problems made it impossible for the scene to be shot when originally intended during spring recess, and thus it was dropped.

THE SHOOTING

Cowriter and coproducer John Carpenter, who had directed the original *Halloween,* visited the set on only two occasions, but his presence was felt throughout the shooting, especially by director Rosenthal. Working closely with cinematographer Dean Cundey, Rosenthal tried to make the film consistent and compatible with Carpenter's style in *Halloween,* such as the use of the moving or subjective camera to convey the killer's presence and point of view, and the creation of images that are shocking in themselves—that grab you viscerally but are not necessarily bloody or violent.

Although Rosenthal was clearly the person in command on the set, there were limits to what he could do. While staging a particular scene he might be reminded by line producer (Hill) or cinematographer (Cundey) that Carpenter would not have done it that way. Or if he tried to add anything new, it would be called to his attention that it was not in the script and that he had better keep in mind the shooting schedule. Nonetheless, there were certain touches to the final film that were distinctively Rosenthal's, particularly the Germanic look. He and art director Mike Riva had a visual concept of what the film should look like—hard-edged shadows—people either in the light or in the dark. Cundey affirms that during the shooting, as well as at the dailies, Rosenthal had considerable control. "John was at the dailies to offer Rick encouragement but pretty much allowed him to do what he wanted."

On the few occasions when Cundey strongly disagreed with Rosenthal's handling of a particular shot, he would try to persuade Rosenthal to shoot it differently. Interestingly, we find that behind these occasional creative differences were differing approaches to the audience. Although both the artistic and marketing strategists agreed that *Halloween II* should be directed toward those people who saw the original, the filmmakers themselves also tried, in varying degrees, to identify their audience in terms of its emotional response to filmic manipulation and how these responses may change over time.

Except for the 20-minute suspense film he had made while still a student at the American Film Institute, Rosenthal had little experience working in the horror film genre. His lack of experience is reflected in the following remark he made to us regarding the audiences for his films: "Maybe I am wrong about this, but I don't think you should make films for audiences. I think you should make a film that entertains you, that you want to make, and that you have to hope that the film finds an audience." In contrast, cinematographer Dean Cundey seemed always aware of creating something for someone other than himself. Before *Halloween II,* he had worked on a number of low-budget horror films, including the original *Halloween, The Fog,* and *Dark Star* and has since worked on *The Thing* (1982), *Halloween III* (1983), and *Psycho II* (1983). Accordingly, Cundey has a remarkable knowledge of how to affect audiences, particularly experienced horror film buffs. In discussing the mechanics of scaring an audience, Cundey commented that if you repeatedly set up scare scenes the same way, you end up building a resistance to the scares. Consequently, "you have to be inconsistent in your consistency."

These differing approaches to the audience are reflected in many of the occasional creative differences between Rosenthal and Cundey that arose during the filming. One scene in the film provides an excellent example of how these alternative views can affect the final product. In it a scare is to be delivered by having a nurse find a dead body. On the day it was filmed there was a great deal of discussion between Rosenthal and Cundey over how to stage it so that the body would be revealed with a maximum impact on the audience. The script had originally called for the dead man's head to be propped up by a lamp, with the nurse then pushing him back to explore his fatal wounds. However, Rosenthal decided that it would be impossible to prop up a man's head on a lamp realistically, and that the revelation should instead be accomplished by having him sitting in an armchair with his back to the nurse, and then having her reach across a desk and spin the chair around to reveal him.

Even though this routine was not unique, having been used so effectively by Hitchcock in *Psycho,* Rosenthal felt that considering horror films are, in his words, "a chilling suspension of disbelief," it would nonetheless work. Cundey, on the other hand, felt that a scene staged like that would only distract audiences:

> If a scene draws the audience out for a moment, if they are suddenly looking at a flaw or a hackneyed gag, if it is running contrary to what

you are trying to create, then it is bad. . . . My feeling is if you are going to ask an audience to believe the impossible you have to make it as believable as possible. You have to answer all their questions.

Creative differences also arose between Rosenthal and Cundey because the former was less able than the latter to anticipate the imagined responses of relevant others, such as the film editor, to his staging of particular scenes. One day on the set, we overheard Rosenthal tell a friend, "I just can't see this movie. I have no idea what this is going to look like." Cundey concurred that Rosenthal's inexperience presented a real problem:

> Horror requires a great deal of knowledge about editing. I think that many films will fail because the director does not understand editing very well and is not able to visualize the movie before it is shot or as it is being shot—even to the point of watching a scene and knowing that you are going to use this piece here and that piece there.

Cundey was not always consistent; he also believed that working for several months in the editing room is an excellent way for a young director like Rosenthal to learn important lessons about filmmaking.

POSTPRODUCTION

> When you consider the fact that making four people sit in an editing room for four months, and look at the picture day after day, and try to anticipate what will make the audience laugh, what will make audiences scared, what will make audiences care for a character, I think we did a pretty good job. (Debra Hill, October 1981)

During postproduction, coproducers Carpenter and Hill's conception of *Halloween II* prevailed over director Rosenthal's. After the shooting, Rosenthal was given about five weeks to prepare his cut (version) of the film. Once his rough cut (minus a sound track) was completed, Carpenter and Hill showed it to high school students, soliciting their opinions. According to Hill, the students wanted more blood and guts. As Rosenthal describes it, Hill and Carpenter became scared that there was not enough blood and gore in their film, so they went out and shot a few new scenes that were extremely violent. Also, they drastically shortened several scenes in which there were no immediate payoffs—that is, in which no grisly killings occurred.

"John and I are very good in the editing room," Hill points out. Indeed, Hill had served as assistant editor on Carpenter's first feature film. "So in *Halloween II,*" as Hill tells it, "we just went in, and we instinctively knew where to cut. Most scenes play the way Rick envisioned them. What John and his editor did was to refine and shorten them here and there." For example, Carpenter and Hill decided that one of Rosenthal's favorite scenes had to be dramatically trimmed. This scene illustrates how Hill and Carpenter's image of *Halloween II*'s potential audience significantly influenced the film's content. Late in the film, one of the female characters is trying to escape from the killer. She gets in a car, tries to start it, cannot start it, and gets out. In Rosenthal's original cut, the scene lasts several minutes and functions to build suspense in the audience. Rosenthal says,

> It goes on and on and on when I cut it. The viewer is supposed to think, "Oh shit, the car doesn't start" and then you say, "Wait a minute. This isn't a scene about a car not starting. He's in the back seat. Get out! Get out of the car!" And just when you are saying, "Oh no! He's coming out of the back seat," she gets out of the car.

According to Rosenthal, because there was no payoff in the scene—that is, the girl was not brutally murdered—Hill and Carpenter shortened it. In the final version, she gets in and out of the car in a matter of seconds—not long enough for the audience to say, "Look out!"

Artistic considerations may have also entered into the decision to trim this scene. Isolated from the rest of the film, the scene may have worked in building suspense, but in the context of the entire film it may have caused the film to drag. In a similar scene that Hill, Carpenter, Rosenthal, and their editor all liked, they unanimously agreed to remove it because at the point when the scene appears, the film should be moving forward and not stopping. Under no circumstances should an audience feel a lag in the momentum.

Executive producer Dino de Laurentiis and Universal's marketing chief Robert Rehme saw early cuts of the film. Although de Laurentiis and Rehme expressed their likes and dislikes about the film, Hill and Carpenter, who had ultimate control over the final cut, were in no way bound by what the businessmen recommended. For example, out of deference to de Laurentiis, Rosenthal cut a scene that de Laurentiis disliked. However, Hill and Carpenter later restored the scene because it was one of their favorites.

When the completed film was submitted to the rating board (CARA), it was assigned an X. CARA indicated that certain violent scenes be toned down and that the "sounds of death" be minimized. After these changes were made, the film received an R.

DISCUSSION AND IMPLICATIONS

Although many scholars (e.g., Gans, 1957; Jarvie, 1970; Schatz, 1981) have commented on the reciprocal relationship between artist and audience in the popular arts, only a few (e.g., Cantor, 1971; Ryan and Peterson, 1982) have actually focused their research on the relationship. Consider, for example, Schatz's (1981) recent book-length study of Hollywood genres, which begins on a promising note:

> The filmmaker's inventive impulse is tempered by his or her practical recognition of certain conventions and audience expectation; the audience demands creativity or variation but only within the context of a familiar narrative experience. As with any such experience it is difficult for either artist or audience to specify precisely what elements of an artistic event they are responding to. Consequently, filmic conventions have been refined through considerable variation and repetition. In this context, it is important to remember that roughly 400 to 700 movies were released *per year* during Hollywood's classic era, and that the studio depended increasingly upon established story formulas and techniques. Thus any theory of Hollywood filmmaking must take into account the essential process of production, feedback, and conventionalization.

Unfortunately, instead of tracing the production of particular genre films from this perspective, Schatz presents a fairly conventional content analysis of once popular Hollywood genres—westerns, musicals, gangster films, screwball comedies, and others—showing how they have changed over time. The artist-audience model is merely invoked as an untested interpretation of why genres change. By contrast, this examination of *Halloween II,* from conception through production, represents to my knowledge the only case study to examine in detail the filmmaker-audience relationship as it evolves during the natural history of a film project.

This study's major contribution is that it illuminates the nature of collaboration in the popular arts. Three models of decision making in the arts were examined. Although all three were found to highlight aspects of the making of *Halloween II,* Becker's (1982) "art world" framework proved the most comprehensive. Although many of the film's personnel put distance between themselves and the object of their labor—making a grisly horror film—they brought to the task an intricate understanding of how one technically goes about putting together such a film. On the surface, the occasional conflicts that arose between the director and the cinematographer seemed to reflect conflicting audience images or opposing reference groups. However, a more fundamental source of conflict was the fact that the cinematographer was an experienced filmmaker, whereas the director, to a considerable extent, was still learning his craft. Differences in opinion over how to stage a scene were more often a reflection of an insider-outsider conflict rather than a clash between filmmakers over how they viewed the potential audience for their film.

Future studies should explore collaborative filmmaking in other genres, such as musicals or comedies, to determine whether these findings are general. For example, attempts to affect audiences should vary depending on the type of film being made. In the case of horror, discussions about the audience tend to revolve around how to set up the audience in order to maximize scaring them. Research is needed to identify the major issues relevant to audience manipulation in other genres.

NOTES

1. Gans writes,

For the purpose our analysis, it must be noted that *The Red Badge of Courage* was in many respects an atypical movie, and the differences in audience images among the participating creators were unusually extreme. Nevertheless, it is likely that the processes described here take place in the making of every movie, though in different ways. In a more representative picture, other kinds and combinations of audience images are likely to be involved. Differences of opinion between creators might focus on such topics as the characteristics and social roles of hero and heroine, the actors to interpret them, the portrayal of complex social relationships and issues, the depiction of emotional and moral conflicts in the story, and the solution of these in the ending. However, what a sociological study of movie-making ought to investigate is precisely what audience images are represented, and what major issues have to be resolved in the more representative kinds of Hollywood movies. (1957, p. 391)

2. Because all content decisions had been made by the time *Halloween II* was marketed, the information about marketing the film is not being reported in this chapter. Interested readers should contact Robert Kapsis, Department of Sociology, Queens College, Flushing NY 11367.

3. For example, one influential paper, *The Los Angeles Times*, has a six-person committee that decides whether a movie ad is acceptable. Until recently, the *Times* accepted any ad that was in "good taste." "But we had games played on us by some of the porn producers and distributors," recalls Gordon Phillips, the paper's director of promotion and public relations. "They would put double meanings in their headlines, and they were using a few pictures we felt were not quite appropriate. So we banned X-rated films and all unrated pornographic films." Today, if ads for G-, PG-, or R-rated films are not in "good taste," they are returned to either the advertising agency or the exhibitor with suggestions on how to make the copy or art acceptable.

Chapter 12

THE COMMODIFICATION OF SPORT

John L. Sewart

THE SOCIAL HEGEMONY OF
THE COMMODITY FORM IN SPORT

"The men of early times," thought Plato, "were better than we and nearer to the gods." Similarly rock stars Paul Simon and Art Garfunkel asked, "Where have you gone, Joe Di Maggio?" These concerns are expressed by many critics today in regard to the character of modern sport in American society. The current situation is contrasted with a vaguely defined "Golden Age" of sport not contaminated by the crass commercialism and sensationalism that characterizes modern professional sport. Today we find exploding scoreboards, nickel-beer night, market-induced rule changes governing the playing of sport, directives issued to fans on multimillion-dollar electronic video screens instructing them when to cheer, the fixing of competitions, gratuitous fan and player violence, the cult of the star, the cult of winning, extreme specialization of athletic talent, and dangerous medical practices. This chapter will present empirical evidence showing the corruption of sport and critically assess the central theoretical issues raised in consideration of the nature and character of modern sport.

As it applies to sport, the debate over mass culture and popular art centers on the problem of manipulation versus personal enrichment and development. This discussion is a necessary first step toward providing a broader base for the study of perhaps the most popular of all popular art forms in contemporary American society: professional sport. It is suggested that this process is best understood from the theoretical vantage point of instrumental rationalism and concomitant consumerism.

The starting point for this analysis is an examination of the extent to which the structure and practice of sport is increasingly shaped by market rationality. As shown in the following sections, when sport becomes a commodity governed by market principles, there is little or no regard for its intrinsic content or form. Although there has always been some concern for market success, several observers have shown that until the twentieth century, the search for profit was mostly indirect (Crepeau, 1980; Vincent, 1981). What is new today is the direct and undisguised primacy of the profit motive. Accordingly, the direction of changes within sport is thoroughly and precisely calculated with the market, especially the market for electronic media, as the normative touchstone. As will be shown, traditional meanings and practices are foreclosed and replaced by a puerile and a Barnumesque ethic of display, titillation, and theatricality.

The social hegemony of the commodity is apparent as the practice of sport is shaped and dominated by the values and instrumentalities of the market ethic. The idealized model of sport, along with its traditional ritualistic meanings, metaphysical aura, and skill democracy, is destroyed as sport becomes just another item to be transported as a commodity. This model views sport as a social phenomenon related to the intersubjective moral order. As opposed to the utilitarian and technical dimensions of life, sport has been identified as a moral, aesthetic, and dramatic phenomenon, as well as a medium of individual self-fulfillment (Huizinga, 1955; James, 1963; Novak, 1976; Weiss, 1969). As a moral phenomenon, sport is oriented toward the dimension of interpersonal bonding. Children's games are considered by G. H. Mead (1934), Jean Piaget (1932), and Lawrence Kohlberg (1969) to be the crucible of social development and the constitution of the social self through symbolic interaction. Because intersubjectivity and symbolic communication are at the center of culture, sport has long been valorized as an important medium enabling social actors to "practice" and "learn" a sense of fair play, justice, and conflict and dispute resolution, sublimating egoistic desires to group needs, as well as generating sociability, solidarity, and communal effort. In this context social behavior is shaped by norms and values informed by intersubjective communication rather than norms and values of a purely instrumental and technical nature. In short, sport is seen as providing a context in which authenticity and self and society may be realized.

The following three sections examine the various ways in which a market mentality has intruded into and subsequently debauched various sports. The commodification of sport is evidenced in the following arenas: (1) changes in rules, format, and scheduling; (2) the abandonment of the ethic of skill democracy (it's not who you know but what you do); and (3) the inclination to spectacle and theatricality. These sections will be followed by an analytical conclusion.

CHANGES IN RULES, FORMAT, AND SCHEDULING

According to Howard Cosell (1973, p. 343), television executives who view sport as merely entertainment will exert tremendous pressure upon the governing bodies of sport in order to attract ever larger advertising revenues. This view translates into action. Changes have occurred that have altered the character of competition and scheduling, such as playing World Series games in the snow, absurdly long playing seasons, more playoff games, bowls, and tournaments. Although the association between broadcasting and sport existed almost from the inception of broadcasting, television was relatively unimportant until the end of the 1950s (Horowitz, 1977). The owners of professional and intercollegiate sport increasingly began to look to television as the major source of revenue. For example, the growth in broadcasting revenues from 1956 to 1976 increased over 1000% (from $10 million to $112 million). More recent figures indicate the financial dependency of sport upon the television industry: In 1982, the National Football League signed a television contract for $2.1 billion for over five years; in 1984, NBC and ABC together paid over $1.1 billion for the rights to broadcast major league baseball; ABC paid $225 million to broadcast the 1984 Summer Olympics; in 1983, ABC paid the National Collegiate Athletic Association $238.5 million for the rights to televise college football (each team competing in a telecast receives $500,000). The fact that sport has become heavily dependent on the commercial broadcast media is evidenced in the comments of Brian Bruns, director of broadcasting for Major League Baseball: "Our people are leaving behind bats, balls, and gloves and are starting to worry about satellites, transponders, and cable" (quoted in Huffman, 1984).

During the early 1970s professional football was criticized as a "boring" game due to the lack of high-score games. Stadia across the country were only partially filled and television ratings dropped to an all-time low. The National Football League Rules Committee responded with a series of rule changes and technical innovations that cumulatively increased the game's scoring and heightened the action for the television audience. For example, the goal posts were moved to the back of the end zones so that field goal kicking would be less utilized, and many penalties were reduced from 15 to 10 or 5 yards. At the time these were changes that made the games more suitable for television. The halftime was reduced from 20 to 15 minutes, increasing the program's salability to sponsors, and the games were rescheduled on Mondays, Thursdays, and Saturdays to attract a wider television audience. In all, 16 changes that radically altered professional football so that it would attract large audiences were adopted in the 1970s.[1]

Similar changes can be identified in other sports—changes that seek to increase "action" and scoring. Professional baseball has witnessed the lowering of the height of the pitcher's mound, which reduces the velocity of the baseball and thus assists the batter; a larger strike zone to encourage more hitting; fewer warmup pitches for relievers; and a livelier ball. These changes also limit managers' trips to the mound to talk with the pitcher and keep the umpires moving at a faster pace. Because of these and other changes, there have been more night games and other innovations that "better" television but not necessarily baseball.

The effort to attract large audiences also degrades the quality of play in a variety of ways. A debauched version of "sideshow" baseball became more evident during the 1982 baseball season, when Rickey Henderson of the Oakland A's was in quest of Lou Brock's base-stealing record. His baseball efforts defied strategy in many situations when he would not stay put at first base in order to chalk up another steal. Sideshow ball became especially apparent on August 24, 1982 in a game with the Detroit Tigers. Henderson had stolen bases 116 and 117 in the first inning. The record at this time was 118. According to Cohn (1982), "When Henderson singled to left in the eighth, magic number 118 was only 90 feet away. Unfortunately so was Fred (Chicken) Stanley who had walked to lead off the inning. He was standing on second base and Rickey was all dressed up with nowhere to steal. Suddenly, Stanley was caught in a rundown between second and third bases. He did not run hard. When Lou Whitaker tagged him out, Stanley jogged briskly off the field, and when he reached the dugout, his teammates welcomed him with warm handshakes."

A similar instance of degradation was also evident in the 1980 National Football League season when the Philadelphia Eagles' Harold Carmichael set a record of pass catching in 123 consecutive games. In the eleventh week of the season (game number 124) Carmichael was shut out until the fourth quarter, when the Eagles ran a special pattern to keep the streak alive. In the twelfth week of the season, the Eagles made certain that this did not happen again by opening the first play of the game with a strategically unsound two-yard completion. This type of debauchery also leads to the fixing of games. Throughout the years ex-athletes, coaches, and trainers periodically reveal instances of fixing. The most recent allegation came from All-Pro Bubba Smith with regard to the 1969 Super Bowl III, when the New York Jets defeated his Baltimore Colts.[2]

The manipulation of sport is not limited to professional athletics. The Los Angeles Olympic Organizing Committee (LAOOC) scheduled the marathon to begin as close to prime television time as possible—5:30 p.m. PST.[3] This is when heat and smog have built up and usually envelop Los Angeles. To make matters worse, marathoners had to run the last 45 minutes of the 1984 Olympics in the heart of downtown's heat and smog because the LAOOC, under pressure from ABC-TV, wanted to have them finish at the L.A. Coliseum, site of the 1932 Games. Australia's Rob de Castella, who has run the world's second-fastest marathon (2:08:18), was incensed when learning of the 5:30 starting time: "I am very disappointed to have the best marathon in the world under adverse conditions. The temperature will be extremely high, and we'll be in dire straits. The race should be run early in the morning or later at night, or at a course near the ocean which is cooler and freer of smog" (McCoy, 1984). Four-time Boston Marathon winner Bill Rodgers suggested that the marathon be held elsewhere: "I think it would be a good idea to hold the marathon in San Francisco . . . but it wouldn't be good for TV. Athletes in America have zero, absolutely zero clout. . . . Given ABC's commitment to money, they won't change" (Broughton, 1983). This situation has been succinctly summarized by Steve Scott, runner of the second-fastest time in the history of the mile race: "The Olympics are just a staging ground for someone's commercial interests. The Games are no longer an event to bring the best athletes together . . . they're a TV extravaganza to sell McDonald's and Xerox" (Cohn, 1984).

In the mid-1960s, ABC-TV began showing documentaries on surfing. These programs attained sufficiently high audience ratings so that network executives attempted to televise and market surfing competitions. However, this required that the competitions be held on a specific site at a prearranged time and date. Regardless of surf and weather conditions, surfers were instructed to begin surfing on cue from television producers. The market orientation of commercial television violated the traditional participatory and democratic norms and rules of surfing competitions that were normally scheduled over a week's period. Each morning surfers would gather on the beach and vote on whether they felt the conditions were appropriate for the contest to begin. If the vote was negative, they would meet for another vote in the early afternoon. This process would be repeated until the competitors reached consensus. If a good surf had not come up during the seven-day period, the contest would be canceled. In the face of capitulating to market demands, many world-class surfers withdrew from these "staged" competitions in order to preserve the creative and self-expressive dimensions of the sport/art form of surfing (Scott, 1971).

THE ABANDONMENT OF
THE ETHIC OF SKILL DEMOCRACY

The most consistent characteristic of sport is that an individual's status is objectively measured in terms of performance or merit according to an agreed-upon set of norms. Subjective factors, family connections, or political influence are of no consequence on the playing field or in the arena: One can hit or catch a ball or not. Commercialization and commodification have steadily eroded the ethic of skill democracy.

The replacement of meritocratic principles by market principles and the canons of entertainment is evident in the sport of tennis. For example, players often "tank" (lose) matches so they can quit a tournament and speed off to another that offers more money; players accommodate to network broadcasting demands for certainty in "air time"—that is, players will split the first two sets and play an "honest" third to ensure filling a time slot and thus guaranteeing advertising revenue for the television networks; players will make advance arrangements to split prize money evenly regardless of the outcome of the match; and preferential treatment in officiating is accorded to big-name players by match umpires who are under heavy pressure from tournament directors to treat them well. Things have become so bad in tournament tennis that M. M. Happer III, administrator of tennis' Pro Council, believes that all exhibition matches are fixed (Mewshaw, 1983, p. 228).[4] In a series of interviews conducted by a sports journalist, these practices are defended by athletes and tennis administrators in the name of tennis being entertainment (Mewshaw, 1983).

The quest for profit and its destructive impact upon the ethic of skill democracy is especially evident in the sport of professional boxing. The scheduling of opponents is ideally determined by an objective selection of the challenger with the best record. However, in the quest to sign lucrative contracts with the television networks, the two boxing associations (the World Boxing Association and World Boxing Council) unabashedly manipulate their rankings of boxers regardless of skill, experience, or competence. Because a titleholder has name recognition and can command lucrative contracts, the choice of opponents often involves bypassing ranked contenders for unknown and unproved boxers who have financial backing. In order to get a title shot, a boxer must be rated among the top 10 contenders in his respective weight division. However, to get into the top 10 ratings of the WBC or WBA it is not necessary to beat anyone, merely to know the right people and "grease" the right palms. An example can be found in boxing when Pete Rademacher, without benefit of a single previous professional fight, was certified to fight Floyd Patterson for the heavyweight crown in 1957. As Patterson's manager at the time, Gus D'Amato argued,

> Professional boxing is like the theater, a business. It's to make money and it doesn't have to be a contest if the public decides to see it. I maintain that a fight is put on to make money. It's no business of any commission—who are only there to see that the rules and regulations are carried out, to see that fighters are physically and medically fit—that no fraud exists and that public is not misinformed. (quoted in Fiske, 1983)

The sport of golf has also undergone similar changes. Match play has been replaced by medal play. Until television began setting the criteria of performance, most tournaments were decided by match play. Medal play always guarantees "the stars" a position in the final competitions regardless of their performance. Match play favors performance; stars such as Sam Snead and Arnold Palmer would have been eliminated if they failed to perform adequately and two "unknowns" would play for the title. Television ratings, it is assumed, would drop accordingly.

In spite of isolated protests from sportswriters concerned with ethical standards of fairness and meritocracy, the modern sporting public fatalistically accepts, with little or no protest, sport dominated by market concerns. However, things have not always been this way. In 1928, for example, the Boston Braves constructed new bleachers in left and center fields in order to shorten the distance required for the newly acquired Roger Hornsby to hit home runs. A columnist called this action "one of the cheapest things ever done in the National

League." A similar outcry erupted among the fans in Boston. After the outcry, the Braves repented and announced they would move the bleachers back (Crepeau, 1980, p. 44). The modern fan views such events quite differently. For example, a fan's response to the base-stealing debauchery described earlier is indicative of the consumerist attitude toward sport as spectacle: "What's all the fuss about Fred Stanley getting picked off base on purpose? . . . Baseball is entertainment. . . . I went to the A's game to see a record broken. . . . I don't care how it happens" (*San Francisco Chronicle,* 1982).[5]

THE INCLINATION TO
SPECTACLE AND THEATRICALITY

With the rapid expansion of pay television and the proliferation of baseball throughout North America on the broadcast media, baseball has been shaped to the need and advantage of the broadcast industry. Baseball was able to overcome its slump in popularity during the 1970s not by enriching the skill level of the sport but through the application of marketing techniques. As Bowie Kuhn, former commissioner of baseball, put it: "The reason baseball has done so well is we've learned to market the product better and we're going to do an even better job at marketing than we are doing now" (Kuhn, 1983, p. 17).[6] Ebbets Field, the Polo Grounds, and Sportsman's Park have been replaced by "entertainment centers" featuring paid cheerleaders and mascots (Krazy George, The San Diego Chicken) who make their entrance in helicopters or parachutes; giant "Diamond Vision" video screens showing replays, the speed of balls thrown by the pitcher, 3-D soft porn images of players, advertisements, commercial lyrics, and jingles; wall-mounted television at concession stands and in bathrooms. In addition, rock music and Las Vegas-style cheerleaders have replaced the time-honored park organist as between-inning pastime. Live rock bands (instead of baseball players) perform as the second "game" of baseball and rock "doubleheaders." The umpire's traditional game-beginning invocation of "Play ball!" has been replaced by human cannonballs shot from center field into a net at the pitcher's mound.

College football is also adopting a sport with live entertainment "lineup" in order to market its product. For example, the 1983 Wake Forest football schedule included fireworks, Bob Hope, the Dallas Cowboy Cheerleaders, the Four Tops, The Temptations, Tanya Tucker, and Fireball.

The North American Soccer League (NASL), established in 1968, has continually struggled for survival in the sport marketplace. Accordingly, this sport has been subjected to the associated processes of commercialization and theatricality. Unable to attract American fans, the owners of soccer have tried to "spice up" the game. The major obstacle to corporatization has come from the inability of the sport to capture the television audience because the sport is not suited for the medium. There are no time-outs in soccer, and if the ball goes out of bounds, it is immediately thrown back into action. There is no "stop and go" action as there is in football, baseball, and basketball. In addition, soccer is a skillful, defensively oriented, low-scoring game. Soccer matches can go several minutes without an offensive attempt to acquire a score—scores of 1-0 or 2-1 are very common. To make things worse, the code of sportsmanship among soccer players is deeply rooted and strictly followed. As a result violence is relatively rare in matches.

In order to add some excitement to the game, the NASL tampered with the world soccer code by eliminating tie games with—what was marketed in typically American style—a "shoot out." The shoot out was devised to be added after the overtime periods. The NASL declared that American spectators needed the added "thrill" of a Matt Dillon-type showdown at high noon (*1982 Soccer Encyclopedia,* pp. 508-512). Other alterations of the sport included moving the off-sides line from the 50-yard line to an arbitrary line 35 yards from the goal. There are also many proposals to widen the goal in order to increase scoring.[7]

Although these and other changes have been made in the NASL, the league has lost millions of dollars on the premise that American fans will learn the subtleties of the outdoor game. The strategy taken up by these frustrated corporate moguls was to invent "the sport of the 80s"—indoor soccer. This game is extremely simple to understand. Played with a bright orange ball on a compressed pitch the size of a hockey rink (200 feet long), the game pits six players on a side with the idea to kick the ball into a 12 × 6½ foot goal. There are time-outs, penalty boxes, and unlimited substitutions. Athletes enter the field of play like rock stars. The lights go off and a spotlight is trained on each player as he is introduced and emerges through a fog fueled by dry ice while the entire arena shakes to the "Eye of the Tiger" blasted over the public address system at a deafening volume. There is a lot of physical contact, the pace of the game is extremely fast, and scoring is high. The end result is a staccato mix of speeding, crashing bodies and ricocheting bright orange balls. As one goalie in the Major Indoor

Soccer League (MISL) put it, "the game is like a human pinball machine ... you've got to have more skills to play outdoor soccer. You can get away with deficiencies playing indoors" (*San Francisco Chronicle,* 1983a).

The Major Indoor Soccer League is the first sport to come into existence with the unmediated view to market itself as any other new commodity in the marketplace. The audience is carefully targeted, the show professionally choreographed, and the entire image marketed according to the techniques of scientific management and appealing to commercialized sex. In New York, the PA announcer constantly advises women attendees as to which bar they can visit after the game to meet players. Players in the League are encouraged to coat their legs with baby oil before a game to make them glisten.[8] A cologne manufacturer sponsors a "10½ competition," wherein female fans are asked to rate the players' sexuality. The executive vice-president of the Chicago Sting has approvingly noted the change in emphasis from soccer to indoor soccer: "I used to say there were 3S's: speed, scoring, and skill. Now I say show, sex, and suburbs" (*Sports Illustrated,* February 28, 1983).

The quest for spectacle and theatricality has worked against an authentic presentation of many dimensions of the new-found interest in women's athletics. For example, in 1979, Grete Waitz set a world record in the New York City Marathon (2:27:33). Because it was being covered live, one would expect to see considerable media coverage of this unusual and spectacular event, but the dictates of the Nielsen ratings resulted in a total neglect of Waitz's athletic skills. Instead, according to Neiderman (1980), "the live coverage ended without so much as a syllable about Waitz. The network signed off at 2:27:00 into the race. Astute tube watchers were able to view a world record being set during the closing credits" (p. 54). Thus, supreme athletic excellence does not qualify as deserving the eye of the spectacle unless it sells.

This lack of coverage is due not only to traditional male-supremacist views regarding the inferiority of women's athletic ability but also to the belief that sweaty, haggard-looking athletes finishing such a grueling event cannot attract an audience. This type of visual imagery does not attract the television audience and advertising monies as do the socially "acceptable" women's sports, such as ice skating, swimming, diving, tennis, gymnastics, and golf. Broadcast executives are much more interested in close-ups of women swimmers and divers in wet bathing suits, Jane Fonda performing leg splits, and pixie-like gymnasts' pelvic movements than the world class displays of aggressive and powerful physicality of women. Accordingly, women athletes who participate in traditionally unacceptable sports that involve aggression and power are neglected. Women's team and contact sports, such as rugby, softball, crew, volleyball, field hockey, and basketball—sports with long traditions and large followings—are neglected by athletic entrepreneurs because they are not marketable to the mass television audience.

Although many regular season competitions of women's sporting leagues are neglected, women athletes are reduced to sideshow freaks when they "compete" in the made-for-TV counterfeit sporting events (such as *Women Superstars* and the *Challenge of the Sexes*) that have little or no relation to the athletic skills of the sport in which the women usually compete. The largest attention given to women's sport has been the 1973 tennis match between world class 29-year-old Billie Jean King and the semiretired 55-year-old Bobby Riggs. Hyped as a "battle of the sexes," this $3 millon competition was promoted and broadcast as a circus event. In the process the full range of women's athleticism is neglected and the integrity of athletic skill is reduced to that which is commodifiable and sold as entertainment.

The logical conclusion of the market inclination to spectacle and theatricality is the creation of "competition" for television in the form of "trash sport." An example of trash sport is found in motorcycle collision distance-jumping tournaments. This so-called sport entails driving a motorcycle into a row of parked cars. The object is to see how many parked cars "athletes" can clear before they tumble onto a mat. To add to the excitement, all contestants wear burning flares attached to their pants. Recently the ante has been upped for this sport—due to flagging fan interest—by clearing buses instead of cars for distance. Fans can also attend the Annual World Belly Flop and Cannonball Diving Championships. A perennial winner in this competition is a 423-pound "athlete" who sets himself on fire as he dives into the water. Or fans can watch "athletes" try to pummel themselves unconscious with their own fists in "Knock Yourself Out Competition."

The supreme trash sport competition is found in All-Star/Big Time Professional Wrestling. This sport is populated by athletes such as Skull Murphy, Gorilla Monsoon, Abdullah the Butcher, Killer Kowalski, Dick the Bruiser, The Destroyer, The Mongolian Stomper, and Dr. X. These athletes compete in a variety of competitions including Texas Bull-Rope Matches, Strap Matches, Indian Death Matches, Chain Matches, 22-Man Battle Royals, Roman Gladiator Matches, and Steel Cage Matches. The premier competition, however, is the

Sicilian Stretcher Death Match, which has the following "rules": no countout, no pin falls, no holds barred, no referee, no rules, no surrender, doctor cannot stop bout, loser must be carried out, and loser must leave town.

What we are witnessing is the reduction of athletic skill, competition, and contest to commodified spectacle sold in the market for mass entertainment. The only guiding principle becomes the highest rate of return on one's investment. This instrumental orientation of today's entrepreneurs of sport stands in sharp contrast with the player orientation to sport as evidenced in the statement from the original creators of the sport of basketball. In the first introduction to the *Basket Ball Cooperating Committee Rule Book* of 1898 it is stated,

> The function of the rules committee is not only to consider and adopt rules that ideally shall be the best for the sport, but the rules committee must, by carefully weighing the evidence and acquaintance with the field, formulate that which represents the best judgment of the *players* of the country; for the games are *not* the product of the makers of the rules. (Gulick, 1898, p. 5, emphasis added)

CONCLUSION

The starting point of this analysis is the Frankfurt School critique of modernity and mass society for its failure to meet the human needs of relatedness, identity, and rootedness (Horkheimer & Adorno, 1972). When confronted with the reality of sensationalism, spectacle, and the predominance of a market mentality in sport, critical theory highlights the extent to which sport has lost its previous autonomy (as represented in the idealized version described above). This autonomy was rooted in a social position in which sport was free from the immediate context of use and exchange. In the process of being subsumed to commodity exchange and instrumental rationalization, sport thus loses its autonomy. Whereas sport had previously presented a partial critique of modernity by virtue of its nonutilitarian form and content, in its new, commodified and degraded version, sport serves to reproduce the modern world. Sport has become increasingly "functionalized" for the existing social order and is valorized by that order precisely for its role as entertainment, distraction, and diversion. Under commodified conditions the form of sport is determined by its value in exchange.

That the meaning of sport is altered by the medium of commodity exchange is evident in the "regression of viewing" sport. Technical standards of intelligibility held by knowledgeable fans are diminished when sport attempts to obtain the widest market possible—that is, appealing to untrained and uninformed eyes. Given the current mode of exchange and distribution of sport, sport is adjusted to attain the greatest market. Such "regression" or "standardization" shifts the reception of sport away from a totalistic understanding to atomized modes of viewing. The modern fan ripped from the wholeness of athletic culture seeks only stimulation and sensation.

Against critical theory's critique of commodified sport, many argue that the public should determine the nature and character of sport in American society (Gans, 1974). On the surface this seems to be sound democratic theory. However, the authentic fulfillment of democratic theory requires that (1) popular taste and judgment be informed and unconstrained and (2) there must be a means by which such judgment can be voiced and implemented. Obviously there is a great disparity between theory and practice in present-day democratic society. The claim that sports industry only gives the public what it wants is a dangerous and misleading half-truth.

In point of fact, the sporting public is by and large totally ignorant of what it might be getting if the profit interests of owners, professional sporting organizations, and the electronic media were different from what they presently are. The human palate is sensitive to a virtually inexhaustible variety of tastes in sport. But it is only as we sample different fares that we are capable of exercising preferences and making discriminatory judgments among them. Today we find a system in which the formulation, refinement, and dissemination of tastes is under a virtual monopoly of commercial and corporate interests. The public's taste is thus shaped with these commercial and corporate interests in mind; secondarily, if at all, is sport's interest taken into account. Unaware of what they might be tasting, it is hardly surprising that most of the public expresses a desire for what they get. In sum, the public's verdict rests on insufficient, distorted, and manipulated evidence. If we are to understand the nature of mass sport, the remarks made by Goethe must be considered: "Formerly there was one taste; now there are many tastes. But tell me, where are these tastes tasted?"

Marx pointed to the enormous transformative power of the market: "All that is holy is profaned. . . . The bourgeois has stripped of its halo every activity hitherto honored and looked up to with reverent awe. It has transformed the doctor, the lawyer, the priest, the poet, the man of science into its paid wage laborer" (Marx, 1978, p. 476). Marx goes on to discuss the economic situation of intellectuals and artists and notes that they are able to "live only so long as they find work, and these workers, who must sell themselves piecemeal, are a commodity like every other article of commerce" (Marx, 1978, p. 479). Similarly athletes can throw passes, execute sky hooks, and hit home runs only if someone with capital will pay them. In the process of subsuming sport to the logic of commodities "what will happen," as Berman (1982, p. 117) has noted in another context, "is that the creative processes and products will be used and transformed in ways that will dumbfound or horrify their creators. But the creators will be powerless to resist, because they must sell their labor power in order to live."

The thesis taken up here is not one of total manipulation and delusion. The manipulative intentions of the designers of culture can never be total in their effects. There remains a subversive potential with the nonutilitarian dimension of sport that enables it to be (potentially) the "antidote to its own lie." There is a limitation to the process of reification "because human beings, as subjects, still constitute the limit of reification. ... Mass culture has to renew its hold over them in an endless series of repetitions; the hopeless effort of repetition is the only trace of hope that the repetition may be futile, that human beings cannot be totally manipulated" (Adorno, 1981-1982, p. 202). Rejecting the thesis of monolithic control, the possibility remains of recovering the emancipatory potential of sport. This potential is located within the absolute practical uselessness of sport. As Ernest Bloch once remarked, even false, crippled needs are needs and contain a kernel of dream, hope, and concrete utopia. The goal of a critical theory of sport is to transform these needs into pressures for changing everyday life.

NOTES

1. The owner-appointed and governing-controlled bodies argue that such changes and innovations have been introduced for the benefit of player safety. However, as former All-Pro player Jack Tatum (1980) has pointed out, the really dangerous aspects of the game are left untouched; e.g., zone defenses, the quick slant passing play, blitzing, steel-hard helmets, dangerous medical practices, artificial playing surfaces, and a win-at-all-cost ethic.

2. Comments made in a television interview on September 26, 1983. According to Smith: "If you remember, if the AFL didn't establish credibility by the end of three years, the merger was null and void. And if you remember, Kansas City got blown out in the first game, Oakland got blown out in the second, and we were the third game" (*San Francisco Chronicle,* 1983).

3. Ironically, women marathoners get a break as a result of the sexism of the networks and the LAOOC. The women marathoners started at 8 a.m. and finished long before the heat and smog buildup.

4. This sort of corruption goes unreported and unnoticed because press coverage is conducted by reporters who are essentially agents for the sponsors and tournament directors. Not limited to the world of tennis, writers and broadcasters who criticize the conduct of their respective sport will suddenly find themselves banned or unwelcome in team club houses, practice sessions, locker rooms, training rooms, hotels, have interviews denied or "unavailable," or find no space available on team buses and planes. Such ostracism, of course, spells the end of any career in sports broadcasting or journalism.

5. However, things could be otherwise. The sole exception to the commercial dominance of sport is found in the Masters Golf Tournament. The Masters is broadcast without gimmickry, hyperbole, reference to money, crowd size, loud voices, or promotions for CBS-TV's next broadcast. This state of affairs is due to the following factors: (1) the stringent insistence of the tournament organizers to keep commercialism out of the picture; (2) a very meager contract with CBS-TV; and (3) an almost guaranteed viewing audience (small but affluent) who CBS can easily sell to advertisers.

6. Many sports writers interpreted Kuhn's forced resignation by the 26 corporate owners of baseball clubs as a matter of Kuhn's underdeveloped business sense.

7. The international governing body of soccer (FIFA) keeps commercialization in check by refusing to allow any player to participate in the prestigious and lucrative World Cup and other international matches if he plays in a league not sanctioned by the Federation Internationale de Football Association (FIFA).

8. MISL crowds are 50% or more women, whereas in other professional sports the crowds are 25% to 30% women.

Chapter 13

THE POLITICAL STRUGGLE FOR PRIME TIME

Kathryn Montgomery

SINCE THE EARLIEST DAYS of network television, "special interest groups"[1] have tried to influence the content of prime-time entertainment programming. Beginning in 1951 with the National Association for the Advancement of Colored People's campaign to force the comedy series, *Amos'n'Andy* off the air, hundreds of organized groups, representing a range of constituencies, have employed various strategies to try to shape program content. These groups proliferated dramatically during the political turbulence of the 1960s and 1970s, and more have emerged in recent years. The goals and concerns of these groups are diverse, and their names reflect the pluralism of American society: the Black Anti-Defamation League; the International Association of Machinists; the National Organization for Women; the National Gay Task Force; the Gray Panthers; the Pro-Life Action League; the National Congress of Parents and Teachers; the Moral Majority.

Although there has been considerable debate about the relation between special interest groups and network entertainment television, little formal research has been conducted in this area. Those scholars who have addressed the issue for the most part have either focused on the activities of only one or two groups (Cowan, 1979; Lewels, 1974; Lewis, 1984; Montgomery, 1979, 1981) or have incorporated discussions of special interest groups into more general works on the television industry (Cantor, 1979, 1980; Gitlin 1983; Rowland, 1983). The present research has involved a comprehensive examination of the role of special interest groups in entertainment television and is based on a wide range of primary and secondary materials, including extensive interviews with network executives, special interest group leaders, government officials, producers, writers, and directors.[2] Two questions were addressed: How has the institution of network television responded to pressure from special interest groups? What impact, if any, have these groups had on entertainment program content?

FINDINGS TO DATE

THE NETWORKS HAVE SUCCESSFULLY INSTITUTIONALIZED THEIR RELATIONSHIP WITH SPECIAL INTEREST GROUPS

Although they were involved with television in the 1950s, special interest groups did not become a serious problem for the television industry until the late 1960s and early 1970s. Many were advocacy groups, representing ethnic minorities, women, and gays. These groups saw the mass media as important targets for their political efforts and sought to eliminate stereotypes and increase positive portrayals in programming. Some of them were part of a larger media reform movement that was aimed at making the television industry more accessible to the public. Several critical court decisions increased the power of these groups to monitor the performance of local broadcast stations (Branscomb & Savage, 1978; Grundfest, 1976; Krasnow et al., 1982). Dealing with special interest groups thus became an increasingly disruptive, costly, and time-consuming task for the networks. Pickets, sit-ins, and threats of violence were not uncommon. Particularly troubling were license challenges against network-owned and -operated stations, challenges that were costly to fight and posed potentially serious economic threats to network corporations. The National Organization for Women, for example, formally petitioned the Federal Communications Commission to deny the licenses of several network-owned stations, because of the "derogatory, demeaning, and stereotyped images of women" in the prime-time programming. Justicia, a group whose name stands for "justice," threatened similar action unless the networks each paid $10 million in "program development funds for shows that feature Chicanos in significant roles in order to restore an image of dignity."

To avoid further confrontations, the networks quickly developed strategies for disarming and containing special interest groups. During the last 15 years, these strategies have evolved into a successful system for "managing" special interest groups.[3] Standards and practices departments have been given primary responsibility for this task.[4] Commonly known as network censors, the executives in these departments set policy for program content and administer it through their supervision of the production process. They also function as a buffer between the public and the networks. The following elements are critical components of the network system for handling special interest groups.

Accessibility

The standards and practices departments maintain an open door policy toward special interest groups. They encourage letter writing, and they frequently meet personally with group leaders. Network representatives say they have had contact with between 100 and 300 groups that have approached them about network programming. When a group protests a program, it is common practice for the standards and practices departments to meet with the protesters to talk about the program in question. If the protest occurs during the production process and appears to be serious, the network executives will sometimes offer to provide the group with the opportunity to review scripts and to preview the program for feedback prior to broadcast. Often this process will result in some modification in content.[5] When black groups launched a major protest against NBC over its miniseries *Beulah Land,* for example, the network met with the protesters, shared the script with them, hired a black historian to work as a "technical consultant," made changes in the program in order to placate the protesters, and previewed the completed series for them.

Cultivation of Permanent Relationships

Rather than just react to special interest groups, the networks have found it to their advantage to seek them out before problems develop and win their support and cooperation. This practice also allows the networks to cultivate permanent relationships with the most moderate of the several groups representing a single constituency. These "insiders" have tended to be the groups most willing to accommodate their goals to fit the demands and needs of network television. These groups have not just been given the illusion of access and input. They are in fact frequently asked to consult on scripts during the writing and production of programs and to preview program materials prior to broadcast. The terms of access and input, however, have been set by the network institutions. The groups fully understand the rules of the game and are willing to play by them. The National Gay Task Force, for example, first made itself known to the networks in 1973 through a protest over offensive portrayals of homosexuals. The group quickly learned that it could be more effective if it adjusted its strategy to the more conciliatory, cooperative approach of an "educational lobby." Gay representatives now serve as "technical consultants" to the networks and the production community on programs that deal with gay characters or issues (Montgomery, 1979, 1981).

The Gray Panthers have a similar relationship with the industry, periodically consulting on the portrayal of the elderly in television programming. Nosotros, a Los Angeles-based group of Hispanic actors, also consults with the networks and the production community on the portrayal of Mexican-Americans in prime time. The groups that have become part of this process are generally pleased with the treatment they have received from the networks. Because of this institutionalized relationship, these groups have internalized the corporate constraints of the networks and scaled down their demands accordingly, even adopting the terminology of the network executives with whom they deal—referring to their role as "sensitizing" the networks through a process of "ongoing dialogue."

Outreach

Standards and practices executives frequently make public appearances at gatherings of special interest groups around the country, assuring them of the networks' commitment to fair representation. From time to time, the networks themselves will set up special meetings with group representatives. NBC recently invited representatives of 35 special interest groups to an all-expenses paid " 'roll up your sleeves' working conference" with network management at Princeton University to discuss "Social Change in the 1980s." In a letter to participants, the network described the event as "a seminar in which NBC executives will learn what the invited conferees have to say about serving a mass audience in a pluralistic society." The meeting was not publicized and was closed to the press in order to "continue and enhance the dialogue and interchange between group leaders and network executives in a forum which provides free and open opportunity for the expression of positive and negative feeling about television and its role in American life."

These outreach efforts, along with the other strategies the networks employ for dealing with special interest groups, have substantially reduced the likelihood of open confrontation. The rare cases in which such confrontations have occurred constitute minor "breakdowns" in an otherwise smooth-running system. Such instances have generally been followed by fine tuning of the procedure in order to preempt any similar mishaps. Special interest groups have become such a permanent fixture in television that broadcasters proudly hail them as proof of the essentially democratic nature of the medium. The following quote from a Television Information Office pamphlet reflects this attitude.

> To assure that entertainment programs are meeting current generally accepted standards, program executives keep in touch with the pluralistic, segmented, incredibly diverse American public. Broadcasters ... meet with groups to discuss, for example, stereotyping of women and minorities, racism, sexism, children's programming, portrayals of the elderly, of Blacks, Italians, Poles, Arab Americans, native Americans, and members of various facets.... Altogether, the groups surveyed represent constituencies of tens of millions of Americans—a substantial and effective means, along with program ratings, by which to gauge people's preferences.

**THIS INSTITUTIONALIZED NETWORK RELATIONSHIP
WITH SPECIAL INTEREST GROUPS
HAS PRODUCED IDENTIFIABLE PATTERNS IN
PRIME-TIME ENTERTAINMENT PROGRAMMING**

Through their continuing interaction with special interest groups, standards and practices executives have developed a keen sense for material that is "sensitive." They have become uniquely skilled at spotting a word, phrase, character, or theme that is a potential "red flag" for any of the groups with which these departments have had contact. The policies that have been developed for special handling of such sensitive program content include elimination of inflammatory material, careful substitution, obfuscation, and alteration.[6] The most significant of these is the policy of "balance."[7] This principle is invoked by the networks to prove they are reasonable and equitable in their treatment of special interest group issues.

"Balance" means that potentially controversial material is carefully structured within each entertainment program so that the program will not appear to be advocating a particular point of view. "Balance" can take a number of forms. If the sensitive issue is racial stereotyping, the network representatives will see to it that any negative stereotype within a program is balanced by a positive representation of that racial group. A network memorandum regarding the ABC comedy series *Soap* included the following mandate: "In order to be able to treat the Mafia storyline here and throughout, it will be necessary to introduce a principal continuing character of Italian descent who is very positive and who will, through the dialogue and action, balance and counter any negative stereotypes" (*Los Angeles Times*, 1977). NBC recently reported that it had ensured racial balance in one of its series by insisting that "if an ethnic character is portrayed in a negative role, at least one additional character of the same ethnicity must be portrayed in the same or subsequent episodes."[8]

In the case of other controversial issues, balance can be achieved by any or all of the following: (1) adding characters to the narrative whose function is to present opposing points of view on the issue; (2) structuring ambiguity into the program by using multiple plot lines to present different positions; and (3) taking special care to leave an issue unresolved at the end of the program. As an example of how the first device might be used, one standards and practices representative recently explained that if a show were being written about a young woman who was contemplating abortion, the network would insist that a character be written into the story, "perhaps an aunt or someone, who would represent the pro-life point of view and counsel the young lady about the moral issues involved in her decision."

As network television has incorporated more and more controversial social and political issues into its entertainment programming, larger amounts of prime-time fare reflect this policy of balance. This has not undermined the ability of programming to generate and maintain large, heterogeneous audiences. In fact, balance may enhance this function. Including elements in each program that represent various points of view on an issue ensures that large segments of the audience will not be alienated and therefore lost. Hence balance has become an important marketing mechanism, as well as a device to protect networks from political protest.

A FEW GROUPS HAVE OPERATED OUTSIDE OF THE NETWORK "MANAGEMENT" SYSTEM

These groups have differed from the majority of special interest groups in several important ways. Rather than making limited demands upon program content, such as the addition of more minority characters or the balanced treatment of a controversial social issue, these groups have demanded sweeping changes in program content. Most of their attention has been focused on reducing what they perceive to be the most troublesome elements in prime-time programming—sex and violence. The organizations in this category have acted on behalf of large liberal and conservative constituencies. Liberal organizations, such as the National Citizens Committee for Broadcasting (NCCB) or the Congress of Parents and Teachers (PTA), have sought reductions in the amount of violent content in network programming (Cowan, 1979). More conservative religious groups, such as the Moral Majority, have taken aim at sexually oriented program content. Despite their diverse political orientations, these groups have employed similar methods to influence network television (Gitlin, 1983).

These groups have operated outside the system because of the nature of the program content they have challenged. Sex and violence permeate a large percentage of prime-time programming. Because these elements often increase ratings, the networks have been very reluctant to eliminate them. Groups seeking a reduction in such content have taken extreme measures to pressure networks, such as threatening to boycott advertisers. The present system of network television advertising makes it difficult to target sponsors for a boycott. Since the early 1960s, advertisers have distributed their messages throughout the programming schedule so that programs typically contain commercial spots from various companies, and these may change from week to week. Therefore, groups have had to develop sophisticated procedures for identifying the advertisers connected with the most offensive content. The NCCB and the PTA have hired experts to conduct scientific content analyses, and volunteers have been employed to do monitoring. Most recently, this method has been employed by the Coalition for Better Television, in which the Moral Majority was a major participant (Gitlin, 1983).

Although there have been clear variations in the tactics used by these groups, their basic strategy has been the same. They have all waged "campaigns" against network television. These campaigns have generally been short term, intense, and heavily dependent on the press. By publicly exposing the advertisers associated with sexual content or the most violent programs and implicitly or explicitly threatening to boycott them, the groups have sought to pressure the networks into reducing such content.

THE NETWORK TELEVISION INDUSTRY
HAS DEVELOPED A SEPARATE SET OF STRATEGIES
FOR HANDLING THESE CAMPAIGNS

The usual procedures employed by standards and practices departments to "manage" special interest groups are not effective when applied to organizations engaged in public campaigns against television. When standards and practices representatives have tried to meet with group leaders in some of these cases, their efforts have largely been unsuccessful. Consequently, alternative strategies have had to be developed. One strategy the networks employ is to discredit the campaigns publicly, making statements to the press about the excessive nature of the demands, the threat of censorship, and the weaknesses in their monitoring methods. In some cases, the networks have used their own in-house social research departments to conduct monitoring and audience surveys to challenge the accuracy and effectiveness of the campaigns.

Because the primary targets of these campaigns have been the advertisers, these companies have developed their own set of strategies. Although advertisers have had virtually no direct influence over the content of prime-time programming since the early 1960s, they have developed mechanisms for reducing their vulnerability to boycott campaigns. As a direct result of special interest group campaigns, most of the major advertisers now have corporate policies about the kinds of programs in which they will buy time (Cowan, 1979; Gitlin, 1983). Many advertisers employ "screening" companies to examine the programs in which commercials are scheduled to appear. Spots may be withdrawn from programs that do not adhere to an advertiser's content policy. During a pressure campaign, this practice can be particularly useful.

**BOYCOTT CAMPAIGNS HAVE REDUCED
OR ALTERED CERTAIN KINDS
OF CONTENT TEMPORARILY BUT HAVE HAD
LITTLE SUBSTANTIAL LONG-TERM IMPACT
ON PRIME-TIME PROGRAMMING**

There is little doubt that the highly publicized campaigns against sex and violence have had some impact on program content. Producers and writers have reported that network policies became stricter during such campaigns, and television critics have noted concurrent changes in content.[9] Standards and practices executives will not readily admit that they act in response to these pressures, but it seems clear that "sex" and "violence" have become more sensitive when groups have publicly campaigned against them. During these campaigns, standards and practices editors have insisted on a reduction in the number of sexual or violent acts in programs and they have given specific instructions to producers to "sanitize" such content.

These changes appear to be the result of generalized pressure from advertisers upon the networks. At the height of a campaign, when advertisers feel most vulnerable to a boycott, they are more inclined to redistribute their ads to what are known within the industry as "clean" shows, those programs that are free of troublesome content. This may inflate the advertising cost of time in clean programs while reducing the cost of time on the troublesome programs. Some advertisers do not care if their spots appear in violent or sexual programs. However, it is the major advertisers in television—those whose expenditures pay for the bulk of network programming—who are most frequently targets of pressure groups. When faced with the choice of paying inflated prices for time on clean shows, or buying time on programs that make them vulnerable to boycotts, these major advertisers have not hesitated to make their displeasure known to the networks.[10] During the height of the campaign by the Coalition for Better Television, several of the largest advertisers in television threatened to take their dollars elsewhere if programming did not change. As a result, some of the more controversial programs on the air were dropped for the next season, despite healthy ratings, and other programs were changed substantially to make them sufficiently clean to be safe for advertisers (Gitlin, 1983).

Unlike the institutionalized content policies that have grown out of the ongoing interaction between special interest groups and standards and practices departments, the impact of campaigns on programming is usually temporary. All campaigns have been limited in duration. It is difficult for a group to sustain interest within the press, its constituency, and the public for long periods of time. In addition, group leadership sometimes changes and other issues become more important than television. Consequently, change in content fluctuates with the ebb and flow of pressures on prime time. In some cases, outside pressure has reduced "gratuitous" violence, only to see a corresponding rise in the amount of gratuitous sex.

**THE STRATEGIES EMPLOYED BY THE
TELEVISION NETWORKS AND THEIR ADVERTISERS
HAVE EFFECTIVELY PROTECTED THE FINANCIAL
WELL-BEING OF THE INDUSTRY FROM
SPECIAL INTEREST GROUP PRESSURE**

Although special interest groups have caused some disruptions for the network television industry from time to time, in the long run they have not constituted a substantial threat to the business of American broadcasting. The industry has proven to be both adaptive and resilient in its dealings with these organizations. Network corporations have adjusted to the continuing presence of special interest groups by finding ways to institutionalize them successfully. The relationship between special interest groups and the networks has had a substantial impact on entertainment programming but has in no way undermined the ability of that programming to generate and sustain the audiences needed by its advertisers. In cases in which the advertisers themselves have been the targets of special interest groups, these companies have managed to reduce their vulnerability to economic threat until the pressure has let up. In the final analysis, the powerful institution of commercial network television has prevailed.

NOTES

1. Sometimes these groups are referred to as "pressure groups," "citizen groups," or "public interest groups." I use the term "special interest groups" because it is how the networks label them.

2. The research has focused only on attempts by special interest groups to influence prime-time program content on the three commercial television networks—ABC, CBS, and NBC. It excludes news and informational programming, local programming, children's programming, and cable television.

3. Grant Tinker, now president of NBC, used this term—during the Proliferation of Pressure Groups Symposium—to describe the way the industry has handled special interest groups (Margulies, 1981).

4. These departments are essentially the same at all the networks, but their labels vary from Broadcast Standards (NBC), to Broadcast Standards and Practices (ABC), to Program Practices (CBS). In this chapter I use the generic term, "standards and practices."

5. There appears to be some variation on this procedure, with both ABC and NBC having previewed programs to special interest groups and CBS saying this is not their policy. In some cases, however, production companies will take on this task either independently or at the suggestion of the network.

6. For a more detailed description of these policies, see Montgomery (1983).

7. This policy appears to have a direct relation to the FCC's Fairness Doctrine, which requires that controversial issues of public importance be treated fairly. This rule generally applies to documentary, news, and public affairs programming, but its application to entertainment programming is sufficiently unclear that network executives themselves disagree about it.

8. This case was cited in an NBC document summarizing that network's treatment of ethical issues.

9. Although these changes may not always be discernible by social science researchers, they have been documented in the press, as well as by industry insiders. In *TV/Radio Age*, O'Toole (1983), for example, attributes a number of changes in program content to the campaign waged by the Coalition for Better Television: "A look at

the new television season in the United States clearly reveals the profound influence of these zealots. *Love Boat* has been cleaned up for the 82-83 season, returning to the light romantic comedy approach with which it began. *Real People* and *That's Incredible* will drop the suicidal in favor of what the network describes as 'the American slice of life.' Bedrooms and bullets have yielded to characterizations, the nature of which are apparent in such program titles as *Mama Malone, Seven Brides for Seven Brothers, Family Ties,* and *Star of the Family.*" Similar changes in program content during the PTA antiviolence campaign in 1976-1977 have been documented by Cowan (1979).

10. For example, Coates (1981) noted during the CBTV campaign that "Agency, network TV, and advertising executives admit that the resurgence of group pressure has made TV users more wary of program content, has caused some to speculate that the networks have passed the word to Hollywood to tone down risque or violent program elements, and that the so-called clean shows, regardless of ratings, may well fetch a premium price in the upfront marketplace because they offend no one."

Chapter 14

CULTURE BY THE MILLIONS
Audience as Innovator

Victoria Billings

THE AUDIENCE, REGARDLESS OF THE MEDIUM, has not historically been passive or inconsequential in shaping its participation in, or the content of, popular culture. Rather, audiences emerge as significant spurs to innovation once they are considered in various media, in a variety of historical settings, and as collectivities rather than an amorphous mass. Furthermore, sociological factors of institutionalization, political consciousness, and collective behavior, rather than the prominent technical feature of directness or indirectness of the medium, account for variations in audience participation.

This stance contrasts sharply with most earlier sociological literature on audiences. Previous work has variously viewed the audience as a mass of powerless individuals (Bell, 1961; Horkheimer & Adorno, 1972; Marcuse, 1964); a consumer group confronted with a limited range of preselected products (Hirsch, 1972); a subordinate class bombarded with hegemonic values (Gitlin, 1979; Sallach, 1974; Tuchman, 1974; Williams, 1977); an image in the producer's mind (Gans, 1975; McQuail, 1969); or a mechanism that provides for "demand" or feedback to culture producers in an indirect, multilayered fashion (Bauer, 1958; Gans, 1957, 1974; McQuail, 1969; Riley & Riley, 1959; Seiden, 1974). With a few exceptions (Balfe, 1981; Greenfield, 1984; Jauss, 1970), the limited scope and depth of the audience's role is a fundamental assumption throughout the literature.

Jarvie (1970), writing on motion pictures, says the audience is typically conceived as an "unstructured group" that has "no social

AUTHOR'S NOTE: I gratefully acknowledge the suggestions of Professors Muriel Cantor and Lynne Zucker in the preparation of this chapter.

organization, no body of custom and tradition, no established set of rules or rituals, no organized group of sentiments, no structure of status roles and no established leadership" (p. 186). The audience is merely an aggregate of demographic characteristics.

Institutional conventions and the social organization of production presumably shape the concept of the audience, which in turn shapes production independent of the audience itself (Cantor, 1980; Hirsch, 1972; Jowett & Linton, 1980). However, not all producers—in particular, entrepreneurs who are self-employed—are as dependent on the hierarchical decision-making processes of the mass media bureaucracies; industries are more receptive to public opinion at less institutionalized points in their development, and even when highly institutionalized, culture industries have means to seek out opinion from the audience (Handel, 1950) or conventions that incorporate historically developed audience preferences.

Some parts of the sociological literature do not portray the audience in faint and ineffectual terms. However, where the audience is treated as more participatory, the literature still stops short of assigning the audience a role as innovator or gives the impression that technological aspects of a medium, such as its directness, may be the sole factor in greater audience participation. For instance, scholars of the performing arts, for whom audience contact is direct, stress the participatory nature of audiences and incorporation of their role into performance conventions (Becker, 1982; Gaylord, 1983; Grotowski, 1927; Piscator, 1949). The audience participates through a sharing of artists' conventions, which puts the audience in the position of sponsor (Becker, 1983) or "witness to the truth of the drama" (Gaylord, 1983).

In contrast to more traditional approaches that minimize the role of popular audiences, the younger generation of Marxists acknowledges that these audiences need to be considered in the production of culture (Cantor, 1980); and social historians have begun to explore the making of culture from the bottom up (Burke, 1981) with fewer preconceptions about the audience's options and participation. But they have not yet provided clear outlines of audience participation or of how class alliances and political consciousness shape that participation.

How can an audience directly cause artistic innovation? In one case, an audience successfully reshaped a stock character into a more complimentary reflection of itself (Griswold, 1983). In seventeenth-century London, young aristocrats whose financial needs forced them to go into commerce patronized the transformation of the old "trickster" character, a financial cheat, into the new "gallant," whose financial sleight of hand was portrayed as clever. But even in this historical case, innovation is still treated as largely in the artists' hands and a prerogative of elites.

Perhaps the best example in the literature of cultural innovation involving a larger class base is the development of novel reading and the production of novels during the eighteenth century in England. Audience-building, an activity of printer-entrepreneurs, had a marked impact on the book trade, expanding the titles available, the repertoire of styles, and the social organization of publishing (Lowenthal, 1961). Literature had been monopolized by the classical language and poetics tradition; now the novel emerged, built on the vernacular and epistolary forms.

The growth of novel reading and production was definitely a class and gender phenomenon, both financially and culturally, aimed at the increasingly affluent and literate middle-class households, particularly housewives and maids (Watt, 1957, pp. 35-59). As novels rose in popularity, the English poor also struggled to learn to read and patronized the circulating libraries despite the disapproval of the upper and middle classes.

Are these examples of audience influence over innovation mere anomalies? To determine how audience segments—in coalition or in conflict—influenced other popular media, I propose to look at the social-historical literature documenting two centuries of audience participation in the direct medium of the theatrical stage and the indirect medium of the theatrical motion picture.

The comparsion of the two media allows a technological variable in audience participation—the directness of the medium—to be compared with sociological features, such as degree of institutionalization of the industry and collective behavior of the audience. To find a conducive environment for audience participation, I have selected media with large collective settings—the theater and motion pictures—but I also trace audience participation over a period of time in which both media moved from low to high institutionalization, as measured by increased capitalization and consolidation of production, distribution, and exhibition. My first goal was to determine the nature and existence of audience participation; my second goal, to isolate factors in its visibility.

AUDIENCE CONTRIBUTIONS TO
LIVE THEATRE: EIGHTEENTH AND NINETEENTH CENTURIES

The nature of audience influence over live theater will be examined primarily in England and the United States, using the heyday of mass theater—the eighteenth and early nineteenth centuries. I will examine access to the theater and the creator-producers, conventions for influencing repertoire and social organization of production, class consciousness and class struggles as motivations, and, finally, limits to audience influence based on evolving social organization of production.

EXPANSION OF ACCESS

Elizabethan theater, particularly Shakespeare, was associated with a cross section of society and pleasing the lower classes by "playing to the gallery" (Funk, 1950, p. 298). When live theater began again after the Puritan Revolution ended, elites predominated as audiences. Theater existed primarily in private settings of country estates and court. Even with the beginning of commercial theater, the emphasis was on small private theaters (Griswold, 1983).

Access for new social gorups increased in the eighteenth century. The sheer number of theaters all over Europe and America expanded between 1850 and 1870. Whereas in the beginning of the eighteenth century London and Paris each had two theaters, by 1860, the number had grown to 30 in each city (Brockett & Findlay, 1973, p. 9). Also, theaters began to expand performances from afternoons into the evening hours to accommodate working persons (Rowell, 1978, pp. 4,7). The number of inexpensive seats increased and the physical distance between performers and the audience decreased. Theaters added pit benches and cut back the stage apron; balconies took on extra tiers. The commercialization of theater entertainment facilitated its development as a mass medium: "anyone who could pay could play" (Porter, 1981, p. 249).

In the United States, the same pattern occurred but later than in England and Europe. Because of the newness of the nation and the persisting influence of Puritanism, the theater was not transformed into a mass medium until the nineteenth century (Hornblow, 1919, p. 46). After the War of 1812, vast numbers of persons crowded into American cities, and from there into theaters that formerly had been patronized only by elites. This flow spawned new and larger theaters and lower ticket prices (Toll, 1976, pp. 3-5).

CHANGING MODE OF AUDIENCE PARTICIPATION

In the early nineteenth century, America had four elaborate theaters; by the late 1830s, New York had the 4,000-seat Bowery Theater. The larger theaters provided the setting and the new audience the participants for collective behavior that was both expressive and instrumental.

Outbursts. Perhaps the most important and, retrospectively, startling aspect of audience participation in the eighteenth and nineteenth centuries is that loud, disruptive participation was accepted as a matter of course, a given of theater attendance. Outbursts preceded the expansion of theaters but also appear to have increased with the influx of new audiences. "In the 1750s when an actor turned to the audience to make a point, a sentence or even a word could bring immediate boos or applause" (Sennett, 1974, p. 206). In 1798, Washington Irving observed in the *New York Chronicle* that audiences in the gallery at a recent performance were "stamping, hissing, roaring, whistling, and when the musicians were refractory, groaning in cadence" (Hornblow, 1919, pp. 253-254). According to Toll (1976),

> Nineteenth-century audiences voiced their feelings about what they saw with a directness and a volume that would startle and outrage mid-Twentieth Century theater goers. Whenever those audiences liked a speech, song or piece of acting, they cheered wildly and demanded encores, regardless of the nature of the performance or the script. ... When displeased, audiences hissed, shouted insults, and threw things at the performers. (p. 7)

The English language itself was affected by the changed conventions of audience participation. The word "explode" or "exploding" originated to describe the audience custom of clapping ("plode") an unpopular act or player off ("ex") stage (Frank, 1950, p. 294; Morris & Morris, 1962, p. 211). Emerging about the same time was the term "encore," which means "again" and "once more," used to demand repetitions of pleasing songs, music, and speeches (Oxford English Dictionary, 1961, p. 149). A journalist, writing in 1712, is cited as saying, "The wretches encored [him] without mercy."

Riots. A less conventional means that the audience had to influence the production of culture in the theater was the demonstration or riot. The prevailing message from the outcome of demonstrations was "the theater public was master" (Moody, 1958, p. 24). Beginning in the mid-eighteenth century in Great Britain, demonstrations and riots became a potent force. Especially important were the 1809 "Old Prices" Riot (new Covent Garden in London) and the 1949 Astor Place Riot (Astor Opera House in New York City).

The "Old Prices" Riot was a demonstration of audiences against higher prices at more than 60 consecutive performances of the premiere production at the refurbished Covent Garden Theater (Moody, 1958; Rowell, 1978, pp. 3-4). Audiences paid admission, filled the pit area (now known as the orchestra) and gallery (balcony), then drowned out all dialogue with the cry, "old prices! old prices!" (Moody, 1958, p. 20). The audience and its leaders eventually won price concessions from the management.

The Astor Place Riot in New York City started as a protest over the appearance of William Macready, an English tragedian, who had a running feud with the popular American actor, Edwin Forrest. Anti-British and anti-aristocratic sentiment had drawn the public into the feud and made touring in America progressively problematic for English actors (Moody, 1958; Toll, 1976; Wolfe, 1975). Between 10,000 and 20,000 angry demonstrators converged on Astor Place during Macready's performance. Excited militia killed 31 persons (Wolfe, 1975, p. 116). The Astor Place Riot convinced theater owners that the upper class and the mass of middle- and lower-class Americans were "impossible to satisfy both in the same place at the same time with the same thing" (Toll, 1976, p. 23).

AUDIENCE-INFLUENCED CHANGES IN REPERTOIRE AND SOCIAL ORGANIZATION OF PRODUCTION

Important changes in the cultural repertoire and social organization of mass theater production can be traced to the new activities of the audience in the eighteenth and nineteenth centuries.

(1) Development of a popular culture in the theater. Popular access to the theater and its repertoire was gained by collective action, such as the outbursts and riots described above, and succeeded at the expense of the conventions of actors and preferences of more traditional elite audiences. Toll (1976) attributes the bifurcation of American culture into elite and popular modes to the Astor Place Riot. Popular audiences rejected wit, in-jokes, satire (Porter, 1982, p. 241), and intellectualized drama in favor of variety exemplified by vaudeville, a collection of acts (Porter, 1982, p. 257), sentiment and spectacle (Rowell, 1978, pp. 2, 38), and humanized drama and actors (Hodge, 1964; Wilson, 1966).

(2) Specific repertorial innovations. These include the Yankee hero (Hodge, 1964) and the heroic style of acting, exemplified by Forrest (Wilson, 1966) and the spread and development of melodrama (Brockett & Findlay, 1973; p. 21; Rowell, 1978, p. 40; Wilson, 1966). Also, encoring stimulated the composition of additional songs for the popular minstrel shows (Toll, 1976).

(3) Changes in the social organization of production. The tendency of audiences to single out actors and pay more to see highly publicized personalities created the foundation for the "star system" (Hornbow, 1919; Toll, 1982, p. 32). A parallel phenomenon was the tendency of audiences to reject one-night performances in favor of long runs for new "hits." This combination contributed to the demise of the old repertorial system, which stressed the rotation of a limited bill of plays presented by actors who functioned as a company of equals (Brockett & Findlay, 1973, pp. 21-25). Several crafts within the theater gained status as a result of the tastes of popular audiences—most prominently, the director (usually an actor who started coordinating spectacles) and the playwright, who wrote the hit plays (Brockett & Findlay, 1973).

The theater professionals who benefited most from the rise of the power of popular audiences was the one who in an entrepreneurial fashion, regardless of original craft, provided new material and settings for popular theater (Hodge, 1963; Hornbow, 1919, p. 272; Toll, 1982).

CLASS ASPECTS OF AUDIENCE PARTICIPATION

Audience participation, particularly when inspired by actual grievances, indicates a clear connection with class consciousness and conflict. Rowell (1978) contrasts "Old Price" Riots with earlier demonstrations, saying that by 1809 "theatre-rioting became a species of class-war," with the prolonged demonstration driving elite audiences from the theater. "For the next fifty years polite society quitted the theater for the opera house and the play for the novel" (Rowell, 1978, pp. 3-4).

Both the "Old Price" Riot and the Astor Place Riot show a gradual rise in lower-class influence in the theater due to particular advantages the masses had in the theater setting. Some were unintentional; some fought for. "The common people were a much larger and louder part of the audience than were the 'better families' " (Toll, 1976, p. 7), ensuring the commoners' influence. The gallery position of cheap seats and the lack of finery among poor theatergoers were advantageous for theater combat; New York elegants who crowded the stage to oggle actresses had to retreat when the gallery pelted them with eggs (Hornbow, 1919, p. 117). And Rowell notes that aristocrats were gradually edged from the front of the pit to boxes at the side, a less strategic place for participation. This gave the cheaper pit and gallery audiences an unobstructed view of—and line of fire to—the stage.

A series of theater demonstrations described by Moody (1958, p. 20) can be interpreted as evidence of declining direct influence by elites over production of live theater. The Lincoln's Inn Theater brawl of 1721, the Drury Lane brawl of 1740, and a Dublin theater fight in 1747 all involved quarrels between actors and aristocrats, whose socializing disrupted plays. After 1748, disturbances involved the whole audience, but particularly the pit and gallery. In 1749, the Duke of Cumberland led a theater riot, but it was a mass protest for compensation after an act failed to appear. In 1760, actor David Garrick tried to abolish the half-price admission after the play's first act. A vociferous protest forced Garrick to retreat.

The possession of technical skills in the arts was related to acceptance of particular performers by the middle and upper classes; possession of these skills gave performers authority. For example, opera-loving elites accepted performers as authorities, exemplified by the autocratic conductor Wagner (Sennett, 1974, pp. 206, 211). By 1754, conflict had shifted to the class issue of whether dandified French performers should appear. The aristocrats fought, literally, for the performers but the "pitties" won.

The popular audience did not yield its expressive and creative authority to the new artistic professionals as readily as the middle- and upper-class audiences did. The arts and sciences, supported by elites, produced impresarios such as Wagner; popular commercial culture produced accessible, "humanized" stars such as Jenny Lind or Edwin Forrest (Porter, 1982, p. 249).

The heroic actor and the melodrama are additional evidence for class-influenced tastes that, thanks to an active popular audience, found their way into the theatrical repertoire. The heroic school of action, exemplified by Forrest, rejected the affected, studied, and aloft classical style in favor of a detailed, realistic, and highly emotional performance (Wilson, 1966, p. 111). A parallel acting type was the female heroine of melodramas adapted from German and French sources (Wilson, 1966, p. 11). "The emotionalistic player abandoned control and surrendered herself to the emotions of the part." Although emotionalism can be interpreted as pandering to the personal at the expense of the political, the style clearly was demanded by the audiences and represents a form of resistance to elite values.

Along the same line, the Yankee hero's appeal was in his freedom from aristocratic corruption; the melodrama pitted the decent rural Yankee's wit against the unscrupulousness of the urban businessman (Hodge, 1964; Toll, 1976, pp. 10-11, 146-147). This popular character is an interesting contrast to Griswold's description of the aristocratically derived gallant.

LIMITS TO AUDIENCE INNOVATION IMPOSED BY THE SOCIAL ORGANIZATION OF PRODUCTION

As institutionalization and concentration of capital increased in live theater production, producers had less interest in modifying productions to suit local audience demands and sought to standardize material that had been successful in the past through publicity, vertical integration of production, distribution and exhibition, and audience segmentation. Early in the development of popular culture, entrepreneurs tried to give the new, larger audiences what they wanted (Porter, 1957; Toll, 1982, p. 4). Later, such forms of popular lower-class entertainment as vaudeville and burlesque were appropriated and sanitized for affluent audiences at expensive, uptown theaters (Toll, 1976, 1982).

By 1870, American entertainment producers had shut out the mass audience for live entertainment by curtailing production of plays and switching capital into accumulation and management of theaters rather than production (Poggi, 1968). Early twentieth-century American theater production was conservative, presenting limited runs of a few plays, due to the power of production and exhibition syndicates, (Brockett & Findlay, 1973, p. 486). Live theater originated with a middle and high-brow New York audience; plays were then peddled to the provinces via road companies. Melodrama virtually disappeared from live theater (Poggi, 1968, pp. 261-263). With these changes the role of the audience in innovation also had diminished.

The diminishment of the audience paralleled a silencing of its voice that had occurred earlier with the middle class in Europe. By the mid-nineteenth century,

> restraint of emotion in the theater became a way of life for middle-class audiences to mark the line between themselves and the working class. A "respectable" audience . . . control[led] its feelings through silence; the old spontaneity was called "primitive" . . . One did not interrupt actors in the middle of a scene but held back until the end to applaud. . . . To cease to express oneself immediately one was moved by a performer was allied to new silence in the theater or concert hall itself. (Sennett, 1974, p. 206)

IMPLICATIONS FOR A MORE
MODERN MEDIUM: THE MOTION PICTURE

Live theater has been replaced as a popular mass entertainment medium by motion pictures and television. Does this mean that the role of audience as innovator died with the advent of more modern media that, by their very nature as indirect forms, rob audiences of the opportunity to interact face-to-face with directors and performers in the performance-by-performance shaping of culture?

Certainly in early motion pictures, the audience reasserted its innovative role. Despite the indirectness of the medium, a less-established social organization of production along with the ingenuity and support of specific audiences helped determine how motion pictures developed. Audiences contributed to popular access, a popular repertoire, and certain features of the social organization of production.

EXPANSION OF ACCESS

The upper class used movies first but mainly as a drawing room novelty (Ramsaye, 1926). The working and middle classes gained access to motion pictures in the first decade of the twentieth century through their support of theaters in entertainment and commercial areas. Merritt (1976), who studied early movie theaters in Boston, views the concentration of motion picture exhibition in new commercial areas as a shift by entrepreneurs to capture middle-class audiences and abandon working-class neighborhood theaters. However, Gomery (1982a) and Allen (1982a), who looked at Milwaukee and New York motion picture exhibition, respectively, found that the early audience as a whole was less securely grounded in the working class from the beginning. A more common denominator among moviegoers was patronage of a commercial and entertainment center and the ability of the better-financed and larger theaters in these locations to supplement movies with the popular but expensive vaudeville acts.

CONVENTIONS FOR AUDIENCE PARTICIPATION

Participation by the motion picture audience in cultural innovation continued certain traditions of the stage audience, despite the physical absence of the players and the unalterable product presented by the movie. In other cases, new forms were invented, partly to circumvent the limitations of the indirect medium.

STAGE TRADITIONS TRANSFERRED
TO MOTION PICTURES

(1) Spontaneous vocal response. Audiences were vociferous in their demands for a variety of attention-grabbing films, just as they had been adamant earlier in their spontaneous demands for fast-paced vaudeville acts (Allen, 1982b, pp. 9-11).

> During the silent era it was considered acceptable for members of the audience to express audibly their views about the action on the screen. ... [Only with the advent of sound were] people who talked aloud ... preemptorily hushed by others who didn't want to miss the dialog. (Sklar, 1975, p. 153)

(2) Patronage of preferred movies. By attending some movies and not others, audiences helped to determine what kind of innovation occurred in early motion pictures. A 1907 attempt by a French film company to produce highbrow cinema for the public did not receive public support, whereas a six-reel version of the popular play *Queen Elizabeth* was a hit, legitimating the use of longer subjects in films (Mast, 1971, p. 43).

NEW FORMS OF PARTICIPATION DEVELOPED FOR
OR ADAPTED TO MOTION PICTURES

(1) Studio contact to promote favored performers. "Before 1910 actors and actresses were not even given billings on their films. Still, audiences began to recognize them and write to studios and movie magazines asking the players' names" (Toll, 1982, p. 27). These new stars, similar to the popular heroic acting type in live theater, were not serious actors in the classical sense, but "projected personal qualities or images that touched the public."

(2) Protests aimed at banning objectionable portrayals. Protests over portrayals of groups by offended members occurred in the theater (Moody, 1958, p. 20). However, justice (from the point of view of the portrayed) was swift and direct through booing and pelting the performers. Movie patrons lacked the satisfaction of face-to-face confrontation. Instead, protests became focused on coordinated efforts to prevent exhibition of the film itself. The first campaign involved blacks' and liberal, northern whites' objections to the portrayal of blacks as incompetent, ignorant, and lustful in D. W. Griffith's *The Birth of a Nation* (DeGrazia & Newman, 1982). Protest took the form of

a nationalized censorship campaign, organized by the National Association for the Advancement of Colored People.

AUDIENCE-INFLUENCED CHANGES
IN THE REPERTOIRE AND SOCIAL
ORGANIZATION OF PRODUCTION

Access to the media by a large, nonelite audience and their conventions for participation resulted in or contributed to specific features of content and social organization of production.

(1) Motion picture content became more diverse and populist. Early industry leaders tried to limit motion picture diversity, but public demand for new and different films, which the competition would deliver if a company wouldn't oblige, forced moviemakers to expand production, distribution, and exhibition. Public demand voiced by vaudeville audiences through exhibitors undermined Vitascope's attempted dominance of early film distribution and helped to promote Lumière, a French film company (Allen, 1982b).

(2) Populist themes. A second aspect of popular culture in motion pictures involved the incorporation of populist themes and characters. Early French films catered to working-class tastes by providing fast-moving action, a simple story, and slapstick comedy that was violent and often disrespectful toward the police and other authority figures (Merritt, 1976, p. 64). Because of early exhibitor interest in attracting a larger middle-class audience by appealing to women, plus the actual patronage of women, the emotional female hero, epitomized by Lillian Gish, became a motion picture staple, similar to the stage type. The melodrama also became incorporated into movies from the stage, most prominently in the films of D. W. Griffith. More currently recognizable aspects of the motion picture repertoire traceable to sponsorship by identifiable and, in many cases vocal, audience segments of the early days include the western (Combs, 1981), the romance (Rose, 1981) and the thriller (Wicking, 1981).

(3) The star system. Social organization institutionalized the audience's interest in stars and left room for continued audience feedback through entrepreneurs and censors. "The star system [is] one of Hollywood's most sacrosanct institutions" (Jowett & Linton, 1980, p. 32). This pattern of film production and promotion based on public recognition of an actor's or actress's persona grew out of early audiences' determination to identify the nameless performers who appeared in films. The box office reliability of "stars" was one of the

reasons Bank of America was willing to finance the film company Famous Players' Lasky in 1918, and stars' reputation based on box office successes remains an important feature of motion picture planning (Pirie, 1981, pp. 106-107).

(4) Independent production. A second aspect of social organization of motion pictures that was influenced by audience support is the persistent sphere of independent production by film entrepreneurs. "The independent has been a factor in Hollywood since the birth of the industry" (Nelson, 1947, p. 50). Several of the major studios began as independents that catered to public interest in innovation. After the largest studios refused to implement sound in movies, a then small producer, Warner Brothers, took sound public with *The Jazz Singer* and received enthusiastic patronage, forcing the industry's leaders to follow (Gomery, 1982b). United Artists also represented an incorporation of the interests of early public stars—Mary Pickford, Charles Chaplin, Douglas Fairbanks, D. W. Griffith, and William S. Hart—who revolted against the Hollywood establishment and formed a distribution company "for the benefit of the great motion picture public" (Balio, 1976, p. 135).

(5) Censorship and rating agencies. A third early audience innovation that became incorporated into the social organization of films was censorship of film content through external censorship boards and internal censorship agencies. The historical example is the Motion Picture Production Code. The current Code and Rating Administration does not censor but does allow public representatives to participate in film evaluation. Although much of the pressure for film censorship came from nonviewers, audience segments also have been displeased from time to time with aspects of films and sought to register their opinion.

SUMMARY

Audiences in eighteenth- and nineteenth-century live theater and early motion pictures contributed to innovations in the repertoire and social organization of production, despite differences in the media. Audiences helped to determine a wide access, a repertoire that was populist, not elitist, and a social organization that was in part institutionalized around audience-supported themes and forms. Although indirectness of feedback to performers and producers in the film medium did limit audience participation in innovation, the audience adapted old and found new ways to influence the repertoire and social organization of production.

The variation in the role of the audience in innovation suggests that audience participation is a matter of a less highly institutionalized organization of production rather than technological factors alone, particularly directness of the medium. Decreases in audience innovation reflect higher institutionalization but also coincide with incorporation of earlier audience preferences into the conventions of the industry.

These findings indicate that the audience's role in innovations in popular culture has considerable range, and its effects can be concretely and specifically located once a highly capitalized and institutionalized setting and a fragmented viewing situation are abandoned and the comparative historical method is applied. The findings also suggest that the entrepreneur is a key figure mediating between the audience and the industry, determining how audience preferences will be institutionalized or whether they will even be acknowledged.

Chapter 15

AUDIENCE COMPOSITION AND TELEVISION CONTENT
The Mass Audience Revisited

Muriel G. Cantor
Joel M. Cantor

ALTHOUGH A HEALTHY INTEREST in media studies has evolved over the past 20 years, few have investigated the topic being considered here. Rather than focus on the effects that television and other media might have on the audience (or audiences) as have so many others, we ask the alternative question—does the *audience* influence media content? How powerful is the audience, if at all, to determine what is broadcast? We do not ask how the audiences' values, beliefs, or behaviors are influenced by what they hear and see. Nor are we interested here in how audience use the media available to them, the gratifications they receive, or what meaning the content has for them.

One of the ongoing debates in mass media scholarship during the last decade has focused on the forces that shape popular culture in general and television dramatic programming in particular. Three explanations prevail, although others have been less widely debated. As we will show, almost no one considers the role the audience itself has in content creation. Some believe that television dramatic presentations reflect their creators' values and norms solely—values and norms fundamentally different from those of the viewing audience (Newcomb & Alley, 1984; Stein, 1979). Others broaden the concept of control to capitalism (Schiller, 1969; Smythe, 1981). To these analysts, the economic structure is the overriding determinant of what is seen and heard. The third (and most prevailing) explanation is that control rests in the organizations primarily responsible for manufacturing and transmitting cultural products (DiMaggio, 1977; Hirsch, 1978).

The first explanation can be dismissed for several reasons: Only those creators who remain in tune with organizational standards and interests aimed at pleasing the audience within approved political and cultural boundaries are allowed to continue to create television programs. The other two explanations are not mutually exclusive and together provide an analytical model applicable to the study of television. Creators (actors, writers, producers, and directors) and other production personnel cannot be studied outside the economic and organizational systems that provide their employment. Those analysts interested in questions of responsibility and control must consider the external forces—the legal, political, and economic constraints within which media organizations and creative personnel operate. However, even those who recognize that larger institutional analysis is essential still present static models, not recognizing that media presentations do change over time. (For an in-depth discussion of how television series have changed see Cantor, 1980, and Cavell, 1982). Neither the underlying (capitalist) system nor the organizations immediately responsible for content are static. Our contention is that all popular cultural products, including television entertainment, will change as the social and material conditions of their audiences change, and if those changes in conditions are not examined, we cannot understand how the social and economic settings in which media products are produced interact with those of the consumers of the products.

We contend that to understand fundamental questions about how content is created and distributed, it is important to recognize that along with understanding the regulations, the organizational structure, and the occupational groups creating television, it is also important to understand its audiences and their contribution to selecting programs and program types.

Two basic propositions underlie this essay: The assumption that there is a "mass" audience for commercial television is false; and program types are more diverse than critics usually recognize. Herbert Gans (1974), Eric Barnouw (1978), and Harold Wilensky (1964) argue that television entertainment, as the most "massified" of all popular culture products, is not culturally diversified. For over 100 years philosophers have devalued all popular culture and critically appraised its contents as low-level and standardized (see Gans, 1974, for review). As Wilensky summarizes the mass society argument, the "mobility, heterogeneity, and centralization of modern society weaken the ties that bind men [sic] to the common life, rendering the mass manipulatable, leaving mass organization and the mass media in control." Wilensky also claims that mass culture tends to be standardized because it strives to please *the average taste of an undifferentiated audience* (emphasis added)—that is, as an undifferentiated mass. His conclusion is based on a study of 1,354 men, representing a cross section of the "middle mass" (his words, see p. 181) in the Detroit area. His findings show, as do many surveys, that there are few differences in program choices between the well educated and those who are not.[1]

Wilensky's article is just one example of how contemporary communication theory has been hampered by the nineteenth-century elitist concepts that originated with those critics who devalued popular culture and looked down on their audiences.[2] According to this definition of mass communications, television (at least the network programming of the recent past) is the "ideal" mass medium. Mass media are defined by their audiences who in turn are defined as large and heterogeneous in composition (Blumer, 1946; Wright, 1975). They are also distinguished from "class" media by the kinds of audiences each attracts. Accordingly, although the audiences for mass media fit the definition of a heterogeneous, undifferentiated mass, the better-educated, smaller audiences for class media such as public television are seen as more homogeneous. Herbert Blumer (1946) claims that a mass is the opposite of a class, without social organization, no body of custom and tradition, no established rules or ritual or organized group sentiments, no structure of status roles, and without established leadership. The mass in contrast to a class is seen as an aggregate of individuals, separate, detached, and *anonymous* to those creating content.

Because social scientists and others as well often confuse the word "large" with the term "mass," most research on how television is created ignores the ultimate audience. Unlike those studying other media who see popular music, books, magazines, and newspapers addressing the needs of different market segments, media researchers who study television often ignore the dynamic interaction among the audience, the market economy, and the larger social structure. Although some researchers understand that a dynamic relationship exists between the audience and the kind of content provided, the many who have studied and reported on television's effects (as one example) often assume it is unimportant to find out which programs are watched and measure just the total amount of time of viewing. Their premise is that because television communicates the same message anyway, the more programs people watch, no matter what they watch, the more likely they are to be affected by television (see Gerbner & Gross, 1976, and Hawkins & Pingree, 1982, for a review of the cultivation literature). However, research on several topics has suggested that the different program types do differ in messages and themes. (For example, see the uses and gratifications studies of Blumler & Katz, 1974, and the few examining specific program types, such as Cantor & Pingree's 1983 work on soaps, and Horsfield's 1984 work on religious programs broadcast on television.) Soap operas provide an excellent example of a program type on television that from its inception targeted a particular market segment: housewives home during the daytime hours.

Both anecdotal reports as well as more rigorous findings show that the television audience may not operate as a single class or as a mass. There are viewers of particular programs or genres who share enough characteristics to make up what are now called "taste segments." This use of the term derives partially from Robert Escarpit's (1977) concept of group sets and partially from Gans's (1974) notion of taste publics. According to Escarpit, what is called "masses" appears to be an intricate system of group sets that are not synonymous with social-economic strata and are clearly not classes. Rather, they are a group of people from different strata that assemble around a particular program type (genre) or single program. As it has been refined, this concept of group sets, or what we call taste segments, has not as yet been adopted by those who study television entertainment.[3] We believe it should because it provides a better fit to the empirical data available from those studies that have examined the television audiences in detail. A taste segment is neither a class nor obviously an undifferentiated mass; rather, it is a cluster of people with both demographic and taste characteristics in common. (Also see Frank and Greenberg, 1980, for another definition of taste segments.) Essentially, by applying such a formulation to the television audience, a researcher admits that diversity exists among television programs and program types, and that at least in the United States it would be appropriate to apply a marketing model to determine whether the audience has influence over the creative process. By definition, taste segments suggest a segmented market for television programs.

In accordance with the premise that no diversity exists among program types, Gans and Barnouw (among others) have argued with some justification that commercial television has not been culturally diversified. However, this lack of diversity could simply demonstrate that certain taste segments have been more powerful than others. Certainly, particular majority values and credos (individualism and capitalism, for example) pervade program types with very few network programs targeted to ethnic groups, the older audience, or the more educated. Most television drama and entertainment is targeted to lower-middle-class viewers, known euphemistically as the "lowest common denominator." (This may be the only legitimate use of the term "mass" to describe the total television audience because it does target that large heterogeneous audience.) However, it would muddle the distinction to call the separate audiences that occasionally assemble for particular programs a "mass." The competition for audiences that networks have more recently been receiving from cable TV, videotape recorders, and the proliferation of independent TV stations has made the idea of cultural diversity more obvious now than it was in the early years of television.[4] However, since television's inception there has been more diversity than such critics recognize. Not only is there diversity among program types, but diversity has also developed among the three television networks. For example, CBS planned a "middle of the road" prime-time schedule for the 1985-1986 season, in several cases using slightly older actors and actresses in lead roles than in previous seasons, in recognition that the affluent population is aging. In contrast, ABC and NBC's focus is on capturing the younger audience, which they consider more desirable (*Broadcasting,* 1985). Market researchers, television producers, network programmers, some critics, and even a few media researchers have long recognized that such audience segments exist, and sometimes the communicators attempted to create those segments deliberately. Along with the soap opera, the broadcasting of professional football and, of course, children's programs serve as examples. Also because the taste segments that assemble or construct around various program types are not made up of just people in the lower socioeconomic strata, there has been a tendency among researchers to exaggerate the number of upper-middle-class viewers in the total audience. Overall, status divisions among the audience become clearer when particular programs are investigated as individual cases. For example, more recently (1985) shows such as *Cheers, Hill Street Blues,* and *Miami Vice* have attracted more affluent viewers than other popular shows. However, the characteristics that seem to separate taste segments more than class or status are age and gender. Of course, the audience does not divide simply by age or gender. As with other forms of popular culture, other characteristics divide the audience as well. The television audience segments not only by age, sex, and class but also by taste. For example, Herbert Gans, in his plea for more cultural diversity, noticed that even *television* (the most massified medium) may program for "cultural tastes." He found a slight trend toward subcultural programming in television. According to Gans (1974),[5]

> Ever since some advertisers discovered that they could best sell their wares by reaching potential buyers rather than the largest number of viewers, they have been interested in programs that appeal to specific age, sex, and sometimes even income groups in the total audience. (p. 157)

Although most network television did (and still does) target the middle and especially the lower-middle economic strata in society (those likely to use the everyday products such as drugs, beauty aids, food, and household items advertised), they recognize that there are other segments within the larger group. Market researchers have long recognized that even the middle and lower-middle economic portions of the population are made up of people with different interests, levels of involvement, and life-styles. Those who study audiences seriously should also recognize that the different program types will attract different aggregates or clusters.

THE SOAP OPERA AS EXAMPLE

Under different governments with different systems of broadcasting, different groups will hold the power to determine its content. In free enterprise under the capitalist system, the important influence on how content is created is who the creators intend to be the *target* audience (or audiences) of consumers, not necessarily the actual audience(s) attracted to particular programs. For purposes of research, however, both audiences must be considered when studying how content is created, evolves, and changes. We do not postulate that there is a direct, immediate, linear causal relationship between the target audiences and the content they receive but rather a dynamic interaction based on several different kinds of feedback from the audience over time to the creators. The soap opera, with its long and rich history in broadcasting, provides an excellent case in point. The form and content of soap operas evolved to their present state partly because certain advertisers and networks originally wanted to attract housewives-consumers. As that core audience changed and as new audiences were attracted, they also changed in subtle but important ways to appeal to the new audiences.

Those who create and finance soap operas (the advertisers, networks, and creators working for those organizations) try to reach 18-

to 49-year-old women, preferably married and raising a family, who consume the household products, beauty aids, feminine hygiene products, and drugs advertised. The audience reached actually does include such women. However, the audiences for soap operas are much more complex. Data show that their audienced not only differ from the audiences for prime time (although some of course are members of both) but that the audience segments among soap viewers also differ. Social scientists often will ignore what has been obvious to the advertising industry and business-oriented magazines that recognize that certain soap operas attract younger viewers, and others, older ones. The majority of viewers for soap operas, such as *General Hospital, The Young and the Restless,* and *All My Children,* are under 35. The others attract more viewers over 50.[6] The Nielsen and other surveys show that although the soap opera creators and distributors *prefer* the 18- to 49-year-old housewife, they actually get more older and younger viewers than they want as their ideal audience. Over time, that reality did not go unnoticed by the advertisers, their agencies, and the producers—particularly ABC, which changed the content of its soaps selectively to keep pace with the survey data and the changing composition of the daytime audience. Younger women not in the labor force who were still at home attending school became a target. That their strategy worked (that is, ratings rose among the younger groups) demonstrates that audiences *over time* can eventually influence content.

Those producers who perceive such taste segments and then act on their judgment prevail. Apparently there is still an older audience that remains the core for certain soap operas, especially those produced by Procter and Gamble, who remain satisfied with the content they receive. Although these soap operas have changed as well, they have not changed as radically as those now targeted to teenagers and young adults. (See Cantor & Pingree, 1983, for a fuller discussion.) It is also possible that as the younger audience itself ages, that soap opera content will again shift to reflect the interests of the older audience as it is then perceived, especially if viewed by the creators as a viable market.

Using soap operas as an example, two aspects stand out that are relevant to our discussion. First, the daytime serials have differed historically both in theme and messages from nighttime (prime-time) programs. Second, although the soap opera's form and formulas have remained relatively constant, their themes and messages did change in ways that are discernible through both quantitative and qualitative content analyses. From the very beginning, when *Betty and Bob,* the first soap opera on national radio in 1932, was introduced, the form and formula for the soap opera had been fixed. Those familiar with the domestic novels of the nineteenth century will recognize the basic theme of *Betty and Bob*. Supposedly a love story, it actually gave moral and social teaching about family problems and appropriate behaviors for women. Sexism and the double standard were implicit. Bob could be unfaithful, but Betty could never be. She (as were all married heroines) was defined as a "good" woman. She was allowed other traits that could be considered "bad," such as acting jealous, being deceitful, or nagging, but she *always* had to be sexually faithful. Bob could sin and be forgiven, but there was a double standard for adultery. Adulterers—especially women adulterers—had to be punished, but men could be forgiven on the condition they were contrite. *Betty and Bob* provided the main story line for the soap opera, on both radio and television: fidelity and infidelity, jealousy, divorce, family problems, illness, career versus marriage, and sometimes romantic love. However, romantic love was rarely presented as it was in the movies, theater, or novels. From the beginning, the interpersonal conflicts involved in heterosexual love relations were stressed. (Homosexual love relations could not exist in radio soaps, of course, and were almost never shown on television either.) What changed over the years was the way these constant themes were translated into current stories about prevailing current personal and sexual relationships (also see Cantor & Cantor, 1984).

There were actually several types of daytime serials on radio. One popular type that did not transfer to television was the "woman alone" story. These were soap operas about single women and their search for happiness (defined as getting a man). Most had careers, but their stories most often revolved around romance and their wish for marriage. The programs could be easily identified through their titles: *The Romance of Helen Trent, Portia Faces Life, Joyce Jordon, M.D.,* and *Young Widder Brown*. Similar to the married heroines, they were also virtuous. They remained pure and virginal while single. The most famous was Helen Trent. Even at the age of a permanent 35, she could tantalize a series of suitors who pursued her from 1933, when the show was first aired, until 1960, when it was finally canceled. Although tempted many times, she never gave in to her sexual impulses. In fact, some argue that she never had any because she was as virginal when the show left the air as she was when it first aired. The absence of sexual activity is indeed remarkable because working as a dress designer in the movie industry, she associated with movie actresses who clearly qualified as "bad"—that is, they were sexually active with partners to whom they were not married.

It is generally agreed that the soap operas currently showing do differ from their predecessors on both early television and radio. The moral teachings have changed. The pure and virginal heroine is gone; premarital sex and adultery have become commonplace acts. Children can be born to unmarried parents, and in at least one famous case of rape, the offender was not punished. In *General Hospital,* "Laura" was raped by "Luke," and they eventually married although when the rape occurred, Laura was married to someone else. (Here is another instance of basic soap opera morality. Luke expiated himself as well as Laura by having "bad" Laura "good" again by marrying her.) More recent episodes of *All My Children* showed "Tad" having affairs with a mother and her daughter concurrently. Separation, divorce, bigamous marriages, and unmarried couples living or sleeping together are everyday occurrences, and it is not unusual for a woman with more than one bed partner having a child whose paternity is in doubt. Although rape, prostitution, lesbianism, adultery, and premarital sex might still be treated (sometimes) as moral problems, the clear-cut distinction between good and bad that distinguished the soap opera of radio and early television has disappeared. Sometimes behavior and verbal messages may still echo the old morality. For example, characters might discuss transgressors as though they had committed bad acts, but the messages are no longer supported by subsequent events. As in the case of Luke, punishment is no longer meted out to the bad characters as it so often was.

Radio soap operas had been clearly targeted to the taste segment of the rural, smalltown housewife. Modern television soap operas still, if pressed, support basic and traditional values but now principally target "emancipated" women who use The Pill (most of the time) and who combine sex with marriage and career. The only explanation that best fits these data is that the production companies themselves recognized these social changes, and the networks then also accepted them as the now-current morality. If the soap operas had retained their melodramatic, overstylized formats, the audiences would probably have rejected them. A content analysis of *Guiding Light* (reported in Cantor & Pingree, 1983) shows that the content followed changes in audience characteristics. For example, as more women entered the labor force, the number of women working in the soaps also increased.

This is not a simplistic reflection hypothesis. Rather we suggest that a complex interrelationship arises between the audience in the heads of the creators and the realities of the marketplace. Viewers' demands do not determine content directly, but rather they could influence content in several ways indirectly. Those interested viewers who communicate their opinions through letter writing or fan magazines and through face-to-face contacts are very important even though they may be a small minority of viewers. All soap opera actors and producers recognize and report anecdotally that some viewers might take the soaps too seriously. Actors report that they are sometimes accosted by viewers on the street who cannot differentiate them from the roles they play. Producers report that they receive letters with advice for the characters on child care, clothes selection, and other personal matters. These viewers are powerful because writers and producers most often keep them in mind when initiating themes or continuing a relatively conservative view of the social world. In addition, ratings (another social construction of reality) are influential because they alert producers to the taste segments being reached by a program. Although decisions on soap opera content are not subject to the same trends as prime-time programs, they do often change and can even be canceled. Innovation is highest when ratings are low. Thus when networks and production organizations decide that a soap is in trouble, the creators no longer use the involved audience as its reference but rather try to reach out to those not yet captured by the traditional stories.

CONCLUSION

In this chapter we contend that the audience should no longer be conceptualized as either a mass or assembly of classes but rather as aggregates or clusters of taste segments. Just as entrepreneurs have always marketed their products to particular consumer groups, so must commercial broadcasters try to reach specific audiences for them, audiences that share the particular characteristics desired. We also suggest that those target audiences participate over time (although indirectly) in the process of content selection. Elsewhere we and others have proposed that prime-time television cannot be understood unless one also examines the legal system and the organizational and economic conditions of production, as well as the work of the creators themselves, for their influence on content. To be complete, that analysis should also now specify how much taste segments in the target audience and their shifts contribute to shaping the final product. Without such added scope of analyses, television will continue to be seen as static and unresponsive to changing social and material conditions, an approach clearly unacceptable given present knowledge.

Moreover, it is no longer possible to understand the relationship between content and its audience without considering each program type individually within prime-time and daytime. Just as prime-time television drama has been found to differ substantially from daytime drama, those differences cannot be specified unless the prime-time programs or program types themselves are analyzed as individual cases. For example, Bradley Greenberg (1980) and George Gerbner and his colleagues (1980a) describe "life on television" by taking *all* fictional programs airing during a certain period of the day as their sample for content analysis. Rather than lump soap operas with rerun movies and series during the day and "specials" with mini- and prime-time series for the evening hours that muddles the data, we recommend that historical content analyses of particular genres and program types be conducted (for example, sitcoms or spy-adventure shows). Historical studies should be conducted of the audiences for those types to parallel the content analyses. This approach to studying content would provide far richer "data" than the usual types of studies undertaken. Although the Nielsen and Arbitron surveys are not ideal sources of data, even their figures could show over time how certain clusters of audience segments have changed over time.

In this chapter, we have argued that even for network television, neither now nor at any time in the past has the mass audience defined by Harold Wilensky and others existed. Our focus has been on the relationship of audience to content, not simply one or the other. We argue that the audience must be included with networks, producers, and advertisers as powerful in determining how programs must change to remain popular or disappear. The question of the interaction among creators, content, and audiences is also central to our understanding of the relation between media and society, although it has rarely been researched. Most media analysts, regardless of their theoretical orientation, have ignored historical and dynamic interaction in favor of a static model. Our soap opera research suggests that in a capitalist economy such as the United States, with changes in demographics, increasing longevity, and the changing composition of the workforce, audience segments form around certain genres and programs and lead to changes in content that would have been unacceptable at an earlier time.

NOTES

1. Wilensky does see some effect of education, but according to him, "the evidence is that the educated display, on balance, a mild tendency toward more discriminating tastes" (p. 191).

2. The results in this study reflect Wilensky's beliefs about the cultural value of prime-time entertainment programs. One of his variables is called "much exposure to poor TV." He defines it by (1) high number of hours per week of television viewing; (2) many westerns as "favorite TV programs—the ones you almost always watch"; and (3) many detective and adventure programs as favorites (see p. 182). Todd Gitlin (1983) also thinks that most TV programs are "bad." He actually calls them "trash." However, the difference between the two is that although Wilensky claims to be value-free and use objective measures, Gitlin does not. Our point is that TV programs may be low-level culture or they may not be, but regardless there is diversity among programs. Neither Wilensky nor Gitlin recognizes much diversity. Gitlin does think *Hill Street Blues* is a "good" program in comparison to most television fare.

3. Recently some anthropologists and "humanists" have been analyzing American and British television from a different perspective. They see television drama as "pluralistic," but they still do not consider the audience. For example, Newcomb and Hirsch (1983a and 1983b), in their plea for qualitative research on television, concentrate on the content and the creators, essentially ignoring the audience. Their work also is somewhat confused in its conceptualization. For example, they claim that cultural diversity is found in television programs but then analyze television as strips, looking at an entire time period (actually prime time) of programs, spot announcements, and advertisements). They say that it is not sufficient to examine particular genres, or even particular series, rather, it is the bulk and body of television that should be analyzed. Implied in that statement is the assumption that television programs, regardless of type, convey similar messages. Actually, Newcomb and Hirsch believe that people watch *television,* not programs. Because these authors refuse to accept any quantitative data, they ignore the empirical reality that most people watch programs or program types (Frank & Greenberg, 1980; Himmelweit & Swift, 1976).

4. It could be argued, as we suggest, that diversity has increased during the years that television has been in existence. That question remains to be answered in future research.

5. In 1974, when Gans wrote these words, the three television networks had a virtual monopoly on the prime-time audience. Since then the audience for network television has contracted, although the audience continues to watch television in large numbers. The trend that Gans noted has become more pronounced.

6. Nielsen data and Frank and Greenberg (1980) show that the audience is segmented according to soap opera type. See Cantor and Pingree (1983, esp. chapter 7, "Soap Opera Audiences") for more details. For an explanation of the relationship between the audience and producers of *Guiding Light,* see Intintoli (1984).

Chapter 16

BEYOND MASS CULTURE AND
CLASS CULTURE
Subcultural Differences in the Structure
of Music Preferences

John P. Robinson
Edward L. Fink

An intellectual is someone who can listen to the William Tell Overture and not think of the Lone Ranger. (Anon.)

As with other material resources in society, cultural artifacts such as works of art, musical instruments, and books are unequally distributed among the population. In addition, the values associated with these cultural products are also unevenly distributed. Cultural products with no apparent survival benefit are evaluated differently by different social groups, as when social climbing for access to better income, housing, education, and the like become associated with socialization to the values of the social group to which one aspires (DiMaggio, 1982). Less tangible cultural products, such as music, differ in their appreciation across social strata (Gans, 1974). This is so even though the costs of such appreciation are minimal in a contemporary society in which radio, television, records, and cassette tapes all make music of great variety universally available.

The American public can listen to music practically everywhere, which, as Konecni (1982) argues, is a new historical phenomenon:

Gone are the days when only the elite could hear high-quality music, while the rest had to await weddings and harvest festivals to hear any music at all.... The most frequent, prototypical situations in which people listen to music have shifted from specialized locations, such as opera houses and concert halls, into informal settings like the home and the automobile. (pp. 498-499)

As a result of the great availability of music, different *styles* of music flourish; with a simple turn of the radio dial, most American communities have access to music from different periods, ethnic groups, age groups, regions, and social classes.

Yet different segments of the public continue to differ in their preferred types of music, apparently consistent with Bourdieu's (1977) definition of cultural capital as "symbolic wealth socially designated as worthy of being sought and possessed." Portrayals of the "high"-culture public note how certain types of music are valued in spite of (or perhaps because of) the lack of popularity of such music. The "highbrow" cultural tasks inherent in appreciating operatic and classical music contrasts with the seemingly less demanding character of "easy listening" mood music, the highly repetitive nature of rock music, and the alleged simplicity of other forms of popular music. Highbrow music is often differentiated into many categories based on nationality of origin, time period of composition, composer, genre, instrumentation, and alleged subtleties of performance. Devotees of highbrow music may not extend such differentiation to other forms of music, perhaps because they believe such analysis is not useful or not possible. They expect that even those who appreciate such music do not make historical or aesthetic distinctions among these genres of music, and they perceive fans of popular or other nonhighbrow music culture as unwilling to be bothered by such distinctions. To the critical tastes in the highbrow audience, these factors confirm the fundamentally nonserious and undemanding character of such music.

The impression we have of those whose cultural appreciation lies outside the realm of highbrow culture is more mixed. On the one hand, such people view most of their critics as snobs while realizing that they may, in turn, be viewed as rowdies, rednecks, boors, or other uncultured personae non grata. They implicitly may take comfort in Becker's (1982) charge that

> the world of symphony music, for instance, has not changed the length of concert programs very much ... [because] it would increase their costs to lengthen the programs, and because audiences expect eighty or ninety minutes of music for the price of a ticket. . . . The basic instrumentation of the orchestra has not changed, nor have the tonal materials used ... or the places in which the music is presented. (p. 135)

On the other hand, because the high-culture adherents can obtain prestige from the tangible as well as the intangible aspects of highbrow music appreciation (e.g., having tickets to prestigious performances), the satisfaction from not being a snob may be mixed with a certain envy about not being *au courant* with high-culture codes and norms. The above is, in large part, the traditional stereotype from both ends of the social continuum in the debate over mass versus class culture. However, it is a stereotype that tends to be reflected in behavior, as DiMaggio and Useem (1978) concluded from their review of over 200 studies of arts participation:

> Available studies repeatedly and consistently demonstrate the ranks of those who attend ... opera, symphony and ballet are dominated by the wealthy and well-educated, most of whom are professionals and managers. Blue collar workers and those with little education are virtually absent. By contrast, the popular arts, such as jazz, rock music and the cinema are consumed at comparable rates by all social classes. . . . *Education seems to be the most salient determinant of arts involvement.* (p. 156, emphasis added)

Yet in a modern, heterogeneous society, culture itself is increasingly composed of blurred distinctions and mixed elements: rock songs that incorporate Bach, or easy listening (or symphonic) orchestrations of the Beatles.

Furthermore, there are various nonhighbrow publics that are far more heterogeneous than we have described. As Gans (1974) has pointed out, because the public for popular forms of culture is so much larger than the public for high culture, the popular culture public will be *more* heterogeneous with regard to taste than the high-culture public. This would be consistent with geographic patterns of American culture described by Blau (in press), who has found American institutions of high culture to be far more widely accessible by region and urbanicity than generally assumed, whereas folk and popular arts were more highly concentrated by geographic factors.

Although music audiences can be expected to be somewhat specialized in their tastes (e.g., rock'n'roll among teenagers), little is known about how preferences for different kinds of music are structured in the wider public (Robinson & Hirsch, 1969). This question has two aspects: First, how and to what extent are preferences for the various musical forms clustered or grouped? Second, how do different segments of the public differ in their music preferences and in the way they structure their music preferences? Is the same configuration of cultural preferences (here, musical types) found in all social groups?

Variables that may be expected to differentiate people in terms of their individual music preferences include both social class factors (educational level, income, occupation) and other factors, such as ethnicity, age, and region of the country. In this study, we will primarily assess the impact of education, the class variable found to be the most predictive by DiMaggio and Useem, and a demographic factor that has been relatively overlooked in previous literature on the sociology of the arts—namely, age. One reason for this is that by focusing on attendance at arts performances, previous empirical studies have overlooked *subjective* differences in responses to various cultural content. In other words, younger and older adults may not differ as much in terms of their behavior as in terms of their appreciation of arts content, much as the generation or cohorts effects for political beliefs depend on the political climate in which young adults become socialized.

This study reports on data collected from a recent survey that will allow us to examine the music preferences of a large and representative national sample. These data are less than ideal in that they examine public response to generic music labels (e.g., "jazz," "classical," "rock") and not specifically to examples of such music. There is considerable disagreement among musicologists about what kinds of music fit into each category and perhaps even greater confusion in the mass audience about which music these terms include. The term "jazz," for example, includes everything from traditional jazz to modern, and members of the public could well decide that artists from Guy Lombardo to Michael Jackson are included under this label. Similarly, some respondents might consider Frank Sinatra, Ray Charles, Bob Dylan, or Hank Williams as representatives of "classical" music. Although examples such as this may be rare, such generic questions do allow for unfortunate ambiguity and idiosyncrasy in response. Nonetheless, these are not unfamiliar terms to the public, and one can expect high agreement about "pure" examples or prototypes of each form of music. Moreover, many of the above idiosyncrasies should cancel each other out in a large survey such as ours.

METHOD

THE SURVEY

The data used in this report are taken from a national probability survey conducted for the National Endowment for the Arts under a grant to the University of Maryland Survey Research Center. This "Survey of Public Participation in the Arts" (SPA 1982) interviewed 17,254 persons. All were age 18 and over, and none lived in group quarters in the United States. Roughly three-quarters of the interviews were collected in person and one-quarter by telephone, with little difference in results found by mode of survey administration.

The survey questioned respondents about their participation in the arts, their arts experiences, and their music preferences. Each month's sample consisted of a national cross-sectional sample of about 1,450 respondents. Earlier reports concerning the survey may be found in Robinson (1983) and Fink, Robinson, and Dowden (1985). The overall survey response rate was over 85%.

The SPA 1982 questionnaire was divided into two types of questions: a set of *core* items on annual arts participation and a set of *rotating* items that surveyed expected correlates and predictors of that participation, including preferences for types of music. Table 16.1 reports the actual music preference question and the overall percentage response for thirteen different types of music. This question was asked only in the April, October, November, and December survey and thus is based on a one-third sample of 5,617 respondents. Respondents simply answered either yes or no to each music item.

RESULTS

Table 16.1 shows the types of music that members of the sample say they enjoy. Although it is possible in the survey context that respondents report their liking for more prestigious types of music, it is reassuring to find in this same data set that self-reported attendance information provided by these same subjects was essentially congruent with the preference information (Fink et al., 1985).

Table 16.1 shows that the proportion of respondents who indicate that they enjoy a given type of music varied from about 10% who report liking to listen to opera, 14% for barbershop music, 58% for liking country-western music, and 48% of respondents reported liking easy listening ("mood") music. Fewer than 2% of the sample reported listening to a type of music not explicitly included on the list in Table 16.1.

STRUCTURE OF PREFERENCE INTERRELATIONSHIPS

There was a rather pronounced tendency for respondents who prefer one type of music to say they enjoyed other types of music,

TABLE 16.1
Preference Proportions by Music Types[a]

Which of these types of music do you like to listen to?

1.	Classical/chamber music?	27.7
2.	Opera?	9.8
3.	Operetta/Broadway musicals/show tunes?	23.2
4.	Jazz?	26.0
5.	Soul/blues/rhythm and blues?	26.4
6.	Big band?	32.5
7.	Country-western?	58.3
8.	Bluegrass?	24.5
9.	Rock?	35.0
10.	Mood/easy listening?	48.1
11.	Folk?	24.9
12.	Barbershop?	14.7
13.	Hymns/gospel?	36.1
14.	Other?	1.6
15.	Every type?	1.8

a. Based on one-third sample (N = 5617).

rather than a clustering of preferences into liking one grouping versus disliking another grouping. Nonetheless, there were some sharp divisions of preference: People who liked classical music were far more likely to say they liked opera than to say they liked country-western music or rock. This was reflected both in terms of the standard correlation coefficients between the types of music and in terms of the odds ratios and other distance measures we examined.

The full spatial configuration obtained by a factor analysis of these correlations is shown in Figure 16.1.[1] To a large extent, the correlation patterns in Figure 16.1 are oriented around a horizontal dimension (explaining 63% of the common variance) defined by *formality and complexity*: Music requiring greater social organization and formality (such as opera and classical) is on one side, and rock and country-western music, which requires less formality and fewer performers, is on the other side. The vertical dimension, explaining 19% of the common variance, seems to reflect the *ecological base of geographic appeal* (rural versus urban) of the music. This would contrast the more rural music (country-western, bluegrass, folk, and hymns) at the upper extreme, with the more urban music (jazz, soul, rock, and classical) at the lower extreme. However, it is also the case that the types of music at the top of this dimension are more likely to be performed as well as listened to by the audience member. The third dimension in the factor analysis (18% of variance)—which is enclosed by the dotted boundary of Figure 16.1 and should be seen as lifting these music forms up from the page—separates three of the more upbeat or "emotional" types of music (jazz, soul, and rock) from the other ten music types.

Although questions may be raised about the appropriateness of factor analysis for dichotomous data, it is important to note that the spatial configuration determined by a multidimensional procedure based on quite different assumptions (GALILEO) produced results similar to the one shown in Figure 16.1 (Fink et al., 1985). This gives us considerable confidence in the robustness of our conclusions, regardless of method. More specifically, however, is the conclusion in both mapping programs that the distance between classical/opera music and other music types is no more pronounced than the distance between other types of less highbrow music—for example, between barbershop and rock, between country-western and show tunes, or between rock and country-western. Put another way, there is as much differentiation between these types of popular culture as between popular culture and high culture.

POPULATION SUBGROUP DIFFERENCES

Table 16.2 shows the relation between the major class variable (education) and preference for the various types of music. Consistent

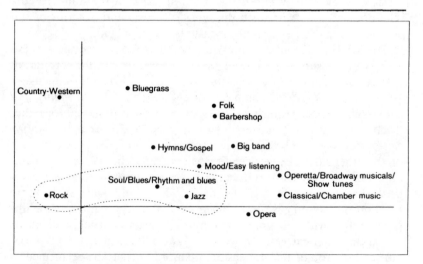

NOTE: Dotted line represents third dimension.

Figure 16.1 First Two Dimensions from Factor Analysis of Music Preferences

with earlier research (e.g., Gans, 1974; Wilensky, 1964), almost all relations between liking the various types of music and educational level are positive. Exceptions include the small turndowns for soul music and easy listening music at the upper end of the educational continuum, the more distinct curvilinearities for country-western and rock music, and the generally negative relation between liking hymns/gospel music and educational level. Thus, increasing educational level is associated with increased proportions not only of individuals who say that they appreciate high-culture products such as classical music, it is also associated with increased proportions of respondents who like *most* kinds of music. This probably reflects social class differences both in purchasing power and in cultural familiarity with examples of each type of music that one *can* like. It may also reflect anything from a greater preference for the symbolic communication inherent in music to an acquiescence to survey questions, although it is usually the less educated who are more susceptible to this form of survey bias (see, for example, Schuman & Presser, 1981).

It is also the case, however, that educational differences are confounded by the factor of age. Because younger adults have higher levels of advanced education, it is unclear how much of the Table 16.2 differences are due to education and not to age differences among those with higher levels of education. Thus, Table 16.3 shows the distribution of preferences across age cohorts. Most of the types of

TABLE 16.2
Percentage Indicating Preference for Music Type,
by Educational Level

Type of Music	Educational Level					
	Grade School	Some H.S.	H.S. Grad.	Some Coll.	Coll. Grad.	Grad. School
Classical	10	15	21	34	47	61
Opera	5	7	7	10	16	23
Musicals	6	11	20	30	40	45
Jazz	10	16	23	35	40	44
Soul, R&B	10	21	25	36	34	33
Big band	10	28	31	35	43	47
Country-western	53	66	62	54	48	49
Bluegrass	18	22	23	26	31	32
Rock	9	22	39	47	46	37
Easy listening	18	33	49	60	63	61
Folk	13	18	21	30	36	47
Barbershop	12	13	13	16	17	18
Hymn/gospel	48	43	34	33	29	32

music exhibit a curvilinear pattern across the age groups. This may reflect socialization to the music type, resulting in an initial positive relation between age and preference, followed by a later withdrawal of interest in music. On the other hand, this nonmonotonic pattern may reflect the fact that the various types of music became popular in different eras, as the age differences in preference are confounded with time period differences.

Of those music types generally showing curvilinearity, peaks occur at different points. For example, classical and big band music peak at age 55-64; musicals, easy listening, and folk at 45-54; soul at 25-34; country-western at 35-44. Opera, hymns/gospel, and barbershop generally show a positive relation with age, whereas rock is the only type clearly showing a negative relation with age.

Nonetheless, it is clear that there are important age differences that need to be examined more closely in conjunction with education. Table 16.4 shows the combined effect of education and age on the thirteen types of music. For six types of music, *both* age and educational level are generally positively related to appreciation: classical, opera, musicals, big band, easy listening, and barbershop. For three other types—jazz, soul, and rock—age is generally negatively related, but educational level is positively related; these types are primarily urban forms with strong roots in black culture. For country-western, bluegrass, and folk music, on the other hand, the pattern is more for

TABLE 16.3
**Percentage Indicating Preference for Music Type,
by Age Group**

Type of Music	Age Group						
	18-24	*25-34*	*35-44*	*45-54*	*55-64*	*65-74*	*75-96*
Classical	17	28	32	31	34	26	23
Opera	3	5	10	15	14	14	16
Musicals	15	19	29	39	29	24	19
Jazz	32	33	23	27	23	17	8
Soul, R&B	32	36	26	26	20	16	5
Big band	16	21	31	45	52	50	27
Country-western	51	56	66	63	58	59	47
Bluegrass	20	28	28	25	26	21	11
Rock	75	56	33	13	8	5	2
Easy listening	42	49	53	56	52	44	13
Folk	14	26	29	30	26	26	20
Barbershop	5	7	12	20	23	27	23
Hymn/gospel	21	28	38	41	46	50	55

age to be curvilinearly related to preference, although educational level is negatively related; these types have a strong rural influence. Finally, for hymns and gospel music, we find a pattern in which age is positively related to preference, whereas educational level is generally negatively related.

It is quite clear, then, that there are important age differences in music preferences, without which it is impossible to interpret meaningfully the differences by education noted in Table 16.2. In other words, age stratification factors are as important to the interpretation of cultural appreciation as is the class stratification factor of education. Whether this is due to the effects of aging per se or to having grown up in a particular age cohort cannot be determined from these data. In either event, age *is* an important factor.

Not only do the aggregate patterns of preferences differ by these age-education categories, but so do the structure of preferences within each category. When separate two-dimensional factor analysis plots for each age × education category are examined, some fundamental differences are found in the Figure 16.1 pattern. In the case of the lowest education groups at all age levels (i.e. cells 1, 4, and 7 in Table 16.4) and middle educated young adults (cell 2), the main horizontal dimension is, as in Figure 16.1, defined by the highbrow-nonhighbrow distinction. That is, we find classical music, show tunes, and opera on the right-hand side of the figure contrasted with country-western, rock, and bluegrass in the middle; the country-western and bluegrass types form the basis of the second (vertical) dimension for cells 4 and 7 whereas big band and easy listening music form that basis for the youngest groups (cells 1 and 2).

In the case of the four older-aged/higher-education categories (cells 5, 6, 8, and 9), on the other hand, the main horizontal distinction is between country-western and bluegrass on the right, and the three highbrow categories classical, opera, show tunes, plus rock in the middle. For these groups, the three highbrow categories form the basis of the top of the second (vertical) dimension, which contrasts with the rock, country, and bluegrass categories in the middle of the diagram.

In other words, these presumably more "experienced" or "sophisticated" listeners (i.e., cells 5, 6, 8, and 9) appear to judge country and bluegrass music as the most distinctive forms of music, whereas the younger, less educated groups rely more on the highbrow-nonhighbrow distinction to organize their music preferences. The older, higher-education groups use this distinction only as a secondary dimension.

TABLE 16.4
Music Across Nine Cohort-Education Categories

I. Positive Age (Cohort) and Positive Education Relations

Age	Classical (1)			Opera (2)			Musical (3)			Big Band (6)			Easy Listening (10)			Barbershop (12)		
	Grade	High	Coll.	Grade	High	Coll.	Grade	High	Coll.	Grade	High	Coll.	Grade	High	Coll.	Grade	High	Coll.
18-29	9	14	33	2	2	6	2	11	26	11	12	26	26	42	55	1	4	1
30-55	12	22	50	4	7	16	11	23	46	24	32	46	31	56	70	12	13	20
56+	14	34	54	7	17	29	11	32	47	34	57	65	31	57	62	20	30	34

II. Negative Age and Positive Education

Age	Jazz (4)			Soul (5)			Rock (9)		
	Grade	High	Coll.	Grade	High	Coll.	Grade	High	Coll.
18-29	17	22	41	21	23	35	52	74	77
30-55	13	17	37	13	18	35	16	33	39
56+	9	19	27	7	19	20	4	6	5

III. Curvilinear Age and Negative Education

Age	Country-Western (7)			Bluegrass (8)			Folk (11)		
	Grade	High	Coll.	Grade	High	Coll.	Grade	High	Coll.
18-29	71	62	50	24	27	32	15	15	29
30-55	82	75	60	30	26	36	18	25	46
56+	67	58	47	24	24	20	18	29	35

IV. Positive Age and Negative Education

Age	Hymns (13)		
	Grade	High	Coll.
18-29	20	15	22
30-55	64	34	32
56+	49	49	42

NOTE: Entries are percentages of each category saying they like each type of music.
a. The cells in this table are labeled as follows:

1	2	3
4	5	6
7	8	9

It is these older, more educated groups, then, whose views seem to underlie the large differences between country and rock music in Figure 16.1. Compared to the older groups, younger groups show much less discrimination among country-western, bluegrass, and rock. Among these younger groups, big band and mood music also emerge as the more important distinctive types of music on the second (vertical) dimension. The final group (cell 3)—the young, college educated—show a unique pattern; classical music is close to both rock and country-western and is quite distant from show tunes, which are closer to both big band and mood music.

SUMMARY AND CONCLUSIONS

We began our discussion in terms of the traditional distinction between high culture and more popular and specialized forms of culture. It seems clear that differences in the public's appreciation of music reflects far more than the class-based distinctions that have been so widely emphasized in the sociological literature on the arts. This conclusion holds as well for the other two empirical indicators of class not analyzed here—namely, income and occupation. Our preliminary analysis indicates that both of these indicators are associated with only about a third as much variance in explaining music preferences as education; in fact, income and occupation explain about as much variance as gender or urbanity. Moreover, the main distinctions in preference for both of these factors occur only in the "elite" groups—those earning over $50,000 per year and those in the professions.

Age, in particular, plays as significant a role in identifying distinctive patterns of music taste. Moreover, the distinctions that various age and education subgroups seem to make in distinguishing the different types of music investigated here are quite different as well; younger and less educated respondents rely more on the traditional highbrow-nonhighbrow distinction than do older or more educated people. They also distinguish less among rock, country, and bluegrass music in their preferences than do older listeners. If these patterns were to continue, it could mean that future music audiences would see less distinction between these popular music forms on the one hand and classical music on the other. In contrast, older and better-educated subgroups of the sample do not distinguish highbrow kinds of music from other types as much as between country music and rock music.

An important implication from these music data concerns the role of age and the sociology of culture. Cultural stability and change can be understood by seeing that music that appeals to a given age cohort in young adulthood continues to have appeal for that cohort as it ages. Thus, we see cultural preferences working their way through history like the devoured prey that passes through a snake. As a result, cultural change is gradual and there is often resistance to new cultural forms. Over time, however, popular music that survives takes on a classic quality that continues to be attractive to a more specialized audience (McPhee, 1963).

In this study we found that the main general structuring dimensions for the evaluative distinctions made by the public in its music preferences are formality, geographical appeal, and emotionality. This was found in both the factor-analytic and multidimensional analyses, which were based on rather different assumptions, measurements, and computational algorithms.

The next steps in our research will involve examining the other background variables that structure the cultural patterns found here. In particular, we plan to examine differences by the third major background factor that relates to music preferences—namely, race. Preliminary analyses suggest that blacks differ widely from whites, as well as from Hispanic and Asian-Americans, in their music preferences (with the latter two groups not differing much from whites in their responses). Blacks, not surprisingly, are most distinctive in their greater liking of soul/blues, jazz, and religious music and their lower preferences for country-western and mood music. Nonetheless, our preliminary analysis of the music preferences of the (more than 500) blacks in our sample reinforces the two main conclusions noted above: (1) Age is associated as much with variation in music preference as is education, and (2) greater differences are found within popular music (country versus rock or soul music) than between popular and highbrow music forms. Both conclusions would seem to require serious reformulations of the portrayals of culture publics, as defined by Gans, Wilensky, and DiMaggio and Useem.

Finally, we hope to conduct parallel analyses with actual examples of the generic music forms described in Table 16.1. In that way we can verify whether the important cultural and subcultural distinctions found here do translate into the world of music as listeners actually experience it. If these results do generalize, observers and entrepreneurs of American culture will need to pay much closer attention to age and cohort differences in cultural appreciation.

NOTE

1. The input for the factor analysis consisted of the simple (dichotomous) correlations between the music preference questions. To create a measure of distance for the multidimensional scaling analysis, we first create a 2 × 2 table for each pairing of music preferences: liking for music type A (yes or no) by liking for music type B (yes or no). In this 2 × 2 table, label the entries a (row 1, column 1), b (row 1, column 2), c (row 2, column 1), and d (row 2, column 2). Thus, if the first column and row represent dislike and the second column and row represent liking, and the columns and rows represent two different types of music, what value should be assigned to represent the relative similarity of these two types of music? If b and/or c were zero, we would consider the two types in the table to be maximally similar. When the cells of the fourfold table (that consist of frequencies) are subjected to the logic of the odds ratio from Goodman's (1972) log-linear model, the suggested measure would be ad/bc. However, this measure has no upper bound. Thus, to provide an upper bound, and to have the measure increase as similarity decreased, the odds ratio was modified as follows:

$$(1 - [ad/(ad + bc)]) = bc/(ad + bc)$$

This results in a metric for distance with a lower bound of 0 realized when b or c is 0, and an upper bound of 1.00 realized when a or d is 0. If the two types of music exhibit a pattern of preference indicating that they were uncorrelated, the distance between them would be 0.50. If, on the other hand, the types of music were negatively related (i.e., liking type A was associated with being less likely to like type B), then the distance measure would be greater than 0.5.

In the course of this research, other distance metrics were examined. Although we cannot claim that the measure that we have chosen to employ is necessarily ideal in all respects, it is a plausible metric derived from the ratio characteristics of the table. We should also note that the multidimensional spaces that we created by using several different metrics (e.g., chi-square, Yule's y correlation coefficient) also resulted in spaces that were all extremely similar to that found in Figure 16.1.

PART IV

MEDIA AND POLITICAL CONFLICT AND CHANGE

> Our lost vision is not the dream of a unified knowledge, but the more modest expectation that we have something to say about freedom and social change. ... The lost vision of communications studies is our failure to concentrate our thinking on social movements and social change that are the testing grounds, if not, the "killing fields" of democratic freedoms. (McCormack, this volume)

We draw this composite quote from Thelma McCormack's chapter (see Part I) because it nicely points to one of the most enthusiastic and, at the same time, most frustrating aspects of research and theory in media studies: How do we come to understand the conditions under which the media serve the forces of "evil" or the forces of "good?" Of course, one's definition of "evil" and "good" varies dramatically by one's conception of the proper social order or one's political ideology. But in a democratic context, we might at least arrive at basic agreement that "good" means freedom and equality and that "good" social change is change that fosters those ends.

As Wright's chapter in Part I and our Introduction implies, our collective effort to understand when and how the media system debilitates or facilitates such social change has been a faltering one, lost, at times, in the miasma of methodological elegance at the expense of theoretical and social relevance. The search for an understanding of "Media and Political Conflict and Change" has taken many diversions from the path of central organizing themes of social change and social control.

The four chapters that constitute this section address these central organizing themes, each in its own way. Jeffrey Alexander asks what propelled one of the most dramatic events of our times—Watergate—into the arena of public opinion formation wherein the American citizenry would be moved to place this "event" on their personal agenda of concern and thus activate processes of social control. He draws our attention to both the media and the political system's role in transforming this "third-rate burglary" into a national issue, and in so doing, he examines the importance of how the event was symbolically structured. D. Garth Taylor also addresses the question of public opinion formation and attempts to sort out the role of the mass media in this process. His substantive focus is busing for the purposes of school desegregation, which was one of the most divisive issues of the 1970s not only in Boston—his empirical site of research—but in the nation generally. He presents evidence on the relative validity of alternative explanations of how public opinion formation and collective action (or inaction) designed to bring about or to prevent this instance of social movement-sponsored change took form.

Gladys Engel Lang and Kurt Lang's chapter presents a strategy for the examination of long-term political effects of the mass media. These scholars argue that our best bet is to focus upon the large and long-term effects of the mass media upon the very nature of the political process, rather than to focus upon short-term effects on audiences. In other words, we should be asking questions about how the media system affects the way politics is conducted (e.g., openly or privately) and the way political decisions are made, because it is these difficult-to-measure, subtle effects of the mass media that matter in the long run. Sandra Ball-Rokeach, Milton Rokeach, and Joel Grube present a chapter that, although not inconsistent with the Langs' call, offers some encouragement to those who would still like to be able to demonstrate socially important and relatively long-term media effects upon the political behaviors and beliefs of individuals. Their chapter addresses both the theoretical and the methodological issues of being able to conduct valid research on the media's potential contribution to purposive social change by way of changing individuals' political beliefs and behavior.

Chapter 17

THE "FORM" OF SUBSTANCE
The Senate Watergate Hearings as Ritual

Jeffrey C. Alexander

IN REFLECTING ON THE ROLE of mass televised media in times of social crisis, it is relevant to recall Andre Bazin's (1958) famous assertion in *What Is Cinema?* that the unique ontology of cinema—as compared to written forms of art, such as novels—is realism. Bazin meant not that art and artifice were absent from cinema but that the end result gave the unmistakable illusion of being "true." Why? Because moving photographic impressions create the sense that there are real people up there saying real things: You cannot distance yourself from such images with the ease that more static, impersonal, and literary forms of communication allow.

This forceful realism is as true for television—particularly documentary or news television—as for the classic cinema, although in this case the medium of contrast is newspapers rather than novels. When political leaders or demagogues want to assert their vision on the populace, they do not write an editorial or an open letter anymore, as Emile Zola did in 1898 when he published "J'accuse" in the French newspaper, *L'Aurore,* and triggered the Dreyfus affair. Today, leaders go on television and speak directly to the people. This General de Gaulle knew; witness his famous speeches calling the French nation back to order after the attempted right-wing generals' coup and after the May revolt in 1968. Richard Nixon also knew this, as he evidenced in the 1952 presidential campaign when he successfully defended himself against charges of corruption in his nationally televised "Checkers" speech. DeGaulle and Nixon were politicians, not aestheticians, but they sensed that command of the television medium, with

the hidden artifice of its mise en scène, means to possess the ontological status of "reality."

But not completely. Here we must move from aesthetics to sociology. We must discuss how contingent is the "possession" of this
medium and how partial and contingent the nature of its truth. To explore the *achievement* of "television truth" is one thing I would like to
discuss in this brief chapter. How precisely this truth—once achieved—
comes to be portrayed is another. I will discuss both in relation to
the Watergate crisis during 1972-1974.

TRUTH DEPENDS ON SOCIAL CONTEXT

Television, even "factual" television, is a medium that depends on
influence, and the willingness to be influenced—to accept statements
of facts at face value—depends on trust in the persuader. The degree
to which factual television is believed—how and to what degree it
achieves the ontological status to which it is, as it were, aesthetically
entitled—depends on the degree to which it is viewed as a differentiated, unattached, and unbiased medium of information. If TV is not
seen as autonomous, but rather as spokesman for church or state, for
political faction or movement, it will be viewed as "true" only by its
sectarian adherents. This is the first proposition about the selectivity
of media truth, and it was absolutely critical for Watergate.

Quantitative analysis of public opinion poll data suggests that in
the Watergate crisis, one of the strongest predictors of support for impeachment was the belief that TV news was "fair." I believe, correspondingly, that one of the primary reasons for the failure to accept
Watergate *as* a serious problem—let alone Nixon's culpability—before the 1972 election was the widespread perception that the media
were not independent but "rad-lib," an identification strongly and
self-consciously promoted by Agnew, Nixon, and their surrogates. By
the time of the 1972 election, indeed, the media's messages about
Watergate were not supported by any major "legitimate" institution
or spokesperson. Congressional committees, courts, and legal bodies
had completely withdrawn from the case, and the media, by continuing to publish Watergate articles, became linked to McGovern and
left-wing Democrats. Between January and April 1973, however, the
media rehabilitated. Feelings of political polarization had greatly
ebbed; other key institutions now seemed to support the media's
earlier reported "facts." Only because the medium of television now
could draw upon fairly wide social consensus, I believe, could its

messages begin to attain the status of "truth." Therefore this shift or change is critical for understanding the impact of the Senate hearings that began in April and May of that first Watergate year.

"TRUTH" CAN BE MORE OR LESS "SERIOUS"

The second proposition I want to introduce about the relativity of truth is this: The truth communicated by the media—even if believed—can be couched at different levels of reality. Most factual messages (e.g., news) are concerned with the immediate and situationally specific relevance of their facts—the "who, what, when, where, why." In a situation of crisis, however, the media can become concerned with more generalized relevance with "values" that define the meaning of nation, the nature of citizenship, the duties of office, or the meaning of life itself. When truth is broadcast on such a generalized level, there is media ritual. *Media truth becomes so generalized in periods of crisis,* periods that involve both social disequilibrium and personal anxiety. The narrative form of values, of course, is myth. On such ritual occasions the media are the forum and the formulator of critical mythical experience.

What began to develop in spring 1973, therefore, was only the relegitimation of the media as a forum for "truth" but had the reconstruction of the media as a forum for certain ritualized value experience. It was precisely this combination of truth and ritualization, I believe, that defined the unique character of the Senate Watergate hearings. That this "event" was not as meaningful for some groups in the population as for others I will note in my conclusion. Here I want to discuss how this unique experience came about and indicate briefly in what it consisted.

THE STRUGGLE FOR A GENERALIZED FORM

The form and substantive content of the televised Watergate hearings were completely intertwined. The form was realism/truth/ritual; the content was "Listen, America, fundamental values are at stake in this crisis, this is not just politics." If the form could be successfully maintained, the substantive content was, to some extent at least, already achieved.

The form of the hearings was a "phenomenological world," a *sui generis,* self-contained sphere of life experience (Schutz, 1967). The world of the hearing was truthful because it succeeded in becoming a world "unto itself." The hearings constituted a world without history; its characters did not have rememberable pasts. It was in a very real sense "out of time." The framing devices of the television medium contributed to this deracinated naturalism—the directing, the in-camera editing, the repetition, juxtaposition, simplification, and so forth are invisible. Add to this bracketed experience the hushed voices of the announcers, the pomp and ceremony of the media event that Katz, Dayan, and Motyl (1977) have described so well, and we have the construction, within the medium of television, of a sacred time and sacred space.[1]

As for content, to create this hearing qua ritual was, as I have said, already to generalize it away from mere politics toward more ultimate concerns. Substantively, what was at stake during the Watergate hearings was a conflict between two ferociously competitive political forces, forces that had a great deal at stake. For Nixon and his political supporters, the issue had to be defined politically. What the Watergate burglars and "cover uppers" had done, they insisted, was "just politics," and they argued that the senators on the Watergate committee, a majority of whom were Democratic, were simply on a political witch-hunt. For Nixon's critics on the committee, by contrast, this mundane political definition had to be opposed. Nixon could be criticized and Watergate legitimated as a real crisis only if the issues were defined as being above politics and involving fundamental moral concerns.

Because form and content were in fact so intertwined, the first issue clearly was whether the hearings were to be televised at all. To allow something to assume the form of a ritualized event is to give participants in a drama the right to forcefully intervene in the culture of the society. It is to give to an event, and to those who are defining its meaning, special, privileged access to the collective conscience. The assumption of "event" status therefore is always a danger and a threat to certain vested interests and groups. We know, in fact, that strenuous efforts were made by the White House to prevent the hearings from being televised, to urge that less TV time be devoted to them, and even to pressure the television networks to terminate their coverage after it had begun. There were also efforts to force the committee to consider the witnesses in a sequence that was far less dramatic than the format that eventually prevailed.

Because these efforts were unsuccessful, the ritual form was achieved. Through television, tens of millions of Americans participated symbolically and emotionally in the deliberations of the committee. On a massive scale, viewing came to be experienced as an obligation. Old routines were broken and new ones formed. What these viewers saw was a highly simplified drama—heroes and villains formed in due course. But this drama was not designed to entertain; rather, it created a deeply serious symbolic occasion. It served to evoke a generalized morality and helped create a mythical level of national self-understanding in a way that few other experiences have in postwar American history.

THE STRUGGLE FOR A GENERALIZED CONTENT

To understand the content of this ritual event, we must appreciate that modern rituals are not so automatically coded as earlier ones. Within the context of the sacred time of the hearings, administration witnesses and senators struggled for moral legitimation, for definitional or ritual superiority and dominance. The end result, in other words, was in no sense preordained: It depended on successful symbolic work. To describe this symbolic work is to embark on the ethnography, or hermeneutics, of a media ritual.

The administration witnesses pursued two strategies. First, they tried to prevent public attention from moving from the political to the value level at all. Thus, they repeatedly tried to rob the event of its ontological status as a ritual. They tried to "cool out" the proceedings by acting relaxed and casual. Robert Haldeman, the Nixon chief of staff who had been portrayed as a straight-laced and arrogant lieutenant, let his hair grow long and smiled meekly throughout his questioning by the committee members. These witnesses also tried to "rationalize" and "specify" the public's orientation to their actions by arguing that they had acted commonsensically according to pragmatic considerations. Consider, for example, the technical rationality invoked when witnesses recalled the arguments for and against Gordon Liddy's plans for massive disruption of the Democratic Convention. It was Liddy who eventually organized the break-in to the Watergate Hotel that actually began the crisis in Washington in June 1972, and by the time of the 1973 hearings he had already become an infamous scoundrel in the public mind. When administrative witnesses recalled the earlier planning discussions with Liddy, however, they described them as focusing primarily on the monetary costs of the disruptions. Even in the moralistic context of the Senate hearings, they never referred to the political, legal, or ideological overtones that such conspiratorial discussions must have contained as well.

Yet the realm of values could not really be avoided—the very form of the "event" ensured their omnipresence. If was within this value realm that the most portentous symbolic struggles of the hearings occurred, for what transpired was nothing less than a struggle for the spiritual soul of the American republic. Watergate had been committed and initially justified in the climate of cultural and political "backlash," values that were in basic ways inimical to the universalism, critical rationality, and tolerance upon which any contemporary democracy must be based. Whether this earlier justifying climate should be evoked in the hearings as legitimate justification was the crucial substantive issue of the hearings.

Administration witnesses evoked this subculture of backlash values. They urged the audience to return to the polarized climate of the 1960s. They appealed to patriotism, the need for stability, to the un-American and deviant qualities of McGovern and the political left. They also argued against the cosmopolitanism that in the minds of the backlash traditionalists, had undermined respect for tradition and had neutralized, for them, the abstract (constitutional) rules of the game. More specifically, they continually appealed to loyalty as the ultimate standard that should govern the relationship between subordinates and authorities. An interesting visual theme that summed up both of these appeals was the passive reference by administration witnesses to family values. Each witness brought his wife and children if he had them. To see them lined up behind him—prim, proper, and devoted—provided symbolic links to the tradition, authority, and personal loyalty that symbolically bound the groups of backlash culture.

The senators, for their part, faced an enormous challenge. They were virtually unknown outside the Senate. Arrayed against them were representatives of an administration that six months before had been elected by the largest plurality in American history. This vote had been, moreover, partly justified by the particularistic sentiments of the backlash, the very sentiments that the senators were now out to demonstrate were deviant and isolated from the true American tradition. What the senators did, in the first instance, was to deny the validity of such sentiments and motives out of hand.

First, they bracketed the political realities of everyday life, particularly the critical realities of political life in the 1960s. Throughout the hearings the senators never referred to the polarized struggles of that day. They literally made those struggles invisible. By so denying any context for the administration's actions, they allowed the witnesses no possible justification.

This strategy of isolating backlash values was supported by the only positive explanation the senators allowed—namely, that the conspirators were just plain stupid. They portrayed the administration witnesses as utterly devoid of common sense, suggesting thereby that no normal person could ever conceive of doing such things. This strategic denial, or bracketing, was coupled with a ringing and unabashed affirmation of the universalistic myth that is the backbone of the American religion. Through their questions, statements, references, gestures, and metaphors, the senators maintained that every American, high or low, rich or poor, acts virtuously in terms of the pure universalism of the civic republican tradition. Nobody is selfish or inhumane. No American is concerned with money or power at the expense of fair play. No team loyalty is so strong that it violates common good or neutralizes the critical attitude toward authority that is the basis of the democratic society.

Passively, this myth was confirmed by the senators' confrontation with family values. Throughout the hearings their families were utterly invisible. We do not know if they had families, but they certainly were not there. Just as Sam Ervin, the southern senator who chaired the proceedings and set before him the Bible and the Constitution, the senators embodied transcendent justice divorced from personal or emotional concerns.

Another confrontation that assumed ritual status was the swearing in of the witnesses. It served no real legal function because these were not legal proceedings. Rather, the swearing in functioned as a process of moral degradation that reduced these famous, powerful people to the status of "everyman," placing them in subordinate positions vis-a-vis the overpowering and universalistic law of the land.

In terms of more direct and explicit conflict, the senators' questions centered on three principle themes, each fundamental to the moral anchoring of a civic democratic society. First, they emphasized the absolute priority of office obligations over personal ones. Several senators repeated over and over again, "This is a nation of laws not men." Second, they emphasized the embedment of these office obligations in a higher transcendent authority. As Ervin particularly emphasized, "the laws of men" must give way to the "laws of God." Ervin's question to Maurice Stans, the treasurer of Nixon's reelection committee, made this hierarchy even more explicit. "Which is more important, not violating laws or not violating ethics?" Finally, the senators insisted that this transcendental anchoring of interest conflict allowed America to be a true "concrete universal." As Lowell Wiecker insisted, in an outraged interruption of the testimony of John Ehrlichman, Nixon's loyal lawyer and troubleshooter: "Republicans don't bug, Republicans don't cheat. They regard their fellow Americans as people to be loved and not as enemies."

In normal times many of these statements would have been greeted with derision, hoots, and cynicism. In fact, many of them were lies in terms of the specific empirical reality of everyday political life, especially in terms of the political reality of the 1960s. Yet they were not laughed at and cynically hooted down, and I think the reason was because this was not everyday life. This was a ritualized, televised event, a period of intense generalization that had "inherent" claims to truth. It was a sacred time and the hearing chambers had become a sacred place. The committee was invoking the most sacred values, not trying to describe empirical fact, and on this mythical level the statements could be seen and understood as true, and they were so seen and understood by significant portions of the population.

CONCLUSION

The hearings ended without laws or specific judgments of evidence, but they had nevertheless profound effects. Here, in conclusion, I would like to qualify further the "truth" that even this most truthful medium in such a white heat can "tell." From an ongoing analysis of various poll data, I venture the following hypotheses.[2] The senate hearings were most powerful in their effect on centrist and left groups (1) among McGovern voters whose outrage at Nixon was splendidly confirmed; (2) among moderate Democrats who, even if they had voted for McGovern, were not outraged at Nixon—some of whom, indeed, had in fact crossed party lines to vote for him; and (3) among moderate or liberal Republicans and Independents who disagreed with many of Nixon's positions but had voted for him anyway, given the choice at the time. The latter two groups were particularly important to the entire process of Watergate. They were prototypically cross-pressured groups. It was the cross-pressured groups that, along with radical McGovern supporters, became most deeply involved in the hearings. Why? Perhaps because they needed the hearings to sort out confused feelings, to clarify crucial issues, to resolve their uncomfortable ambivalence. Their greater relative stake can be found in the poll data. In the period mid-April 1973 to late June 1973—the period of the hearings' beginning and its most dramatic revelations—the growth among Republicans who thought Watergate "serious" was 20%; among Independents it was 18%; among Democrats, just 15% (although, of course, many more of the latter had thought Watergate serious before the hearings).

The "truth telling" of the hearings must be modified in another way—not just to encompass variation among groups but to allow for the varying relevance of different parts of the story itself. Although the meaning of the hearings was highly generalized, in both form and content, I believe this generalization had an impact more on the

"Watergate" symbol itself than on the characters involved, particularly on the character of the president. That this impact on the Watergate symbol was enormous and fateful is revealed by the fact that there was, from the beginning of the Watergate crisis until its end in August 1974, only one period of great increase in the number of Americans who believed Watergate to be "serious." This occurred precisely during the first two months of the Watergate hearings, April through early July 1973. Before the hearings, only 31% of Americans thought it serious; by early July nearly 50% did, a figure that remained solid until the end of the crisis. Although the meaning of "Watergate" became enormously clarified, the linkage between Nixon and Watergate was not made until later. Nixon's October 1973 firing of Archibald Cox, his own special prosecutor on the Watergate case, put him on the wrong side of the mythical antinomies that had been established during the hearings themselves. Although support for Nixon's impeachment went up just a few points during the hearings, after the "Saturday night massacre"—when Cox was fired—it increased by more than 10%.[3]

It would be a mistake, therefore, to view media ritual as an all-embracing experience that has a univocal meaning for an entire population. It would be just as mistaken, however, to argue that the hearings had no ritual status at all. True, they affected cultural meanings as distinct from concrete persons, and certain groups in the population more than others. Within these parameters, however, the form and content of "media truth" during the Watergate events can—and must—be treated in terms of ritual experience, and with the interpretive, hermeneutical tools such experience demands. Only by doing so can we understand the deep importance that this mass-mediated experience had for American democratic culture.

NOTES

1. For the concept of bracketing, and other devices that allow actors to maintain a "naive" attitude toward reality, see Husserl (1931).

2. This analysis is based on data from the 1972-1974 panel sample taken by the American National Election Study and conducted by the Center for Political Studies of the Institute for Social Science Research, University of Michigan. The analysis was conducted with the assistance of Maria Iosne and Eric Rambo.

3. The figures in these last two paragraphs are drawn from Gallup, Harris, and other poll data analyzed by Gladys and Kurt Lang (1983, pp. 88-93, 114-117). The Langs appropriated the term "seriousness" from the polls; by contrast, I have differentiated the symbolic elements emphasized by distinct events.

Chapter 18

AWARENESS OF PUBLIC OPINION AND SCHOOL DESEGREGATION PROTEST

D. Garth Taylor

SOLIDARITY AND MOBILIZATION

Americans who oppose desegregation often believe they are part of a conflict between "the people" and "supporters of integration" that has characterized racial politics in this country for more than 100 years. At the heart of the matter is the issue of whether a community has the right to embody its values in the law or whether civil rights take precedence over local mores. The Supreme Court once ruled, in *Plessy* v. *Ferguson*, that solidarity of community opinion legally prevents the court from barring local-level discrimination:

> So far, then, as a conflict with the Fourteenth Amendment is concerned, [this] case reduces itself to the question whether the statute ... is a reasonable regulation. ... In determining the question of reasonableness [a legislature] is at liberty to act with reference to the established usages, customs and traditions of the people, and with a view to the promotion of their comfort. ... Gauged by this standard, we cannot say that a law which authorizes or even requires the separation of the two races in public conveyances is unreasonable.

The view that majority opinion should determine the rights of the minority was echoed in a memo to Justice Robert Jackson from his

AUTHOR'S NOTE: This chapter is based upon Taylor (in press, chapter 6).

clerk, William Rehnquist, who wrote at the time the *Brown* case was beginning its journey to the Supreme Court:

> To the argument made by Thurgood, not John Marshall, that a majority may not deprive a minority of its constitutional right, the answer must be made that while this is sound in theory, in the long run it is the majority who will decide what the rights of the minority are.

School boards once sought to defend themselves with the argument that widespread opposition to desegregation constitutes prima facie evidence of the reasonableness of their actions. In the 1950 case of *Sweatt* v. *Painter*, the state of Texas produced a public opinion poll showing that most of the people wanted to maintain segregation. In its final argument in *Brown* v. *Board of Education*, the state of Florida produced a poll showing that three-quarters of the "white leaders" in the state disagreed with the Brown decision, 30% disagreed "violently," and only 13% of peace officers intended to enforce state attendance laws at racially mixed schools.

The principal focus of attention in this chapter is the Boston school desegregation controversy in the middle 1970s. Boston residents were primed to view the conflict over mandatory desegregation as a contest between authorities and solidified community opposition. The view that local autonomy is continually subject to encroachment by the state government, the Protestant establishment, and other "outsiders" was widespread in Boston. In the middle 1960s the Massachusetts state legislature passed the Racial Imbalance Act (RIA), a law with stringent requirements for desegregation and busing. The impact of this law, however, was almost entirely focused on Boston and no other Massachusetts city because of the demographic concentration of minorities in that part of the state. Boston neighborhood residents, working through their representatives in the state legislature, successfully avoided implementation of the RIA until June 1974. At that time Federal Judge Arthur Garrity found the Boston school board guilty of segregative action and imposed the RIA plan as Phase I of the remedy, to be begun in autumn 1974, and ordered an even more inclusive plan as Phase II to be implemented the following year. This chapter is a small part of the story of public opposition to Judge Garrity's order. I focus particularly on how awareness of public opposition increases the willingness of neighborhood residents to oppose a social policy they consider to be unjust.

AWARENESS OF PUBLIC OPINION
AND INCENTIVES TO PROTEST:
THREE THEORIES

THE SPIRAL OF SILENCE

Noelle-Neumann analyzes the relation between perception of majority public support and willingness to express one's views on matters of public choice (1974, 1977, 1979; see also Taylor, 1982). She finds that those who believe the majority agrees with them, and/or who believe the trend is toward majority support for their position, are more likely than others to be willing to express their views publicly on the policy matter in question. This theory is labeled the "spiral of silence" because of a tendency for those who believe they are in the minority to become less and less likely to advance their views affirmatively.

The theme of intimidation by the majority is common in historical analyses of American racial politics. W. J. Cash (1941), writing of the South during the period before the Civil War, notes the progressive social isolation of the moderates:

> The defense of slavery not only eventuated ... in a taboo on criticism; in the same process it set up a ban on all analysis and inquiry. . . .In a world in which patriotism to the South was increasingly the first duty of men, in which coolness about slavery was accounted treason, [detachment] was next to impossible. (p. 101)

Martin Luther King wrote of the same phenomenon occurring more than 100 years later. The spiral of silence not only eliminates the appearances of divisions of opinion among whites but also, by doing so, minimizes the opportunity for a coalition to form between blacks and white moderates:

> As a result of the Citizens Councils' activities most white moderates in the South no longer feel free to discuss in public the issues involved in desegregation for fear of social ostracism and economic reprisals. What channels of communication had once existed between whites and Negroes have thus largely closed. (King, 1958)

Virginius Dabney, editor of Richmond's *Times-Dispatch*, spoke ominously of the "thunderous silence" of his friends and colleagues on southern newspapers. George Washington Cable's 1890 lament on this subject was titled *The Silent South*.

As a tool for understanding intimidation in racial politics, the theory of the spiral of silence is quite valuable. But as a tool for explaining the relation between perception of public opinion and willingness to protest, the spiral of silence is quite limited. The theory explains why people *do not* express themselves when they think they are in the minority. In the smallest, daily kinds of interactions with one's neighbors and associates—that is, in the realm where ideas about race become fashionable or unfashionable—the spiral of silence may explain why integrationist ideas cease to be expressed and why segregationist ideas acquire their apparent grip on the popular imagination.

The theory does not explain, however, why those who believe they are in the majority may be *more* likely to act. One could argue that the reason some people express their views is the opposite of the reason other do not—perhaps an absence of fear of isolation. But this is not an adequate explanation. Absence of fear is not a sufficient motivational basis for action. The next two theories suggest a positive motivational basis for the relation between perception of public opinion and willingness to protest.

REINFORCING VERSUS DIVIDING COMMUNITY CLEAVAGE

Gamson et al. (1982) argue that the likelihood of joining a protest depends, to some extent, on how a person believes the community to be divided. Two patterns of community cleavage are depicted in Figure 18.1. The symbol "P" stands, in the terminology of Gamson et al., for "potential challengers." For understanding school desegregation politics, these are the residents of a community facing a court order. The symbol "A" stands for "authorities"—that is, those mandating desegregation. Gamson et al. argue that those who believe there is a reinforcing cleavage have a greater incentive to protest than those who believe there is a dividing cleavage.

In the "reinforcing" pattern, the courts (and others who support integration) are on one side of the line and the residents of the community are on the other. Perception of a reinforcing cleavage makes protest more likely because it helps establish a collective group identity. A sense of group solidarity means that people do not think it likely that the "outsiders" will be able to co-opt "loyalists" within the group. Divisions are not expected to become strong within the community. People's loyalties to individuals and institutions in the group motivate actions on behalf of the group.

1. A Reinforcing Cleavage

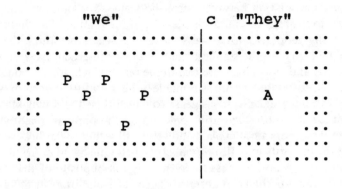

2. A Dividing Cleavage

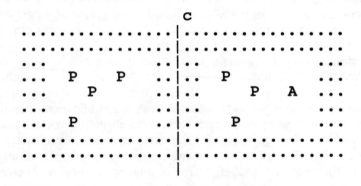

```
c = Social cleavage
A = Authorities
P = Potential challengers
```

NOTE: Drawing is based on Gamson et al. (1982, p. 78).

Figure 18.1 Possible Cleavage Patterns: Two Ideal Types

In the "dividing" pattern, the salient cleavage partitions the participants into a set that includes the courts and some community residents who favor desegregation and another set that includes other community residents who oppose desegregation. Someone who believes there is a dividing cleavage is less likely to protest than someone who thinks there is a reinforcing cleavage because (a) the sense of group identity does not develop; (b) there is a clearly recognized possibility of a coalition between some members of the community and the advocates of desegregation; and (c) therefore there is less reason to believe protest activities will be successful.

SOLIDITARY AND THE ABILITY TO IMPOSE COSTS

Albert Hirschman wrote a short book (1970) about collective action that suggests that the reward people expect from joining a protest is directly proportional to the cost they believe can be imposed on authorities. He suggests that in situations of community conflict, the higher the proportion who are believed to be protesting, the greater the cost an individual expects can be imposed by joining as well. Therefore, the higher the proportion believed to be protesting, the greater the expected reward to the individual from joining. By these bonds of rational calculation and reward-based incentive, the decision to take part in anti-busing protest is most likely to occur when someone believes the community is unanimously or predominantly opposed to desegregation.

Hirschman's model assumes that each person who is opposed to busing and has an impression of how the community is reacting to it. Each person's impression of the relation between the imposition of an unpopular public policy and the extent of public opposition to it can be represented on a graph such as those in Figures 18.2a and 18.2b, based on Appendix A of Hirschman's book (1970).

Figures 18.2a and 18.2b represent the impressions two different people have of how the rest of the community is reacting to school desegregation. The x-axis of Figure 18.2a represents the percentage expected to *not* protest school desegregation. Q0 is the percentage not protesting before the court order—that is, 100%. Q1 is the percentage expected to not protest after the court order. The percentage who are believed to protest is therefore (Q0 − Q1).

The y-axis represents the amount of dissatisfaction a person experiences with the "proponents of integration." The level before busing is L0. The level after court-implemented desegregation is L1. As Y increases on the graph, the level of dissatisfaction increases.

The dependent variable in the analysis, the likelihood that an individual will protest, is represented as the region labeled Pr{VU}. It is assumed that the likelihood of action is a function of the level of dissatisfaction and the percentage of others expected to protest. When many others are protesting, the individual believes that significant

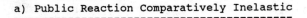

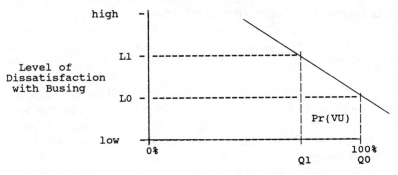

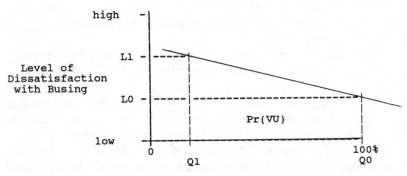

NOTE: Pr {VU} = the likelihood that an individual will protest. Drawing is based on Hirschman (1970, p. 130).

Figure 18.2 Graphs Showing Perceived Public Reaction and the Likelihood of Protest

costs are quite likely to be imposed on authorities and that joining the action can significantly increase those costs.

Given an individual's level of dissatisfaction, the proportion expected to protest depends on the slope of the line relating the level of dissatisfaction (L) to the percentage protesting (Q). The slope of this line is what Hirschman calls the "quality-elasticity of demand" (Hirschman, 1970, p. 130). The quality-elasticity of demand is an individual's sense of the volatility of public opinion. It is the person's estimate of the extent of community conflict that is likely to erupt as a result of a given level of dissatisfaction with busing.

The importance of the perceived volatility of public response can be seen by comparing Figure 18.2a with Figure 18.2b. Both represent individuals who have the same level of dissatisfaction with busing. A person who believes he or she is in the minority or that there is a dividing cleavage perceives a low elasticity of public response. This person is represented in Figure 18.2a. The proportion engaging in protest as a result of the court order, (Q0 - Q1), is believed to be relatively small. The likelihood that the community can impose significant costs on authorities or that an individual can contribute in a significant way is therefore believed to be low. The region labeled Pr{VU}, showing the likelihood that this individual will engage in illegal protest, is comparatively small.

A person who believes he or she is in the majority or that there is a reinforcing cleavage perceives a high elasticity of public response. This is represented in Figure 18.2b. This person believes the proportion engaging in illegal protest as a result of the court order, {Q0 - Q1}, is relatively high. The likelihood that the community can impose significant costs on authorities and that an individual can contribute in a significant way is therefore believed to be high. The region Pr[VU], corresponding to the likelihood of participating in illegal action, is also comparatively large.

What, exactly, do people attend to when judging the costs likely to be imposed by community protest and the value of joining? There is a difference between nonpublic goods and public goods in the kinds of costs created for authorities. There is no simple "unit" cost for each person who decides to stop "buying" and to start protesting against school desegregation. The costs of this kind of action, especially its illegal varieties, are borne by those responsible for the day-to-day operation of the schools, the police, and other community institutions.

Even though there is no simple "unit rule" relating public opposition to the costs that can be placed in the way of school desegregation implementation, there is no doubt that Boston residents were aware that costs were associated with protest actions. Mayor White repeatedly requested funds and police from other jurisdictions to defray the costs of enforcing public order during the period of demonstrations, boycotts, and defiance. On several occasions he publicly discussed the financial burden on the city and the school district from having to pay the costs associated with public resistance to school desegregation implementation (Richard, Knox, & Oliphant, 1975).

In this situation, in which higher costs are known to be associated with higher levels of public opposition, Hirschman's model elegantly describes the reward-based relation between perceived levels of public opposition and a person's willingness to protest.

THE ROLE OF MEDIA

Each theory analyzed here relies significantly, albeit indirectly, on effects of mass media and mass communications. Each theory analyzes how *perceived* opinions *perceived* alignments of the community against "outside" forces, and *perceived* levels of opposition in the community affect the willingness of individuals to take part in protest actions. Media play a potentially significant role in shaping these perceptions.

Each theory points to a different way in which the media might influence perceptions and thereby affect the level of mobilization in a community. In the spiral of silence, the principal impact of the media is on the perception of the opinions of one's neighbors. With Gamson's theory, the principal impact of media would be on people's awareness of an alignment of the community against unjust, "outside" authorities. In Hirschman's theory, the primary influence of media would be on perceptions of the proportion of the community already mobilized and the net costs and benefits that might follow from joining in.

The theories and research in this chapter show a number of significant ways in which media effects on mobilization might be conceptualized and studied. The Boston survey was not designed principally as a media analysis. The analyses in this chapter suggest, however, that media effects can significantly reinforce community tendencies toward mobilization.

AWARENESS OF PUBLIC OPINION AND
DESEGREGATION PROTEST: EMPIRICAL FINDINGS

PUBLIC OPINION ABOUT PUBLIC OPINION

The data analyzed in this chapter are from a five-wave panel survey of approximately 500 Boston neighborhood residents conducted during 1974 and 1975. Data were collected by the National Opinion Research Center based on a questionnaire and sample designed by J. Michael Ross. The first two waves of the survey were collected in September 1973 and April 1974—before Judge Garrity's order but after at least 10 years' conflict over desegregation and implementation of the RIA. The third wave of the survey was collected in July 1974, just after Judge Garrity's order. The final waves were collected in November 1974, the beginning of Phase I, and in July 1975, the end of Phase I. Because of the design of the survey, the responses are not representative of Boston in its entirety but, rather, of a collection of neighborhoods within the city (Stinchcombe & Taylor, 1980; Taylor & Stinchcombe, 1977). The data are used to explore and test the three theories of public opinion discussed in the previous section of this chapter.

The independent variable in each of the three theories is the same—that is, public perception of public disagreement with and reaction to desegregation. Table 18.1 shows the results for a number of measures of people's perceptions of community opinion and neighborhood action during the time of the Boston school desegregation controversy. Neighborhood residents who perceive widespread opposition to the court order, a reinforcing pattern of community conflict, and/or an elastic public response to busing are those who said

(1) public opinion is predominantly opposed to busing;

(2) the percentage boycotting the public schools is high and/or increasing;

(3) their neighbors will work to resist, avoid, or otherwise oppose the court order.

The first row of Table 18.1 shows that in each wave, nearly 100% of the respondents in the Boston sample have the impression that public opinion in their neighborhood is predominantly opposed to two-way busing to achieve school desegregation. The second row of Table 18.1 shows people's perception of neighborhood support for Judge Garrity's decision. People were asked to estimate the proportion of their neighbors agreeing with the court order. The second row of Table 18.1 shows that during the time of the wave 3 interview, the average of these estimates is 15%.

The next five questions in Table 18.1 deal with the topic of school boycotts. The third row shows that during the beginning months of Phase I (wave 4), residents of the Boston neighborhoods estimated that, on average, 19% of their neighbors were not sending their children to public school regularly. During this same time 19% said the level of boycott participation increased since the beginning of the school year (see row 4 of Table 18.1) and 26% said the school boycott would become even more extensive (see row 5). During the summer

TABLE 18.1

Neighborhood Perception of Public Opinion, Public Action, and Trends Regarding Support for Desegregation

	Wave 1	Wave 2	Wave 3	Wave 4	Wave 5
Percentage saying opposition is dominant opinion for neighbors (actual: 95% opposed)	94	98	98		96
Average percentage of neighbors believed to agree with Judge Garrity (actual: 16% agree)			15%		
Average percentage believed to be boycotting in early fall, 1974 (actual: 12% boycott)			19%		
Perceived trend in the school boycott					
Percentage "increasing"				19	
Percentage "no change"				45	
Expected future trend in the boycott					
Percentage "increase"				26	
Percentage "no change"				59	
Average percentage believed boycotting in 1974/1975 school year (actual: 27% boycott)					33%
Expected future trend in the boycott					
Percentage "increase"					52
Percentage "no change"					36
Percentage of neighbors expected to resist, defy, openly oppose, or avoid Phase I			65		
Percentage of neighbors believed to have defied, demonstrated against, avoided, interfered with, or worked against Phase I				79	
Percentage of neighbors expected to avoid, demonstrate against, openly oppose, or create problems to hinder Phase II					75
Percentage saying preference for separation of the races is the dominant opinion among neighbors	61				58

NOTE: Data are combined from samples of white residents of six Boston neighborhoods.

after Phase I (wave 5) residents of the Boston neighborhoods estimated, on average, that 33% of their neighbors had not sent their children to public school regularly (row 6). During the next school year (row 7), 52% expected the boycott would increase.

The next three questions in Table 18.1 have to do with the perception respondents had of their neighbors' actions regarding the court order. Just before the beginning of Phase I (wave 3), 65% said their neighbors would "resist," "defy," "openly oppose," or "find a way around" the court order (row 8 of Table 18.1). By the end of the first few months of Phase I (wave 4), 79% of the respondents said their neighbors were actually participating in "demonstrations," "defiance," "interference," "avoidance," or were "actively working to reverse the Phase I decision" (row 9). This level of perceived neighborhood reaction remains steady. At the end of the 1974-1975 school year (wave 5), 75% said their neighbors would engage in a similar inventory of actions to hinder implementation of the Phase II plan (row 10).

PERCEPTION OF OPPOSITION AND MOBILIZATION

Each of the three theories offers a different explanation of the relation between perceived support for one's point of view and willingness to protest. According to the spiral of silence, those who believe they are in the minority fear social isolation and so do not risk exposing themselves to the disapproval of their neighbors. According to the theory advanced by Gamson et al., someone who believes the public is strongly opposed to a policy tends to perceive a reinforcing cleavage. This activates group loyalties and increases the salience of any past conflicts between insiders and outsiders as a way of understanding the issue. According to Hirschman's theory, the higher the proportion believed to oppose a policy, the more certain an individual is that protest can impose significant costs on authorities, and therefore the more likely an individual is to join.

During the period of time spanned by the wave 1 to wave 4 surveys—from before Judge Garrity's order until the beginning of Phase I—the pattern is strongly in the direction predicted by each theory. Perception of the strength of public opposition to busing is strongly, monotonically related to people's willingness to protest. Data from the wave 1 interviews are shown in Table 18.2.

The percentages in Table 18.2 and in the next two tables are for respondents *opposed to busing*.[1] In principle, analyses could be done to show the effect of perceived community opinion on willingness to act on behalf of the court order for neighborhood residents who favor busing. Given the sample size, however, there are too few pro-busing respondents to do so.[2]

The first column in Table 18.2 shows the percentage saying they would encourage defiance of the court order if they were members of

TABLE 18.2
Perceived Public Opposition and Willingness to Protest,
Wave 1

	Percentage Willing to Support Defiance	Percentage Willing to Support Boycott
Perceived level of opposition to busing among neighbors		
Very strongly opposed	61	48
Less strongly opposed	47	25
Neutral, favorable	37	27

NOTE: Data are combined from samples of white residents of six Boston neighborhoods. Data show responses of those personally opposed to busing at the time of the interview. Patterns shown are significant (.05) when racial prejudice/fear and strength of anti-busing opinion are controlled.

the Boston school board. Overall, 57% of the Boston neighborhood residents opposed to busing said they would. The first column in Table 18.2 also shows how this measure of willingness is related to perceived levels of public opposition to busing. As the perceived level of public opposition diminishes, so does the percentage willing to defy the court.

The second column in Table 18.2 shows a similar analysis for the percentage saying they would support a school boycott if they were members of the Boston school board. Overall, 43% said they would. Willingness to support a school boycott is also strongly related to the level of perceived public opposition to busing during this stage of the controversy. Among those who believed the public was "very strongly opposed" to busing, 48% supported the boycott. As the perceived level of public opposition diminished, support for the boycott did as well.

The data from waves 1-4, without exception, support the three theories discussed in this chapter. Those who saw support for their views in the social environment, those who saw a reinforced cleavage, those who thought that protest was widespread were all more likely than those who did not to support protest against desegregation. The data from the wave 5 interviews, shown in Table 18.3, also tend to support the three theories, but not completely. As before, findings are shown for Boston neighborhood residents personally opposed to busing at the time of the current interview.

The second column in Table 18.3 shows the percentage saying they "frequently" or "very frequently" talked with their neighbors about

TABLE 18.3
Perceived Public Opposition, Willingness to Protest, and Willingness to Express Anti-Busing Views, Wave 5

	Percentage Willing to Support Boycott	Percentage Discussing Opinions Frequently or Very Frequently with Neighbors
Perceived level of opposition to busing among neighbors		
Very strong opposed	46	68
Less strongly opposed	31	54
Neutral, favorable	46	18
Percentage of neighbors believed to have boycotted during 1974-1975		
45% or more	49	73
15% to 44%	44	71
14% or less	43	57
Expected action of neighbors regarding the court order		
Antagonistic	48	69
Neutral, favorable	29	51
Expected future trend in the school boycott during 1975-1976		
Increase	49	85
No change	31	51
Decrease	54	71

NOTE: Data are combined from samples of white residents of six Boston neighborhoods. Data show responses of those personally opposed to busing at the time of the interview. Patterns shown are significant (.05) when racial prejudice/fear and strength of anti-busing opinion are controlled.

"how the events of the past year have affected the quality of the Boston schools." The frequency of discussing anti-busing opinions with the neighbors is highest for those who believed their neighbors were "very strongly opposed" to busing; those with very high estimates of the proportion of neighbors participating in the school boycott; and for those expecting their neighbors to take anti-busing actions during Phase II. These findings support the three theories: Perceived support is related to individual willingness to express one's views. Other evidence in Table 18.3, however, is inconsistent with these results.

The percentage discussing their anti-busing opinions with the neighbors is especially high for those who expected increased support for the boycott during Phase II, but it is also especially high for those who expected decreased support. This suggests a pattern of rearguard action.[3] During the late stages of the anti-busing conflict, willingness to express anti-busing views was especially high for those who thought the trend was in their favor, but it was also especially high for those who thought their opinions were against the trend.

Other evidence in Table 18.3 also illustrates a rearguard pattern. The percentage supporting the school boycott is especially high for those who expected increased boycotting but is also especially high for those who expected a decrease in neighborhood boycott participation. Likewise, the percentage in favor of the boycott is especially high for those who perceived "very strong" neighborhood opposition to busing but is also especially high for those who thought their neighbors were neutral or positive on busing.

Why should there be a rearguard pattern? The literature on the spiral of silence suggests one explanation for the deviant patterns in Table 18.3. Those who believe they are in the minority may still be especially likely to speak out if they believe the trend of public opinion is in their favor or if they believe, for some other reason, that they will ultimately be successful. The Boston "rearguarders" may have had the impression that public opinion was changing in the anti-Garrity direction.

Other evidence, however, does not support this explanation. The wave 5 interviews were conducted after the first year of court-ordered desegregation was complete. During this time boycotts and defiance had been contained by public authority, and the threat of receivership had been announced (but not yet implemented) by Judge Garrity. By the time of the wave 5 interviews, most Boston neighborhood residents had given up on the idea of delaying desegregation. The rearguard pattern in Table 18.3 is evidence of support for a lost cause during the final stages of a conflict. This phenomenon contradicts the three theories of mobilization analyzed here. The pattern suggests that the three theories are most applicable during earlier stages of a community conflict.

ON THE ACCURACY OF PUBLIC PERCEPTIONS

Misperception of the direction of public opinion is referred to as "pluralistic ignorance" (Allport, 1924; Isenberg, 1980; Krech &

Crutchfield, 1948; Merton, 1968). This phenomenon is important for studies of mobilization because people may be willing to protest based on their perceptions of community opinion but, because of pluralistic ignorance, may be greatly mistaken in that perception. Survey studies of the accuracy of public assessments of public opinion agree that misperception is, in certain circumstances, widespread. Fields and Schuman (1976) and O'Gorman (1975, 1976, 1979) report quite high levels of public misperception of community opinion, particularly with regard to matters of racial politics and racial preferences.

The figures in Table 18.1 show, however, that Boston residents have a quite accurate picture of the level of opposition to busing and the dynamics of protest against the court order during the period covered by these surveys. The first two rows of Table 18.1 show that about 95% said community opinion was predominantly opposed to two-way busing and that only a small percentage favored Judge Garrity's order. About 85% to 90% of neighborhood residents actually were opposed to busing during this period. To assess the accuracy of the perception of community opposition to Judge Garrity's order (row 3 of Table 1), people were asked whether they themselves were for or against the court's decision. At the time of the wave 3 interview, 16% agreed with the court, a result that is quite close to the average percentage perceived to agree with Judge Garrity—15%.

Public estimates of boycott participation are also quite accurate. Neighborhood residents estimated, on average, a boycott participation rate of 19% at the beginning of Phase I and a rate of 33% by the end of the first year. Public school enrollment was actually down 12% during the first few months of Phase I and down 27% by the end of the 1974-1975 school year. With respect to the boycott, the only figure that might be called inaccurate is the high percentage expecting more extensive participation during the next school year. This, in fact, did not happen.

There are no objective standards for measuring the accuracy of the last three measures of perceptions shown in Table 18.1. Survey analysts are loath, for a number of reasons, to inquire too deeply about participation in protest actions that are a violation of the law. Therefore, we cannot tell if the percentage believed to be participating in such action is too high or too low.

Why is the apparent level of pluralistic ignorance lower in the Boston data than in other surveys having to do with some of the same topics? Some of the previous research is based on national surveys conducted during times of relative calm, compared to the situation in Boston in the mid-1970s (e.g., O'Gorman 1975, 1976, 1979). It may be that communication patterns are more dense and better informed during times of community crisis, thus leading to more accurate perceptions of public opinion and public action. A second reason that other studies of racial opinions show high levels of pluralistic ignorance may be that these studies ask about private behavior ("Would your neighbors allow their children to play with children of another race?") and general feelings ("Are your neighbors generally for or against separation of the races?"), rather than about public behavior (protests) and opinions on concrete political issues (the court order). The high levels of pluralistic ignorance about racial issues found in other surveys may not characterize the situation in more geographically concentrated areas when detailed questions are asked about (1) public opinion regarding local issues that have been a matter of controversy for some time and (2) public participation in particular actions, such as school boycotts, in which information regarding neighbor's actions may have been a topic for coverage by mass media.

One question asked in the Boston survey is more similar to the general questions used in the earlier studies of pluralistic ignorance and shows a higher level of public misperception of public opinion. The eleventh row of Table 18.1 shows that about 60% said their neighbors were predominantly in favor of separation of the races. Belief in separation of the races is actually the minority opinion in these neighborhoods—favored by 5% to 10%. It may be that perceptions of public opinion on racial matters are accurate for questions about implementation of minority rights (where public opinion is generally opposed) but pluralistically ignorant for questions about endorsement of general principles about racial equality (where public opinion is generally tolerant).

CONCLUSION

PUBLIC OPINION AND SCHOOL DESEGREGATION ENFORCEMENT

The Supreme Court, in its 1955 ruling in *Brown II*, allowed that "a variety of obstacles" justified delay by local officials in implementing desegregation. The court did not, however, recognize public opinion as a valid reason for delay:

> It should go without saying that the vitality of these constitutional principles cannot be allowed to yield simply because of disagreement with them.

The argument that public opposition justifies delay was specifically tested in the Little Rock case and found unacceptable.

In spite of unfavorable legal precedent, opponents of desegregation still search for evidence of the extensiveness of public opposition and school boards still introduce that evidence into federal court hearings on desegregation. Such actions, of course, have no legal standing. They do, however, provide vivid public documentation of widespread community opposition to busing and may prolong any period of public conflict that attends mandatory desegregation.

PUBLIC OPINION AND THE MOBILIZATION OF DISCONTENT

Hirschman's model argues that those who are more certain of public opposition are more certain that meaningful social costs can be imposed on authorities by participation in school desegregation protest. Since they are more certain their actions will be effective, they are more likely to join. The work by Gamson et al. suggests that the perception of widespread community opposition to busing creates a vested interest in a group identity—defined on the basis of opposition to busing and other historically similar intrusions of "outside" powers. The spiral of silence suggests that those who accept desegregation may become intimidated from expressing their views after discovering evidence of their minority status.

These explanations of the relation between perception of community opposition and willingness to take part in anti-busing protest are not mutually exclusive. People's beliefs in the elasticity of public response is probably related to their beliefs about the extent to which the current community conflict follows "historical" lines of cleavage. An excitable public is likely to be aroused again by a court order. People's sense of the level of arousal of the "excitable" public is also proportional to their sense of the social harm that is done by the court order. This sense of harm is, of course, subject to manipulation by media, authorities, and other sources of information and impression management. People's sense of the exact level of public participation is influenced by their sense of the harm done, the level of excitability of the community, as well as other sources of information such as school board surveys or pronouncements by public officials. The theory of the spiral of silence explains how, in the end, dissent from the majority view against busing can become locked out because of intimidation, frustration, and, finally, loss of interest.

Unless steps are taken to discourage and discredit opposition to integration, unless efforts are made to preserve and publicize diversity of opinion in a community, and unless attempts are made to build coalitions on the desegregation issue in a new way so that busing does not seem to be a new version of the "same old conflict," the dynamics of compliance will not be smooth. Instead, the more or less practical, sometimes "rational" choices of most individuals will encourage the development of an antagonized community with a sense of its identity as such, a predisposition to join protests that seem likely to inflict harm, and an intolerance for opposing points of view that is reinforced by the gradual weakening of the forcefulness with which the opposition pursues its argument.

NOTES

1. Data are analyzed separately for anti-busing respondents for a number of reasons. Most important, it is necessary to control for the fact that one's opinion on busing is related to one's perception of the level of anti-busing sentiment in the community. This phenomenon, known as the "looking glass" effect, is well documented in the literature on pluralistic ignorance and the theory of the spiral of silence. Second, it is necessary to establish the discriminant validity (Cronbach, 1971) of the measures of perceived public opinion and willingness to voice publicly one's views against busing. It is necessary to show that perception of public opposition and willingness to take part in anti-busing actions are not simply as measures of extreme anti-busing opinion. Panel analyses were also performed to determine whether the conclusions hold up when adjustments are made for cross-lagged effects and instability of response. Although any such procedure cannot, in principle, determine the direction of a causal relationship (Duncan, 1972, 1975), the pattern of coefficients in the panel models shows that the strongest effects are the ones suggested by the findings as they are presented in Tables 18.2 and 18.3.

2. This is unfortunate because one of my earlier studies finds that the effect of perceived support for one's views is sometimes different for those who are actually in the majority than for those actually in the minority (Taylor, 1982).

3. The term "rearguard" is relative. The first four waves of the Boston panel survey are "early" measures with respect to the timing of the data collection but not with respect to the 10-year history of the school desegregation controversy in Boston.

Chapter 19

SOME OBSERVATIONS ON THE LONG-RANGE EFFECTS OF TELEVISION

Gladys Engel Lang
Kurt Lang

THE SUMMER OF 1984 was a time of nostalgia for old media research hands. It was a time to look back and reflect on the long-range and cumulative effects of television on political life and political participation. The future we had anticipated some three decades ago had become the present. Having cut our eyeteeth as researchers on the national party conventions of 1952, we had survived to see television, for the first time, abandoning full coverage of the very events through which that medium first established itself on the political scene.

Pondering the effects of these televised ritualistic gatherings that culminate in the nominating process, it became apparent that over the long haul, the most lasting effect of these broadcasts had been on the institution itself. Back in 1952, the convention telecasts had been a proving ground for producers, reporters, technicians, and politicians. The coverage had set the style for the televising not only of future conventions but of all other political events as well. At that time the networks, but CBS in particular, had insisted that it was not their task to make a good show out of the conventions. The irony resides in the way that the political parties, in the years since 1952, have done the job for them. These meetings have become more and more staged, exactly as if they were nothing other than shows for television. Speeches have been pared to the bone; delegations have been polled off camera so as not to interrupt the smooth progress of the proceedings; convention highlights have been prescheduled for prime time. The party and its soon-to-be-crowned candidate are touted in films ostensibly projected for the delegates in the hall but actually designed to exploit to the fullest the free air time granted by the definition of the convention as a genuine news event. In fact, all too often in recent times, with the outcome a foregone conclusion, prospects for any self-generated news break have been almost nil. Thus it was that for the first time in 1972, when Richard Nixon was renominated, the production of a convention could be scripted in advance. As we have been able to observe, this happened again with Reagan's renomination. What the networks transmitted in 1984 was not the drama of a contested nomination but two political spectacles designed as the kickoff to the electoral campaign.

It also seems ironic that just as the center of gravity of the nominating process had shifted away from the conventions to the various state primaries where, assumedly, there is more potential for citizenship participation in the process, the networks chose to withdraw from their original commitment to televise the conventions in their entirety as a means for increasing citizen participation.

Before taking up the implications of these and similar developments, let us make some general observations on communication research. For a long time, and surely three decades ago, those investigating the effects of mass communication on politics were concentrating on directly observable short-term effects, most often on the impact of media exposure during an electoral campaign in relation to vote decisions as these affected the outcome of an election. It was nevertheless acknowledged, even by such scholars as the late Joseph Klapper, whose name will forever be associated with the minimal effects theorem (see the introductory chapter), that there were indeed other, and perhaps even more serious, long-term effects that ought to have a valid claim on the attention of researchers. If many scholars failed to address this broad range of effects, as they did, it was in large part—or so we believe—because these more indirect and social effects of the media, television in particular, were difficult to demonstrate through a single survey or experiment or even a series of such surveys and experiments. Efforts to infer them were considered "soft" and, thus, like some of our own work, were not counted among the established findings of research, as in the review of tested propositions in behavioral research carefully catalogued by Berelson and Steiner in the mid-1960s.

In assessing long-term effects, one must realize first that they involve more than just the *passage of time;* it is not just a matter of the difference between an "immediately after" and a "delayed" measure after an exposure. With time there is an opportunity for repeated exposure either to the same message, similar messages, certain types of messages, or to the message content of a particular medium, so that a second kind of effect or influence is likely to become *cumulative*. Habits, expectations, and frames of reference change in ways that are not always apparent and often are not able to be anticipated in a study of short-term effects that takes them as given. This leads to a third phenomenon that has to be considered—namely, *spillover*. With saturation—that is, when almost everyone has heard about an event or issue (an example would be the break-in at Watergate; see Alexander's chapter)—some of the distinctions between those directly exposed and those not so exposed, or between heavy users and light users, or those with preferences for different media, become blurred. Fourth and last, in addition to time, cumulation, and spillover—all of which have to be considered in assessing long-term effects—there are *reciprocal effects,* whereby the televising of an event (or of proceedings) reacts back on the event being televised, thereby changing its nature.

Reciprocal effects came in for attention quite early in the history of televised politics. Thus, it was noted that the presence of TV cameras on any occasion elicits reactions from those upon whom they focus. These reactions range from the minute and trivial (such as "acting for the camera" in what purports to be a spontaneous expression of anger or enthusiasm or, alternatively, improved decorum at a political function) to the more serious (such as the use of the TV presence by leaders or would-be leaders without any real constituencies to accommodate to the demands of the medium and thus gain publicity for themselves). Time-honored institutions such as the presidential press conference have been reciprocally affected by the presence of television. When Eisenhower first allowed cameras in, some feared lest this dampen the give-and-take between the press and the president. There is no evidence that this has been a consistent trend, only that some presidents have been more reluctant than others to meet with the press. Moreover, on occasion these televised press conferences have taken on a confrontational tone, especially during the years of Watergate. Yet in at least one respect, in response to being televised, one major function of these press conferences has been lost: They no longer serve as off-the-record briefings for reporters as they did in the pretelevision era. No longer can a president, assured that he will not be quoted, rely on this form for frank discussion with reporters on matters of serious public concern. The real briefings these days still tend to take place in private; what used to emerge formerly from the free-ranging press conference is now made public in the form of leaks. The official press conference has become little more than a platform available to presidents for statements to which they wish to give wide play. A president appearing before television must carefully weigh his replies; an unfortunate remark cannot be stricken from the public record once it has been broadcast. The mere attempt to do so would make headlines and, like any departure from the previously released speech, quickly catch every observant reporter's eyes. In these and similar instances, the impact of the medium on the event itself cannot readily be extricated from the impact of transmitting the event.

Over the years the whole pace and style of national political campaigning has been adapted to television. It has even been said that there is no campaign in the old-fashioned sense of taking to the stump; rather, the campaign exists for and on television alone. Among the traditions that have gone by the wayside is the custom of ceasing to campaign before the eve of election in order to avoid sensational but unanswerable charges that make news on election morning when they can no longer be answered. Nowadays, candidates vie for television time right up to the hour the polls open, and their managers continue with statements, issued right through election day, with an eye toward forestalling any potentially adverse effects of early returns and projections of the outcome by networks.

These and other developments point to the appropriateness, now that the future is here, of an effort toward systematic evaluation of the role that television has played in them. We do not contend that the sole cause for any of these changes is to be found in television, but any inquiry has to center on the documentation of actual links between the increasingly ubiquitous presence of the video medium and the kind of developments we have alluded to. A systematic mining of data already available could do much to clarify the image of politics to which political actors, the press, and to a degree even the public at large are continually reacting.

In the rest of this chapter, we do no more than present some admittedly sketchy thoughts on long-term changes in political life, whose existence has been pretty well documented, and suggest their relation to the growth of television. These changes are

(1) the increasing personalization of politics

(2) the nationalization of political discourse, and

(3) volatility in electoral behavior

THE PERSONALIZATION OF POLITICS

One of the most pervasive reciprocal effects of television on electioneering and political debate has been to make the candidate's personality the major determinant of electoral choice. Could this have come about even without television? Would a Ronald Reagan, for example, have fared just as well with another medium—that is, as well as Roosevelt did with radio? TV, from its very beginning, has tended to personalize politics through closeups that allow and encourage viewers to scrutinize the faces and mien of those who present themselves on the screen. Though most viewers evidently lack an insider's knowledge, television nevertheless allows viewers to circumvent the representational party structure that mediates between them and the "issues." They no longer feel the need for ward heelers or union leaders to tell them what to think or how to vote. Yet their judgments are often little more than evaluations based on a faith instilled by the style of the candidates as to whether they can be trusted, on impressions of honesty or sincerity projected via the TV screen with correspondingly less attention paid to past records and/or political associates. Nevertheless, there is no compelling evidence that more sophisticated voters who pay more attention to issues and print media and who value the independence of their own judgments actually lean less than others on television to assess the candidates.

Without question, personalized politics preceded the arrival of television on the political scene, but at least two aspects of this phenomenon seem, if not altogether new, at least accentuated. First, from the standpoint of the citizens, there is the greater confidence people can now have in their acumens when it comes to assessing the character and ability of a candidate. This self-confidence is bolstered by what viewers see as "happening before their very eyes," even though they may lack the technical background or insider knowledge to fully comprehend what has been opened up to them.

Second, with so many relative unknowns now willing to contest a political primary, we appear to have entered a new phase of politics. Being a viable candidate has come to depend less on the support of a party organization than on the ability to sell oneself through a media campaign. There are many political action committees ready to distribute resources for such a campaign to anyone with promise. Regardless of which was the initial impetus, the relation between the weakness of the American parties and the availability of television for the waging of maverick campaigns appears to be a mutually reinforcing relation. The greater the disarray of the parties, the more important television becomes as a means for short-circuiting what used to be normal political channels. Conversely, television, by giving outsiders a far better chance than they would have had under the old system dominated by the organizations, serves to weaken the party system further.

We have all noted how a telegenic personality combined with a carefully crafted set of slogans can catapult a virtual unknown into the limelight and to victory against a well-respected establishment figure. Thus, John Kennedy, the scion of a multimillionaire family, managed in 1960 to outpoll Senator Hubert Humphrey, long a champion of the poor, in West Virginia, a state that should have been his home ground because of its long-standing poverty and considerable unemployment. Similarly, people like Senator Eugene McCarthy (in 1968), Senator George McGovern (in 1972), ex-governor Jimmy Carter (in 1976), and Senator Gary Hart (in 1984) emerged from practically nowhere to challenge seriously, though not invariably to defeat, the better-known front-runner by appealing to voters over the heads of the party leaders.

Although past research has admirably succeeded in documenting media effects in the latter phases of political campaigns, the personalization of politics is especially evident in the early presidential primaries before preferences have firmed up to a point at which people tend to perceive mostly the things that validate their prejudices. It is the media effects in these earlier phases that most need research attention.

THE NATIONALIZATION OF POLITICS

Television, because it is preeminently a national medium, has contributed to a corresponding nationalization of politics. By this we mean the tendency for what in the past would have remained political developments of purely local or regional interest to become involved in public debate at the national level. There is nothing intrinsically either good or bad about this development, the beginnings of which could be observed back in 1952. At that time, television was the medium through which those promoting the Eisenhower candidacy were able to elevate what was essentially an internal dispute within the Republican Party of Texas into an issue of national concern. The dispute was of a kind likely to surface every four years in those states where the "Grand Old Party" had no real roots, so that leadership was almost always up for grabs when the presidential nomination was at stake. By the effectiveness with which they managed to present their case on television as a "fair play" amendment, the Eisenhower supporters were able to generate considerable pressure on delegates from other states to cast their vote on a number of procedural questions, which ultimately assured the nomination of their candidate.

That was the beginning. Later, when the TV cameras caught glimpses of southern police brutally harassing civil rights workers in peaceful demonstrations, it helped make whites there conscious that segregationist practices in their own states, however firmly rooted in local custom, could no longer be considered a strictly local concern. A good deal of fury was consequently directed at northern reporters and camera crews for showing the South in what now appeared in a "bad light." On the other hand, images of police action as unfair could easily be generalized to make any kind of crowd control appear intrinsically arbitrary, in this way supplying an implicit justification for the antipolice riots that scarred many cities, mostly in the North, during the mid-1960s.

This kind of nationalization of politics is but a specific reflection of the more general disposition of television news to cover the world from a position close to the national establishment, to which it is tied in numerous ways, formal and informal. The importance of these ties for the flow of news can hardly be exaggerated. From this establishment perspective, a large part of the world goes unnoticed. Washington is always big news, because that is where a large part of the press corps is located and one can always find something worth reporting between Pennsylvania Avenue, where the White House is, and Capitol Hill, the seat of Congress. Developments more remote from the centers of power are less likely to receive the same publicity, except when there is an unusually dramatic event. Hence, television news typically focuses on highly visible antiestablishment figures. This small group of persons then become the issue makers who, in tacit collaboration with the media that rely on them for news, then define the lines along which political debate takes place.

VOTER VOLATILITY

The third long-range effect of the advent of television we shall touch on only briefly—the connection is more convoluted. There have been, since 1952, significant increases in the size of the floating vote, the number of self-styled independents, the amount of ticket splitting, as well as other indicators of the loosening of traditional party loyalties. On the surface this development only reflects the personalization of politics, already mentioned, but it is also related to the marked decline in public trust and confidence in almost every American institution. One can, as always, find a good many concrete reasons for this growth of distrust. Among those frequently mentioned have been the much-publicized duplicity over the conduct of the war in Vietnam; the broken promises over such things as civil rights, environmental protection, and other matters of direct concern to many people; the public scandals associated with Watergate and Abscam; the obvious frustration over the manifest inability of government to solve fundamental economic problems; and the very evident foreign policy failures of the past decade or so. The decline may have leveled off, but despite continued assurances by the Reagan White House, there is no firm basis for believing that it has been reversed.

The point here is that the general demoralization has gone hand in hand with the emergence of television as the dominant news medium. Although this coincidence should not by itself be taken as evidence of a causal relation, television has contributed to the spread of distrust by sharpening the disparity between what citizens can observe about the political process and their visible power to affect outcomes. That such disparity exists and is aggravated by television is undeniable, even though only a few studies so far have sought evidence on this disparity and its effects. In other words, it is a question not only of where (or in whom) people place their trust in their search for answers or as a way out of the morass, but more especially why the issue of credibility should have become so important in the age of television.

Parenthetically, Michael Robinson, who reanalyzed data from the 1968 election study by the Center for Political Studies, University of Michigan, found that those who relied upon television in following politics were more cynical than those who did not. Those who relied entirely upon TV were the most cynical of all. Later, he became more specific in pinpointing this relation between lowered confidence in the institutions of government and television viewing. He traced it to the onset of expanded network news and what he saw as its emphasis on all that is negative and conflictful. Along with some of the other think tankers associated with the conservative American Enterprise Institute, Robinson has been insisting that network news, as a genre, has changed the incumbent presidential candidate. That television news has always been harder on the incumbent than has print news is a question subject to empirical proof. A case can also be made that television has acted, on occasion, to unify the nation and to restore confidence in political institutions, as it did during the impeachment controversy.

The main point of this admittedly nostalgic essay—to end on a programmatic note—is that, as researchers, we can do more than speculate about the process through which television, in conjunction with other developments, has contributed and will continue to contribute to these long-term political changes: the personalization, the nationalization, and the volatility of politics. There are two general strategies for research that will address these issues. One is to design studies not simply for measurement but so as to observe in detail the different ways in which participants at the various political levels of politics interact in terms of the symbolic environment constructed for them by the news media. The other strategy, and the one that served as the catalyst for this chapter, and the one that has been called, for want of a better description, the inverse analytic deductive approach, is to exploit the vast array of material, both processed and unprocessed, that has been collected over the years. We need to go beyond the kind of naive inductionism that does little more than align the evidence for and against a few rather simplistic empirical generalizations. The issues relating to long-term effects can be answered only through some kind of creative synthesis. Both strategies, it seems to us, call for imaginative case studies and, preferably, for collaborative effort on a large scale.[1]

NOTE

1. We covered a conference on "long-term political effects of television" in May 1985 under the auspices of the School of Communications at the University of Washington. The goal of this conference was to stimulate and to articulate exactly the kind of collaborative research effort that we call for here. This strategy is illustrated in Lang and Lang (1983, 1984).

Chapter 20

CHANGING AND STABILIZING
POLITICAL BEHAVIOR AND BELIEFS

Sandra J. Ball-Rokeach
Milton Rokeach
Joel W. Grube

IN RECENT DECADES, social scientists have either grown weary of or become pessimistic about the chances of being able to demonstrate effects of the media on individuals' political beliefs and behavior. Such weariness has led media researchers to all but abandon the effort to demonstrate political effects on individuals. Attention has turned to either nonpolitical effects (e.g., literacy, aggression, or health behavior) or to more abstract effects of the media on political processes, such as those addressed in two of the chapters in this volume—Alexander's analysis of the media's role in the Nixon Watergate event or Gladys and Kurt Lang's analysis of the media's cumulative effects upon the conduct of political life. Thus, the effort to demonstrate that the media make a difference in the formation and change of individuals' political values, attitudes, and behavior has, at least temporarily, lost its historical prominence in American inquiry into media effects (see the introductory, Wright's, and McCormack's chapters in this volume, and Ball-Rokeach, 1986).

In this chapter we contend that abandoning the effort to demonstrate political effects on individuals is both premature and unwarranted. We share McCormack's dismay at the loss of the "vision" of those pioneering researchers (also discussed by Wright) who had

AUTHORS' NOTE: This chapter is based on material published in *Psychology Today*.

hoped to contribute to an understanding of social change by elucidating the media system's influence upon Americans' political behavior. In the final analysis, an understanding of the conditions and the processes that inhibit, facilitate, or even reverse social change requires an understanding of how large structural or macroprocesses affect individuals.

RESEARCH AIMS AND
THEORETICAL ORIENTATION

In this chapter we present theory and research findings about how television can be employed to influence some of the most controversial and perennial political and social change questions of our time; namely, racism, sexism, and environmentalism. In our research we have tried to overcome one of the major sources of discontent about media effects research of the past; namely, that the artificiality of laboratory experiments precludes the making of convincing research findings. When people are invited into laboratories to watch commercial or "research" programming; they are observed, questioned, and paid for their efforts. As a result, the natural self-selection process whereby people decide what and how to expose themselves to the media is obscured. With our methodology, we studied voluntary viewers; people who choose to watch a particular program in the privacy of their own homes, alone, or with friends, or family, with their normal level of attention; people who retain the option of turning the set off, who might be interrupted by any number of everyday incidents and who, finally, are not worried about being observed. Another source of discontent about prior research has been that the effects studied tend to be trivial because they do not last long and because they do not concern socially important behavior. In our research we examined relatively long-term and substantively important media effects on political beliefs and behavior.

We ground our research on two theories—*media system dependency theory* (Ball-Rokeach, 1985; Ball-Rokeach & DeFleur, 1976; Ball-Rokeach et al., 1984) and *belief system theory* (Ball-Rokeach et al., 1984; Rokeach, 1973, 1979). We wanted to test the idea that the way people relate to television can make a difference in whether they decide to watch a program, their level of attention and involvement while watching, and the probability of that exposure having effects on their political values, attitudes, and behavior.

The particular aspect of the way people relate to television that we examined is called *media system dependency*. Whereas media dependency refers to how we relate to all kinds of media, we examined television. Television dependency is defined as the extent to which the attainment of personal goals is contingent on the information resources of television. When the information that TV provides in the form of news or entertainment is necessary to people being able to understand, act, and play, we say that they have established dependency relations with television. We found three major types of TV dependency relations (Ball-Rokeach et al., 1984) that we call "social understanding" or understanding the world around us; "self-understanding" or understanding our minds, bodies, and emotions; and "orientation/play" or acting and interacting with others, including private or social play activities.

We also wanted to test an idea that comes from belief system theory—that people change their values, attitudes, and ultimately their behavior when they are forced to confront themselves —to assess honestly whether or not their values are consistent with their conceptions of themselves as moral and competent people. If people recognize an inconsistency between what their beliefs are and how they see themselves, we believe that they experience a sense of dissatisfaction with themselves, a condition for reassessment and change. If, on the other hand, people recognize a consistency between what their beliefs are and how they see themselves, we believe that they experience a sense of satisfaction with themselves, a condition for stabilization.

To test these ideas in as natural a setting as possible, we designed an elaborate experiment involving thousands of viewers who, one day in 1979, sat down in their own homes and tuned in a show called *The Great American Values Test*. Actually, we had something to do with who tuned in. Through a conventional ad campaign, we tried to draw into our audience people who had established dependency relations with television for social understanding and self-understanding. In this way, we were trying to exert some control over what is called the *selective exposure process*. Our reasoning was that people with strong social understanding and self-understanding TV dependencies would be likely to watch the program with high levels of attention and involvement and would thus be more likely to be affected by the program. By using statements in our *TV Guide*, newspaper, and TV ads such as "learn about you, your neighbors, and American values" and "this may be the most important test you will ever take," we succeeded in drawing into our voluntary audience a disproportionate number of people with strong social understanding and self-understanding TV dependencies.

THE TV PROGRAM
AND THE TARGET VALUES

The Great American Values Test[1] is a program that we had produced especially for this experiment. It is cohosted by Ed Asner, former star of *Lou Grant*, and Sandy Hill, the former anchor of ABC's *Good Morning America*. In the course of this 30-minute program Asner and Hill discuss values, generally at first, and then with an emphasis on three basic ones—*freedom, equality*, and a *world of beauty*. They gently prod viewers to examine their own commitment to these target values, which we as researchers wanted to influence.

The first 15-minute segment of our TV program is purely introductory in nature, designed to capture and then to hold the viewer's interest. Asner and Hill discuss what human values are and how social scientists measure them. They also talk about various findings from a national survey of American values conducted several years ago by the National Opinion Research Center, which showed differences in values between blacks and whites, men and women, young and old, rich and poor, and among citizens of different countries. Biographical inserts with residents of our "experimental city" talking about their values, file film of relevant historical news events (e.g., civil rights marches), scenes of children talking about what is most important to them, and other visual material are incorporated to keep up the pace and the interest value of the program without interfering with the communication of the messages that we wanted to get across.

These messages came in the latter part of the program and focused upon the three target values—freedom, equality, and a world of beauty. By "needling" viewers to examine their own commitment to these values, we hoped to make them satisfied or dissatisfied, depending on how well they thought they measured up to their ideal conceptions of themselves as moral citizens in a democratic society. For instance, Asner attempts to influence viewers' value priorities for freedom and equality by drawing attention to certain findings from the national survey:

> Americans feel that freedom is very important. They rank it third. But they also feel that equality is considerably less important; they rank it

12th. Since most Americans value freedom far higher than they value equality, the question is: What does this mean? Does it suggest that Americans as a whole are much more interested in their own freedom than they are in freedom for other people? Is there a contradiction in the American people between their love of freedom and their lesser love for equality?

All this was designed to arouse the TV viewers' feelings about their own consistency or lack of it. Viewers who recognized a discrepancy between their notion of an ideal moral citizen and their own value priorities for freedom and equality would experience consternation, causing them—we theorized—to reexamine their beliefs. Viewers who examined their values and found them consistent would also be aroused—satisfied in this case—reinforcing (perhaps even increasing) their commitment.

Asner and Hill then discuss the national survey results further, pointing out to viewers that equality rankings, but not freedom rankings, had a lot to do with attitudes toward racism and with differences in emotional reaction to the assassination of the Reverend Martin Luther King, Jr. They noted that the higher people rank equality, the more favorable are their attitudes toward civil rights issues and the more antiracist is their behavior. Hill then poses the following question to the viewers:

> This raises the question whether those who are against civil rights are really saying they care a great deal about their own freedom but really don't care that much about other people's freedom.

All told, the equality-freedom segments, designed to persuade viewers to increase their commitment to these two values, total six minutes. Interspersed are the proenvironmental segments, designed to increase the value people place on a world of beauty. Totaling four and a half minutes, these segments are again designed to arouse in viewers feelings of either satisfaction or dissatisfaction, depending upon their own environmental values. The following comment by Hill illustrates the "needling" process:

> Young people start out with a natural appreciation of beauty. But in the process of growing up this appreciation is somehow knocked out of them. Eleven-year-olds rank a world of beauty 7th in importance. Fifteen-year-olds rank it 14th. And by the time they reach adulthood, a world of beauty has plummeted to 17th down the list of importance, and there it remains for most adult Americans. Perhaps that explains why so many Americans are willing to live with pollution and ugliness.

A world of beauty is a socially desirable value, but, as Hill and Asner go on to discuss, it often conflicts with the desire for material comfort. They note that while environmentalists rank a world of beauty 6th, on the average, and a comfortable life 17th, people who are unconcerned with the environment rank comfort higher and a world of beauty much lower. Asner then concludes the segment with these remarks: "Also, people who prefer products that can be recycled place a higher value on a world of beauty. So do people who favor laws to ban throw-away beverage containers."

RESEARCH METHODOLOGY

The Great American Values Test was shown at 7:30 on the evening of February 27, 1979. In the Tri-Cities area of eastern Washington—our experimental site—all three commercial channels carried the program, limiting the residents' viewing options to independent and public stations or alternative access to network channels for those with cable. In Yakima, a city with a very similar population 80 miles away, the show was blacked out. Yakima was our control city. We chose for study random samples of adults in the Tri-Cities area and Yakima selected from telephone directories. Unlike subjects in the classic laboratory experiment, however, our research participants were not recruited or contacted in advance. Because they did not know they were being studied or that the program had anything to do with research, they were free to watch or ignore our TV program in the privacy of their own homes, just as they might treat any other program. By creating such a natural experiment we also created a number of research problems that we had to overcome. First, we had to find ways to maximize the probability that our preselected participants would be sufficiently interested in *The Great American Values Test* to watch it voluntarily when it aired. That is one reason we recruited the popular Ed Asner and Sandy Hill to be our cohosts. We also persuaded the station managers of the local ABC, CBS, and NBC affiliates to show our program at the same time; we conducted a typical promotional campaign in *TV Guide* and the local newspaper and aired promotions on TV and radio; and we aired the program as close to prime time as possible and gave it a title that we thought would have wide appeal.

Our next challenge was to find out whether our preselected participants did in fact watch our program and, if so, whether they watched without interruption. To do this we hired 30 trained telephone interviewers, who called the 1,699 respondents in the Tri-Cities samples immediately after the program. To keep this phone call separate from the research enterprise in the minds of respondents, interviewers identified themselves as calling from the Washington State University TV station (KWSU), which had participated in the making of the program. In the phone call, lasting about a minute and a half, they also obtained information about whether the preselected participant or anyone else in the household had watched the TV program; how much of the program had been seen and with what level of involvement and attention; whether the viewer had been interrupted and, if so, the reason for the interruption. We also collected basic demographic information (age, sex, education, ethnicity).

In addition, we had to discover whether the basic values, related social attitudes, and, most important, political behavior of our viewers had changed. All participants in both experimental and control cities received an opinion survey from Washington State University that asked for a ranking, in order of importance, of the 18 values studied in the national survey—including freedom, equality, a world of beauty, and others such as wisdom, salvation, and mature love (see Table 20.1). The survey also measured related attitudes, specifically toward racism, sexism, and environmental conservation. We also measured the extent to which each participant depended on television for information leading to self-understanding, social understanding, orientation, and play.

Half of the participants in both Tri-Cities and Yakima received this survey seven weeks before our TV program aired, and the remaining half received it four weeks afterwards. Although we could not get a record of any individual viewer's values both before and after the program, we had a sufficiently large sample of randomly selected subjects that any significant change in collective values or attitudes was most likely caused by having watched our program.

Finally, we had to determine whether our TV program had also influenced the viewers' political behavior. To find out, we mailed three solicitations for money to all of our preselected participants in the experimental and control cities 8, 10, and 13 weeks after our TV program had aired. Two of these solicitations were designed to assess the long-term behavioral effects of the freedom-equality segment; the third was designed to assess the effects of the proenvironmental segment. All three solicitations were mailed out from (and with the cooperation of) actual organizations, headquartered (and thus post-

TABLE 20.1
Rokeach Value Survey:[a] Terminal Values of Americans

Rankings of a National Sample of Americans[b]	Terminal Values (arranged alphabetically)
8	A comfortable life
17	An exciting life
7	A sense of accomplishment
2	A world at peace
15	A world of beauty
12	Equality
1	Family security
3	Freedom
5	Happiness
11	Inner harmony
14	Mature love
13	National security
16	Pleasure
10	Salvation
4	Self-respect
18	Social recognition
9	True friendship
6	Wisdom

a. Copyright, Milton Rokeach, 1982.
b. Respondents are asked to "rank these values in order of their importance to you as guiding principles in your life." The most important value is 1 and the least important is 18.

marked) in different cities in the state of Washington. One came from the Afro-American Players in Yakima, a cultural organization devoted to providing opportunities for black children to participate in music, drama, and dance. The second came from the Women's Intercollegiate Athletics Program at Washington State University in Pullman. The third was mailed out from the Committee for Initiative 61 in Seattle, an organization formed to secure passage of an antipollution measure requiring mandatory deposits on beer and soft drink bottles; it was to appear on the ballot in November 1979 elections in the state of Washington.

Thus, even though we had no direct contact with our participants before *The Great American Values Test* had aired, we were able to find out whether they watched the show, whether they watched it with or without interruption, whether their basic political values and attitudes had undergone change, and, most important, whether their political behavior—namely, donating money to political causes—had been affected.

RESEARCH FINDINGS

Our findings exceeded our wildest expectations. We estimate that our Nielsen rating" was a whopping 65%; that is, 65% of all Tri-Cities participants who watched TV at 7:30 p.m. on February 27, 1979, watched our program. Nonetheless, many of our participants did not watch television at all because they were doing other things: eating, cleaning up in the kitchen, attending to the children, working, shopping, and so on. Thus, we estimate that only about 26% actually watched, and that only about half of those watched without any interruption. Notwithstanding this low proportion of uninterrupted viewers (about one in eight), our data on the responses to the three solicitations mailed two to three months after the program aired usually showed significant differences between our experimental sample and controls. There were significantly more responses, in the form of donations from Tri-Cities residents. And there were also signficantly fewer negative responses. Some people could not resist the temptation to mail back the return envelope with such negative remarks as: "Teach the blacks to work. If that doesn't work, shoot them"; "I am strictly opposed to this program. I think God made women for home and family and I am very much against women's lib"; and "I would like to help with the expenses of getting Initiative 61 to fail by making a contribution against it." Significantly fewer of such negative responses came from the Tri-Cities area. We refer to this as the "Asner effect." Both Asner and Hill volunteered to help in this research, and Asner told us he had decided to participate not so much because he expected positive changes but because he hoped the show "would at least shut up the bigots." To a significant extent, Asner was right in that our results suggest that the program led to significantly fewer "bigoted" responses in the experimental city than in the control city.

Even more dramatic were the results obtained when we compared the uninterrupted viewers with interrupted viewers and with nonviewers. The interrupted viewers were those who intended to watch our program but were interrupted by circumstances beyond their control, such as the telephone ringing, a fight between the children, or a knock at the door. They offer an important comparison because although they were presumably as highly motivated as the uninterrupted viewers to tune in, they did not receive full exposure to the program and were not exposed to the "needling" messages presented in the last half of the program. Interestingly, we discovered that uninterrupted and interrupted viewers did not differ from the nonviewers in experimental and control cities in basic political values or in attitudes toward racism, sexism, and the environment before the TV show had aired. Interrupted viewers and, of course, nonviewers exhibited no before-to-after changes in their political values and attitudes. By contrast, those who watched the entire show did change significantly. Before the show their political behavior, values, and social attitudes were like the others, but weeks and months later they were more egalitarian and more proenvironmental.

Surely the most impressive of our findings have to do with the money collected. As a group, viewers who watched *The Great American Values Test* without interruption contributed on the average about four to six times as much money as did the nonviewers in both the Tri-Cities and in Yakima, and about nine times as much as did the interrupted viewers. Moreover, the uninterrupted viewers contributed more money on the average to each of the three solicitations—proenvironment, antiracism, and antisexism—than did any of the remaining three groups. Furthermore, the average per capita contribution was generally greater.

Beyond these behavioral differences, our findings show that the three values targeted in our TV program also underwent the expected changes. Uninterrupted viewers significantly increased their rankings of two target values, freedom and equality, and less dramatically increased their ranking of the third, a world of beauty. In contrast, the remaining three groups showed not a single significant change. The three social attitudes that are related to these three basic values were also affected. Two of these three attitudes—attitude toward the environment and attitude toward blacks—changed significantly, with viewers (and only viewers) becoming more proenvironment and more antiracist. Considering that the Tri-Cities is home to Washington's Hanford nuclear power plant and that its people, for understandable economic reasons, have been traditionally pronuclear and resistant to environmental activism, the shift toward a proenvironmental position is particularly interesting. Viewers' attitudes toward women also became more favorable, although the change was not so striking.

Finally, participants' dependency on TV also played an important role. Those who were highly dependent on TV for understanding themselves and society were more likely to watch in the first place. And when they watched, they watched with very high levels of attention and involvement of their mind and their feelings. As expected, these high TV dependency viewers were more affected by the program; they contributed more money, rearranged their fundamental values more noticeably and became more antiracist, antisexist, and proenvironmental in their attitudes than did those who were less dependent on TV for social understanding and self-understanding.

CONCLUSIONS

Although alternative interpretations of such findings are always possible, we believe that the most plausible explanation is that *The Great American Values Test* caused the changes we see. We think it led some of the viewers to become dissatisfied with their values, thus prompting a change in values and related attitudes and behavior in a direction that would make them feel better about themselves. Alternatively, our program could have made those who already valued freedom, equality, and beauty highly feel good about themselves, thus making these values more salient and more likely to be acted upon when solicitations came from organizations specializing in implementing these values. Findings from a separate, smaller study indicate that the TV program did indeed arouse the predicted feelings of dissatisfaction and satisfaction that we regard as the mechanism of the belief and the behavior effects that we observed in the larger study.

The findings and conclusions stemming from our work with *The Great American Values Test* force us to a conclusion that many will consider to be very strong: A single 30-minute exposure to TV can significantly alter basic beliefs, related attitudes, and behavior of large numbers of people for at least several months. For us this seems to have important implications—scientific, political, and ethical—all of which are discussed at length in Ball-Rokeach et al. (1984). For the purposes of this volume, however, the clearest implications are (1) that researchers can demonstrate relatively long-term media effects on socially important political beliefs and behavior and do so in natural research settings that increase confidence in the validity of the findings; (2) the combination of media system dependency theory and belief system theory may provide a generally useful way to articulate and to study the effects process from initial exposure decisions to effects on real behavior; and (3) even a 30-minute TV program may have powerful political effects on individuals, if its content is designed and guided by relevant theory.

NOTES

1. Inquiries about how to obtain this program should be sent to Director, Department of Radio and Television Services, Washington State University, Pullman, WA 99164.

2. Distributed by Halgren Tests, N.E. 1145 Clifford, Pullman, WA 99163.

PART V

MEDIA CONTENT

THE OFFERINGS IN THIS SECTION are just a small sample of what could be included under the title "Media Content." We chose these chapters not because they represent research on all of America's most popular media, not because they represent necessarily main stream ideas on what is seen on the screen, printed in our newspapers and magazines, or heard on the air. Rather, they represent primarily new work and new ideas.

Eleanor Singer and Phyllis Endreny show how journalists interpret and report social science findings as "news." Addressing the question of what is news and why some information is reported in the press and why some is not, they show the control journalists (and their editors) have over what is made known and how much is known. This chapter shows how much power rests in the "system" rather than in the individual reporters. They find, for example, that news values rather than the values of the social science community clearly determine the content of social science stories. One problem that Singer and Endreny pose is that the lay public's perceptions of social science and scientists is largely based upon what is learned from the media. Thus, this content analysis raises clear policy questions for both the social science community and the media system, questions that concern whether the "picture" of social science formed in the public's mind is a valid and desirable one.

In her chapter, Andrea Press directs our attention to how the portrayal and image of women in the movies have changed since the end of World War II. She demonstrates a connection between changes in movie content and contemporaneous changes in the social and political climate. Press concludes that such changes may be regressive and have political ramifications for women who seek equal rights with men. She remains speculative but points to a need to place research on movie content and back as a high priority on our research agenda. The interaction between film and social change has resumed some of its earlier import because movies have, through cable and video recorders, regained a larger and more diverse home and theater audience than they had even a decade ago.

Ann Swidler, Melissa Rapp, and Yasemin Soysal suggest that the "format" of television content is as important to research as is the content itself. Their chapter illustrates how aesthetics and control go hand in hand. Among the many questions that could be addressed, none is more intriguing than theirs: Why is romance neglected on television? That question is surprising because so many researchers believe that all of prime-time television is simply about either romance or violence. Reading this chapter, we believe that people will gain new insights into the organizational controls and limits on creativity that are reflected in the formats, as well as the choice of actual stories, portrayals, and images.

The final chapter in this section by Philip Lamy and Jack Levin is a strong example of how content analysis can serve as an ideal tool to study cultural change and diversity. The authors and their colleagues have conducted several content analyses that examine the values communicated in the publications that serve punks, hippies, and other alternative youth cultures. In this chapter they compare punk values to those found in *Reader's Digest,* and they confirm earlier studies showing that the values of punk and hippie publications are expressed in sharp contrast to the dominance of instrumental values in middle-class publications. Their research illustrates the importance of a program of research in which each new research effort serves in some way to replicate the findings of earlier studies.

Chapter 21

THE REPORTING OF SOCIAL SCIENCE RESEARCH IN THE MASS MEDIA

Eleanor Singer
Phyllis Endreny

SINCE 1980 we, together with Carol Weiss, have been engaged in a study of the reporting of social science. The study looked at social science reporting in ten news media: *The New York Times, Washington Post, Wall Street Journal, The Boston Globe, Newsweek, U.S. News and World Report,* and the three network evening newscasts. The study consisted of two major components: a content analysis of the media in 1982 and a corresponding period in 1970, and interviews with reporters, social scientists, and editors on selected social science stories.[1] In this chapter, we examine the transformation of social science research that takes place when it is reported in the mass media and speculate about some consequences of this transformation.

Robert Darnton's richly evocative article, "Writing News and Telling Stories" (1975), develops the thesis that although "the context of work shapes the content of news . . . stories also take form under the

AUTHORS' NOTE: This chapter is based on a larger study, with Carol Weiss of Harvard University, of the reporting of social science in the mass media. The support of the Russell Sage Foundation is gratefully acknowledged. We would like to express our appreciation to our research assistants, Kathleen Allen, Kathy Cole, Anna DiLellio, Diane Elebe, Doris Newman, Anastasios Kalomiris, and Thuy Tranthi, and to Marc Glassman for statistical consultation and data processing. An earlier version of this chapter was delivered at the American Sociological Association meetings in San Antonio, Texas, in August 1984. Portions are reprinted, with permission, from Chapter 3 of *Social Science in the Media,* by Weiss and Singer with Endreny (in press).

influence of inherited techniques of storytelling.'' He concludes, ''as the reporter passes through his formative phases he familiarizes himself with news, both as a commodity that is manufactured in the newsroom and as a way of seeing the world that somehow reached *The New York Times* from Mother Goose.'' Other analysts of why news is the way it is have sought to explain it by reference to a cultural action perspective that points out that a news story is, in part, a *story*—that is, a distinct and rather stereotyped form, governed by literary conventions as well as organizational necessities.

Both of these perspectives argue that news is, in part, a contrivance that, regardless of substance, must be given the form of ''a good story'' and ''a good read.'' The essential aim of science, on the other hand, is the production of new knowledge and its subsequent sharing with the community of one's peers. The details that the scientist regards as essential to this communication may well be deemed inessential by the journalist and perhaps detrimental to the obligation to write a good story. Elsewhere we consider in some detail the mechanisms by which social science research finds its way into the mass media (Weiss, Singer, with Endreny, in press). Here we will say only that media needs and interests, rather than those of the social scientist, are crucial and that a process of negotiation between reporters and their scientist sources, and of competition and negotiation between editors and reporters, is involved (Epstein, 1973; Gans, 1979; Sigal, 1973; Tuchman, 1978).

To the extent that reporters of science are becoming better educated and more specialized, they may show greater appreciation for the values of science, but as Dunwoody and Stocking (in press) have aptly noted, the science reporter's abstract respect for such values may be sorely tested under the real-world pressures of the work place. Moreover, anecdotes (Darnton, 1975) as well as systematic study (Johnson, 1963) indicate that even when science reporters' values display considerable congruence with the values of the domain of science that is their beat, editors reveal primary concern with the storytelling, readability dimensions of the news account. And although the importance of the topic may also count, it is importance in a general sense, and not importance within some social science discipline. Writing in the *Newsletter* of the National Association of Science Writers, Joel Shurkin (1979), then a science writer for *The Philadelphia Inquirer,* made a similar point when he wrote about the recently concluded American Association for the Advancement of Science (AAAS) meetings:

> It is undeniably true that the stories filed were second-rate in terms of cosmic importance. . . . Most of our customers and editors have forgotten that we have done the climate story every year for the last four years. They still like it.

Although reporters and editors may search for functional equivalents, there is nothing like "peer review" to assure the quality of the research being reported, unless the research is drawn from a scholarly journal.[2] Only rarely does a dimension of judgment often used by referees for scholarly journals—namely, methodological soundness—seem to be an explicit journalistic criterion.[3] Although all editors and reporters interviewed expressed concern about the validity of the social science research they were reporting, they appear not to link validity with the methods used by the researcher. Instead, one common way of assessing validity[4] is to talk to other researchers in the field. Concluding his examination of what he calls "the hoofprints of a distinct case of herd journalism," for example, Petit (1979) writes that the public relations man who triggered the flurry of reporting on a mutant depressive gene "risked stampeding a story prematurely into print *when it cried out for solicitation of opinions from researchers other than the author*" (emphasis added).

In the remainder of this chapter we do three things. First, we examine some characteristics of the social science research reported in the media, both "focus" stories in which some aspect of social science is the subject of the story and "ancillary" stories in which social science is brought in as subsidiary to the main topic. Second, we contrast in some detail the presentation of social science research in the media with the norms for its presentation in scholarly journals. The implicit question addressed by the comparison is this: If the public had access only, or primarily, to the mass media for information about current social science research, what conception would they be likely to form? How does social science in the media differ from social science as portrayed in the scholarly literature, a portrait presumably closer to the "real thing"? Finally, we look at some instance of the reporting of social science that we consider problematic, and ask what the consequences of such reporting are likely to be for the public and for social science as an institution. The focus of this chapter is obviously selective. We have emphasized some of what we consider to be problematic in the coverage of social science research instead of highlighting its positive aspects or attempting a more balanced view. Similar to other social science research, it thus offers a partial perspective and should be understood as such.

SOME CHARACTERISTICS OF
SOCIAL SCIENCE RESEARCH
REPORTED IN THE MEDIA

In 1982, the modal newspaper story focused on social science research was about some aspect of economics, followed closely by stories about research on politics and government; these figures parallel those for social science stories as a whole (see Table 21.1).[5] On the other hand, both in the newsmagazines and on television, the modal story focused on social science research and was about some aspect of health, followed by stories about social control, politics, and government. Newsmagazines and television newscasts in 1982 were thus much more likely than newspapers to feature social science research in the "back of the book" rather than in the hard news sections (economics having become hard news).[6]

In 1982, most social science identified as research in the media was based on survey research,[7] much of it consisting of privately sponsored opinion polls. In this respect, little had changed since 1970. Presser's (1985) investigation of the frequency with which articles based on survey data have appeared in the leading journals of four disciplines—sociology, political science, economics, and social psychology—allows us to compare the use of survey research in the mass media with its use in scholarly journals. In 1979-1980, 55.8% of the articles in sociology, 35% of those in political science, 28.7% of those in economics, and 10.1% of those in social psychology were based on survey research. The proportions of articles based on survey data increased notably in all fields except social psychology between 1949-1950 and 1979-1980. But substantial though the scholarly use made of survey research is, its reporting by the mass media is greater still, accounting in 1982 for 81.8% of all focus stories for which some method was identified.

Although half of all focus studies reported in newspapers or magazines in 1982 originated either with the government or with some other research organization, about 17% originated at a university. On TV, government accounted for 36.4% of all focus studies reported and universities for another 13.6%; media-initiated and executed studies accounted for 22.7% of all focus social science studies reported on TV and for 28.6% of all ancillary studies. Between 1970 and 1982, media-initiated and executed studies increased in frequency in all media. Overwhelmingly, these studies were opinion surveys or polls.

TABLE 21.1

1982 Study[a] Topic, by Type of Media and Whether
Story Is Focused or Ancillary (in percentages)

Study Topic	Focus			Ancillary		
	News-papers	News-Magazines	TV	News-papers	News-Magazines	TV
U.S. economy	27.1	16.7	4.5	23.0	33.3	21.4
Foreign economics	4.4	0.0	—	2.9	1.9	—
Government and politics	23.0	12.5	22.7	19.3	22.2	0.0
International affairs	1.9	0.0	0.0	13.0	13.0	50.0
Integration	10.0	12.5	18.2	13.8	5.6	7.1
Social control	6.4	8.3	4.5	5.6	5.6	14.3
Health	16.3	29.2	45.5	14.0	1.9	7.1
Demographics	4.2	12.5	—	3.2	7.4	—
Relationships and lifestyles	6.4	8.3	4.5	5.0	9.3	0.0
Miscellaneous	0.3	—	—	0.3	—	—
(N)	(361)	(24)	(22)	(378)	(54)	(14)

a. Up to three studies were coded for each story; 79.4% of the stories mentioned only one study, and the analysis in this chapter is based only on the first study coded. In 374 of the 407 focus stories, the study was the main focus of the article.

SOCIAL SCIENCE RESEARCH
FOR TWO AUDIENCES

By far the most significant difference between social science research as written for the general public and for other social scientists has to do with the way research findings are presented. In newspapers, newsmagazines, and on television, findings resulting from one piece of research, done in a particular time and place, with a distinct sample and a specified research instrument, are often presented as if they were universal truths, holding for all people everywhere. As Rick Flaste, science editor of *The New York Times,* put it at a Hastings Center conference, "We wouldn't take caveats very seriously; we don't especially like caveats." The result is a news item such as the following:

> Racial patterns in health care show that blacks and other minorities often need care more than whites, but generally get less and of a lower quality, a National Academy of Science report said. The study cited "striking" differences in dental and nursing home care, and cited strong evidence of racial bias. (*Wall Street Journal,* February 9, 1982, p. 1)

In what follows, we identify several media practices that contribute to this image of social science and contrast them with the norms governing the reporting of social science research in scholarly journals. Unfortunately, we do not know how frequently such norms are obeyed in practice. But Presser's study (1985) of the reporting of survey research in the leading journals of four social science disciplines is instructive in this regard.

IDENTIFICATION OF A PUBLISHED SOURCE

When an article in a scholarly journal presents findings from prior research, the source of those findings is expected to be clearly indicated, either in a footnote or in a list of references. That these findings may not be accurately reported (Garfield, 1977-1978) may be determined by the reader going back to the original source. In media reports of research, on the other hand, a published source for research results is indicated only about 40% of the time in focus stories and fewer than 20% of the time in ancillary stories.

We are not the first to have noted this phenomenon. Garfield (1977-1978), for example, writes,

> Most newspapers and magazines—even those that purport to cover scientific and technical news—are almost completely void of references. This omission not only throws doubt on the reporter's authority and credibility, but can also be extremely frustrating to those readers with a real interest in the subject. It seems like links to the primary literature sometimes are deliberately eliminated to add to the mystique of the reporter's sources. Some newspapers and magazines—notably *The New York Times* and *Science News*—usually supply at least one reference in text for major articles. It usually consists of a statement such as "in the latest issue of the *New England Journal of Medicine.*" But this amounts to little more than a token effort. (pp. 217-218)

Dunwoody (1984) has made a related point. Noting that the media constitute primary sources of scientific and technical information for nonscientists, she urges the media to provide the kind of information—namely, references—that will enable the reader to pick up "where the news stories leave off."

We also asked whether or not it was possible to locate the published source of the research from the information given in the news story. There were no significant differences in this respect among media, between focus and ancillary stories, or over time. In about 80% of the cases in which a source was mentioned, the information given in the news story was adequate for locating it, although it took precisely the form Garfield has described.

IDENTIFICATION OF THE RESEARCHER

Citation of scientists responsible for prior relevant research is, of course, prescribed behavior when writing for a scholarly journal (e.g., Garfield, 1977-1978; Kaplan, 1965). But identification of the scientists who carried out the research being reported is far from accepted practice in the media (Borman, 1978). In 77.5% of the studies coded it was impossible to tell how many people had been responsible for carrying out the research, although one or more social scientists may have been named in connection with the project. "'Black Americans are four times more likely than whites to suffer severe kidney disease.' a study from Alabama said today," announced a UPI dispatch in the *Washington Post* of May 27, 1982, identifying the investigators only as "researchers at the University of Alabama at Birmingham and the Birmingham Veterans Administration Medical Center." Together with the other tendencies described, the failure to identify the research findings as resulting from the efforts of a particular social scientist contributes to their image as disembodied facts—facts the authenticity of which is legitimated by reference to the institution under whose auspices the study was done. For example, consider this item, reprinted in its entirety from the *Wall Street Journal* of March 23, 1982:

> Unemployed workers' children are more likely to get ill and for longer periods than the offspring of those still working, a University of North Carolina study suggests. The youngsters seem most vulnerable at the time of a layoff. Afterwards, the risk drops. (p. 1)

DISCUSSION OF METHODS USED

Very few social science stories in the media discuss the methods used. Only 17.8% of the studies we analyzed in 1982 made any detailed mention of the methods used,[8] and only 30 stories contained any evaluation of those methods. Newspapers were more likely to provide such details than either of the other media, but even among those newspapers stories we have classified as "focus" social science, only 30.7% gave any detail about methods in 1982. Magazines and television were much less likely to do so, and these media were even less likely to provide details about research methods in ancillary than in focus stories.

In a study of how polls were reported on the NBC and CBS TV evening newscasts and by *The New York Times,* Paletz et al. (1980, p. 505) reported that during the mid-1970s, 67% of the articles in the *Times* drawing on survey data reported sample size and 43% gave the dates of the survey; the figures for the NBC and CBS evening news programs were lower. But aside from sample size and survey dates, methodological information was minimal. In 95% of the TV stories and 70% of those in the *Times,* for example, none of the polling questions was quoted in its entirety.

As it turns out, however, the media differ less in this respect from scholarly journals than might have been supposed. In a recent study of the reporting of surveys in social science journals, Presser (1985) found that fewer than half of the articles based on survey data reported on each of the following: sampling method, response rate, wording of any question, year of the survey, or interviewer characteristics. "These reporting levels," writes Presser, "are not markedly better than those of the much criticized mass media, despite the considerably greater space available in journals" (quoted in Turner & Martin, 1985, p. 106).

Although scholarly journals are apparently not much better than the mass media in providing details about methods, at least so far as survey research is concerned, it is difficult to conceive of an article in a scholarly journal that did not at least name the method used. Nevertheless, in 1982, between 21.4% and 54.5% of social science stories (depending on the medium and whether the story was focus or ancillary) did not even name the research method used in the study. News stories tell us that a "report" predicts a high failure rate for small businesses (*Washington Post,* April 13, 1982, p. C7), or that a "study" predicts unemployment will stay high for years (*Washington Post,* May 5, 1982, p. D10), but fail to tell us what methods were used in arriving at these predictions and therefore give readers no chance to evaluate how plausible they are. Once again, there has been little change in this regard since 1970.

PLACING RESEARCH FINDINGS IN CONTEXT

In scholarly journal articles, it is customary to provide an indication of whether one's findings are in accord with, or depart from, the findings of related research (Kaplan, 1965; Wilson, 1952). Although we do not know how regularly this norm is obeyed in practice, we do know that the proportion of media stories that provide such a context is very small. In 1982, between 4.2% and 18.2% of focus stories, depending on the medium, provided discrepant information, and between 0% and 4.5% of ancillary stories did so; the figures were somewhat higher for supporting information.

Among the relatively few news stories that provided such a context during our monitoring period, and did so superbly, was one by Harold M. Schmeck, Jr. in *The New York Times* of June 18, 1982 on a four-year study demonstrating a reduced risk of ovarian cancer among women who used birth control pills. Schmeck quotes the researchers as saying, "Our figures agree with those earlier studies that estimated a reduction of 40 percent to 50 percent in the risk of ovarian cancer among oral contraceptive users." Schmeck then continued,

> However, a study done by epidemiologists of the New York State Health Department and reported earlier this week at a meeting in Cincinnati did not show a protection effect of oral contraceptives against ovarian cancer, according to Dr. Solley, who said he had no explanation for the discrepancy. (p. B10)

So far we have identified five media practices that alone or, especially, in combination, contribute to what we have referred to as the image of a disembodied, timelessly true social science, "without caveats." The number of news stories lacking one or more of the qualifications that would help to put the research in context is not trivial. Just about half of the newspaper and newsmagazine stories focused on a social science study in 1982 were lacking all, or all but one, of the elements that help put social science in perspective: identification of the researchers, naming of the method used, mention of supporting and discrepant information, and indication of a published source.[9] Note that these are minimal requirements: for example, the method used must only be named, not discussed in any detail.

However, it would be misleading to imply that all media reports of social science research contribute to this impression. On the contrary, there are reports of research that, in the space of a few column inches, clearly convey complex and subtle information that many social scientists would be at a loss to present in several pages. For example, an Associated Press (AP) story run in the *Times* of October 12, 1980 under the headline "Study Shows London Executions May Have Affected Murder Rate," manages, in 10¾ column inches, to tell readers the conclusion of the study (highly publicized executions of convicted killers in London from 1858-1921 deterred other murders, but for no longer than two weeks), the name and institutional affiliation of the researcher (David Phillips of the University of California at San Diego), a published source (the current issue of the *American Journal of Sociology*), the possible limitations of the findings ("Dr. David

Phillips ... cautioned that the London findings might not necessarily apply to contemporary America"), the methods used (tracing statistics through local coroners' offices to develop weekly murder rates, rather than the monthly or yearly figures used by other researchers, and restricting the study to executions that received extensive newspaper coverage), apparently discrepant research done by others, and an explanation for the discrepancy, as well as an interpretation of the significance of the findings ("Dr. Phillips noted that political conservatives believed a deterrent effect existed while liberals generally did not. He called both sides' views accurate").

Although we could give other examples of this kind of reporting, it is relatively rare. We estimate that no more than 7% of studies in 1982 focus social science stories included all five of the elements mentioned above. A disproportionate number of these, however, are what might be called "core" social science stories—that is, dealing with concerns central to social science as a discipline (e.g., divorce, delinquency, suicide, TV and crime, or race differences in educational achievement), rather than evaluations of social programs, polls of public opinion, and the like.[10] In 1982, we identified 105 *Times* stories that were classified as featuring a social science study. Of these, at most 11 could be construed as "core."

When we compared these 11 stories with all focus social science studies reported in our sample of newspaper stories in 1982, we found sizable differences as far as the inclusion of key elements was concerned. For the most part, these differences were in the direction of much greater specificity for the "core" stories (which were also considerably longer than the average 1982 *Times* focus story): the number of investigators was much more likely to be indicated (82% vs. 23%) and at least one of them was almost always named; published sources were much more likely to be referred to (73% vs. 42%); an interpretation of the findings was much more often offered (73% vs. 39%); and discrepant as well as supporting findings from other research were more likely to be included (27% vs. 9% and 46% vs. 15%, respectively). The "core" studies were also much more likely to be done under university auspices then the general run of studies (64% vs. 17%). Only with respect to methods was there little difference: 27% of core studies, compared with 31% of all studies, described the method in any detail, and the number of stories in which no information about methods was provided at all was actually greater for the "core" studies than for the average story about social science research (55% vs. 34%).

NEWS VALUES AND SCIENCE VALUES

Most of the scientists who were interviewed about the reporting of their research in the media expressed satisfaction with its accuracy, and that has generally been found in other studies as well (Dunwoody & Scott, 1982; Ryan, 1979; Tankard & Ryan, 1974).[11] In this section, however, we talk about instances of the reporting of social science that, for one reason or another, we consider problematic. We discuss such reporting under two headings: call-ins, write-ins, and "electronic polls"; and disagreement among social scientists or social science studies.

CALL-INS, WRITE-INS, AND "ELECTRONIC POLLS"

An unknown proportion of "studies" reported in the popular media consists of activities that most social scientists would agree do not constitute "research" at all: "surveys" of a magazine's readers based on responses by self-selected subscribers, phone-ins to 900 (or 800) numbers sponsored by television networks, or interviews with convenience samples. Even though the number of respondents to such surveys can sometimes reach several hundred thousand, the method of phone-ins or write-ins violates all the rules of sampling on which legitimate surveys are based.

Although the two procedures may, by accident, yield the same or similar results, there is no way of knowing when that will happen. For example, after the speech in which a U.S. ambassador all but urged the removal of the UN from the United States, ABC conducted both a 900-number phone-in and a telephone survey conducted in accord with established sampling and interviewing procedures. Whereas 67% in the phone-in (with more than 100,000 telephone calls) said the UN should leave the United States, 66% in the poll said the UN should stay (rising to 72% when the "don't know's" were eliminated). "We had the spectacle of two ABC polls asking essentially the same question on the same day showing more than diametrically opposed results," Roper (1983) pointed out,

> What is the effect of this on the public? ... And what sociologically useful purpose does ABC perform by putting two so-called polls on the air which show diametrically opposite results? Journalists correctly make the point that the public has a right to know. By providing diametrically opposite polling results, is ABC fulfilling the right to

know? Or is ABC convincing people that you can prove anything you want with a poll?

In our count of social science content in the media, such instances of pseudo-social science as instant polls, write-ins, and the like have been included. We have done this both because we assume that is how they are perceived by the general public and also because it is often impossible, given the paucity of information about methods, to know when a news story reports the results of a legitimate survey and when it represents the write-up of a piece of pseudo-research.

Call-ins often make dramatic copy. But what is interesting to readers and viewers is not necessarily either good science, in the sense that the methods can withstand scrutiny, or important science, in the sense that it makes a significant contribution to knowledge about social life. For example, Dunwoody (1983), who analyzed press coverage of the 1977 and 1979 AAAS meetings, suggested two reasons why science reporters, who profess to dislike social research and find it difficult to evaluate, nevertheless give it good play. One is that many social science stories have obvious reader relevance. The second is that social science is easier to understand than other scientific research, and reporters in a hurry to meet a deadline may be drawn to papers that they can easily comprehend. But neither of those criteria is necessarily designed to assure the quality of scientific importance of the social science reported.

"WHEN THE MASTERS ALL FALL OUT. ..."

Most social scientists probably agree that phone-ins do not constitute legitimate social science research, and at the other end of the scale, there are undoubtedly studies that all (or most) social scientists would agree had been competently done and resulted in valid information. In between lie those studies—probably the most numerous category—that are subject to divergent evaluations by social scientists themselves and that find their way into the popular press either through prior publication in a scholarly journal or through press releases issued at professional meetings or by the researcher's institution, or perhaps through some of the specialized journals devoted to the dissemination of science information (*Psychology Today, Human Behavior, Science News, Science 85,* and the like).

Although publication in a refereed journal should afford some protection against egregious error, studies of the journal review process have documented the existence of substantial disagreements among reviewers in some fields (Zuckerman & Merton, 1971, n. 3). Cole et al. (1981), in a study of peer review at the National Science Foundation, have documented similar disagreements in the evaluation of proposals in the physical as well as the social sciences. Given these disagreements among experts, it is inevitable that research finding its way into the popular press will be at best contingent and partial and, at worst, flawed in at least some respects. For the same reasons, two studies may report conflicting findings (as two surveys of public opinion not infrequently do), or come to different conclusions on the basis of the same findings. How the media deal with such inevitable instances of conflict is crucial, we believe, for the public's image of social science.

Shortly before we began this study, sociologist James S. Coleman was in the news because of a recently completed story for the National Center for Education Statistics that compared the performance of public and private school pupils. At first Coleman emphasized the fact that students in private and parochial schools learned more than those in public schools. Subsequently, after these findings aroused considerable controversy in the press, he explained that it was the characteristics of the schools, and not their auspices, which made the difference. "Good public schools do just as well as those in the private sector," he was quoted in *The New York Times* of April 26, 1981, as saying,

> It is not insignificant that these characteristics are more often found in the private sector, but if I were writing the report again I would focus more on how public policy can help schools in both sectors to be more effective.

During the 1982 period when we were monitoring social science coverage in the media, the country was treated to the spectacle of a parade of eminent psychiatrists testifying for both the prosecution and the defense in the widely publicized trial of John Hinckley for the attempted assassination of President Reagan. On December 11, 1983, the *Times* began a story on the Shoreham nuclear plant as follows:

> The Long Island Lighting Company generated a bevy of experts last week—sociologists, pollsters, attorneys—to argue that the utility could safely evacuate people living near its Shoreham nuclear reactor.... A sociologist testifying on Lilco's behalf said emergency workers would fulfill their responsibilities in the event of a serious reactor accident. Sociologists consulting for Suffock maintained, however, that workers would experience "role conflict" and foresake their duties to take care of their own families first.

But disagreements among social scientists are not confined to policy research. Shortly after we had stopped monitoring media coverage of the social sciences came the publication of Derek Freeman's book, *Margaret Mead and Samoa* (1983), which challenged not only Mead's interpretations but also, and more seriously, her objectivity and the accuracy of her observations. The story broke on the front page of *The New York Times* of January 31, 1983, and for several weeks received prominent attention in the daily press, the news weeklies, and on television.

Even when the personalities and policies are less prominent, the clash of expert opinion is news. In *The New York Times* of April 30, 1982 (p. A30), Nicholas Wade scathingly commented on a story in the May 1982 issue of *Psychology Today,* in which "'eleven of the best minds in the field' describe what each considers to be 'the most significant work in psychology over the last decade and a half.'" Under the headline, "Smart Apes or Dumb?" Wade rhetorically asks, "Can psychology be taken seriously as a science if even its leading practitioners cannot agree on its recent advances?" Although a more dispassionate reading of the *Psychology Today* article tells a somewhat different story, Wade had deliberately chosen to emphasize areas of disagreement among social scientists.

We do not want to be misunderstood as blaming the press for bad reporting when it features disagreements among social scientists. Rather, we see in the combination of several ingredients—the partial knowledge achieved by the social sciences, the often conflicting perspectives social scientists bring to their work, the apparently commonsensical nature of much social science content, the characteristics of social science reporting described earlier in this chapter, and the news value of conflict and dissent—the potential for increasing public skepticism about the validity and utility of the social sciences:

> When the masters all fall out,
> What can the student do but doubt?

The Special Case of the Polls

Our monitoring of the reporting of social science "poll" stories, explicitly identified as such, made up 35.9% of the 521 stories that contained any mention of a social science study in 1982 and identified the research method used; surveys or polls of public opinion, as already noted, together made up 81.8%.[12] Turner and Martin (1985) estimated that over 200 million copies of newspapers containing poll results reached the American public in a one-month period (July 1 to July 30) in 1980. According to Gollin (personal communication), representatives of over 100 newspapers indicated, at a meeting of the Newspaper Research Council in 1982, that they conduct their own polls. In presenting the results of their own polls, the media tend to be meticulous in reporting sample size and sampling error, and not much else. But in the process of stressing sampling error, to quote Roper (1983) again:

> They have not warned the reader or viewer of error as they have intended. Instead, they have implied an unwarranted degree of accuracy. They have, in effect, said "This finding is within three percentage points of what the entire American public thinks on this subject"—when in fact a differently worded question might, and often does, produce a result that is 25 to 30 points different from the reported result.

> The media—particularly the broadcast media—almost never tell their readers or listeners what the question they asked was. They merely come up with their conclusion and the percentage results from an unknown question. Thus, the listener or reader has no way of evaluating the result.

Of course, question wording is not the only factor other than sampling design that may affect the results of a public opinion poll. If one poll offers three choices for an office and another offers five, percentages for any single candidate are bound to differ. If one poll includes "leaners" and another only decided voters, the percentages are not comparable. If a candidate is identified as an independent in one poll but not another, that fact will affect response.

Thus, the polls—the most ubiquitous example of social science in the media—illustrate dramatically some of the problems with social science reporting identified in the preceding section. In 1967, Philip Meyer, then a Nieman fellow at Harvard and a member of the Washington Bureau of Knight Newspapers and now William Rand Kenan, Jr. Professor in the School of Journalism at the University of North Carolina, published an article titled "Social Science—A New Beat?" In it he pointed to the transformation of social science from an armchair to an empirical science with "immediate practical application," and he urged journalists to develop the critical sophistication needed to separate the wheat from the chaff. "Social science," he said,

> has not yet shaken down to the point where it is easy to identify the fringe operators. There is no equivalent of a local medical society to put the finger on a quack pollster.

"Many newspapers," he went on to point out,

> blandly report the outcomes of polls as if all polls were alike. ... Earlier
> this year, Harris and Gallup produced opposite results on the relative
> popularity of Richard Nixon and George Romney among Republican
> voters. Papers which subscribed to both polls shrugged their editorial
> shoulders and ran the conflicting reports side by side without comment,
> in the time-honored tradition of "letting the reader decide." If the
> highly educated staff of a metropolitan newspaper cannot interpret such
> a discrepancy, how can the poor reader be expected to do it?

There are some indications that this situation is beginning to
change, albeit slowly. During the entire sampling period of 1982, less
than a handful of methodological social science stories appeared
anywhere in the media. But on August 15, 1984, the *Times* ran a front-
page story by Robert Reinhold that examined at length the methodological variations that might have accounted for the discrepant
presidential poll results then being reported. On the following day, the
Wall Street Journal featured, on page 2, a similar analysis by political
scientist Carl Everett Ladd, executive director of the Roper Center for
Public Opinion Research. And in reporting the results of the *Times*-
CBS polls, the *Times* now regularly includes a boxed statement indicating that sampling error is only one part of total survey error.

SOME IMPLICATIONS OF THE FINDINGS

In 1981, there appeared an article in the *Journal of the Market
Research Society* (23; pp. 209-219) titled "Analyzing Data: or Telling
Stories?" In a way, that is an apt description for the disparate functions of the social scientist and the journalist. The scientist aims to get
closer to the truth and to tell others about it. The journalist aims to tell
an interesting story—a true one, it is hoped. These aims are not an-
tithetical, but they differ in the priorities they assign to the elements
involved.

These differences in priorities have consequences both for the kind
of social research that gets reported in the mass media and for the way
it is reported. *General* criteria of newsworthiness, not those specific to
the realm of social science, govern *what* social science is reported
in the media. And journalistic tradition, rather than social science
norms, governs *how* such research is reported. Those qualifications so
dear to the heart of social scientists—that these findings hold for this
sample, in this place and especially under these conditions—are
almost universally ignored.

But few facts established by social scientists attain universal validity. As a result, mass media audiences not infrequently encounter research findings that appear to contradict earlier research. And because conflict, rather than consensus, is "news," journalists are likely to highlight such disagreements among social scientists. Add to this the fact that an unknown amount of what passes for social science research in the media is in fact "pseudo" research or research of poor quality and dubious validity. The most blatant recent examples of such research are call-ins, but ordinarily errors are much more subtle and may not be easy to detect even by social scientists unless they are expert in the particular area of the research.

Furthermore, because media coverage has long been considered desirable by university press offices and is coming to be considered as a "good" by social science organizations as well, there is a tendency to adapt academic press releases to media values and to feature what is obviously interesting instead of making accessible research findings that may be more difficult to communicate to a mass audience. But to the extent that rewards from other social spheres follow attention by journalists, the values of social science may well be distorted by this process. If funding follows newsworthiness and reader interest—and our respondents tell us that it sometimes does—the cause of social science is not necessarily well served. Putting all of this another way, we can say that social scientists and journalists are subject to different normative expectations so far as communication behavior is concerned. In addition, journalists operate under structural constraints—limitations of time and space for the preparation and presentation of stories—to which social scientists are not subject. And although social science techniques are increasingly sophisticated, the training of reporters is neither designed nor intended to keep pace with them.

As a result, whereas some reporting of social science research in the mass media is superb, journalistic norms and structural constraints, along with certain characteristics of the organization and present state of development of the social sciences themselves, militate against the kind of social science coverage that is routinely true as well as good. Can anything be done to improve it? We will briefly mention four things we believe can be done even in the short run. We avoid long-range considerations and emphasize that other social scientists differ from us, both in their definition of the problem and in their proposals for a solution.

First, we recommend better training for reporters in the methods of social research—training designed to help them sort wheat from chaff.

The Detroit *Free Press,* for example, sponsors a seminar taught by scientists from the University of Michigan Survey Research Center for its editors and reporters. And the Russell Sage Foundation, mindful of the extraordinarily complex skills needed in the reporting of risks, is helping Victor Cohn, a veteran science reporter for the *Washington Post,* develop a primer for reporters on the statistical methods scientists (including social scientists) use. Should all reporters learn such skills? The answer is probably yes, because they apply to all empirical research, not only that done in the social sciences.

Second, we recommend more attention by social scientists to accurate reporting—to the inclusion of qualifications and caveats in the material prepared for the press. Although some social scientists hypothesize that a tendency to hedge may keep them from their fair share of attention in the media, we believe that the delimiting of research findings in the media is absolutely essential for the proper regard and future esteem of the social sciences. Social scientists have to learn how to qualify their findings when talking to reporters, and reporters have to learn to probe and report the reasons for discrepant results. Only in this way can we help the public to develop realistic, instead of inflated, conceptions and expectations of social science research.

Third, we need cooperation by social scientists, social science organizations, and media organizations to eliminate the reporting of "pseudo" research. When ABC conducts a phone-in and subsequently reports the results on television, it is not the ABC reporters who are to blame. It is the network that must be persuaded to abandon a practice it considers lucrative. There are of course, plenty of "surveys" reported in the media that are not surveys at all and that better methodological training for reporters might eliminate from public view. But the issues often go beyond methodological sophistication to competition between individual and organizational interests, a competition in which social science values may well lose. And the solution may have to come as a result of deliberate public relations efforts by survey and other social science organizations to educate the public about the differences between social science and entertainment, rather than in attempts to get media and other organizations to abandon practices they consider economically attractive.

Finally, we need more efforts by university press officers and public relations offices of social science organizations to publicize "important" social science studies in addition to those that easily lend themselves to journalistic adaptation. That means more input from social scientists themselves, rather than reliance on the journalists who ordinarily staff these positions. And, in the long run, it implies more linkage between the media and the social sciences, more positions that straddle both worlds, and, perhaps, more efforts to develop a social science "beat."

NOTES

1. Eleanor Singer and Phyllis Endreny carried out the content analysis and interviews with editors at Columbia University; Carol Weiss and her assistants at Harvard University conducted the interviews with social scientists and journalists.

For the content analysis, we selected every story that met our definition of social science during a five-month period in 1982 and three-month period in 1970 in which we monitored every third week of media coverage—a total of 3,105 stories in all. We defined social science as the intersection of two dimensions: every story that mentioned a social science element (research, a social scientist, data, a social science organization, theory, method, or institutional concerns) in some 17 specified social science fields (e.g., economics, psychology, sociology) was included in our sample. For each time, we coded a set of media variables—the media name and date, the amount of space or time devoted to the item, the prominence with which it was featured, and so on. For each item, we also coded a set of content variables, including such information as the topic of the story and the nature of the item (book reviews, obituary, news story, etc.). The remaining information coded varied depending on the particular social science element involved. For research reports, we coded such information as the institutional origins of the study, the discipline of the investigator, whether or not the investigator was named or identified as a social scientist, whether or not information was given about the methods used in the study, the topic of the study, and so on. For further details about the research design as well as the findings, see Weiss, Singer, with Endreny (in press).

2. Relatively few stories about social science research identify a published source. Of the 29% that do, only 21.6% cite a journal article, whereas 51.6% cite a project report and 11.2%, a book.

3. Most of the literature that comes closest to touching on this does so only inferentially, by way of case studies, or indirectly (accuracy studies, dimensions of judgment). Furthermore, most of these references pertain to natural science, and even the more explicit ones address *inclusion* of methodological information in an article rather than evaluation of it. Some anecdotal references are Weigel and Pappas (1981, esp. p. 485) and Tankard and Showalter (1977). Indirect references come from Tichenor et al. (1970), Johnson (1963), Tankard and Ryan (1974), Ryan (1979). One indirect reference leading to a contrary conclusion is Rich (1986), who suggests high attention to technique.

4. How journalists go about establishing validity is discussed in much greater detail in Endreny (1985).

5. The analyses in this chapter are based on the first study coded for each story; 79.4% of study stories mentioned only one study.

6. In all, 853 stories involving social science research were analyzed in 1982; 407 of these were what we have called "focus" stories and the remainder were "ancillary" stories. The corresponding figures for 1970 were 139 and 106. For the 1970-1982 comparison, we selected a three-month subsample of 1982 stories and excluded the *Boston*

Globe, as well as the three network broadcasts. For those stories in which it was possible to identify the number of researchers associated with the study, we coded the discipline of the social scientists involved. The four most frequently represented were sociologists (24%), economists (20%), psychologists (14%), and "pollsters" (10%).

7. Some research reported in the media was undoubtedly overlooked. For example, we probably missed many economic forecasting studies done by business forecasting firms, when the media presented only the forecasts without reference to a study. On the other hand, some studies were picked up as social science studies only because they had been done by a social scientist, even if they did not qualify on the basis of subject matter.

8. For studies mentioned in an ancillary role only, the figure drops below 8%. Newspapers provide more detail than either newsmagazines or TV newscasts.

9. In 1970, this was true of 57.5% of the newspaper stories and 40.0% of (15) newsmagazine stories.

10. We are grateful to Robert K. Merton and Harriet Zuckerman for suggesting this line of analysis. The selection of core studies was done independently, with a fair amount of agreement, by Eleanor Singer and Phyllis Endreny, without regard to how they were reported. *The New York Times* was selected because we assumed, on the basis of impressions formed during the study, that social science reporting would be most comprehensive there.

11. A consistently reported corollary of this finding is that satisfaction is generally higher with the story on which the scientist was a source than with science news in general.

12. Although most surveys in our sample are polls of attitudes and opinions, these terms are not altogether synonymous.

Chapter 22

IDEOLOGIES OF FEMININITY
Film and Popular Consciousness in the Postwar Era

Andrea L. Press

THEORETICAL AND METHODOLOGICAL CONSIDERATIONS

In examining the changes in the representation of women in film over the past two generations, one sees clear shifts in the content[1] of Hollywood films that seem to correspond with changes in the social and political climate of American women during this period. In this chapter, I will identify the broad outlines of three eras in the representation of women in post-World War II Hollywood films. I will then sketch the relationships that I see between these shifts in the representation of women to shifts in the political climate as it affected American women during this same period of time.

The following events are most relevant to my argument: (1) women's booming employment during the war, and their increasing domesticization in the years immediately following—I coin the term "prefeminist" to describe this period of time that extends roughly from the early 1940s through the early 1960s; (2) the rise of a consciousness of feminist concerns in the public discourse corresponding with the rise of the civil rights movement of the early to mid-1960s and the feminist political activity it spawned[2]—I term this the "feminist period," which extends roughly from the mid-1960s through the late 1970s; and (3) the rising backlash among women, especially younger women[3] against the ideals of liberal feminism—for lack of a better term, I call this period of the 1980s the "postfeminist" period.

In the chapter, I discuss two Hollywood genres of the postwar period: the "strong-woman" films that flowered in the postwar period and were revived in a different form during the late 1960s and early 1970s, and the "woman's film," which actually originated during the 1930s but continued through the 1940s and the 1950s, and is currently being revived in a different form in the "postfeminist" 1980s. As I define them, both strong-woman films and woman's films are characterized by the fact that their central characters are female. The primary difference between them is that strong-woman films picture women in the public sphere and feature working women as their main characters, whereas woman's films depict the private, domestic sphere and usually feature nonworking women. I discuss the earlier and later form of each genre and draw some limited connections between their shifting emphases in the portrayal of women with the shifting political climate of women.

For reasons that would require further research to uncover, few representatives of either of these genres made it to the top 10 or 15 on *Variety*'s annual list of top-grossing films, particularly in the 1940s and 1950s. I cannot, therefore, justify my choice of these genres on the basis of popularity. In fact, in examining *Variety*'s 10 highest-grossing films for each year throughout the last four decades, one rarely finds films that feature females as leading characters of any sort. I am thus forced to seek another justification for choosing to examine the strong-woman and woman's film genres. My reason is simply that they are well suited to a detailed study of ideologies of femininity in Hollywood film in the sense that they offer more opportunity, both numerically and substantively, to study depictions of females than do the other genres in which females often occupy minor roles (Press, 1986). The genres I have chosen also tend to deal specifically with "female" problems: For the strong-woman picture, this is often the problem of combining work and family, and for the woman's picture, this is often domestic drama or love-related difficulties. These situations, absent from many other genres, offer better substance for the study of ideologies of femininity.

I have identified several (alas, too few) "representative" films for each of the two genres. I have tried to choose films that can be seen as "classic" strong-woman films, or "classic" woman's films, films that contain all or almost all of the essential elements of each genre as I have defined them.[4] I realize that this criterion does not meet the representativeness criterion of traditional sampling procedures. My selection procedures may, however, be regarded as appropriate to the focused aims of a case analysis strategy. More pragmatic financial limitations also operated against my gaining access to the total populations of Hollywood films from which to sample.

THE PREFEMINIST PERIOD

The ideological manipulation of women in the United States during and after World War II has been discussed widely in the feminist literature.[5] Briefly, feminists have argued that women in advanced capitalist society serve as a reserve army of labor called upon when needed by the economy—for example, during wartime, when production needs were heavy and labor was scarce. The "Rosie the Riveter" ideology—essentially an ideology of female strength—predominated in government propaganda and advertising campaigns during this time.[6] After the war, when women workers were perceived by men in power to be economic threats, another ideological campaign was launched by government and industry to urge women to give up their paid jobs and return to the home.

During the 1940s, at the apex of women's wartime success in the sphere of wage labor, we see the rise of several very strong female stars—Kathryn Hepburn, Bette Davis, Rosalind Russell, and Barbara Stanwyck, for example—starring in a number of films in which women play strong and independent, yet passionate, lead characters. Some examples are the Hepburn-Tracy films, *Woman of the Year* (1942), *Adam's Rib* (1949), and *Pat and Mike* (1952), and Rosalind Russell in *His Girl Friday* (1940). Such "strong-women" films essentially dropped out of the Hollywood scene during the 1950s and early 1960s. As we will see, however, they reemerged in a new form during the "feminist" period.

The strong-woman films were progressively replaced by another genre that became popular during the 1940s and 1950s—the "woman's film." The woman's film became a distinct genre during this period. It is characterized by a focus upon one or several female characters who are shown engaging in very traditional female pursuits—usually trying to catch a man or suffering through some love-threatened tragedy with a husband or a lover. Woman's films as I have defined them span the two traditional genres of drama and comedy. Often they are melodramatic, but sometimes the traditional elements of the woman's melodrama—specifically, the "woman tries to catch man" angle—are spoofed in a comic product. Sometimes called "weepies" in the more melodramatic form, the woman's picture offers audiences (on the surface at least) a very traditional image of women and often a very conservative view of family life.

Early examples of the "woman's film" include Cukor's *The Women* (1930), distinguished by an entirely female cast and advertised at the time to concern "135 women with men on their minds,"[7] and Vidor's *Stella Dallas* (1937) with Barbara Stanwyck. Later instances of the genre include *Now Voyager* (1942) with Bette Davis, *Mildred Pierce* (1945) with Joan Crawford, the Douglas Sirk melodramas *Magnificent Obsession* (1954) and *All That Heaven Allows* (1955) with Jane Wyman, and *There's Always Tomorrow* (1956) with Barbara Stanwyck, and, finally, the comedy *How To Marry A Millionaire* (1953), a good spoof on the genre, with Lauren Bacall, Marilyn Monroe, and Betty Grable.

This era of the woman's film is particularly interesting because, in contrast to later Hollywood products, there is an undercurrent within the film that can be brutally critical of the traditional family and of woman's role within it.[8] For example, Douglas Sirk directed a series of films that well illustrate the concept of the "dual message" present in many woman's films. His 1956 melodrama, *There's Always Tomorrow,* starring Barbara Stanwyck and Fred MacMurray, is a good case in point. A short plot summary and brief description of some of the uses of cinematic techniques in this film will serve to illustrate my category of the dual message woman's film. MacMurray plays a married man feeling trapped by his wife, who pays more attention to the children than to him. Stanwyck, his high school sweetheart, shows up and they fall in love once again. But out of respect for "the family," she convinces him to stay married. The narrative would have us believe that he is choosing the truly moral alternative by remaining with his family. However, camera angles that frame his home as a symbol of confinement express a different and very critical perspective on such traditional morality. The camera reveals his home to be a prison and his wife and children his jailers. Such is the film's dual message regarding the traditional American family.

The question of how films of this period were received by audiences is an important one but quite complicated to answer. It is difficult, if not impossible, to discover in retrospect whether such films as *There's Always Tomorrow* were received in terms of their narrative message, or in terms of that message which is communicated through camera and other cinematic forms.[9]

Both the strong-woman films and the woman's film genres of the prefeminist period are interesting for another reason. On the whole, these older genres portray women as sharing collective membership in a common female class. Whether rich or poor, women share their quest for and dependence upon men, both financially and socially, sometimes emotionally. The ambivalence and ambiguity inherent in such dependence shows clearly in many films of the genre. There is thus another dual message. In *There's Always Tomorrow,* for example, Barbara Stanwyck shows dependence, but she also shows loyalty to MacMurray's wife, whom she knows not at all personally. Stanwyck gives him up to some degree out of concern for another woman's situation.

THE FEMINIST PERIOD

A hegemony emerged in the films of the 1960s and 1970s regarding women, work, and family—women can "do it all" or they can have a successful, interesting career, as well as raise a happy and loving family, preferably with the help of an enlightened, liberal husband. In 1964, Friedan in *The Feminine Mystique* criticized the ideological messages in American culture that told women they must limit their choices to either family or career. Having worked as an editor of a woman's magazine for a number of years, Friedan was in a particularly good position to criticize the contours of the "feminine mystique" as it was built by the media and as it took effect in women's consciousness. She articulated an alternative position that was deceptively simple, a position that deemphasized class differences between women and neglected problems inherent in the traditional middle-class *male* role in American society. Friedan painted a rosy picture of the busy, affluent, and fulfilled lives women would have when, having been liberated from the strictures of the feminine mystique, they adopted both the traditional female and the traditional male social roles as their own. Although a more comprehensive discussion of the liberal feminist position[10] is not possible here, I will briefly summarize some of the points most relevant to the present analysis.

Liberal feminism shares most of the inherent contradictions and limitations of the liberal political theory generally (Eisenstein, 1981, 1984). For feminism, these translate into the paradox that liberal society's abstract ideal of "equality of individuals" is based upon a male model of the individual in the sense that such an individual is not assumed to be saddled with domestic chores, child care responsibilities, or nurturant duties. Successful career people, by definition, are forced by the demanding structure of virtually all professions and by the inflexible structure of most mere jobs, to devote most of their working hours to professional pursuits in order to remain competitive. What this adds up to for women is that they are being advised to embrace what was formerly "male"—instrumental activity is to take precedence over other aspects of their lives. In addition, liberal feminism did not even begin to address the problems of working-class women who have always had to balance roles in both the public and the private spheres, with a female ideal that was culturally middle class. For these women, then, the messages of liberal feminism were even more contradictory.

Although other themes have been advocated for women in other schools of feminist theory and practice, this liberal feminist message had the most significant and recognizable effect on our dominant mass media. Scanning *Variety*'s list of the top-grossing films of the 1970s, we find several clear examples of the liberal feminist influence, particularly among films that were heralded as path breaking for feminists. For instance, *Klute* (1971) and *An Unmarried Woman* (1977) expose some of the conflicts facing women, yet they make a mockery of the search for a truly new gender identity. These films adhere to essentially traditional solutions to their protagonists' dilemmas (Gledhill, 1980; Lesage, 1982). On the surface, the female protagonists seem to adopt many male character and/or personality traits, but there is a strong covert message indicating that, at base, the protagonists remain women and the men remain men in the most traditional and stereotypical senses.

In addition to the obvious incompatibilities between the overt ideological messages of liberal feminist films and films of the original woman's picture era, I contend that there is an even more fundamental way in which the films of these two eras differ. In the 1970s' feminist films, the tension essentially dropped out of the female personality as it was portrayed in the prefeminist films. In the woman's films, women's *passion* itself is seen to be divided: The social structure ties women to home and family, yet often women's passions drive them toward independence, either in deed or in thought. When work becomes a stronger theme, as it does in the films of the 1970s, this passionate independence tends to disappear. Compare the characters of Rosalind Russell in *His Girl Friday* (1940) with that of Jane Fonda in *Klute* or Jill Clayburgh in *An Unmarried Woman*. Russell plays a fiery newspaper reporter who claims that she yearns to marry and give up her work. But in neither work nor love is her passion ridiculed. Both are pictured to constitute integral sides of a formidable character to be taken seriously in all her endeavors.

In contrast, Fonda's Bree Daniels collapses into the most passive image of the traditional woman when finally confronted with Klute, a "real man" (Donald Sutherland). By the film's end she appears drained of emotional strength as she follows Sutherland off to a "little house in the country," a path she swore earlier in the film that she would never follow. Clayburgh, in *An Unmarried Woman,* fares no better—she makes a fainthearted stab at independence following her divorce, but she is never convincing. Unlike Russell, she is not a character one takes seriously. She has no definite career plans and barely attempts to make any during the film. Passion for both Fonda and Clayburgh's characters dissolves into, at best, a passive position within a very traditional relationship with a traditional male. The fiery undercurrent of independence that characterized the Hollywood women of former eras has dropped out. In its wake we find a one-dimensional character, an image corresponding to either the extreme male or the extreme female side of the traditional male-female dichotomy.

THE POSTFEMINIST BACKLASH

I have argued elsewhere (Press, n.d.) that many young women, particularly those from a working-class background, are rejecting liberal feminist values in favor of a return to more traditional views of gender role differences. I interpret this backlash as a reaction against the rife contradictions inherent with the liberal feminist ideology. As previously stated, these contradictions are particularly severe for working-class women. This is consistent with my finding of a stronger backlash among working-class women.

Two of the most popular films of the 1980s serve to illustrate the filmic expression of the backlash characteristics of this decade. I will first describe these films and the ideological elements that qualify them as "backlash" forms. I will then make a case for calling them "woman's films" of the 1980s or, in accordance with my observations of an antifeminist backlash in our present culture, the postfeminist period.

In the huge box-office smashes *An Officer and A Gentleman* and *Terms of Endearment,* Debra Winger plays extraordinarily regressive female roles, extraordinary because these roles occur in the 1980s yet fail to pay even lipservice to the strong feminist movement in this country. In both films Winger is the woman who fights for the right to be traditional in relation to work, men, and family. It's not that the characters she portrays are necessarily one-dimensional; both are likable, high-spirited women, drawn with humor and dignity. Yet clearly these characters are materially, emotionally, and ideologically the traditional American women for whom relationships with men and family take precedence above all other factors in the definition of their identities as adult women.

These characters, however, are not entirely the mirror image of Hollywood women of the 1940s and 1950s. In concrete terms, one important change is that the traditional woman of the 1980s is a more overtly sexual figure. More interesting is that although these films resemble the earlier woman's films in important surface respects—that is, the female protagonists are motivated by love and are structurally defined in terms of their relationship to men and family—in a deeper sense, the new films are quite different. Morally it seems that the characters of the 1980s are driven by their very inner passions toward rather than away from the traditional social structure. This drive occurs despite the feminist movement's demonstration of the oppressiveness of the social structure for women. In earlier films, there was discernible at least some level of consciousness among the main characters of their oppression as women. Their passions often directed them to react against this, to seek greater freedom and self-expression.

Such rebellion is missing in films of the 1980s. Thus, Winger's Paula in *An Officer and A Gentleman* seeks to escape her dreary working-class life through marriage to an officer-candidate; yet she is allowed no consciousness that this is an escape route for her. When her friend Lynette is more honest in admitting her desire to use marriage as an escape, she is condemned by the film for being a person of no integrity.

One can imagine this essentially traditional plot in a woman's film of the 1940s or 1950s with one important difference: In the woman's picture, the common plight of women would be emphasized. Certainly the women would not be set in opposition to each other. The moral crimes that would be serious in a woman's picture would be those against one's fellow woman, not those like Lynette's aimed at men.

CONTRASTING PREFEMINIST AND POSTFEMINIST WOMAN'S FILMS

The 1950 film, *All About Eve,* serves as a good contrast to the 1980s', *An Officer and A Gentleman.* In *All About Eve,* Bette Davis plays Margo, a very worldly, manipulative, successful actress. Anne Baxter plays Eve, a woman who appears to befriend Margo but secretly envies her position. Eve betrays Margo and manipulates her to Eve's own advantage. She becomes successful, but at Margo's expense. Eve is clearly identified in the film to be the villain. Margo is the wronged woman. What differentiates Eve's character from that of Margo is, in essence, the sex of the person or persons at whom crimes are directed. Margo has manipulated the men in power to get where she is. Eve uses many of Margo's tricks, but uses them against Margo, betraying a fundamental moral stricture of the woman's picture by wronging another woman. This moral scenario stands in stark contrast to that presented in *An Officer and A Gentleman.*

Another instructive comparison with *An Officer and A Gentleman* are the two 1950 comedies, *Gentlemen Prefer Blondes* (1950) and *How To Marry A Millionaire* (1953). Both of the 1950s films resemble the 1980s film in some plot essentials, so that although *Gentlemen Prefer Blondes* is a musical comedy, *How To Marry A Millionaire* is a comedy, and *An Officer and A Gentleman* is a drama, all are woman's pictures by my definition. *How To Marry A Millionaire* follows the adventures of three young models—Lauren Bacall (Schatzy), Marilyn Monroe (Pola), and Betty Grable (Loco)—as they search for rich husbands. Their aims are similar to those of Paula and Lynette in the later film; namely, the dual pull of money, status, and romance in attracting a woman to a potential husband. Yet in *How To Marry A Millionaire,* the women are shown actively planning their futures together and taking care of each other in their quest. Such an entirely unsympathetic character as Lynette is avoided.

Gentlemen Prefer Blondes features Marilyn Monroe and Jane Russell, again as two women out to trap husbands. And again, the women in this film form a strong, united group, although they do disagree on points of strategy, money, and morality. What unites them is their common position as women. At one point in the film, Russell exclaims in response to a criticism of her friend Monroe, "Nobody criticizes Lorelei but me!" The strongest emotion shown in this film, as in *How To Marry A Millionaire,* is the support offered by the women to one another. Such a theme is characteristic, I have argued, of prefeminist woman's films.

This theme of unity among women is absent in films of the 1980s. The extraordinarily low image of female friendship in *An Officer and A Gentleman,* for example, would be unthinkable in these earlier woman's pictures. The comaraderie and sense of women's unity in their common experience has entirely dropped out of the later film. *An Officer and A Gentleman* is indeed a "romance" in an extreme sense of the word—romance exists in a vacuum, and no other factors (e.g., social structure or class) can or should have any reality where romance is concerned.

Terms of Endearment, another 1980s film, features similarly regressive female characterizations in which any common class consciousness among women is conspicuously absent. Debra Winger's character presents an interesting paradox. Again, Winger plays the woman who fights to be traditional. Unlike the novel, Winger's character is drawn to be much stronger than is that of her mother in the film,[11] and both lack class consciousness. Winger marries, has three children, and has money worries, but unlike most American women, she never considers working. Nor does she consider an abortion, exclaiming in horror when her own mother suggests it. The one scene in which career women are featured portrays them as shallow, stupid, and essentially unhappy, a portrayal drawn in sharp contrast to Winger's character. The paradoxical pieces of Winger's characterization in this film add up to a clear message for American women: You will be a better person if you fight to retain the traditional woman's role of the nonworking wife and mother. Never mind that you may be poor and oppressed in that role. The role, itself, is its own compensation.

Even in prefeminist days the drama of women's lives was vividly portrayed in at least some films on the Hollywood screen. As for the "postfeminist" era, it seems that the woman's film has returned in a new and vulgarized form that is compatible with the apparent backlash reaction to the messages of liberal feminism. The true drama of women's lives has been exchanged for a picture that is, in some respects, even more romanticized than that offered in Hollywood's Golden Age. We can only conjecture as to the regressive political effects such a trend in Hollywood's mode representation might have.

NOTES

1. I wish to stress here that in this chapter I discuss primarily film content and to a very limited extent the use of certain cinematic techniques. Changing conditions of film production—the decline of the studio system, declining film audiences, and many other factors relevant to the economy and politics of film production—are undoubtedly relevant to explanations of the shifts in film *content* that I identify. Unfortunately, these elements of the story are beyond the scope of this chapter.

2. For a fuller discussion of these historical events, see Evans (1979).

3. I am not arguing that there has been a broad *political* shift to the right among women in the United States. This claim has been attacked and rightly so. See, for example, Stacy (1983). My claim is that on the *ideological* level I have found in the course of

my dissertation research (Press, in press), a movement away from the ideas espoused by many liberal feminists during the early 1970s. A good example of this shift may be seen in Betty Friedan's recent book, *The Second Stage* (1981).

4. For a similar rationale see Cavell (1981, p. 2). In choosing films for the "feminist" and "postfeminist" periods, I have found representatives that are among the top 10 highest-grossing films listed by *variety*, and I have chosen to discuss these whenever possible.

5. For a more complete discussion of this point, see Milkman (1980) and Sokoloff (1980).

6. For an excellent illustration and analysis of the propaganda relating to women's work during this era, see *Rosie the Riveter*, a feminist documentary.

7. Quoted in Halliwell (1977, p. 1,193).

8. Film scholars in this country have tended to adopt the "auteur theory" in their approach to film criticism. It emphasizes the importance of the director in creating the film and thus in establishing its "quality." For example, see Sarris (1968). I do not entirely concur with this theory, but it does seem to explain why most of the dual-message woman's films that I identify have been made by a handful of directors—for instance, Sirk, Cukor, and Wyler.

9. I do attempt, in the full report of my dissertation research (Press, 1986), to develop a methodology capable of addressing the question of how these messages were actively interpreted and used by the women who received them.

10. For a discussion of liberal feminism in relation to liberalism, see Eisenstein (1981, 1984).

11. I am indebted to Professor Carolyn Porter (Director, Women's Studies, University of California at Berkeley) for this observation.

Chapter 23

FORMAT AND FORMULA IN
PRIME-TIME TV

Ann Swidler
Melissa Rapp
Yasemin Soysal

THIS CHAPTER EXPLORES how television content is shaped by
the interaction of *format* and *formula,* the structural and aesthetic
constraints within which television programming is created. We are interested in explaining why television develops some themes in our
social and cultural repertoire while slighting others. We are also interested in the ways standard dramatic conventions are altered when
they are adapted to television's frameworks.

We were initially led to examine the interaction of format and formula on television by a puzzle: Why does the traditional love story,
which provides the major fodder for other formula media such as pulp
fiction, play a more limited role on prime-time television? But to
understand the relative neglect of the love story on television, we must
consider more generally the route by which popular social, psychological, or moral concerns affect the content of American television.

Those who study the content of television programming use two
different models to account for that content. One is "reflection
theory" (Albrecht, 1954), in which the content of American television

AUTHORS' NOTE: An earlier version of this chapter was presented at the an-
nual meeting of the American Sociological Association, San Antonio, Texas,
August 1984. It has benefited greatly from the comments of Howie Becker, Bill
Bielby, Fred Block, Muriel Cantor, Claude Fischer, Wendy Griswold, Lisa
Heilbron, Kathryn Henry, Arlie Hochschild, Carole Joffe, Susan Krieger,
Richard A. Peterson, and Gaye Tuchman.

reflects the fundamental preoccupations of the American people. The second, more often associated with those critical of television, is one version or another of "manipulation theory," in which what appears on television is determined by the choices of those who control television production and programming. Of course, the models do not differ so greatly in their actual claims, because the manipulation theorists agree that a central concern for media decision makers is satisfying popular taste, even if ignorance, timidity, political bias, or commitment to capitalism distort the version of that taste that actually appears on television (Gitlin, 1983).

The problem is that neither manipulation theory nor reflection theory is very helpful without careful consideration of the organizational forces that constrain American television on the one hand (Cantor, 1980) and the problems of television as an aesthetic form on the other (Newcomb, 1974). We examine here how the content of television is shaped by the need to make television entertaining—essentially the problem of aesthetic form—within the constraints and opportunities of the organization of television programming.

FORMATS

An important but relatively neglected aspect of television's organization is the *format* of television programming. By formats, we mean the units in which television programs are constructed and their continuity through time. We will analyze how format constrains the formulas that will work effectively on television and thus constrains the ways in which television can either reflect or shape popular imagination.

The most prevalent formats on American television are (1) the episodic *series* and (2) the continuing *serial*. Both series and serials provide continuity for viewers, attempting to "hook" them into watching the same show week after week. Both series and serials employ a stable group of core characters who (often with changing "guest stars") engage in broadly similar encounters from show to show. The serial differs from the series in that the serial develops suspenseful plot complications that continue from week to week, whereas the series resolve all or most of the plot threads of a given episode within that episode. Until recently American prime-time television has been dominated by the weekly series format, whereas daytime TV has specialized in the daily serial (Cantor, 1980; Cantor & Pingree, 1983).

Other formats besides the serial and the series also play a role on American television. (3) *One-shot* programs: Television could, at least in principle, be made up entirely of unrelated shows and dramas—like the format of one movie after another on cable movie channels. Some sporting events, made-for-TV movies, and "specials" are one-shot programs, with the advantage of providing variety and the disadvantage that they require special advertising to attract viewers. (4) *Anthologies:* Early in the history of American television there was frequent use of the anthology format—a series of dramas, each with its own cast and plot, often introduced by the same host (*The Loretta Young Show, Dick Powell's Zane Grey Theater, The Dupont Show with June Allyson*), and sometimes specializing in a particular plot formula (love stories on "Loretta Young", science fiction/fantasy on *The Twilight Zone,* westerns on "Zane Grey"). With Steven Spielberg's *Amazing Stories* and the new *Twilight Zone,* among others, the 1985 season saw a remarkable revival of the anthology format. (5) *Miniseries:* The most significant recent format innovation has been the miniseries, a single drama shown over several closely spaced evenings. These series allow complex dramas, sustained over time, that still come to a conclusion.

LOVE ON TELEVISION

On television, format constrains plot formula—and thus thematic content—in significant ways. (We speak here of dramatic and comedy shows because such TV genres as game shows and variety shows are very differently affected by format constraints.) Most striking is the fate of the love story on American television.

In *The Rise of the Novel* (1957), Ian Watt outlines the plot of the classic love story, exemplified by Samuel Richardson's *Pamela.* A virtuous servant girl resists her wealthy employer's advances; he is finally won over by her virtue and marries her. The love story involves courtship and marriage, thus uniting a drama about the inner lives of individuals with problems of social destiny. In the formula love story, individual character is tested (and sometimes transformed), so that love is both a stimulus to and a reward for virtue. In other versions of the love formula, individuals fight against social or personal obstacles to marry the person they have chosen, thus again posing the problem of the relationship of individual character and social destiny (Swidler, 1980).

Outside of television, the most popular formula stories in America are love stories—the Harlequin and Silhouette romances that sell by the millions to subscribers and in supermarkets and drug stores, best-selling melodramas, from *Marjorie Morningstar* to *Princess Daisy,* and, of course, love in the movies. But classic romantic love stories—about courtship, attempted seduction, and marriage—have played a limited role on American television, although they still thrive in other media. (Witness the recent success of the movie, *An Officer and A Gentleman,* that has all the elements of the bourgeois, romantic love story, including the moral transformation of the male hero and the triumphant marriage of the heroine.) As we shall see below, even the obsession of daytime TV with problems of love and personal relationships gives love a peculiar twist. This anomaly of the missing love story well illustrates how format constrains television content.

SERIES

The problem with love stories, of course, is that they end. Courtship loses its meaning if it goes on indefinitely. Yet it is essential to the self-contained weekly episodes of the series format that particular conflicts or misunderstandings be resolved each week, whereas the underlying tensions on which the show is based persist without being resolved. Love stories are not easily adapted to produce the continuing conflicts series demand. Marry off the hero(ine) of a romance, and the drama is over.

As Ian Watt (1957) argues, the drama of courtship provided an ideal thematic resource for the novel because it was a single, unified action that culminated in a decisive resolution—marriage—that simultaneously resolved problems of personal and social destiny. One can certainly have stories about love, even on series television, but these cannot be full-blown love stories involving core series characters. Thus, Ricky Nelson can fall in and out of puppy love during a single episode of *The Adventures of Ozzie and Harriet,* but he cannot be married off—or even fight to win the girl he loves—week after week.

On a show that is basically about something besides love—the comedy detective series *The Rockford Files,* for example—the hero can pursue an occasional love interest, but these must not be too frequent and they must usually end with a poignant parting.[1] Otherwise we have a series about a compulsive womanizer or a married detective, neither a basis for further love stories. Even series that have played out a love story over several episodes—*Rhoda,* for example—have found that the resolution of love stories interferes with the continuity of characters and situations required by a series. (Rhoda's marriage deprived the series of one of its fundamental sources of humor—the tribulations of single womanhood—and the producers' solution of divorcing her again simply cast a pall over the show.)

At the deeper level of underlying social and moral meanings, love stories are about the resolution of problems of individual character. They are satisfying only if they have decisive resolutions, not only because love often leads to marriage but because love tests and often alters character (Swidler, 1980). It is this revelation or transformation of character—whether in marriage and happiness ever after, renunciation (as in *Casablanca*), or tragic loss (*Love Story*)—that makes love stories poor material out of which to construct the continuing conflicts on which series television depends.

In the early years of American television, there was some room for love stories, primarily within the anthology format. *The Loretta Young Show,* for example, featured a different drama every week, many about love. Prestigious dramatic anthologies such as *Playhouse 90* featured varying weekly dramas, some of which were love stories (the classic being "Marty"). But the anthology format was abandoned during the 1960s[2] in favor of the series for evening TV and the serial for daytime viewing. Whatever the reasons for the anthology's decline, it had important consequences for the love story, and for other formulas as well. The movie shown on television became the only format that could accommodate a full-blown love story.

WHERE HAS LOVE GONE?

What, then, has happened to love themes on American television since the early 1960s? First, we would argue that there was simply an unsatisfied appetite for love stories, which has reemerged with force in the great popularity of TV miniseries, from *Roots* and *Holocaust* to *Shogun* and *Rich Man, Poor Man.* Indeed, it may be the craving for love stories, as much as the lavish productions or the occasional resonances with social issues, that accounts for the popularity of miniseries on TV. Kunta Kinte met, almost lost, and finally won his wife in a dramatically satisfying courtship, and love stories also animated the narrative of the lives of his children and grandchildren.

Second, love reappeared in a form more suitable to the series format—in the affectionate love of the domestic comedy. Situation comedies began on American television as vehicles for comedic performers—one wacky spouse who created predictable hilarity week after week. It is this high comedy that made *The George Burns and Gracie Allen Show, The Life of Riley, I Love Lucy, I Married Joan,* or *The Honeymooners* funny. More abrasive than loving, spouses operated like vaudeville comedy teams (Hough, 1981, p. 208). But in the later domestic comedies, as several commentators have noted (Grote, 1983, p. 60; Newcomb, 1974, pp. 43-58), nothing about the families themselves was inherently funny. These were normal people, trying to raise their children well and to work out the misunderstandings that each week ruffled their domestic harmony. In some sense *The Adventures of Ozzie and Harriet, Father Knows Best, My Three Sons,* and *Leave It to Beaver* were love stories, although they were not shows about romance and courtship leading to marriage but about having, losing, and winning again a very domestic kind of love.

Students of situation comedy have pointed out (Grote, 1983, p. 59; Mitz, 1983, p. 3) that it is the genre in which nothing ever really happens. Its appeal, in Hollywood's conventional wisdom, is that viewers become attached to the characters and want to invite them into their homes week after week (Gitlin, 1983, p. 64). The drama and the humor these shows offer come from experiences that teach individuals moral lessons about themselves or others, or from the growth of understanding and acceptance among the members of a loving group. The apparently static situation comedy, with its small difficulties and small triumphs, is in some ways the adaptation of the love formula to a series format.

In the plot of the traditional love story the character of a hero or heroine is tested—his usually by fighting for the woman he loves; hers by resisting seduction or by marrying for love despite pressure from parents or society. Love is the reward for true worth. In the domestic comedies of the 1960s and 1970s, something like this love drama, in which character is formed and tested and love is the reward for virtue, is played out in the small setting and in the little ups and downs of family life. It loses the dramatic tension and satisfying resolution of the traditional love story but preserves its concern with character development, the reward of virtue, and the mutuality of affection. The series format, however, will not accommodate the more decisive testing or transformation of character, and the dashing or fulfillment of personal and social hopes, that characterized the traditional drama of courtship and marriage.

Finally, two significant format innovations have allowed a resurgence of the love story on prime-time TV. First is the somewhat surprising reappearance of the anthology format or, rather, a series "sandwich" with an anthology "filling." The Aaron Spelling shows

The Love Boat, Fantasy Island, and *Hotel* developed premises that allowed the insertion of several minidramas (or comedies) every week into a series format.[3] Thus, the regular crew of the Love Boat are there to provide the continuing attachments that presumably sustain regular viewing while new stories unfold each week. Primarily involving guest characters, these stories can actually end. The premises, the settings, and the continuing characters of the Spelling-produced anthologies are often implausible and the dramas forced. Nevertheless, we would argue, the demand for love stories on prime-time television has made these series-anthology shows very successful, despite their aesthetic limitations.

SERIALS

The other recent format innovation (besides the miniseries and the sandwich anthology) has been the prime-time serial. As the daytime romance of Luke and Laura on *General Hospital* showed, a stormy courtship can be sustained on a serial and even provide a tremendous short-term ratings success. Indeed, one might say that love has been the central preoccupation of the daytime serial, with individual elements of the traditional love formula—seduction, longing, lovers frustrated by social obstacles—providing its bread and butter. Nonetheless, the serial format makes it own special demands, which push stories of love in peculiar directions.

In principle, a serial can present an occasional love story, ending and all, as long as it has a large enough cast that when a love drama is resolved, it can be "moved to the back burner." But love in the serial is usually more troubled. Those who marry must break up again in order to be available for new romantic entanglements. Lovers overcome obstacles, find true love, only to change character almost miraculously some weeks later, as the virtuous wife becomes the guilty adulteress, or the passion that has consumed a man for months is forgotten when an old love reappears on the scene.

Serial love is deprived of satisfying endings, but it is also driven—and sometimes driven out—by the need for suspense. The serial depends on continuing stories suspenseful enough to carry viewers from one episode to the next. And as Alfred Hitchcock, the master of suspense, has argued, the key to suspense (as opposed to mystery) is that the audience knows disaster is imminent and can only wait and watch the often unsuspecting victim.[4] A murderer stalking his prey, a bomb ticking away, a rescuer desperate to get there in time—these are the elements of which suspense is made. So serial drama, even when it deals with personal relationships, focuses persistently on disasters waiting to happen.[5]

Television serials, which often treat love, marriage, and sex, bear little resemblance to the traditional love story.[6] Instead they focus on terrible secrets that would destroy someone's life if they were revealed—secrets the audience knows and waits in fascinated horror for the characters to learn (his child was fathered by another man; her gangster ex-husband is alive after all; her husband is in love with her best friend; her seducer that drunken night was ...). Serials also create suspense through evil conspiracies that entrap the unsuspecting victims. The serial drama's reliance on suspense thus pulls it continuously toward plot devices almost unknown in other television formats—terrible secrets and evil conspiracies. Even more strikingly, serial dramas are full of truly villainous characters, who hatch the plots and perform the twisted deeds that have to be kept secret.

TELEVISION'S DIVIDED WORLD

One striking feature of the aggregate pattern of television programming is the peculiar division of cultural labor between situation comedies, with their commitment to fundamentally good characters among whom nothing ever really goes wrong, and both daytime and now evening "soaps" in which cruel, malicious characters continually create real havoc.[7]

Newcomb and Hirsch (1983) have advanced the image of television as a "cultural forum," in which the multiplicity of messages and points of view, rather than some unity of perspective, creates the larger meaning of television viewing. But consideration of the constraints created by television formats suggests that the specialization of vision among different television genres—the happy community of the sit-com and the evil turmoil of the soap—has another logic as well. In nearly opposite ways, the format constraints of the series and the serial truncate the range of dramatic possibility each can explore.

In contrast, the changing weekly dramas on action-adventure series permit these series to draw in the wider repertoire of dramatic formulas available to such genres as novels, plays, and movies—whose stories end. Occasionally, they can even deal with love. The dramas in action-adventure series tend to pit good against evil and to involve a struggle with a decisive outcome. Traditionally, however, they have taken little advantage of the dramatic possibilities of the relationships among core series characters themselves. Thus, in the western (*The Lone Ranger*) and the police show (*Dragnet*), the drama came from the action itself, not from Elliot Ness's relationships with his men, a misunderstanding between Tonto and the Lone Ranger, or Sergeant Friday's personal life.

More recently, however, there has been a mingling of television forms along two dimensions. The action-adventure series has taken up elements of situation comedy, and series television has experimented with some continuing plots.

Thus, some recent action-adventure series have developed a dual structure, with a kind of sit-com framework among the principal characters, who make dramatic fun of getting along in spite of their differences, and an action component in which the heroes chase the bad guy of the week. The hero of the action-adventure series is replaced by a group of heroes who have complex (or at least amusing) relationships (beginning with such shows as *77 Sunset Strip* or *Bonanza*). The heroes develop idiosyncratic charm, peculiar hangers-on (*Rockford Files*), and occasional personal involvement with the varied action situations they encounter each week (*Lou Grant, Cagney and Lacey*). In these recent series it has been possible for the core characters to develop more complex and sometimes difficult relationships than occur on traditional situation comedies—perhaps precisely because the core group does not have to sustain the entire burden of the show from week to week.

The increasingly adept fusion of plots based on the personal relationships of a core group with dramas that change from week to week has meant a blurring of the line between comedy and adventure. Like comedy hits such as *M*A*S*H*, most of the successful recent adventure shows combine the funny with the grim. The sit-com formula of humor binding together a group in which each member learns to love the others' peculiarities characterizes recent action-adventure series as diverse as *Lou Grant, Cagney and Lacey*, and *The A-Team* (in contrast with the earlier *Mission Impossible* or *Police Woman*, for example).

In some of these series the division between series and serial is breached as well. *Hill Street Blues*, with its introduction of continuing plots into a series format, is only the most extreme of a group of innovative shows, going back at least to *M*A*S*H*, that have allowed richer dramatic development of the lives of the principal characters.

FORMAT AND FORMULA

Consideration of how the format of television programming constrains the formulas that can succeed is just one of several issues that link sociological analysis of organizational constraints to an understanding of the aesthetic and entertainment aspects of television as a cultural form. In *Television: Technology and Cultural Form* (1975), Raymond Williams pioneered a fuller sociological understanding of television by putting television as a technology in a *comparative* framework. He showed (using considerable ingenuity and the simplest of evidence—a log of a day's television viewing in England versus the United States) that the characteristics of television programming are not inherent in the medium, or even in its mass audience, but depend also on the organizational context in which they are developed and marketed. American television, he argues, has been fundamentally shaped by its use as a vehicle for advertising, but also by government regulation that has protected the dominance of the network system.

A fuller sociological understanding of television requires comparison—the kind of cross-national comparison Williams has begun, but also comparison with other mass media that appeal to popular taste within different organizational constraints. Such comparisons give perspective and suggest questions, such as the one with which we began, about why a kind of love story that has enormous popular appeal in pulp fiction and the movies is virtually absent on "regularly scheduled" TV.

An issue such as television format forces one to rethink both the reflection theory and the manipulation theory accounts of the content of American television. Let us take manipulation theory first. Television's critics are universally concerned with the ways in which American television both reflects and reproduces American capitalism. But one of the most fundamental consequences of the way television is paid for in America has been precisely the heavy emphasis on *regularly scheduled* programs. Programs that can be spun out in endless series are not required by television as a medium or by anything in our cultural appetites. (Indeed, the dominance of the miniseries on British television and of the 13-week, nightly *telenovela* in Latin America suggest the need for historical and comparative research on how format constraints develop.) Despite a limited number of specials—movies, miniseries, major sporting events, pageants, and so forth—but as the stable base of their operations, networks rely on selling advertisers slots on regularly scheduled programs.[8]

Second, considering format can lead us to rethink arguments about what it is that television "reflects." Whether it is a direct embodiment of popular taste or a reflection distorted by the biases and blind spots of producers and directors, we have too easily taken for granted that what we see on television is the picture either that the aggregated mass of Americans or the producers and directors who serve them have of their society. In *Inside Prime Time,* for example, Gitlin (1983) writes that for television characters, "personal ambition and consumerism are the driving forces in their lives" (pp. 268-269). This is *not,* of course, an accurate characterization of prime-time television, in which, if anything, a kind of smarmy moralism has long held sway, with characters on both sit-com and adventure *series* inevitably making the "right" decision, putting principle and group welfare above personal ambition. But it is an excellent characterization of the moral world of the enormously popular prime-time *serials,* such as *Dynasty, Dallas, Flamingo Road,* and *Knots Landing.* As we have argued, it is in the serial format that villains are so useful as creators of suspenseful conspiracies and secrets.

Gitlin acknowledges a few lines later that greed and ambition are not all of American TV; people also "care about love, friendship, safety, trust, adventure, the nurture of the weak, not just material wealth" (p. 269). Attention to format and formula can bring some analytic order to such conflicting descriptions of the central themes of American television, suggesting that there are organizational factors at work behind both the greed and ambition and the self-sacrificing concern for the weak on prime-time TV. Even more important, format may also account for why still other themes, such as the love story, are largely neglected.

Consideration of format and formula also corrects reflection theories in a second way, by giving us new insights into the problems of television as an aesthetic form. As Horace Newcomb (1974) reminds us, television is entertainment, and as entertainment it has its own distinctive aesthetic difficulties. In any medium the formulas that entertain are not a direct reflection of underlying social concerns, so "reading" a society from its arts requires care. In particular, one can read "social meanings" only against a background of the available repertoire of dramatic formulas on which culture creators draw.

Important formulas in American popular culture include the love story (Watt, 1957), the western (Wright, 1975), mysteries, detective stories, and popular melodramas (Cawelti, 1976). But how those meanings will be cast on American television depends not only on contemporary social concerns (divorce, autonomous women, race relations) and on the deep, underlying issues that give popular formulas their vitality. It depends also on such apparently trivial but in fact significant matters as the need for most television programs to attract a regular audience that will tune in to the same shows week after week. This constraint, deriving from the way television is financed, means that some formulas with potentially wide popular appeal are neglected on television, whereas others with less popular resonance may become very important.

We argue that for American television, the commitment to continuing series and serials has restricted the ways television can use the traditional formulaic resources of the culture. Detective and western stories can draw on formulas from popular fiction, but without the possibility of a decisive ending even the core meanings of these formulas are gutted. Series cowboys can deliver a knockout punch, but they cannot fully make the transition Will Wright (1975) describes from being lonely individuals whose special skill keeps them outside society to heroes who use their special skill to save society and are thus welcomed into it. The television detective cannot follow the widening spiral of the hard-boiled detective formula (Cawelti, 1976), in which the detective's relentless pursuit of justice reveals the entire society as corrupt and brings down the power structure with the criminal. (Compare, as examples, the catastrophic ending of the movie *Chinatown* with the continuing amiable relationship between Rockford and his frequent antagonists on the local police force.) And, of course, the most central meanings of the love story are lost in both the stable domesticity of the sit-com and the steamy sex of the soaps.

Both Horace Newcomb (1974) and David Thorburn (1976) argue that television formats also create new aesthetic possibilities. Newcomb (1974) stresses the long time frame of soap opera stories, which can "grow and develop over periods of months and years" (p. 163), and Thorburn focuses on the intensified portrayal of character by series actors. Both point to new possibilities created by television's use of "endless" time. The evening soaps have also reintroduced richly developed villains, restoring what had been a central dramatic resource of premodern theater. (Think of Iago, Richard II, or the schemers of Moliere's comedies.) Both the "trickster" archetype (Griswold, 1983) and the particular form of satiric social critique it made possible had virtually disappeared from our cultural repertoire until the emergence of "J.R." of *Dallas*.

In thinking about both the possibilities and the limits of American television, it is important to remember that television creates entertainment and social meanings within a distinctive set of constraints, one of which is the formats the system of television production allows.

NOTES

1. Recent detective shows, most notably *Remington Steele,* create at least partial exceptions to this rule. They develop continuing romantic tension between a man and woman who are series principals, even if the romance is not the main focus of the show and can never be finally resolved.

2. The reasons for the decline of the anthology format remain mysterious. The prestige anthologies, original dramas produced live in New York, have received the most attention. Barnouw (1975, pp. 154-167) argues that these anthologies declined due to sponsor interference, the switch from live production in New York to film production in Hollywood (undermining the anthologies that had New York theater as their base), and the commercial advantages of series—"identification with a continuing, attractive actor" (p. 166), and predictable program content. But neither fear of controversy nor commercial advantages should explain the decline of formula anthologies such as *Loretta Young* and *Zane Grey,* which had attractive hosts and predictable formula plots.

3. Asked whether *Love Boat, Fantasy Island,* and *Hotel* were anthologies, Aaron Spelling answered: "Yes. The only way you can do anthologies now is if you have continuing characters going through them, so the audience has someone to hang on to each week" (*American Film,* 1984, p. 12). Each of the anthologies has several minidramas per episode, and on some shows (such as *Fantasy Island*), only one of these dramas is likely to be about love.

4. Hitchcock (quoted in Chatman, 1978, pp. 59-60) says,

> It is possible to build up almost unbearable tension in a play or film in which the audience knows who the murderer is all the time, and from the very start they want to scream out to all the other characters in the plot, "Watch out for So-and-So! He's a killer!" There you have real tenseness and an irresistible desire to know what happens.

Or, as a book on scriptwriting (Root, 1979, p. 54) puts it, create suspense by "letting the audience in on something that your characters don't know."

5. Cantor (1979) suggests other important differences between evening series and daytime serials. Daytime serials are produced primarily in New York, whereas evening series are produced in Hollywood. Although they have relatively low production budgets, serials have large casts, whereas episodic series are often built around one or a few continuing characters who are the center of the series. In serials, individual actors can be replaced or written out of the story, whereas the success of series often depends on its individual "stars."

6. A major exception to this rule is the important role courtship played in the radio serial (Stedman, 1971). Radio serials (the queen of the genre was *The Romance of Helen Trent*) often used a formula quite close to the plot of *Pamela,* with a cad-seducer pursuing a virtuous woman. And these dramas did *end*—with the virtuous woman retaining her purity and the seducer spurned. It would be interesting to ask why the radio serial was able to sustain endless "courtships," whereas the television soap opera did not. One reason may be simply that the radio era was a more staid one, in which the titilla-

tion of attempted seduction was enough to sustain interest, whereas the rape, incest, and adultery of the television soap would have offended audience sensibility. There are also two possible explanations related to the format of radio versus television. First, radio soap operas were usually only 15 minutes long and so could more easily focus on the perils of a single heroine than can the multistranded dramas of 90-minute daytime television. Second, the radio soap operas used a narrator, whose commentary on the ongoing action could create suspense without the complex intrigue of television soap operas.

7. An early manual for television scriptwriters (Seldes, 1953) described writing for series versus serials:

> The group of minor characters so familiar in the series drama, so confidently expected that people would miss them if they were kept out for weeks at a time, need not be constantly present in the serial, need not be made so attractive. The enemies rather than the friends of the heroine are important. (p. 126)

8. Focusing on the consequences of television formats suggests asking what accounts for the range of formats available on American television. The way advertising is sold no doubt has had a major effect, particularly in establishing the initial dominance of series and serials. As Cantor (1980, pp. 67-70) reminds us, from the origins of television at least until the 1960s, advertisers controlled and often paid for the programs they sponsored. A continuing program, associated with a given product, was what the sponsor bought. Only after the mid-1960s, according to Cantor, was the "magazine concept" in which "sponsors would buy inserts in programs produced by the networks or by independent producers under network control" (p. 68) fully established. When advertisers buy blocks of viewers rather than particular programs, networks may show whatever programming will attract large audiences, even if it offends some viewers.

The continued reliance on series and serials may also have more purely organizational explanations. As both Hirsch (1972) and Peterson and Berger (1975) have pointed out, culture-producing organizations must continually offer new products with high uncertainty about their success. The difficulty with miniseries and movies is that even when successful, they can be evaluated only in retrospect. Showing a successful movie, for example, still gives the network no way to evaluate the likely success of any new movie or miniseries. Movie studios that do cope with such uncertainties also have huge instabilities in their fortunes—and in the careers of their top executives.

Chapter 24

PUNK AND MIDDLE-CLASS VALUES
A Content Analysis

Philip Lamy
Jack Levin

PUNK OFFICIALLY DEBUTED as the "new wave" in youth sub-culture in the later months of 1976 through its discovery by the media as a movement with "social significance" (Baker & Cope, 1981; Coon, 1977; Hebdige, 1979; York, 1978). During a long, hot London summer, marked by drought, economic recession, racial violence, and crumbling urban neighborhoods, the British public was further distressed to learn that angry mobs of "disaffected" youth from inner-city working-class backgrounds had declared war on contemporary society, its institutions, and its dominant cultural values. The "punks" had affected a behavior and lifestyle in mock defiance of what is generally associated with British formalism and conservatism. They were the antithesis of all that they felt society stood for and thus they assumed the identity of society's alienated outcasts.

Television news programs and newspapers were filled with the bizarre pictures of costumed, zombielike, X-rated cartoon characters who stalked the twilight streets of London, hanging out in the rock clubs and shops that catered to their new, adopted lifestyle of punk. The young rock fans (who were the punks) had copied and exaggerated the style, dress, and behavior of their idols, the pub-playing punk rock bands. The result was the infamous punk "look": a curious montage of 1950s revivalist, fetishist, and paramilitary imagery, coupled with safety pin, razor blade, and spiked "jewelry," zippers (for tearing), and "angry shades." Hair was closely cropped, teased, feathered, and often dyed bright shocking colors; faces were made up in the gaudy and grim starkness suggestive of death itself.

The origins of the punk phenomenon can be found in the counter-cultures and youth subcultures of both America and England of the past 25 years (Coon, 1977; Hebdige, 1979). Its direct relationship to the rock culture is not surprising; other countercultures of recent years including the beats and hippies have also had their ideological and expressive centers in music (Yinger, 1977).

In the mid- to late 1970s the British punks, whose ages ranged between 13 and 19, came from white working-class backgrounds and were more self-consciously proletarian. By contrast, their American cousins came from primarily middle-class backgrounds, and the average age in the punk community was in the mid-20s (Hebdige, 1979).

In England the punks were largely ignorant of politics, philosophy, and literature. But as time passed and the music and movement became more sophisticated, so did its base of adherents. "One middle-class son of the artegentsia described his get-up as a 'complex statement of alienation'" (York, 1978, p. 135). British punks never did reach the intellectual levels that the Americans did, but the sources and feelings of alienation were the same. The punks vehemently reacted against the norms and values of the dominant culture, which they saw as repressive and inauthentic. They mocked and spat on conservative, capitalist big business that dictated what they must wear, buy, and listen to in music. They were cynical about the media, the police, and the entire social system for which no one (including themselves) wanted to be responsible.

THE PUNK AND
MIDDLE-CLASS PATTERNS IN AMERICA

The punk movement claims to be an alternative society practicing alienation from and rejection of the value system of the American middle-class culture. But because punk grew out of the American middle-class culture, it cannot be accurately understood in isolation from it. Among sociologists the value system of the middle class is generally defined as instrumental in nature. The instrumental orientation, formally defined by Talcott Parsons (1951), characterizes the dominant American value pattern as emphasizing utilitarian or instrumental activism as the cognitive or rational solution to life's tasks. Instrumental values are held as a means toward achieving "a goal which is an anticipated future state of affairs" (Parsons, 1951, p. 48). This goal-oriented rational behavior is a product of the Protestant ethic that has as its primary focus a ceaseless and generalized obligation to "worthwhile" achievement (Kerr, 1962; Levin & Spates, 1970; Reich, 1970).

In America, the main instrumental concerns are those dealing with economic achievement—that is, rationally constructed efforts to increase economic production, profits, and occupational status by means of extended formal education and hard work. The demands placed on the individual require two essential conditions: individual achievement in terms of personal wealth, power, or status and achievements as a moral obligation to contribute to the building of American society (Parsons & White, 1964). Thus, middle-class achievement cannot be purely utilitarian, using any means possible to a particular end, but must function through legitimized and socially sanctioned avenues. Success in America is defined in social as well as personal terms. Earning a decent living and contributing to the growth and expansion of the American dream place the individual in an upstanding and responsible position in society. The primary features of the middle-class pattern—economic, cognitive, and achievement values, all of which posit a goal-oriented ethic within the system—can be designated as the basic categories of "instrumentalism" (Levin & Spates, 1970; Parsons & White, 1964).

Perhaps no other subculture has sought with more grim determination than the punks to alienate itself from traditional forms of meaning and to bring down on themselves such furious disapproval. The punks clearly regard the value structure of the dominant culture as repressive, decadent, and obsolete, and offer instead a world made up of "anti-values." Vulgarity, cynicism, sexual perversion, twisted politics, and apocalyptic prophecy express much of the world view the punk sees. These are labels that the punks would also place on middle-class society. The punks have taken to expressing their disillusionment with society by mocking it in exaggerated style. Punk breaks all the codes of accepted behavior and lifestyle and reproduces the entire philosophical and sartorial history of subcultures in "cut-up" form, combining elements that had originally belonged to completely different epochs (Baker & Cope, 1981; Coon, 1977; Hebdige, 1979).

Such a negative reaction to society's dominant values has caused the punk movement in America to form a lifestyle and philosophy very different from that which predominates—the American ideal of the "hard working," self-denying, rational middle-class citizen. The punks present little in the form of a party manifesto or a positively directed alternative plan for a better society. Hebdige has described the ideal punk as "one forever condemned to act out alienation . . . to mime his imagined condition,'' and as a prophet "with the prescient knowledge of society's evident anarchy, surrender, and decline" (1979, p. 26).

This alternative mode of existence deemphasizes the economic, cognitive, and achievement value structure of the dominant culture and focuses instead on all objects and actions as ends in themselves and as necessary foci of present-time orientation and immediate gratification. Rather than attempting to deal with their affairs on a cognitive-rational level, or in terms of economic value, the punk's ideals stress the tearing apart of traditional meaning and the worthlessness of materialism. In addition, the achievement aspects of the middle-class pattern are replaced by almost total reliance on self-expression as experienced during the present moment (that is, by dressing in the punk "look," getting into punk music, art, drugs, etc.). And where middle-class individuals are expected to pursue goals through socially legitimized routes, punks choose a path as far outside accepted norms as they can discover or create themselves. The essential element of the punk value pattern as indicated by self-expression can be characterized by the term "expressivism" (Levin & Spates, 1970; Zelditch, 1955).

METHOD

The purpose of the present study was to examine punk values in relation to values of the American middle class and the hippie movement of the late 1960s. To define the value structure of the American punk subculture, a sample was taken from punk periodicals published in 1982 from major centers of punk activities. Much of the literature produced within the punk underground press exists in the form of hastily photocopied, limited edition, "little" magazines popularly called "fanzines." Literally hundreds of fanzines exist in America and England that focus primarily on the music and art scene of the punk community (records, concerts, new bands, art shows, etc.).

Because the content of the fanzines, as well as many of the other "regular" magazines, is purely expressive, they were not chosen for analysis. The punk magazines that were finally chosen—*NOMAG* (Los Angeles), *The East Village Eye* (New York City), and *Take It!* (Boston)—reflected the punk lifestyle—that is, they displayed a variety of subject matter other than music and art and seemed to be highly representative of the communities they serviced.

A single issue of each punk periodical from every second month in the year 1982 was selected on a random basis. Every second nonfictional article appearing in this sample of issues, excluding poetry and letters to the editor, was subjected to analysis (n = 117). Comparisons with hippie values were made possible by Levin and Spates's (1970) content analysis of the underground press. Using a procedure identical to that followed in the present study, they examined 316 articles from *Avatar* (Boston), *Distant Drummer* (Philadelphia), *East Village Other* (New York), *Los Angeles Free Press, San Francisco Oracle,* and *Washington Free Press* published during 1967-1968. In the late 1960s, these periodicals were read almost exclusively by political and apolitical contingents of hippies (Levin & Spates, 1970).

To provide a comparable sample of articles representing middle-class values, an analysis was also conducted on concurrently published issues of the *Reader's Digest,* selected for its variety of middle-class articles from different sources. Excluding fiction and poetry, every second article appearing in every other issue of *Reader's Digest* was studied (n = 89).

The major value-themes of articles in both punk and middle-class samples were coded by means of a modified version of Ralph K. White's "value catalogue" (1951), the same catalogue employed by Levin and Spates in their earlier study of hippie values. All materials were coded using a detailed set of definitions of the value-themes and appropriate coding sheets. Because of the presumed violent content of the punk subculture, an additional set of categories examining violence in the punk and middle-class literature was utilized.

Following the lead of earlier research, the categories "self-expressive," "concern for others," "affiliation," and "religious-philosophical" were treated as expressionism, whereas the categories "achievement," "cognitive," and "economic" became the basis for instrumentalism. Categories of the value analysis are listed below.

Instrumental

(a) *Achievement:* Values that produce achievement motivation for the individual in terms of hard work, practicality, economic value through occupation, and regard for ownership.

(b) *Cognitive:* These represent the drive for learning as a means for achieving success, welfare, happiness, or as an end in itself.

(c) *Economic:* These values are at the collective level, such as state, national, or industrial, thus differing from individual goals such as achievement.

Expression

(d) *Self-expressive:* These values include humor, play, fun in general, relaxation, new discoveries, travel, art, beauty, sexual expression or fulfillment.

(e) *Affiliative:* This category focuses upon the gregariousness of individuals and the friendships that they develop. The affiliative aim may be conformity, loyalty to the group, friendship, other-directedness, or group activity.

(f) *Concern for others:* This category includes feelings toward particular groups or humanity in general. These objectives are more abstract than affiliation.

(g) *Religious-philosophical:* This category includes values concerning the ultimate meaning of life, the role of deity, after-life, and so on.

Other

(h) *Individualistic:* These values stress the importance of the individual, the development of personality, independence, personal fulfillment, including rebellion.

(i) *Physiological:* These values are created by physiological drives such as hunger, sex, physical safety, and health. These elements can be clinical or medical.

(j) *Political:* These are collective values such as state, community, national, and international in reference to group decision-making processes.

(k) *Miscellaneous:* Values not covered above such as hope, honesty, purity, modesty, and manners.

Categories of the analysis of violence were as follows:

Violence as Major Factor

(a) *Violent content:* This area includes elements of physical or psychological injury to oneself, other persons, or animals. Also included in this category are sadomasochistic behavior, sexual perversion, and destruction of property.

(b) *Nonviolent content:* These were elements that were clearly peaceful, complacent, restrained, respectful, and mannerly.

(c) *Uncertain:* Articles in which the content could not be determined as being violent or nonviolent were placed in this category.

The reliability of the value analysis was tested by having three coders independently code 20 articles from both the alternative press and the *Reader's Digest* samples. Using a "two out of three" criterion (that is, two of three coders agreed), agreement concerning the value

TABLE 24.1
Value-Themes in the Punk Press and *Reader's Digest*
(in percentages)

Value-Theme	Punk Press		Reader's Digest	
Expressive	80		27	
Self-expressive		65		16
Concern for others		7		6
Affiliative		6		4
Religious-philosophical		2		1
Instrumental	4		38	
Achievement		2		17
Cognitive		2		17
Economic		0		4
Other	16		35	
Individual		4		11
Political		9		6
Physiological		1		15
Miscellaneous		2		3
Total		100		100
(N = 206)		(117)		(89)

NOTE: A Chi-square analysis was conducted by comparing the alternative punk press and *Reader's Digest* on the two major value-themes, Expressive and Instrumental (χ^2 = 52.84, df = 1, p < .001).

analysis reached 95%, total agreement was 65%. For the category of violence "two out of three" agreement was 100%, and total agreement was 75%.

RESULTS AND DISCUSSION

Results obtained in an analysis of the punk press clearly suggest that expressivism occupies a central position, whereas instrumentalism is virtually nonexistent, in the punk value structure. As shown in Table 24.1, expressive concerns accounted for 80% of the value-themes in the punk press, whereas instrumental concerns were the major focus of only 4% of these articles. In sharp contrast, instrumental concerns represented the major value-theme in the *Reader's Digest* sample (38%), whereas expressive concerns were less important (27%).

Within the expressive category of the value catalogue the dominant content in the punk literature was on "self-expression" (65%). For example, in both the Boston and New York punk press there were columns dealing with movies, fashion, art, and music. Typical articles described the relationship of early avant-garde personalities to the punk movement (such as Andy Warhol, Allen Ginsberg, and William Burroughs) and presented interviews with contemporary punk rock performers and other punk personalities. In all of the punk literature, articles were often written in such a confusing, outrageous, perhaps experimental manner that it was often difficult to know when the writer was seriously discussing a subject or was creating art. There were many book and record reviews in the punk literature and avant-garde, experimental, and punk futuristic art constituted a significant amount of the self-expressive category.

Concerning the other expressive categories, there were few articles in significant numbers to warrant discussion, save for a fair representation of humanistic articles dealing with the poor and derelict of the New York and Boston punk communities as reflected in the category "concern for others" (7%).

In the *Reader's Digest* sample, "achievement" and "cognitive" were the dominant components of instrumentalism, each representing 17% of all value-themes. Typically, *Reader's Digest* articles emphasized new or revised methods for occupational achievement, including business enterprises, advice on financial investments and taxes, the careers of well-known persons who had achieved occupational success, and so on. Cognitive concerns were manifested in self-improvement columns and articles such as enriching vocabulary or speech, handling relationships, and in articles describing new science and technology. "Self-expression" (16%) was the most significant expressive category in the *Reader's Digest* sample. The majority of articles in this category were related to laughter, games, cooking, and playing with pets.

No significant difference was uncovered between the punk and middle-class samples with respect to violent content (χ^2 = 1.65, df = 1, p > .05). Specifically, 35% of the articles in the punk sample and 26% in *Reader's Digest* contained violence.

Punk's detractors accusingly point to the killing of animals on stage during (some) punk performances, decorative self-mutilation, "slam dancing," violent deaths in the punk community, a punk cult of neo-Nazis, and the whole anarchic philosophy of the movement as evidence of punk's thoroughly violent nature. However, in the punk literature, violence most often took its form in artistic expression. The postapocalyptic look, the punk version of what everyone will be wearing once "they" drop "the big one," is essentially punk fashion. It is a cynical political statement of decaying Western society, but it is also personal aesthetic expression. "The punks wanted to look good and to shock, but in that order" (York, 1978, p. 137). Much of the violent nature of the punk movement is psychological. The literature presented many articles that railed against the violence being perpetrated on the American public by the media, the government, and the dominant culture.

In the *Reader's Digest,* violence was prevalent in articles describing Central American turmoil, the buildup of nuclear weapons, crime, disasters, and personal calamity. The manner of presentation in the middle-class sample is more objective and desensitized, even sanitized, whereas the punks illustrate violence in an exaggerated and sarcastic tone. People are perhaps more disturbed by the punk "in your face" attitude and the stark realism they attempt to portray than by the constant but socially acceptable outpouring of violence in the mainstream media. The punks mock the violence and apathy they see as integral to the dominant culture, and the fact that they have evoked such vehement criticism from society is evidence that they have succeeded in making their point.

In their earlier study, Levin and Spates (1970) found that expressive concerns were the "staple of great magnitude" for readers of the hip underground press and the hippie movement as a whole. Expressive values accounted for 46% of their sample, with more than half of that in the subcategory, "self-expressive" (28%).

As shown in Table 24.2, punk expressivism (80%) is almost twice that of the hippie value content. Moreover, individual and political concerns accounted for 20% and 19%, respectively, of all value categories in the hippie press, but only 4% and 9% in the punk press.

As reflected in their periodicals, the hippies developed an activist radical fringe, something the punks have yet to display in any advanced form. This obviously has much to do with the political and social climate of the turbulent 1960s and with the emphasis the hippies, and the subsequent hip generation, placed upon individualism and the "do your own thing" ethic (Levin & Spates, 1970). The punks, however, see this ethic as contributing to the alienation of people and as generating the "me generation," all of which they revolt against. And to become part of the "me generation," one has to cultivate and improve the self by adopting instrumental goals. Furthermore, it is evident that punk's roots in England and America are predominantly artistic; thus, it follows that the movement as a whole will also be largely expressive.

TABLE 24.2
Value-Themes in the Punk and Hippie Press
(in percentages)

Value-Theme	Punk Press		Hippie Press	
Expressive	80		46	
Self-expressive		65		28
Concern for others		7		8
Affiliative		6		4
Religious-philosophical		2		6
Instrumental	4		10	
Achievement		2		3
Cognitive		2		5
Economic		0		2
Other	16		44	
Individual		4		20
Political		9		19
Physiological		1		4
Miscellaneous		2		1
Total		100		100
(N = 433)		(117)		(316)

NOTE: Data for the hippie press were taken from Levin and Spates (1970, p. 396). (Chi-square: $\chi^2 = 8.04$, df = 1, p < .01).

CONCLUSION

Results obtained in the present content analysis suggest that the punk movement is more expressive, and less instrumental, than its middle-class counterpart. This confirms earlier studies comparing the expressive nature of beats and hippies to the American middle class (Levin & Spates, 1970; Miller, 1977; Spates, 1976; Spates & Levin, 1971). Alternative youth countercultures typically react against middle-class values that they view as conservative in expressive and artistic disposition and thus compensate for that fact by downplaying instrumental goals and amplifying expressive ones.

Similar to the hippie movement of the 1960s, which evolved into a "hip generation" of middle-class fashion, music, and dance, the punks have inspired a "new wave" in middle-class lifestyles. In its basic form, punk was too "vulgar" and "crude" for conventional, middle-class taste. By contrast, new wave eliminates the most extreme and deviant elements of punk while preserving its core expressivism. For example, whereas punk bands such as The Dead Kennedys might offend and infuriate "middle-of-the-road" listeners, new wave groups such as The Police and Devo are widely accepted. Similarly, drastic punk hairstyles such as the "skinhead" and "Mohawk" are regarded as perverse, whereas a neatly cropped, short haircut is seen as fashionable.

Unlike its hippie predecessors, however, the punk movement does not have an "alternative plan" in the form of communitarian farms, cooperatives, and yippie radicals of the 1960s generation. Instead, the punks generally resigned themselves to parodying the entire "hopeless" situation that they see as their present and future state of existence.

At the same time, there is some ambiguity within the punk movement and its ideology. Despite punk's basic expressivism, much of its art and music contain social and political commentary ranging from neo-Marxism to racism and fascism. Moreover, the punk phenomena in Europe and America have played a significant role in the anti-nuclear rallies of recent years. Punks have been prominent among the protestors and have contributed to the apocalyptic "style" of the rallies. The skeletal, white-painted "faces of doom," and the mutilated and bloodied bodies of a holocaust scenario are a direct influence of the punk aesthetic. Punks have also figured prominently in the "rock against racism" campaign set up to combat the growing influence of National Front activity in working-class communities in England during the late 1970s (Hebdige, 1979). Although the punk philosophy preaches a nihilistic philosophy and calls for total rejection of society's norms, it is, in its negative way, positively directed. The punk movement succeeds in calling attention to itself and is able to spread its message of discontent, alienation, and uncertainty about humankind's future.

CONCLUSION

Going Beyond Contemporary Media Theory and Research

THE CHAPTERS AND COMMENTARIES included here present a small but significant part of the research under way in the field of mass communications. Our intent in selecting these pieces was to show that the "famine" in research has passed and that the field of mass communications has expanded from its initially narrow but important 1940s and 1950s focus on audience characteristics and effects on individuals. When Herbert Gans commented on the famine in American mass communication rescarch in 1972, he said that we need to know how mass media function as institutions and why they function the way they do; how they determine content and what cultural and interest groups influence this determination, directly or indirectly; and, most important, how the media relate to their audiences in this process. From this collection it is clear that researchers have taken his suggestions seriously in most areas. We need to continue to "rediscover" these and other classical questions that prompted the research interests of so many pioneers of the pre-1940s era. The questions were good and our answers to them are getting better.

The chapters in this book, for example, not only show the progress we have made toward understanding both how content is created and its distribution but also provide models of future research (see especially the chapters by Swidler et al., Lamy and Levin, Singer and Endreny, Billings, Cantor and Cantor, Kapsis, Gray, Parker, and Sewart). In different contexts, Cantor (1980) and DeFleur and Ball-Rokeach (1982) have emphasized the importance of understanding the system in which content is created and distributed. We hope that this book will help clarify the processes by which contents change. One thing is clear: We cannot divorce the question of content change from the political, social, and economic realities of the media system, their audiences, and the larger society. Once these linkages are made, we may be in a better position to broaden our vision to comprehend the conditions under which content changes in some essential way but also when it remains the same.

This collection also demonstrates that the seminal work of Lazarsfeld and his colleagues continues to influence the direction of media research, although the scope has broadened considerably. No longer is the term "social" narrowly applied to mean simply demographic characteristics. The definition of "social" has expanded to include history, industrial relations, culture, social structure, political economy, and social process. Only market researchers can now limit themselves to demographic characteristics of viewers as "independent variables" in their efforts to discover "target audiences" for advertisers. The social scientist's effort to uncover the reciprocal relations between the media and social processes of change, conflict, integration, and control requires moving beyond demographics of audiences to questions of the structural position of the media in social life and its cumulative, as well as its more immediate, effects on belief, behavior, culture, and process. Going hand in hand with our expansion of the concept of social is the need to improve upon the methods of our inquiry; especially historical and comparative, case study, field survey, and quasi-experimental methods. Examples of such improvements are well represented in this volume, but the challenge of making valid observations of the media's influence on the changing fabric of our information society will require even more improvement. We endorse Lang and Lang's call made in their chapter in this volume for a collaborative effort to develop such strategies.

It is notable that we have not included any work that examines probably the most talked-about media effects: effects of media violence and pornography on individuals. Although this psychologist-dominated examination of specific and short-term effects of the media on politically defined "problems" of violent, erotic, or pornographic media content (see Wright's chapter in this volume) will continue to be pursued as long as legislators and interest groups find it in their interests to do so, it is our view that these questions should not be left at the psychological level of analysis. We should reformulate the way these questions are posed and couch them in more sociologically relevant terms so as to be able to uncover the social and cultural consequences of the way violence and sex is treated in media content (Ball-Rokeach, 1971). In addition to those chapters that touch upon such issues—for example, the nature of sport (Sewart), female sex role stereotypes (Press), and the portrayal of the criminal (Parker)—we should seek answers to such questions as these: How does the media world of violence and/or sex affect the citizen's, law enforcement organizations', and the state's willingness to approve and use violence in interpersonal, intergroup, and international relations? Or following the lead of Gerbner and his colleagues, how does the symbolic construction of the media world affect levels of fear, alienation, and anxiety and the even more basic question of political ideologies? Or how can we explain why the incredible amount of research done on the question of media violence and sex has had virtually no effect on either legislative policy or media content; that is, what are the political economic functions of asking these questions and researching them over and over gain? These illustrative recommendations for future research suggest that the previously distinct arenas of inquiry into news construction (Gans, 1979; Tuchman, 1978, and many others) could be profitably joined with the search for the effects of violence-sex media content in news and entertainment, and with a new line of research coming out of the sociology of knowledge tradition on the politics of how media effects research questions are posed.

Perhaps our couching of the media system as an economic agency in the business of creating, gathering, processing, and disseminating information in the form of cultural products called "news" and "entertainment" may also encourage us to move into other areas of theory and research that are not well represented in this volume. Of these, we would point to the need to buttress the fragments of available research on the media system's relations to other social systems. For example, what difference do these relations make not only for the kind of content that is created but also for the structure and conduct of basic political, economic, familial, educational, legal, military, religious, and recreational life? In addition to the concept of structural dependency or interdependence that has been suggested here, we need to develop other concepts that will allow us to examine the media system as part of a relation rather than as an isolated system. This problem takes us back, as Schudson has noted, to fundamental questions posed by Weber, Durkheim, and Marx. Both Rosengren's and Beniger's chapters may be seen as attempts to deal with such difficult questions, and McCormack calls for such an approach with regard to the question of social change.

Another obvious line of theory and research that is only touched upon in this volume is the social and cultural determinants and consequences of the "new" information-communication technologies. The questions that are pressing at this point in time include the following: How is the media system adapting (or failing to adapt) to the emergence of these technologies? What is and will determine which of these potential "mass" communication technologies will realize their technological potential? What will "mass" communication mean in the future, and will it make sense to even speak of "mass" communication? Will the technological potential for narrowcasting (moving from "mass" audiences to specialized audiences, e.g., see Robinson and Fink) and its parallel in the print media fundamentally alter the structure of the media industry and our conception of the media "audience"? We see in some of the chapters (e.g., Cantor and Cantor, Billings, Robinson and Fink) a serious questioning of the idea of the "mass" audience as usually defined. We suspect that the very meaning of media audience will change even more dramatically as new technologies become commonplace.

In this book we have not focused on new technologies per se because their adoption and potential consequences are always grounded in the power relations between the media system and other social systems and within the media system itself. For example, some groups and organizations have more power than others to select and create which of the potential technologies will be adopted and what content or information services will thus be made available. Studies and projections of new media technologies are therefore necessarily wedded to understandings of power relations, competition, and conflict. The Information Age emerged as part and parcel of social control forces (see Beniger's chapter in this volume), and we expect it will continue to take shape under the same sort of social forces.

One of those forces that has received much public attention in recent years is the combined thrust of legal and corporate attempts to exert more control over the media system, particularly the major networks. The attempt by Ted Turner (head of the Cable News Network) to take over CBS, for example, was unsuccessful, but apparently it forced CBS to cut personnel so that funds could be accumulated to buy back its stock. Of course, Senator Jessie Helms's attempt to take over CBS is explicitly justified as a way to exert the control necessary to make CBS a spokesperson of the "far right." The legal right of the journalist to keep sources and notes secret is being challenged in the courts around the nation. These few examples of the many attempts to exert control over media content suggest a potentially important area of inquiry into the consequences of such "pressures" on the practices, policies, and structure of media organizations. Following Cantor's (1980) lead, we could go beyond Montgomery's analysis of the consequences of interest group pressure to an even more general appreciation of the external forces that shape media organizations. Of course, such pursuits would also have to incorporate those cases in which the legal-political forces seem to be operating to reduce the amount of government control over the media system, such as the Federal Communications Commissions' recent deregulation moves.

Despite the complicated pushes and pulls of external and internal forces that affect the way in which new media technologies will be developed, we think that it is a good bet that computer-based information technologies that serve as information utilities for communities will continue to be developed. Both the Turner and Paz and the Hirschburg et al. chapters demonstrate the heavy media system dependency that individuals and communities have under conditions of threat or experience of a natural disaster. The Taylor chapter addresses a related community problem of public opinion formation under conditions of intergroup conflict. The conventional one-way media of today, however, are not well suited to the tasks of ambiguity resolution and rumor control that individuals, groups, and communities need performed under such conditions. We suggest that three usually separate lines of inquiry could be fruitfully brought together to explore the possibility that community-based interactive media systems could be developed to handle these tasks better. The three lines of inquiry are media system dependency theory applied to the community level of analysis, a social impact of new information-communication technologies approach, and public opinion formation.

As with so many things in life, the very things that are most provocative and exciting are also the sources of incredible frustration. The study of media systems and mass communications is no exception. The field is so diverse and unwieldy that it provokes both the exciting freedom to create and the frustrating challenge of getting a handle on what the most compelling questions are. In this brief conclusion, we have had the frustration of having to select only a few of what we regard as compelling questions to be addressed in future theory and research. But as coeditors of this volume, we also have the excitement of hoping that the contents of this volume will provoke others to pursue these and other questions identified by the many fine scholars represented herein.

REFERENCES

Adams, J. B., Mullen, J. J., & Wilson, H. H. (1969). Diffusion of a "minor" foreign affairs news event. *Journalism Quarterly, 46,* 545-551.

Adler, B. (1981). WVSP: Voices serving people. *Southern Exposure, 9,* 23.

Adorno, T. (1981-1982). Transparencies on film. *New German Critique, 24,* 20-31.

Albrecht, M. C. (1954). The relationship of literature and society. *American Journal of Sociology, 59,* 425-436.

Alicote, J. (Ed.). (1936-1964). *Film daily yearbook of motion pictures.* New York: Film Daily.

Allen, R. C. (1982a). Motion picture exhibition in Manhattan, 1906-1912: Beyond the nickelodeon. In G. Kindem (Ed.), *The American movie industry: The business of motion pictures* (pp. 12-24). Carbondale: Southern Illinois University Press.

Allen, R. C. (1982b). Vitascope/cinematographe: Initial patterns of American film industry practice. In G. Kindem (Ed.), *The American movie industry: The business of motion pictures* (pp. 3-11). Carbondale: Southern Illinois University Press.

Allport, F. (1924). *Social psychology.* Boston: Houghton Mifflin.

American Film. (1984). Dialogue on film: Aaron Spelling. Vol. *55,* 10-14.

Andren, G. (1984). The cement of society: On causation and technology between patterns of culture and production/reproduction structures. In G. Melischek, K. E. Rosengren, & J. Stappers (Eds.), *Cultural indicators: An international symposium* (pp. 33-48). Vienna: Akademie der Wissenschaften.

Avery, R. K., & Pepper, R. (1980). An institutional history of public broadcasting. *Journal of Communication, 30,* 126-138.

Baker, G. A., & Cope, S. (1981). *The new music.* New York: Bay.

Balfe, J. (1981). Social mobility and modern art: Abstract expressionism and its generative audience. In L. Kriesberg (Ed.), *Research in social movements, conflict and change* (Vol. 4, pp. 235-251). Greenwich, CT: Jai.

Balio, T. (1976). Stars in business: The founding of United Artists. In T. Balio (Ed.), *The American film industry* (pp. 135-152). Madison: University of Wisconsin Press.

Ball, S. J. (1969). Television entertainment and violence. In R. K. Baker & S. J. Ball (Eds.), *Mass media and violence: A staff report to the National Commission on the Causes and Prevention of Violence* (pp. 235-236). Washington, DC: Government Printing Office.

Ball-Rokeach, S. J. (1971). The legitimation of violence. In J. F. Short, Jr., & M. E. Wolfgang (Eds.), *Collective violence* (pp. 100-111). Chicago: Aldine.

Ball-Rokeach, S. J. (1973). From pervasive ambiguity to a definition of the situation. *Sociometry, 36,* 378-389.

Ball-Rokeach, S. J. (1985). The origins of individual media system dependency: A sociological framework. *Communication Research, 12,* 485-510.

Ball-Rokeach, S. J. (1986). The media and the social fabric. In J. F. Short, Jr. (Ed.), *The social fabric: Dimensions and issues.* Beverly Hills, CA: Sage.

Ball-Rokeach, S. J., & DeFleur, M. L. (1976). A dependency model of mass media effects. *Communication Research, 3,* 3-21.

Ball-Rokeach, S. J., Rokeach, M., & Grube, J. W. (1984). *The great American values test: Influencing behavior and belief through television.* New York: Free Press.

Barnouw, E. (1975). *Tube of plenty: The evolution of American television.* New York: Oxford University Press.

References   355

Barnouw, E. (1978). *The sponsor: Notes on a modern potentate.* New York: Oxford University Press.
Barr, K. (1979). Long waves: A selected annotated bibliography. *Review, 2,* 675-718.
Barton, A. H., Denitch, B., & Kadushin, C. (1973). *Opinion-making elites in Yugoslavia.* New York: Praeger.
Bauer, R. (1958). The communicator and the audience. *Journal of Conflict Resolution, 2,* 66-78.
Bazin, A. (1958). *Qu' est-ce que le cinema?* (Vol. 1). Paris: Editions du Cerf.
Becker, H. (1982). *Art worlds.* Berkeley: University of California Press.
Becker, H. (1983). Foreward. In J. B. Kamerman & R. Martorella (Eds.), *Performers and performances: The social organization of artistic work* (pp. x-xi). New York: Praeger.
Bell, D. (1960). *The end of ideology: On the exhaustion of political ideas in the fifties.* New York: Free Press.
Bell, D. (1965). *The end of ideology: On the exhaustion of political ideas in the fifties.* (rev. ed.). New York: Free Press.
Bell, D. (1973). *The coming of post-industrial society: A venture in social forecasting.* New York: Basic Books.
Bell, D. (1976). *The cultural contradictions of capitalism.* New York: Basic Books.
Bell, D. (1979). The social framework of the information society. In M. L. Dertouzos & J. Moses (Eds.), *The computer age: A twenty year view* (pp. 163-211). Cambridge: MIT Press.
Berelson, B. (1959). The state of communication research. *Public Opinion Quarterly, 23,* 1-6.
Berelson, B. R., Lazarsfeld, P. F., & McPhee, W. N. (1954). *Voting: A study of opinion formation in a presidential campaign.* Chicago: University of Chicago Press.
Berger, P. L., & Luckman, T. (1967). *The social construction of reality: A treatise in the sociology of knowledge.* Garden City, NY: Doubleday.
Berman, M. (1982). *All that is solid melts into air: The experience of modernity.* New York: Simon & Schuster.
Best, J. (1981). The social control of media content. *Journal of Popular Culture, 14,* 611-617.
Blanqui, J. A. (1880). *History of political economy in Europe* (E. J. Leonard, Trans.). New York: G. P. Putnam. (Original work published 1837)
Blau, J. (in press). The geography of culture. In J. P. Robinson (Ed.), *Social science and the arts: 1984.* Lanham, MD: University Press of America.
Block, E. (1984). Freedom, equality, etcetera: Values and valuations in the Swedish domestic political debate, 1945-1975. In G. Melischek, K. E. Rosengren, & J. Stappers (Eds.), *Cultural indicators: An international symposium* (pp. 159-176). Vienna: Akademie der Wissenschaften.
Block, P. (1984). Newspaper content as a secularization indicator. In G. Melischek, K. E. Rosengren, & J. Stappers (Eds.), *Cultural indicators: An international symposium* (pp. 195-216). Vienna: Akademie der Wissenschaften.
Blumer, H. (1946). Collective behavior. In A. M. Lee (Ed.), *New outline of the principles of sociology* (pp. 167-222). New York: Barnes & Noble.
Blumer, H., & Hauser, P. M. (1933). *Movies, delinquency, and crime.* New York: Arno.

Blumler, J. G. (1969). Producers attitudes toward television coverage of an election campaign: A case study. *Sociological Review Monograph: Sociology of Mass Communications, 13*, 85-115.

Blumler, J. G., & Katz, E. (Eds.). (1974). *The uses of mass communications: Current perspectives on gratifications research.* Beverly Hills, CA: Sage.

Bogart, L. (1950). The spread of news on a local event: A case history. *Public Opinion Quarterly, 14,* 769-772.

Bogart, L. (1956). *The age of television.* New York: Ungar.

Bogart, L. (1981). *Press and public: Who reads what, when, where, and why in American newspapers.* Hillsdale, NJ: Erlbaum.

Bogart, L. (1984). The public's use and perception of newspapers. *Public Opinion Quarterly, 48,* 709-719.

Bonjean, C. M., Hill, R. J., & Martin, H. W. (1965). Reactions to the assassination in Dallas. In B. S. Greenberg & E. B. Parker (Eds.), *The Kennedy assassination and the American public* (pp. 178-198). Stanford, CA: Stanford University Press.

Borman, S. C. (1978). Communication accuracy in magazine science reporting. *Journalism Quarterly, 55,* 345-346.

Boulding, K. E. (1953). *The organizational revolution: A study in the ethics of economic organization.* New York: Harper.

Bourdieu, P. (1977). Cultural reproduction and social reproduction. In J. Karabel & A. H. Halsey (Eds.), *Power and ideology in education* (pp. 487-511). New York: Oxford University Press.

Bouwman, H. (1984). Cultivation analysis: The Dutch case. In G. Melischek, K. E. Rosengren, & J. Stappers (Eds.), *Cultural indicators: An international symposium* (pp. 407-422). Vienna: Akademie der Wissenschaften.

Bower, R. T. (1973). *Television and the public.* New York: Holt, Rinehart & Winston.

Bower, R. T. (1985). *The changing television audience in America.* New York: Columbia University Press.

Branscomb, A. W., & Savage, M. (1978). The broadcasting reform movement: At the crossroads. *Journal of Communication, 28,* 25-34.

Breed, W. (1955). Social control in the news room: A functional analysis. *Social Forces, 33,* 326-335.

Broadcasting. (1985). Ready, set and almost go on TV's new year. Vol. *109*: 34-35, 38.

Brockett, O. G., & Findlay, R. R. (1973). *Century of innovation: A history of European and American drama since 1870.* Englewood Cliffs, NJ: Prentice-Hall.

Broughton, D. (1983, July/August). Dirty Air: The biggest hurdle? *Not Man Apart,* pp. 18-21.

Brzezinski, Z. (1970). *Between two ages: America's role in the technetronic era.* New York: Viking.

Budd, R. W., MacLean, M. S., & Barnes, A. M. (1966). Regularities in the diffusion of two major news events. *Journalism Quarterly, 43,* 221-230.

Bunge, M. (1981). *Scientific materialism.* Dordrecht: Reidel.

Burchfield, R. W. (Ed.). (1972). *A supplement to the Oxford English Dictionary* (Vol. 1). Oxford: Clarendon.

Burgoon, J. (1980). Predictors of newspaper readership. *Journalism Quarterly, 57,* 589-596.

Burke, P. (1981). The "discovery" of popular culture. In R. Samuel (Ed.), *People's history and socialist theory* (pp. 216-226). London: Routledge & Kegan Paul.

Burrell, G., & Morgan, G. (1979). *Sociological paradigms and organizational analysis.* London: Heineman.

Cantor, M. G. (1971). *The Hollywood TV producer: His work and his audience*. New York: Basic Books.

Cantor, M. G. (1979a). Our days and our nights on TV. *Journal of Communication, 29*, 66-72.

Cantor, M. G. (1979b). The politics of popular drama. *Communication Research, 6*, 387-406.

Cantor, M. G. (1980). *Prime-time television: Content and control*. Beverly Hills, CA: Sage.

Cantor, M. G., & Cantor, J. M. (1984). Do soaps teach sex? *Television and Children, 7*, 29-38.

Cantor, M. G., & Pingree, S. (1983). *The soap opera*. Beverly Hills, CA: Sage.

Carlsson, G., Dahlberg, A., & Rosengren, K. E. (1981). Mass media content, political opinions, and social change: Sweden 1967-1974. In K. E. Rosengren (Ed.), *Advances in content analysis* (pp. 227-240). Beverly Hills, CA: Sage.

Cash, W. (1941). *The mind of the South*. New York: Knopf.

Cassady, R., Jr. (1982). Monopoly in motion picture production and distribution: 1908-1915. In G. Kindem (Ed.), *The American movie industry: The business of motion pictures* (pp. 25-67). Carbondale: Southern Illinois University Press.

Catton, W. R., Jr. (1969). The worldview presented by mass media. In R. K. Baker & S. J. Ball (Eds.), *Mass media and violence: A report to the National Commission on the Causes and Prevention of Violence* (pp. 473-486). Washington, DC: Government Printing Office.

Cavell, S. (1981). *Pursuits of happiness: The Hollywood comedy of remarriage*. Cambridge, MA: Harvard University Press.

Cavell, S. (1982). The fact of television. *Daedalus, 111*, 75-96.

Cawelti, J. G. (1976). *Adventure, mystery, and romance: Formula stories as art and popular culture*. Chicago: University of Chicago Press.

Chaffee, S. H., McLeod, J. M., & Wackman, D. B. (1973). Family communication patterns and adolescent political participation. In J. Dennis (Ed.), *Socialization to politics* (pp. 349-364). New York: John Wiley.

Chatman, S. (1978). *Story and discourse: Narrative structure in fiction and film*. Ithaca, NY: Cornell University Press.

Coates, C. (1981, March 30). Scramble under way for "clean" tv shows. *Advertising Age*.

Cogley, J. (1972). *Report on blacklisting: Part 1. The movies*. New York: Arno.

Cohn, L. (1982, August 26). A game is smeared. *San Francisco Chronicle Sporting Green*, p. 35.

Cohn, L. (1984, April 20). Steve Scott's path to glory. *San Francisco Chronicle Sporting Green*, p. 41.

Cole, S., Cole, J. R., & Simon, G. A. (1981). Chance and consensus in peer review. *Science, 214*, 881-886.

Combs, R. (1981). Westerns. In D. Pirie (Ed.), *Anatomy of the movies* (pp. 201-219). New York: Macmillan.

Conant, M. (1960). *Antitrust in the motion picture industry: Economic and legal analysis*. Berkeley: University of California Press.

Cooley, C. H. (1956). *Social organization: A study of the larger mind*. New York: Free Press.

Coon, C. (1977). *The new wave punk rock explosion*. London: Omnibus.

Cosell, H. (1973). *Cosell*. New York: Pocket Books.

Coser, L. (1975). Publishers as gatekeepers of ideas. *Annals of the American Academy of Political and Social Science, 42,* 14-22.

Cowan, G. (1979). *See no evil: The backstage battle over sex and violence on television*. New York: Simon & Schuster.

Creel, G. (1972). *How we advertised America*. New York: Arno.

Crepeau, R. (1980). *Baseball: America's diamond mind, 1914-1919*. Orlando: University Presses of Florida.

Cronbach, L. (1971). Test validation. In R. Thorndike (Ed.), *Educational measurement*. Washington, DC: American Council on Education.

Darnton, R. (1975). Writing news and telling stories. *Daedalus, 104,* 175-194.

Davison, W. P. (1965). *International political communication*. New York: Praeger.

DeFleur, M. L., & Ball-Rokeach, S. J. (1982). *Theories of mass communication* (4th. ed.). New York: Longman.

DeFleur, M. L., & Larson, O. N. (1958). *The flow of information: An experiment in mass communication*. New York: Harper.

De Grazia, E., & Newman, R. K. (1982). *Banned films: Movies, censors and the First Amendment*. New York: Bowker.

de Sola Pool, I. (1983, August). Tracking the flow of information. *Science.*

de Sola Pool, I., Inose, H., Takasaki, N., & Hurwitz, R. (1984). *Communications flows: Census in the United States and Japan*. Amsterdam: North Holland Press.

Deutsch, A. (1948). *The shame of the states*. New York: Harcourt, Brace.

Deutschmann, P. J., & Danielson, W. A. (1960). Diffusion of knowledge of the major news story. *Journalism Quarterly, 37,* 345-355.

Dillman, D. A. (1978). *Mail and telephone surveys: The total design method*. New York: John Wiley.

Dillman, D. A. (1980). *After Mt. St. Helens: Seven gray days in May* (mimeo). Pullman: Washington State University, Department of Rural Sociology.

DiMaggio, P. (1977). Market structure, the creative process and popular culture: Toward an organizational reinterpretation of mass culture theory. *Journal of Popular Culture, 11,* 436-466.

DiMaggio, P. (1982). Cultural capital and school success: The impact of status culture participation on the grades of U.S. high school students. *American Sociological Review, 47,* 189-201.

DiMaggio, P., & Powell, W. (1983). The iron cage revisited: Institutional isomorphism and collective rationality in organizational fields. *American Sociological Review, 48,* 147-160.

DiMaggio, P., & Useem, M. (1978). Social class and arts consumption: The origins and consequences of class differences in exposure to the arts in America. *Theory and Society, 5,* 141-161.

Djilas, M. (1957). *The new class: An analysis of the communist system*. New York: Praeger.

Duncan, O. D. (1972). Unmeasured variables in linear models for panel analysis. In O. D. Duncan, *Sociological methodology 1972* (pp. 36-82). San Francisco: Jossey-Bass.

Duncan, O. D. (1975). Some linear models for two-wave, two-variable panel analysis, with one-way causation and measurement error. In H. M. Blalock, A. Aganbegian,

F. M. Borodkin, R. Boudon, & V. Capecchi (Eds.), *Quantitative sociology: International perspectives on mathematical and statistical modeling* (pp. 285-306). Chicago: Aldine.

Dunwoody, S. (1983). *Mass media coverage of the social sciences: Some new answers to old questions.* Paper presented at the annual meetings of the Association for Education in Journalism and Mass Communications.

Dunwoody, S. (1984). *Communicating risk information: What role do the media play?* Paper presented at the annual meetings of the American Association for the Advancement of Science.

Dunwoody, S., & Scott, B. T. (1982). Scientists as mass media sources. *Journalism Quarterly, 59,* 52-59.

Dunwoody, S., & Stocking, S. H. (in press). Social scientists and journalists: Confronting the stereotypes. In E. Rubinstein & J. Brown (Eds.), *The media, social science, and social policy for children: Different paths to a common goal.* Norwood, NJ: Ablex.

Durkheim, E. (1935). *The division of labor in society* (G. Simpson, Trans.). New York: Free Press. (Original work published 1893)

Ebert, R. (1981). Why movie audiences aren't safe any more. *American Film, 6,* 54-56.

Eisenstein, Z. (1981). *The radical future of liberal feminism.* New York: Longman.

Eisenstein, Z. (1984). *Feminism and sexual inequality: Crisis in liberal America.* New York: Monthly Review Press.

Elliot, P. (1972). *The making of a television series: A case study in the sociology of culture.* London: Constable.

Endreny, P. (1985). *News values and science values: The editor's role in shaping news about the social sciences.* Unpublished doctoral dissertation, Columbia University.

Epstein, E. J. (1973). *News from nowhere: Television and the news.* New York: Random House.

Escarpit, R. (1977). The concept of "mass." *Journal of Communication, 27,* 44-47.

Evans, C. R. (1979). *The micro millennium.* New York: Washington Square/Pocket Books.

Evans, S. (1979). *Personal politics: The roots of women's liberation in the civil rights movement and the new left.* New York: Knopf.

Fabricant, S. (1949). *The changing industrial distribution of gainful workers: Some comments on the American decennial statistics for 1820-1940.* New York: National Bureau of Economic Research.

Facey, P. W. (1974). *The legion of decency: A sociological analysis of the emergence of a social pressure group.* New York: Arno.

Farber, S. J. (1981). Why do critics love trashy movies? *American Film, 6,* 65-68.

Faris, R.E.L. (1967). *Chicago sociology, 1920-1932.* Chicago: University of Chicago Press.

Federal Council of Churches of Christ in America. (1931). *The public relations of the motion picture industry.* New York: Author.

Fields, J. M., & Schuman, H. (1976). Public beliefs about the beliefs of the public. *Public Opinion Quarterly, 40,* 427-448.

Fink, E. L., Robinson, J. P., & Dowden, S. (1985). The structure of music preference and attendance. *Communication Research, 12,* 301-318.

Fiske, J. (1983, November 19). Boxing week. *San Francisco Chronicle,* p. 37.

Frank, R. E., & Greenberg, M. G. (1980). *The public use of television.* Beverly Hills, CA: Sage.

Freeman, D. (1983). *Margaret Mead and Samoa.* Cambridge, MA: Harvard University Press.

Freidson, E. (1953). Communications research and the concept of the mass. *American Sociological Review, 18,* 313-317.

Friedan, B. (1981). *The second stage.* New York: Summit.

Funk, W. (1950). *Word origins and their romantic stories.* New York: William Funk.

Galbraith, J. K. (1967). *The new industrial state.* Boston: Houghton Mifflin.

Galbraith, J. K. (1978). *The new industrial state* (3rd rev. ed.). Boston: Houghton Mifflin.

Gamson, W. (1975). *The strategy of social protest.* Homewood, IL: Dorsey.

Gans, H. J. (1957). The creator-audience relationship in the mass media: An analysis of movie-making. In B. Rosenberg & D. M. White (Eds.), *Mass culture: The popular arts in America* (pp. 315-324). New York: Free Press.

Gans, H. J. (1966). Popular culture in America: Social problem in a mass society or social asset in a pluralist society? In H. S. Becker (Ed.), *Social problems: A modern approach.* New York: John Wiley.

Gans, H. J. (1972). The famine in American mass communication research: Comments on Hirsch, Tuchman, and Gecas. *American Journal of Sociology, 77,* 697-705.

Gans, H. J. (1974). *Popular culture and high culture: An analysis and evaluation of taste.* New York: Basic Books.

Gans, H. J. (1979). *Deciding what's news: A study of CBS Evening News, NBC Nightly News, Newsweek and Time.* New York: Pantheon.

Garfield, E. (1977-1978). *Essays of an information scientist* (Vol. 3). Philadelphia: ISI.

Gaylord, K. (1983). Theatrical performances: Structure and process, tradition and revolt. In J. B. Kamerman & R. Martorella (Eds.). *Performers and performances: The social organization of art* (pp. 135-149). New York: Praeger.

Gerbner, G. (1959). Mental illness on television: A study of censorship. *Journal of Broadcasting, 3,* 293-303.

Gerbner, G. (1969). Toward "cultural indicators": The analysis of mass mediated public message systems. *AV Communication Review, 17,* 137-148.

Gerbner, G. (1984). Political functions of television viewing: A cultivation analysis. In G. Melischek et al. (Eds.), *Cultural indicators: An international symposium.* Vienna: Akademie der Wissenschaften.

Gerbner, G., & Gross, L. (1976). Living with television: The violence profile. *Journal of Communication, 26,* 173-199.

Gerbner, G., Gross, L., Morgan, M., & Signorielli, N. (1980). The mainstreaming of America: Violence profile No. 11. *Journal of Communication, 30,* 10-29.

Gerbner, G., Gross, L., Morgan, M., & Signorielli, N. (1981a). Final reply to Hirsch. *Communication Research, 8,* 259-277.

Gerbner, G., Gross, L., Morgan, M., & Signorielli, N. (1981b). Health and medicine on television. *New England Journal of Medicine, 305,* 901-904.

Gerbner, G., Gross, L., Signorielli, N., & Morgan, M. (1980). Aging with television: Images of television drama, and conceptions of social reality. *Journal of Communication, 30,* 137-148.

Gerbner, G., & Tannenbaum, P. H. (1962). Mass media censorship and the portrayal of mental illness: Some effects of industry-wide controls in motion pictures and television. In W. L. Schramm (Ed.), *Studies of innovation and of communication to the public.* Stanford, CA: Stanford University Press.

Giddings, H. (1916). *The principles of sociology: An analysis of the phenomena of association and of social organization.* New York: Macmillan.

Gitlin, T. (1979). Prime time ideology: The hegemonic process in television entertainment. *Social Problems, 26,* 251-266.

Gitlin, T. (1980). *The whole world is watching: Mass media in the making and unmaking of the New Left.* Berkeley: University of California Press.

Gitlin, T. (1981). The new crusades: How the fundamentalists tied up the networks. *American Film, 7,* 60-64, 80-81.

Gitlin, T. (1983). *Inside prime-time.* New York: Pantheon.

Gledhill, C. (1980). "Klute" 1: A contemporary film noir and feminist criticism. In E. A. Kaplan (Ed.), *Women in film noir.* London: BFI.

Goffman, E. (1979). *Gender advertisements.* Cambridge, MA: Harvard University Press.

Goldman, W. (1983). *Adventures in the screen trade: A personal view of Hollywood and screenwriting.* New York: Warner.

Goldmann, K. (1984). World politics and domestic culture: Sweden, 1950-1975. In G. Melischek, K. E. Rosengren, & J. Stappers (Eds.), *Cultural indicators: An international symposium* (pp. 195-216). Vienna: Akademie der Wissenschaften.

Goltz, J. D. (1984). Are the news media responsible for disaster myths? A content analysis of emergency response imagery. *Mass Emergencies and Disasters, 2,* 345-368.

Gomery, D. (1982). *A history of Milwaukee's movie theaters.* Unpublished manuscript, University of Maryland.

Goodman, L. A. (1972). A general model for the analysis of surveys. *American Journal of Sociology, 77,* 1035-1086.

Gouldner, A. (1979). *The future of intellectuals and the rise of the class.* New York: Seabury.

Gray, H. (1983). *Independent culture production: Theresa Records, case study of a jazz independent.* Unpublished doctoral dissertation, University of California at Santa Cruz.

Greenberg, B. S. (1964). Person-to-person communication in the diffusion of news events. *Journalism Quarterly, 41,* 489-494.

Greenberg, B. S. (1980). *Life on television: Content analysis of U.S. TV drama.* Norwood, NJ: Ablex.

Greenberg, P. (1977, November 11). Wild in the stands. *New Times,* pp. 50-57.

Greenfield, L. (1984). *The role of the public in success of artistic styles.* Paper presented at the annual meeting of the American Sociological Association, San Antonio, TX.

Griswold, W. (1983). The devil's techniques: Cultural legitimation and social change. *American Sociological Review, 48,* 668-680.

Gross, L. (1984). The cultivation of intolerance: Television, blacks, and gays. In G. Melischek, K. E. Rosengren, & J. Stappers (Eds.), *Cultural indicators: An international symposium* (pp. 345-364). Vienna: Akademie der Wissenschaften.

Grote, D. (1983). *The end of comedy: The sit-com and the comedic tradition.* Hamden, CT: Archon.

Grotowski, J. (1927). *Towards a poor theater.* New York: Simon & Schuster.

Grundfest, J. (1976). *Citizen participation in broadcast licensing before the FCC.* Santa Monica, CA: Rand Corporation.

Guback, T. H. (1969). *The international film industry: Western Europe and America since 1945.* Bloomington: Indiana University Press.

Guimery, D. (1975). *Citizens' groups and broadcasting.* New York: Praeger.

Gulick, L. (Ed.). (1898). *Spalding's official basket ball guide.* New York: American Sports Publishing.

Guttman, L. (1954). A new approach to factor analysis: The radex. In P. F. Lazarsfeld (Ed.), *Mathematical thinking in the social sciences.* New York: Free Press.

Habermas, J. (1960). *Toward a rational society: Student protest, science, and politics.* Boston: Beacon.

Halliwell, L. (1977). *Halliwell's film guide: A survey of 8,000 English-language movies.* New York: Scribner.

Handel, L. (1950). *Hollywood looks at its audiences: A report of film audience research.* New York: Arno.

Hankiss, E., Manchin, R., Furstos, L., & Szakolczai, A. (1984). Modernization of value systems: Indicators of change in cross-cultural comparisons. In G. Melischek, K. E. Rosengren, & J. Stappers (Eds.), *Cultural indicators: An international symposium* (pp. 461-472). Vienna: Akademie der Wissenschaften.

Harris, M. (1980). *Cultural materialism.* New York: Vintage.

Hawkins, R. P., & Pingree, S. (1982). Television's influence on social reality. In D. Pearl, L. Bouthile, & J. Lazar (Eds.), *Television and behavior: Ten years of scientific progress and implications for the eighties* (Vol. 2). Washington DC: Government Printing Office.

Hawkins, R. P., & Pingree, S. (1984). The effects of television-mediated culture. In G. Melischek, K. E. Rosengren, & J. Stappers (Eds.), *Cultural indicators: An international symposium* (pp. 317-328). Vienna: Akademie der Wissenschaften.

Hays, W. (1945). *Annual report of the president, 23rd anniversary year, 1944-1945.* New York: Motion Picture Producers and Distributors of America.

Hebdige, D. (1979). *Subculture: The meaning of style.* London: Methuen.

Hedinsson, E. (1981). *TV, family, and society: The social origins and effects of adolescents' TV use.* Stockholm: Almqvist & Wiksell International.

Hedinsson, E., & Windahl, S. (1984). Cultivation analysis: A Swedish illustration. In G. Melischek, K. E. Rosengren, & J. Stappers (Eds.), *Cultural indicators: An international symposium* (pp. 384-406). Vienna: Akademie der Wissenschaften.

Hill, R. J., & Bonjean, C. M. (1964). News diffusion: A test of the regularity hypothesis. *Journalism Quarterly, 41,* 336-342.

Himmelweit, H., & Swift, B. (1976). Continuities and discontinuities in media usage and taste: A longitudinal study. *Journal of Social Issues, 32,* 133-156.

Hirsch, P. M. (1972). Processing fads and fashions: An organization-set analysis of cultural industry systems. *American Journal of Sociology, 77,* 639-659.

Hirsch, P. M. (1975). Organizational effectiveness and the institutional environment. *Administrative Science Quarterly, 20,* 327-344.

Hirsch, P. M. (1978). Occupational, organizational and institutional models in mass media research. In P. Hirsch, P. Miller, & F. G. Kline (Eds.), *Strategies for mass media research.* Beverly Hills, CA: Sage.

Hirsch, P. M. (1980). The scary world of the nonviewer and other anomalies: A reanalysis of Gerbner et al.'s findings on cultivation analysis. *Communication Research, 7,* 403-456.

Hirschburg, P. L., & Dillman, D. A. (1983). *News value and diffusion of information.* Paper presented at the annual meetings of the Southern Sociological Association.

Hirschman, A. O. (1970). *Exit, voice and loyalty: Responses to decline in firms, organizations, and state.* Cambridge, MA: Harvard University Press.

Hodge, F. (1964). *Yankee theatre: The image of America on the stage, 1825-1850.* Austin: University of Texas Press.

Holz, J. R., & Wright, C. R. (1979). Sociology of mass communications. *Annual review of sociology* (Vol. 5, pp. 193-217). Palo Alto, CA: Annual Reviews.

Horkheimer, M., & Adorno, T. W. (1944). *The dialectic of enlightenment.* New York: Herder & Herder.

Hornbow, A. (1919). *A history of theater in America from its beginnings to the present time* (Vol. 1). New York: Benjamin Blom.

Horowitz, I. (1977). Sports telecast: Rights and regulations. *Journal of Communication, 27,* 160-168.

Horsfield, P. G. (1984). *Religious television: The American experience.* New York: Longman.

Horton, D., Mauksch, H. O., & Lang, K. (1951). *Chicago summer television.* Chicago: National Opinion Research Center.

Hough, A. (1981). Trials and tribulations—thirty years of sitcom. In R. P. Adler (Ed.), *Understanding television: Essays on television as a social and cultural force* (pp. 201-223). New York: Praeger.

Huettig, M. (1944). *Economic control of the motion picture industry, a study in industrial organization.* Philadelphia: University of Pennsylvania Press.

Huffman, L. (1984, March 27). Pay ball. *Village Voice,* pp. 68-69.

Hughes, H. M. (1940). *News and the human interest story.* Chicago: University of Chicago Press.

Hughes, M. (1980). The fruits of cultivation analysis: A re-examination of some effects of television watching. *Public Opinion Quarterly, 44,* 287-302.

Huizinga, J. (1955). *Homo ludens: A study of the play element in culture.* London: Routledge.

Husserl, E. (1977). *Cartesian meditations: An introduction to phenomenology.* The Hague: M. Nijhoff. (Originally published in 1931)

Hyman, H. H. (1959). *Political socialization: A study in the psychology of political behavior.* New York: Free Press.

Hyman, H. H. (1961). The role of the mass media in the formation of public opinion. In D. C. Reddick (Ed.), *The role of the mass media in a democratic society.* Austin: University of Texas Press.

Hyman, H. H., Levine, G. N., & Wright, C. R. (1967). *Inducing social change in developing communities: An international survey of expert advice.* Geneva: United Nations Research Institute for Social Development.

Inglehart, R. (1977). *The silent revolution: Changing values and political styles among Western publics.* Princeton, NJ: Princeton University Press.

Inglehart, R. (1984). Measuring cultural change in Japan, Western Europe and the United States. In G. Melischek, K. E. Rosengren, & J. Stappers (Eds.), *Cultural indicators: An international symposium* (pp. 473-498). Vienna: Akademie der Wissenschaften.

Inglehart, R. (1985). Aggregate stability and individual-level flux in mass belief systems: The level of analysis paradox. *American Political Science Review, 79,* 97-116.

Intinloli, M. J. (1984). *Taking soap operas seriously: The world of Guiding Light.* New York: Praeger.

Isenberg, D. (1980). Levels of analysis of pluralistic ignorance phenomena: The case of receptiveness to interpersonal feedback. *Journal of Applied Social Psychology, 10,* 457-467.

James, C.L.R. (1963). *Beyond a boundary.* London: Stanley Hall.

Janowitz, M. (1952). *The community press in an urban setting.* New York: Free Press.

Jarvie, I. C. (1970). *Movies and society.* New York: Basic Books.

Jauss, H. R. (1970). Literary history as a challenge to literary theory. *New Literary History, 2.*

Johnson, K. (1963). Dimensions of judgment of science news stories. *Journalism Quarterly, 40,* 315-322.

Johnsson-Smaragdi, U. (1983). *TV use and social interaction in adolescence: A longitudinal study.* Stockholm: Almqvist & Wiksell.

Johnston, E. (1949, March 9). *Variety,* pp. 1-24.

Johnstone, J.W.C., Slawski, E. J., & Bowman, W. W. (1976). *The news people: A sociological portrait of American journalists and their work.* Urbana: University of Illinois Press.

Jowett, G., & Linton, J. M. (1980). *Movies as mass communication.* Beverly Hills, CA: Sage.

Kadushin, C. (1966). The friends and supporters of psychotherapy: On social circles in urban life. *American Sociological Review, 31,* 786-802.

Kaplan, N. (1965). The norms of citation behavior: Prolegomena to the footnote. *American Documentation, 16,* 179-184.

Kapsis, R. E. (1982). Dressed to kill. *American Film, 7,* 52-56.

Katz, E., Gurevitch, M., & Haas, H. (1973). On the use of the media for important things. *American Sociological Review, 38,* 164-181.

Katz, E., & Lazarsfeld, P. F. (1955). *Personal influence: The part played by people in the flow of mass communications.* New York: Free Press.

Katz, E., Wedell, G., Pilsworth, M., & Shinar, D. (1977). *Broadcasting in the Third World: Promise and performance.* Cambridge, MA: Harvard University Press.

Kendall, P. L., & Wolf, K. M. (1949). The analysis of deviant cases in communication research. In P. F. Lazarsfeld & F. N. Stanton (Eds.), *Communications Research 1948-1949.* New York: Harper.

Kerr, W. (1962). *The decline of pleasure.* New York: Simon & Schuster.

Kindem, G. (1982). Hollywood's movie star system: An historical overview. In G. Kindem (Ed.), *The American movie industry: The business of motion pictures* (pp. 79-93). Carbondale: Southern Illinois University Press.

King, M. L. (1958). *Stride toward freedom: The Montgomery story.* New York: Harper.

Klapper, J. T. (1960). *The effects of mass communication.* New York: Free Press.

Kleinknecht, A. (1981). Innovation, accumulation and crisis: Waves in economic development. *Review, 4,* 683-711.

Klingemann, H. D., Mohler, P. P., & Weber, R. P. (1982). Das reichstumsthema in den thronreden des kaisers und die soziookonomische entwicklung in Deutschland 1871-1919. In H. D. Klingemann (Ed.), *Computerunterstutzte inhaltsanalyse in der empirischen sozialforschung.* Kronberg: Scriptor.

Kohlberg, L. (1969). Stage and sequence: The cognitive-development approach to socialization. In D. A. Goslin (Ed.), *Handbook of socialization theory and research* (pp. 347-480). Chicago: Rand McNally.

Konecni, V. J. (1982). Social interaction and musical preference. In D. Deutsch (Ed.), *The psychology of music* (pp. 497-516). New York: Academic.

Koppes, C. R., & Black, G. D. (1977). What to show the world: The Office of War Information and Hollywood, 1942-1945. *Journal of American History, 64,* 87-105.

Krasnow, E. G., Longley, L. D., & Terry, H. A. (1982). *The politics of broadcast regulation.* New York: St. Martin's.

Krech, D., & Crutchfield, R. (1948). *Theory and problems of social psychology.* New York: McGraw-Hill.

Kroeber, A. L., & Kluckhohn, C. (1952). Culture: A critical review of concepts and definitions. *Harvard University Peabody Museum of American Archaeology and Ethnology Papers, 47*(1).

Kroeber, A. L., & Parsons, T. (1958). The concepts of culture and of social system. *American Sociological Review, 23,* 582-583.

Kuhn, B. (1983, September). An interview with Bowie Kuhn. *Sport,* pp. 6-12.

Lang, G. E., & Lang, K. (1983). *The battle for public opinion: The president, the press, and the polls during Watergate.* New York: Columbia University Press.

Lang, K., & Lang G. E. (1968). *Politics and television.* Chicago: Quadrangle.

Larsen, O. N., & Hill, R. J. (1954). Mass media and interpersonal communication in the diffusion of a news event. *American Sociological Review, 19,* 426-433.

Lasswell, H. D. (1948). The structure and function of communication in society. In L. Bryson (Ed.), *The communication of ideas: A series of addresses* (pp. 37-51). New York: Harper & Brothers.

Lasswell, H. D., & Namenwirth, J. Z. (1968). *The Lasswell value dictionary, 1-3* (mimeo). New Haven, CT.

Lazarsfeld, P. F. (1940). *Radio and the printed page: An introduction to the study of radio and its role in the communication of ideas.* New York: Duell, Sloan & Pearce.

Lazarsfeld, P. F. (Ed.). (1942). *Radio research 1941.* New York: Duell, Sloan & Pearce.

Lazarsfeld, P. F. (1963). Afterward: Some reflections on past and future research on broadcasting. In G. A. Steiner (Ed.), *People look at television: A study of audience attitudes.* New York: Knopf.

Lazarsfeld, P. F., Berelson, B., & Gaudet, H. (1944). *The people's choice: How the voter makes up his mind in a presidential election.* New York: Duell, Sloan & Pearce.

Lazarsfeld, P. F., Berelson, B., & Gaudet, H. (1948). *The people's choice: How the voter makes up his mind in a presidential election* (2nd. ed.). New York: Columbia University Press.

Lazarsfeld, P. F., & Field, H. (1946). *The people look at radio.* Chapel Hill: University of North Carolina Press.

Lazarsfeld, P. F., & Kendall, P. L. (1948). *Radio listening in America: The people look at radio—again.* Englewood Cliffs, NJ: Prentice-Hall.

Lazarsfeld, P. F., & Merton, R. K. (1948). Mass communication, popular taste and organized social action. In L. Bryson (Ed.), *The communication of ideas.* New York: Harper.

Lazarsfeld, P. F., & Stanton, F. N. (Eds.). (1944). *Radio research 1942-1943.* New York: Duell, Sloan & Pearce.

Lazarsfeld, P. F., & Stanton, F. N. (Eds.). (1949). *Communication research 1948-1949.* New York: Harper.

Lebergott, S. (1964). *Manpower in economic growth: The American record since 1800.* New York: McGraw-Hill.

Lesage, J. (1982). The hegemonic female fantasy in *An Unmarried Woman* and *Craig's Wife. Film Reader, 5,* 83-94.

Levin, J., & Spates, J. L. (1970). Hippie values: An analysis of the underground press. *Youth and Society, 2,* 59-72.

Lewels, F. J. (1974). *The uses of the media by the Chicano movement: A study in minority access.* New York: Praeger.

Lewis, C. (1984). *Television license renewal challenges by women's groups.* Unpublished doctoral dissertation, University of Minnesota.

Lord, D. A. (1946, November 23). Production code, a "product of industry." *Motion Picture Herald,* p. 22.

Los Angeles Times. (1977, June 27). Taming a lusty show: Censor's memo tells how.

Lumsden, C. J., & Wilson, E. O. (1981). *Genes, mind, and culture.* Cambridge, MA: Harvard University Press.

Lynd, R. S., & Lynd, H. M. (1929). *Middletown: A study in contemporary American culture.* New York: Harcourt, Brace.

Lynd, R. S., & Lynd, H. M. (1937). *Middletown in transition: A study in cultural conflicts.* New York: Harcourt, Brace.

Machlup, F. (1980). *Knowledge: Its creation, distribution, and economic significance* (Vol. 1). Princeton, NJ: Princeton University Press.

Maisel, A. Q. (1946, May 6). Bedlam, 1946. *Life,* pp. 102-118.

Marcuse, H. (1964). *One-dimensional man: Studies in the ideology of advanced industrial society.* Boston: Beacon.

Margulies, L. (Ed.). (1981, Summer). Proliferation of pressure groups in prime time symposium. *Emmy.*

Martin, O. (1937). *Hollywood's movie commandments.* New York: H. W. Wilson.

Mast, G. (1971). *A short history of the movies.* New York: Pegasus.

McClelland, D. C. (1953). *The achievement motive.* New York: Irvington.

McClelland, D. C. (1961). *The achieving society.* Princeton, NJ: Van Nostrand.

McClelland, D. C. (1975). *Power: The inner experience.* New York: Irvington.

McClure, A. F. (1971). Censor the movies! Early attempts to regulate the content of motion pictures in America, 1907-1936. In A. McClure (Ed.), *The movies: An American idiom.* Rutherford, NJ: Fairleigh Dickenson University Press.

McCombs, M. E., & Shaw, D. (1972). The agenda-setting function of mass media. *Public Opinion Quarterly, 36,* 176-187.

McCombs, M. E., & Weaver, D. (1985). Toward a merger of gratification and agenda-setting research. In K. E. Rosengren, L. A. Wenner, & P. Palmgreen (Eds.), *Media gratifications research: Current perspectives* (pp. 95-108). Beverly Hills, CA: Sage.

McCoy, P. (1984, March 3). Marathon madness. *Sporting News,* p. 28.

McCron, R. (1976). Changing perspectives in the study of mass media and socialization. In J. D. Halloran (Ed.), *Mass media and socialization* (pp. 13-44). Leeds: Kavanagh & Sons.

McLuhan, M. (1964). *Understanding media: The extensions of man.* New York: McGraw-Hill.

McPhee, W. N. (1963). *Formal theories of mass behavior.* New York: Free Press.

McQuail, D. (1969). Uncertainty about the audience and the organization of mass media communicators. In P. Halmos (Ed.), *The sociology of mass communications* (pp. 75-84). Hanley: F. H. Brooks.

Mead, G. H. (1934). *Mind, self, and society.* Chicago: University of Chicago Press.

Mead, M. (1970). *Culture and commitment: A study of the generation gap.* New York: Natural History Press.

Medalia, N. Z., & Larsen, O. N. (1958). Diffusion and belief in a collective delusion: The Seattle windshield pitting epidemic. *American Sociological Review, 23,* 180-186.

Melischek, G., Rosengren, K. E., & Stappers, J. (Eds.). (1984). *Cultural indicators: An international symposium.* Vienna: Akademie der Wissenschaften.

Mendelsohn, H. (1964). Broadcast vs. personal sources of information in emergent public crisis: The presidential assassination. *Journal of Broadcasting, 8,* 147-156.

Menninger, W. C. (1948). *Psychiatry in a troubled world.* New York: Macmillan.

Merritt, R. (1976). Nickelodeon theaters, 1905-1914: Building an audience for the movies. In T. Balio (Eds.), *The American film industry* (pp. 59-79). Madison: University of Wisconsin Press.

Merton, R. K. (1949). Patterns of influence: A study of interpersonal influence and of communication behavior in a local community. In P. F. Lazarsfeld & F. N. Stanton (Eds.), *Communication research 1948-1949.* New York: Harper.

Merton, R. K. (1968). *Social theory and social structure* (3rd. ed.). New York: Free Press.

Merton, R. K., Fiske, M., & Curtis, A. (1946). *Mass persuasion: The social psychology of a war bond drive.* New York: Harper.

Mewshaw, M. (1983). *Short circuit.* New York: Atheneum.

Meyer, P. (1967, June). Social science: A new beat. *Nieman Reports,* pp. 3-8.

Meyersohn, R., & Katz, E. (1958). Notes on a natural history of fads. *American Journal of Sociology, 62,* 594-601.

Milavsky, J. R., Stipp, H. H., Kessler, R. C., & Rubens, W. S. (1982). *Television and aggression: A panel study.* New York: Academic.

Milkman, R. (1980). Women's work and organizing the sexual division of labor: Historical perspectives on the American labor movement. *Socialist Review, 10,* 95-150.

Mill, J. S. (1848). *Principles of political economy, with some their applications to social philosophy* (2 vols.). Boston: Little.

Miller, R. (1977). *Bohemia: The proto-culture, then, and now.* Chicago: Nelson Hall.

Mills, C. W. (1951). *White collar: The American middle class.* New York: Oxford University Press.

Mills, C. W. (1956). *The power elite.* New York: Oxford University Press.

Mills, C. W. (1963). The cultural apparatus. In I. L. Horowitz (Ed.), *Power, politics and people: The collected essays of C. W. Mills* (pp. 405-422). New York: Oxford University Press.

Mitz, R. (1983). *The great TV sitcom book.* New York: Perigree.

Mock, J. R., & Larson, C. (1968). *Words that won the war: The story on the Committee on Public Information, 1917-1919.* Princeton, NJ: Princeton University Press.

Montgomery, K. (1979). *Gay activists and the networks: A case study of special interest pressure in television.* Unpublished doctoral dissertation, University of California at Los Angeles.

Montgomery, K. (1981). Gay activists and the networks. *Journal of Communication, 31,* 49-57.

Montgomery, K. (1983, April). *The treatment of controversial issues in entertainment television.* Paper presented at the conference on New Directions in Television Research.

Moody, R. (1958). *The Astor Palace riot.* Bloomington: Indiana University Press.

Moody's Industrial Manual of Investments. (1930-1965). New York: Moody's Investment Service.

Morgan, M. (1980). *Longitudinal patterns of TV viewing and adolescent role socialization.* Unpublished doctoral dissertation, Annenberg School of Communications, University of Pennsylvania.

Morgan, M. (1984). Symbolic victimization and real world fear. In G. Melischek, K. E. Rosengren, & J. Stappers (Eds.), *Cultural indicators: An international symposium* (pp. 365-376). Vienna: Akademie der Wissenschaften.

Morris, W., & Morris, M. (1962). *Morris dictionary of word and phrase origins.* New York: Harper & Row.

Motion Picture Producers and Distributors of America, Inc. (1935). *Progress and trends of motion picture entertainment: Annual report.* New York: Author.

Mukerji, C. (1977). Film games. *Symbolic Interaction, 1,* 20-31.

Mulder, R. (1980). Media credibility: A use-gratification approach. *Journalism Quarterly, 57,* 474-477.

Mullally, D. P. (1980). Radio: The other public medium. *Journal of Communication, 30,* 189-197.

Namenwirth, J. Z. (1973). Wheels of time and the interdependence of value change in America. *Journal of Interdisciplinary History, 3,* 649-683.

Namenwirth, J. Z., & Bibbee, R. C. (1976). Change within or of the system: An example from the history of American values. *Quality and Quantity, 10,* 145-164.

Neiderman, T. (1980). Waitz sets world record. *N.Y. Running News, 21,* 20-22.

Nelson, D. M. (1947). The independent producer. *Annals of the American Academy of Political and Social Science, 254,* 49-57.

Neuman, W. R. (1982, September). *Communications technology and cultural diversity.* Paper presented at the annual meeting of the American Sociological Association.

Newcomb, H. (1974). *TV: The most popular art.* Garden City, NY: Doubleday.

Newcomb, H., & Alley, R. (1984). *The producer's medium.* New York: Oxford University Press.

Newcomb, H., & Hirsch, P. M. (1983a, April). *A qualitative approach to television research.* Paper presented at the conference on New Directions in Television Studies, University of Michigan.

Newcomb, H., & Hirsch, P. M. (1983b). Television as a cultural forum: Implications for research. *Quarterly Review of Film Studies.*

NFCB Newsletter. (1981, May 11). FCC eases limits on donors, promos. Vol. 7.

Noble, G. (1975). *Children in front of the small screen.* Beverly Hills, CA: Sage.

Noelle-Neuman, E. (1974). The spiral of silence: A theory of public opinion. *Journal of Communication, 24,* 43-51.

Noelle-Neuman, E. (1977). Turbulences in the climate of opinion: Methodological applications of the spiral of silence theory. *Public Opinion Quarterly, 41,* 143-158.

Noelle-Neuman, E. (1979). Public opinion and the classical tradition. *Public Opinion Quarterly, 43,* 143-156.

Noelle-Neuman, E. (1983). *The spiral of silence.* Chicago: Chicago University Press.

Nora, S., & Minc., A. (1978). *The computerization of society: A report to the president of France.* Cambridge: MIT Press.

North American Soccer League. (1982). *Soccer encyclopedia.* New York: Dutton.

Novak, M. (1976). *The joy of sport: End zones, bases, baskets, balls, and the consecration of the American spirit.* New York: Basic Books.

Nowak, K. (1984). Cultural indicators in Swedish advertising, 1950-1975. In G. Melischek, K. E. Rosengren, & J. Stappers (Eds.), *Cultural indicators: An international symposium* (pp. 217-236). Vienna: Akademie der Wissenschaften.

Ogburn, W. F., & Gilfillan, S. C. (1933). The influence of invention and discovery. In *Recent trends in the United States: Report of the President's Research Committee on Social Trends* (pp. 122-166). New York: McGraw-Hill.

O'Gorman, H. J. (1975). Pluralistic ignorance and white estimates of white support for racial segregation. *Public Opinion Quarterly, 39,* 313-330.

O'Gorman, H. J. (1979). White and black perceptions of racial values. *Public Opinion Quarterly, 43,* 48-59.

O'Gorman, H. J., with Garry, S. L. (1976). Pluralistic ignorance: A replication and extension. *Public Opinion Quarterly, 40,* 449-458.

O'Toole J. I. (1983, January 17). Article in *TV/Radio Age.*

Oxford English Dictionary. (1961). (Vol. 3). Oxford: Clarendon.

Paletz, D. L., & Entman, R. M. (1981). *Media power politics.* New York: Free Press.

Palmgreen, P., Wenner, L. A., & Rosengren, K. E. (1985). Uses and gratifications research: The last ten years. In K. E. Rosengren, L. A. Wenner, & P. Palmgreen (Eds.), *Media gratifications research: Current perspectives.* Beverly Hills, CA: Sage.

Park, R. E. (1922). *The immigrant press and its control.* New York: Harper.

Parker, J. J. (1983). *Box office madness: Industry/institution/audience and the formulating of delinquency, crime and mental problems in American film, 1930-1950.* Unpublished doctoral dissertation, University of Colorado.

Parker, J. J. (1984). *The social control of delinquency images in American motion pictures, 1930-1955.* Paper presented at the meeting of the Society for the Study of Social Problems, San Antonio, TX.

Parsons, T. (1951). *The social system.* New York: Free Press.

Parsons, T., & White, W. (1964). The link between character and society. In *Social structure and personality.* New York: Free Press.

Pekurny, R. (1977). *Broadcast self-regulation: A participant-observation study of the National Broadcasting Company's broadcast standards department.* Unpublished doctoral dissertation, University of Minnesota.

Peterson, R. A. (1979). Revitalizing the culture concept. In A. Inkeles, J. Coleman, & R. H. Turner (Eds.), *Annual review of sociology* (Vol. 5, pp. 137-166). Palo Alto, CA: Annual Reviews.

Peterson, R. A., & Berger, D. G. (1975). Cycles in symbol production: The case of popular music. *American Sociological Review, 40,* 156-173.

Petit, C. (1979). Mutant depressive gene stampedes writers at AAAS. *Newsletter of the National Association of Science Writers, 27*(1).

Phillips, K. P. (1975). *Mediacracy: American parties and politics in the communication age.* Garden City, NY: Doubleday.

Piaget, J. (1932). *The moral judgment of the child.* New York: Free Press.

Pirie, D. (1981). *Anatomy of the movies.* New York: Macmillan.

Pisacator, E. (1949). Objective acting. In T. Cole & H. K. Chinoy (Eds.), *Actors on acting* (pp. 285-291). New York: Crown.

Poggi, J. (1968). *Theater in America: The impact of economic forces, 1870-1967.* Ithaca, NY: Cornell University Press.

Porat, M. U. (1977). *The information economy: Definition and measurement.* Washington, DC: U.S. Department of Commerce, Office of Telecommunications.

Porter, R. (1982). *English society in the eighteenth century.* London: Allen Lane.

Postman, N. (1979). *Teaching as a conserving activity.* New York: Delacorte.

Pred, A. R. (1973). *Urban growth and the circulation of information: The United States system of cities, 1790-1840.* Cambridge, MA: Harvard University Press.

Press, A. (1986). *Ideologies of work, family, and femininity in three generations of American women in relation to the dominant visual media in the post-war United States.* Unpublished doctoral dissertation, University of California at Berkeley, Department of Sociology.

Press, A. (n.d.). *Women and work in ideology and reality: Romance and work for the working-class woman.* Unpublished manuscript, University of California at Berkeley, Department of Sociology.

Presser, S. (1985). The use of survey data in basic research in the social sciences. In C. F. Turner & E. Martin (Eds.), *The survey measurement of subjective phenomena.* New York: Russell Sage.

Quarles, R., Jeffres, L. W., Sanchez-Ilundain, C., & Neuwirth, K. (1983). News diffusion of assassination attempts on President Reagan and Pope John Paul II. *Journal of Broadcasting, 27*, 387-394.

Ramsaye, T. (1926). *A million and one nights: A history of the motion picture.* New York: Simon & Schuster.

Rankin, W. L., & Grube, J. W. (1980). A comparison of ranking and rating procedures of value system measurement. *European Journal of Social Psychology, 10,* 233-246.

Redlich, F. (1968). *The molding of American banking: men and ideas.* New York: Johnson Reprint Corporation. (Original work published 1951)

Reich, C. A. (1970). *The greening of America: How the youth revolution is trying to make America livable.* New York: Random House.

Rich, J. T. (1981). A measure of comprehensiveness in news magazine science coverage. *Journalism Quarterly, 58,* 248-253.

Richard, R., Knox, R., & Oliphant, T. (1975, May 25). The first year. *Boston Globe,* pp. A1-A24.

Richta, R., (Ed.). (1969). *Civilization at the crossroads: Social and human implications of the scientific and technological revolution.* White Plains, NY: International Arts & Science.

Riley, J. W., & Riley, M. W. (1959). Mass communication and the social system. In R. K. Merton, L. Broom, & L. S. Cottrell, Jr. (Eds.), *Sociology today: Problem and prospects* (pp. 537-578). New York: Basic Books.

Robinson, J. P. (1983). Culture indicators from the leisure activity survey. *American Behavioral Scientist, 26,* 543-552.

Robinson, J. P., & Hirsch, P. (1969). It's the sound that does it. *Psychology Today, 3,* 42-45.

Robinson, W. S. (1942). Radio comes to the farmer. In P. F. Lazarsfeld (Ed.), *Radio research 1941.* New York: Duell, Sloan & Pearce.

Roe, K. (1983). *Mass media and adolescent schooling: Conflict or co-existence?* Stockholm: Almqvist & Wiksell International.

Rokeach, M. (1973). *The nature of human values.* New York: Free Press.

Rokeach, M. (1974). Change and stability in American value systems, 1968-1971. *Public Opinion Quarterly, 38,* 222-238.

Rokeach, M. (Ed.). (1979). *Understanding human values: Individual and societal.* New York: Free Press.

Root, W. (1979). *Writing the script: A practical guide for films and television.* New York: Holt, Rinehart & Winston.

Roper, B. W. (1983, November). *Polls and media: For good or ill?* Talk presented to the National Council on Public Polls.

Rose, C. (1981). Romance. In D. Pirie (Ed.), *Anatomy of the movies* (pp. 232-241). New York: Macmillan.

Rosenblum, R., & Karen, R. (1980). *When the shooting stops ... the cutting begins: A film editor's story.* New York: Penguin.

Rosengren, K. E. (1973). Diffusion of news: An overview. *Journalism Quarterly, 50.*

Rosengren, K. E. (1981). Mass media and social change: Some current approaches. In E. Katz & T. Szecsko (Eds.), *Mass media and social change.* Beverly Hills, CA: Sage.

Rosengren, K. E. (1983a). Communication research: One paradigm or four? *Journal of Communication, 33,* 185-207.

Rosengren, K. E. (1983b). *The climate of literature.* Lund: Studentlitteratur.

Rosengren, K. E. (1984a). Cultural indicators for the comparative study of culture. In G. Melischek, K. E. Rosengren, & J. Stappers (Eds.), *Cultural indicators: An international symposium* (pp. 11-32). Vienna: Akademie der Wissenschaften.

Rosengren, K. E. (1984b). Time and culture: Developments in the Swedish literary frame of reference. In G. Melischek, K. E. Rosengren, & J. Stappers (Eds.), *Cultural indicators: An international symposium* (pp. 236-258). Vienna: Akademie der Wissenschaften.

Rosengren, K. E., & Windahl, S. (1972). Mass media use as a functional alternative. In D. McQuail (Ed.), *Sociology of mass communications* (pp. 166-194). Harmondsworth: Pengiun.

Rosengren, K. E., & Windahl, S. (1977). Mass media use: Causes and effects. *Communications, 3,* 336-351.

Roshco, B. (1975). *Newsmaking.* Chicago: University of Chicago Press.

Ross, E. A. (1940). *New-age sociology.* New York: Appleton-Century.

Ross, L. (1952). *Movie.* New York: Harcourt, Brace.

Rothschild, N. (1984). Small group affiliation as a mediating factor in the cultivation process. In G. Melischek, K. E. Rosengren, & J. Stappers (Eds.), *Cultural indicators: An international symposium* (pp. 377-388). Vienna: Akademie der Wissenschaften.

Rous, G. L., & Lee, D. E. (1978). Freedom and equality: Two values of political orientation. *Journal of Communication, 28,* 45-51.

Rowell, G. (1978). *The Victorian theater, 1792-1914: A survey.* Cambridge: Cambridge University Press.

Rowland, W. (1983). *The politics of TV violence: Policy uses of communication research.* Beverly Hills, CA: Sage.

Rubin, A. M. (1985). Media gratifications through the life cycle. In K. E. Rosengren, L. A. Wenner, & P. Palmgreen (Eds.), *Media gratifications research: Current perspectives* (pp. 195-208). Beverly Hills, CA: Sage.

Rubin, A. M., & Windahl, S. (1982). *Mass media uses and dependency.* Paper presented at the annual meetings of the International Communication Association, Boston.

Rubinstein, B. (1983). Financing community radio. *NFCB Newsletter, 9,* 6-7.

Ryan, J., & Peterson, R. A. (1982). The product image: The fate of creativity in country music songwriting. In J. S. Ettema & D. C. Whitney (Eds.), *Individuals in mass media organizations: Creativity and constraint* (pp. 11-32). Beverly Hills, CA: Sage.

Ryan, M. (1979). Attitudes of scientists and journalists toward media coverage of science news. *Journalism Quarterly, 56,* 18-26.

Sallach, D. L. (1974). Class domination and ideological hegemony. In G. Tuchman (Ed.), *The TV establishment* (pp. 161-173). Englewood Cliffs, NJ: Prentice-Hall.

Sanders, C. (1982). Structural and interactional features of popular cultural production: An introduction to the production of culture perspective. *Journal of Popular Choice, 16,* 66-75.

San Francisco Chronicle. (1982, August 28). Letters to the editor, p. 51.

San Francisco Chronicle. (1983a, February 11). Box scores, p. 48.

San Francisco Chronicle. (1983b, September 27). Box scores, p. 55.

Sarris, A. (1968). *The American cinema: Directors and directions, 1929-1968.* New York: Dutton.

Schatz, T. (1981). *Hollywood genres: Formulas, filmmaking, and the studio system.* Philadelphia: Temple University Press.

Schiller, H. I. (1969). *Mass communications and the American empire.* New York: A. M. Kelley.

Schrader, P. (1972). Notes on film noir. *Film Comment, 8,* 8-13.

Schudson, M. (1982). The politics of narrative form: The emergences of news conventions in print and television. *Daedalus, 111,* 97-112.

Schuman, H., & Presser, S. (1981). *Questions and answers in attitude surveys: Experiments on question form, wording, and context.* New York: Academic.

Schutz, A. (1967). *The phenomenology of the social world.* Evanston, IL: Northwestern University Press. (Original work published 1932)

Schwartz, D. A. (1973). How fast does news travel? *Public Opinion Quarterly, 37,* 625-627.

Scott, J. (1971). *The athletic revolution.* New York: Free Press.

Scott, W. R., & Meyer, J. W. (1983). *The organization of societal sectors.* Unpublished manuscript, Stanford University.

Seiden, M. H. (1974). *Who controls the mass media? Popular myths and economic realities.* New York: Basic Books.

Seldes, G. (1953). *Writing for television.* Garden City, NY: Doubleday.

Selznick, P. (1984). *TVA and the grass roots: A study of politics and organization.* Berkeley: University of California Press.

Sennett, R. (1974). *The fall of public man.* New York: Vintage.

Sheatsley, P. B., & Feldman, J. J. (1964). A national survey on public reactions and behavior. *Public Opinion Quarterly, 28,* 189-215.

Shepard, R. N. (1978). The circumplex and related topological manifolds in the study of perception. In S. Shye (Ed.), *Theory construction and data analysis in the behavioral sciences* (pp. 29-80). San Francisco: Jossey-Bass.

Shurkin, J. (1979). The science writers still go to the AAAS Meetings: Some answers to "why?" *Newsletter of the National Association of Science Writers, 27*(1).

Sigal, L. (1973). *Reporters and officials: The organization and politics of newsmaking.* Lexington, MA: D. C. Heath.

Signorielli, N. (1984). The demography of the television world. In G. Melischek, K. E. Rosengren, & J. Stappers (Eds.), *Cultural indicators: An international symposium* (pp. 137-158). Vienna: Akademie der Wissenschaften.

Simonet, T. S. (1978). Industry. *Film Comment, 14,* 72-73.

Sklar, R. (1975). *Movie-made America: A social history of American movies.* New York: Random House.

Small, A. W., & Vincent, G. E. (1894). *An introduction to the study of society.* New York: American Book Co.

Smythe, D. W. (1981). *Dependency road: Communications, capitalism, consciousness and Canada.* Norwood, NJ: Ablex.

Sochen, J. (1979). The new woman and twenties America: "Way down East." In J. E. O'Conner & M. A. Jackson (Eds.), *American history/American film* (pp. 1-16). New York: Frederick Ungar.

Sokoloff, N. (1980). *Between money and love: The dialectics of women's home and market work.* New York: Praeger.

Sorokin, P. (1937-1941). *Social and cultural dynamics* (4 vols.). London: Allen & Unwin.

Spates, J. L. (1976). Counterculture and dominant culture values: A cross-national analysis of the underground press and dominant culture magazines. *American Sociological Review, 41,* 868-883.

Spates, J. L., & Levin, J. (1972). Beats, hippies, the hip generation, and the American middle class: An analysis of values. *International Social Science Journal, 24,* 326-353.

Spitzer, S. P., & Spitzer, N. S. (1965). Diffusion of news of the Kennedy and Oswald deaths. In B. S. Greenberg & E. B. Parker (Eds.)., *The Kennedy assassination and the American public* (pp. 99-111). Stanford, CA: Stanford University Press.

Sports Illustrated. (1983, February 28). Scorecard.

Stacy, J. (1983). The new conservative feminism. *Feminist Studies, 9,* 559-584.

Stedman, R. W. (1971). *The serials: Suspense and drama by installment* (2nd ed.). Norman: University of Oklahoma Press.

Stein, B. (1979). *The view from Sunset Boulevard: America as brought to you by the people who make television.* New York: Basic Books.

Stevenson, R. (1980). The cummulative audience of network television news. *Journalism Quarterly, 57,* 477-481.

Stinchcombe, A., & Taylor, D. G. (1980). On democracy and school desegregation. In W. Stephan & J. Feagin (Eds.), *School desegregation: Past, present and future* (pp. 157-186).

Stone, P. J., Dunphy, D. C., Smith, M. S., & Ogilivie, D. M. (1966). *The general inquirer: A computer approach to content analysis.* Cambridge: MIT Press.

Swidler, A. (1980). Love and adulthood in American culture. In N. J. Smelser & E. H. Erikson (Eds.), *Themes of work and love in adulthood* (pp. 120-147). Cambridge, MA: Harvard University Press.

Tankard, J. W., & Ryan, M. (1974). News source perceptions of accuracy of scientific coverage. *Journalism Quarterly, 51,* 209-225.

Tankard, J. W., & Showalter, S. W. (1977). Press coverage of the 1972 Report on Television and Social Behavior. *Journalism Quarterly, 55,* 293-298.

Tatum, J. (1980). *They call me assassin.* New York: Everest House.

Taylor, D. G. (1982). Pluralistic ignorance and the spiral of silence: A formal analysis. *Public Opinion Quarterly, 46,* 311-335.

Taylor, D. G. (in press). *Public opinion, collective action and anti-busing protest: The Boston school desegregation controversy.* Chicago: University of Chicago Press.

Taylor, D. G., & Stinchcombe, A. (1977). *The Boston school desegregation controversy.* Chicago: National Opinion Research Center.

Thorburn, D. (1976). Television melodrama. In R. Adler & D. Cater (Eds.), *Television as a cultural force* (pp. 77-94). New York: Praeger.

Thunberg, A. M., Nowak, K., Rosengren, K. E., & Sigurd, B. (1982). *Communication and equality: A Swedish perspective.* Stockholm: Almqvist & Wiksell International.

Tichenor, P. J., Olien, C. N., Harrison, Q., & Donohue, G. (1970). Mass communication systems and communication accuracy in science news reporting. *Journalism Quarterly, 47,* 673-683.

Toffler, A. (1971). *Future shock.* New York: Bantam.

Toffler, A. (1980). *The third wave.* New York: William Morrow.

Toll, R. (1976). *On with the show: The first century of show business in America.* Oxford: Oxford University Press.

Toll, R. (1982). *The entertainment machine: American show business in the twentieth century.* Oxford: Oxford University Press.

Tomita, T. (1975). The volume of information flow and the quantum evaluation of media. *Telecommunications, 42,* 339.

Touraine, A. (1971). *The post-industrial society, tomorrow's social history: Classes, conflicts, and culture in the programmed society.* New York: Random House.

Toynbee, A. (1920). *Lectures on the industrial revolution of the eighteenth century in England: Popular addresses, notes, and other fragments.* London: Longmans, Green. (Original work published 1884)

Tuchman, G. (1974). Introduction. In G. Tuchman (Ed.), *The TV establishment* (pp. 1-40). Englewood Cliffs, NJ: Prentice-Hall.

Tuchman, G. (1978). *Making news: A study in the construction of reality.* New York: Free Press.

Turner, C. F., & Martin, E. (Eds). (1985). *Surveying subjective phenomenon.* New York: Russell Sage.

Turner, R. H., Nigg, J. M., Paz, D. H., & Young, B. S. (1980). *Community response to earthquake threat in Southern California.* Los Angeles: University of California Institute for Social Science Research.

Turner, R. H., Nigg, J. M., & Paz, D. H. (in press). *Waiting for disaster: Earthquake watching in Southern California.* Berkeley: University of California Press.

Tylor, E. B. (1958). *Primitive culture.* New York: Harper. (Original work published 1871)

U.S. Bureau of the Census. (1942-1952). *Statistical abstracts of the United States.* Washington, DC: Government Printing Office.

U.S. Bureau of the Census. (1975). *Historical statistics of the United States, colonial times to 1970* (Bicentennial ed., part 1). Washington, DC: Government Printing Office.

U.S. Department of Justice. (1936). *Proceedings of the attorney general's conference on crime.* Washington, DC: Government Printing Office.

U.S. Department of Justice. (1940). *U.S. v. Paramount Pictures, Inc., et al.,* S.D.NY, Amended and supplemental complaint.

U.S. Department of State. (1946, May 3). Letters, J. M. Begg to [major company presidents]. 811.42700 (F)/5-346, RG 59. Washington, DC: National Archives.

U.S. Department of State. (1947, September 8). Telegram, Marschall, Department of State to American Legation, Dublin. 811.4061 MP/8-1147, RG 59, NA.

U.S. Department of State. (1948a, circa April 1). Memo, Sandor Fodor [MPEA] to American Legation, Budapest. 811.4061 MP/4-148, RG 59, NA.

U.S. Department of State. (1948b, June 8). Letter, W. L. Thorp to Eric Johnston. 811.4061 MP/6-848, RG 59, NA.

U.S. House, Special Committee on Postwar Economic Policy and Planning. (1947). *Postwar economic policy and planning, Part 9: Export of information media, both government and private* (Hearings, 79th Congress, 1st and 2nd Sessions, December 20, 1946). Washington, DC: Government Printing Office.

U.S. Office of Censorship. (1943). File: *Shipping date of disapproved films, July-September 1943.* Box 570, Entry 12E/1, RG 216, NA.

U.S. Office of Censorship. (1944). File: *Showing of disapproved films at foreign points, February 1943 to March 1944.* Box 570, Entry 12E/1, RG 216, NA.

U.S. Office of Censorship. (1945a). File: *Disapproved: August 1942-April 1945.* Box 570, Entry 12E/1, RG 216, NA.

U.S. Office of Censorship. (1945b). File: *Form OC 77, NY Board of Review, March 1943 to May 1945.* Box 570, Entry 12E/1, RG 216, NA.

U.S. Office of Censorship. (1946). *A history of the Office of Censorship [1941-1945], IV.* RG 216, NA.

U.S. Office of War Information, Domestic Branch, Bureau of Motion Pictures. (1942). *Two Mrs. Carrolls."* Box 3514, Entry 567, RG 208. WNRC.

U.S. Office of War Information. (1945b, June 7). Memorandum, Cunningham to Barnard. File: *"Chief's office."* Box 3509, Entry 566, RG 208, WNRC.

U.S. Office of War Information. (1945c, September 18). Report of activities, 1942-1945. File: *History-Miscellaneous Divisions.* Box 65, Entry 6, RG 208,WNRC.

U.S. Office of War Information, Domestic Branch, Bureau of Motion Pictures. (1942). *Government information manual for the motion picture industry.* File: Hollywood Information Manual, Box 1517, Entry 285, RG 208. Suitland, MD: National Records Center.

U.S. Office of War Information, Overseas Branch, Bureau of Motion Pictures. (1944, October). Survey of films viewed in the year September 15, 1943 to September 15, 1944. File: *Inventory of feature pix, August 1944.* Box 3509, Entry 566, RG 208, WNRC.

U.S. Senate, Subcommittee of the Committee on Interstate Commerce. (1942). *Propaganda in motion pictures* (Hearings, 77th Congress, 1st Session, on S. Res. 152, September 9-26). Washington, DC: Government Printing Office.

U.S. Senate, Temporary National Economic Committee. (1941). *Investigation of concentration of economic power: The motion picture industry—a pattern of control* (Monograph No. 43, 76th Congress, 3rd Session). Washington, DC: Government Printing Office.

Value Survey (1982). Halgren Tests. N. E. 1145 Clifford, Pullman, WA 99163.

Van den Ban, A. W. (1962). A revision of the two-step flow of communication hypothesis. *Gazette, 10,* 237-249.

Vermeersch, E. (1977). An analysis of the concept of culture. In B. Bernardi (Ed.), *The concept and dynamics of culture* (pp. 9-73). The Hague: Mouton.

Vincent, T. (1981). *Mudville's revenge: The rise and fall of American sport.* New York: Seabury.

Wade, J. (1833). *History of the middle and working classes.* London: E. Wilson.

Wade, J. (1835). *History of the middle and working classes.* (3rd. ed.). London: E. Wilson.

Warner Brothers Studio Records. (1946). Appendix to brief for the Warner defendants, *U.S. vs. Paramount Pictures et al.,* Exhibit W-5, p. 3: *Total film rentals received from domestic and foreign, circa 1946.* Warner Brothers Legal Department Files, Theater Collection, Firestone Library, Princeton University.

Warner Brothers Studio Records. (1950). *Catalog of classified story resumes, circa January 1950.* Los Angeles: University of Southern California, Robert Sisk Collection, Archives of Performing Arts, University Library.

Warner Brothers Studio Records. (1958). Senate Small Business Committee, L. Philips-White paper, 1958. Box 12777, File: *Television and corporate files.* Warner Brothers Legal Department Files, Theater Collection, Firestone Library, Princeton University.

Warshow, R. (1948). The gangster as tragic hero. *Partisan Review, 15,* 240-244.

Wasko, J. (1982). *Movies and money: Financing the American film industry.* Norwood, NJ: Ablex.

Watt, I. (1957). *The rise of the novel: Studies in Defoe, Richardson and Fielding.* Berkeley: University of California Press.

Weaver, W. R. (1943, July 3). Studios headed for cycle of juvenile vandals. *Motion Picture Herald,* p. 31.

Weber, M. (1968). *Economy and society: An outline of interpretive sociology* (3 vols., G. Roth & C. Wittich, Eds.). New York: Bedminster. (Original work published 1922)

Weber, R. P. (1981). Society and economy in the Western world system. *Social Forces, 59,* 1130-1148.

Weber, R. P. (1984). Content-analytic cultural indicators. In G. Melischek, K. E. Rosengren, & J. Stappers (Eds.), *Cultural indicators: An international symposium* (pp. 301-314). Vienna: Akademie der Wissenschaften.

Weigel, R. H., & Pappas, J. J. (1981). Social science and the press. *American Psychologist, 36,* 480-487.

Weiss, C., Singer, E., & Endreny, P. (in press). *Social science in the media.*

Weiss, P. (1969). *Sport: A philosophic inquiry.* Carbondale: Southern Illinois University Press.

White, R. K. (1951). *Value analysis: The nature and use of the method.* New York: Society for the Study of Social Issues.

Whitney, S. (1958). *Antitrust policies: American experience in twenty industries.* New York: Twentieth Century Fund.

Whyte, W. H., Jr. (1956). *The organization man.* New York: Simon & Schuster.

Wicking, C. (1981). Thrillers. In D. Pirie (Ed.), *Anatomy of movies* (pp. 220-231). New York: Macmillan.

Wiener, N. (1948). *Cybernetics: Or control and communication in the animal and the machine.* Cambridge: MIT Press.

Wiener, N. (1961). *Cybernetics: Or control and communication in the animal and the machine* (2nd ed.). Cambridge: MIT Press.

Wilensky, H. L. (1964). Mass society and mass culture: Interdependence or dependence. *American Sociological Review, 29,* 173-197.

Wiley, M. M., & Rice, S. A. (1933). The agencies of communication. In W. F. Ogburn (Ed.), *Recent social trends* (pp. 167-217). New York: McGraw-Hill.

Williams, R. (1975). *Television: Technology and cultural form.* New York: Schocken.

Williams, R. (1977). *Marxism and literature.* Oxford: Oxford University Press.

Wilson, E. B., Jr. (1952). *An introduction to scientific research.* New York: McGraw-Hill.

Wilson, G. B. (1966). *A history of American acting.* Westport, CT: Greenwood.

Windahl, S., Hedinisson, E., & Hojerback, J. (1984). *Adolescents without TV: A study of media deprivation* (media panel report No. 13). Lund, Sweden: University of Lund, Department of Sociology.

Winner, L. (1977). *Autonomous technology: Technics-out-of-control as a theme in political thought.* Cambridge: MIT Press.

Wober, J. M. (1984). Prophecy and prophylaxis: Predicted harms and their absence in a regulated television system. In G. Melischek, K. E. Rosengren, & J. Stappers (Eds.), *Cultural indicators: An international symposium* (pp. 423-440). Vienna: Akademie der Wissenschaften.

Wolfe, G. R. (1975). *New York: A guide to the metropolis.* New York: McGraw-Hill.

Wright, C. R. (1959). *Mass communication: A sociological perspective.* New York: Random House.

Wright, C. R. (1960). Functional analysis and mass communication. *Public Opinion Quarterly, 24,* 605-620.

Wright, C. R. (1975). Social structure and mass communication behavior. In L. Coser (Ed.), *The idea of social structure: Papers in honor of Robert K. Merton.* New York: Harcourt Brace Janovich.

Wright, C. R. (1985). *Mass communication: A sociological perspective* (3rd ed.). New York: Random House.

Wright, R. L. (1984). Personal correspondence, January 26, February 19.

Yinger, J. M. (1977). Presidential address: Countercultures and social change. *American Sociological Review, 42,* 833-853.

York, P. (1978). The post-punk mortem: Harpers & Queen, 1977. In *Style wars* (pp. 129-144). Salem, NH: Merrimack.

Young, M. (1961). *The rise of meritocracy 1870-1933: An essay on education and equality.* Harmondsworth, England: Penguin. (Original work published 1958)

Zelditch, M., Jr. (1955). Role differentiation in the nuclear family: A comparative study. In T. Parsons & R. F. Bales (Eds.), *Family: Socialization and interaction process.* New York: Free Press.

Zuckerman, H., & Merton, R. K. (1971). Patterns of evaluation in science: Institutionalization, structure, and functions of the referee system. *Minerva, 9,* 66-100.

NAME INDEX

SUBJECT INDEX

ABOUT THE CONTRIBUTORS

Jeffrey C. Alexander is Professor of Sociology at the University of California, Los Angeles. He has written *Theoretical Logic in Sociology* (4 volumes), *Twenty Lectures: Sociological Theory since World War II* and *Structure and Meaning: Essays in Sociological Theory* (both forthcoming, Columbia University Press), and edited *Neofunctionalism* (Sage, 1985) and, with Giesen, Münch, and Smelser, *The Micro-Macro Link* (forthcoming, University of California Press). Past Chair of the Theory Section of the American Sociological Association, he is currently (1985-1986) a Fellow at The Institute for Advanced Studies in Princeton, New Jersey. His research on Watergate was facilitated by fellowships from the Guggenheim and Ford Foundations.

Sandra J. Ball-Rokeach is Professor of Sociology at Washington State University and, at present, a Visiting Professor at the Annenberg School of Communications at the University of Southern California. She received her Ph.D. in 1968 from the University of Washington. Her previous works include *Violence and the Media* (1969), *Theories of Mass Communication* (1982), and numerous journal articles on the subjects of media system dependency, theory, and research, interpersonal and collective violence, social change, and ambiguity. Her most recent book is *The Great American Values Test: Influencing Behavior and Belief Through Television* (with M. Rokeach and J. W. Grube, Free Press, 1984). Ball-Rokeach has been a Fulbright Scholar at the Communications Institute of Hebrew University and a Rockefeller Fellow at the Bellagio Study Center in Bellagio, Italy.

James R. Beniger is Associate Professor at the Annenberg School of Communications, University of Southern California. He is a member of the editorial board of *Public Opinion Quarterly* and the Board of Overseers of the General Social Survey, NORC, Chicago. For the past eight years he has taught sociology and statistics at Princeton University, where he helped to establish an undergraduate communications program. His second book, *The Control Revolution*, is an elaboration of ideas presented in his contribution to this volume. A graduate of Harvard University in history, he has an M.S. in statistics and a Ph.D. in sociology from the University of California, Berkeley.

Victoria Billings is a graduate student in the Department of Sociology at the University of California at Los Angeles. Her recent articles include "Why Pornography? Models of Functions and Effects," with Neil M.

Malamuth in the Journal of Communication. She is working on her dissertation, entitled, "Making Demands: Female Enterprise and the Expansion of the Service Sector of the Economy."

Joel M. Cantor (M.A., anthropology, American University; Ph.D., psychology, University of Minnesota) consults in the areas of cross-cultural counseling and communications.

Muriel G. Cantor received her Ph.D. in sociology from the University of California, Los Angeles and is currently Professor of Sociology at the American University, Washington, DC. Her published works have appeared in *Communication Research, Journal of Communication, Journalism Quarterly,* and several collections of readings. Her dissertation was later published as *The Hollywood TV Producer*; other books include *Prime-Time Television* and *The Soap Opera.* Cantor has been a consultant for the Corporation for Public Broadcasting, the National Institute of Mental Health, the U.S. Office of Education, and the National Organization for Women. In addition, she contributed to the Report to the Surgeon General on Television and Social Behavior in 1972 and to the update of that report, *Television and Behavior* (1982).

Ithiel de Sola Pool was Ruth and Arthur Sloan Professor of Political Science and founder and director of the Research Program on Communications Policy at Massachusetts Institute of Technology until his death.

Don A. Dillman is Director of the Social and Economic Sciences Research Center and Professor of Sociology and Rural Sociology at Washington State University in Pullman. He is widely known for his book, *Mail and Telephone Surveys: The Total Design Method* (John Wiley, 1978). His research interests are in the improvement of survey methods and the impact of information technologies on human behavior. He is a past president of the Rural Sociological Society.

Phyllis Endreny is Assistant Professor in Mass Communication at the University of Illinois at Chicago. She received her M.A. and Ph.D. in sociology from Columbia University. She is currently collaborating with Eleanor Singer on a study of the reporting of risk in the mass media. She is the author of *Pictorial Communication with Illiterates: An Introductory Investigation of the Issues* (a Ford Foundation study for the Population Resources Center, 1978) and an article entitled, "How the Times and CBS Report Their Own Polls," published in *Journalism Quarterly* in 1982.

Edward L. Fink (Ph.D., University of Wisconsin—Madison) is Associate Professor of Communication Arts and Theatre at the University of Maryland. His research interests involve the measurement and modeling of cognition and attitude change, interpersonal communication, and issues in theory construction and data analysis. His work has been published in *Human Communication Research, Sociological Methods and Research, Journal of Experimental Social Psychology, Behavioral Science, Communication Monographs,* and *Communication Yearbooks* 6, 7, 8, 9, and 10. He is also coauthor (with J. Woelfel) of *The Measurement of Communication Processes.*

Herman Gray is Assistant Professor at Northeastern University in Boston, Massachusetts. His current research interests focus on the ideological impact of minority representations and the treatment of racial inequality in entertainment and news media, alternative media and cultural organizations, and the social circumstances surrounding the social production of avant garde jazz.

Joel W. Grube is a Postdoctoral Research Fellow at the School of Public Health, University of California, Berkeley. Previously he was Senior Research Officer at the Economic and Social Research Institute in Dublin, Ireland and Assistant Director of the Social Research Center, Washington State University. He received his Ph.D. from Washington State University in 1979, specializing in social psychology. His current research interests include values and attitudes, value and attitude change, and adolescent smoking, drinking, and other drug use. He coauthored *The Great American Values Test: Influencing Behavior and Belief Through Television* (with S. J. Ball-Rokeach and M. Rokeach) and has published extensively in his areas of interest.

Peter L. Hirschburg received his Ph.D. in sociology from Washington State University and is Assistant Professor of Sociology at Southeast Missouri State University. He is currently analyzing data from a social impact study of the eruption of Mount St. Helens. Previous writing has been in the area of deviant behavior.

Robert Kapsis teaches sociology of film and mass communications in the Department of Sociology and Film Studies at Queens College of the City University of New York. Since 1981 he has been conducting research in Hollywood on genre filmmaking and how industry organizational factors influence film aesthetics. Dr. Kapsis is currently working under a fellowship from the National Endowment for the Humanities to complete a book on how marketing practices shape the production of

Hollywood feature films and the reputation of filmmakers. He is also engaged in a study of Alfred Hitchcock that will focus on how Hitchcock used publicity to reshape his reputation among influential members of the American and international film world.

Philip Lamy is working toward his Ph.D. in the Department of Sociology and Anthropology at Northeastern University, Boston. His areas of specialization include mass communications and the media, social movements, and popular culture.

Gladys Engel Lang holds a B.A. degree from the University of Michigan, an M.A. from the University of Washington, and a Ph.D. from the University of Chicago. For a number of years on the faculty at Stony Brook, she is currently Professor of Communications, with joint appointments in Political Science and Sociology, at the University of Washington. She has taught at a number of other academic institutions, including Columbia University, Queens College, and Carleton University in Ottawa, and held research posts with a number of governmental and quasi-governmental agencies, including the Office of War Information, the Office of Strategic Services, and the Center for Urban Education in New York City.

Kurt Lang, who is on the faculty at the University of Washington as Director, School of Communications, was Professor of Sociology and Political Science at Stony Brook for many years. His B.A., M.A., and Ph.D. are from the University of Chicago. After military service in World War II, he worked as public opinion and media analyst for the U.S. Office of Military Government for Germany and, during the 1950s, as research sociologist for the Canadian Broadcasting Corporation. He is the author of *Military Institutions and the Sociology of War*.

Jack Levin is a Professor in the Department of Sociology and Anthropology at Northeastern University, Boston. He is the author and coauthor of numerous books and articles, including *Mass Murder: America's Growing Menace* (with James Fox, 1985) and *Prejudice and Discrimination* (with William Levin, 1983). His areas of specialization include mass communications, the sociology of youth, and social psychology.

Thelma McCormack is a Professor of Sociology at York University in Canada, President of the Canadian Sociology and Anthropology Association, and Distinguished Chair in Women's Studies at Mount St. Vincent University in Halifax. Her recent work, emerging from the feminist colloquy on pornography, has been to develop a feminist understanding of civil liberties. A recent publication, "Blood Libel," is a discussion of the Sharon trial and the media. An American expatriate, now a Canadian citizen, she has been active in the women's movement in Canada and other just causes.

Kathryn Montgomery, formerly Director of Broadcasting, California State University, Los Angeles, is now an Assistant Professor in the Department of Theater, Film and Television at the University of California, Los Angeles. She is the author of a book on advocacy groups and network entertainment television entitled *Target: Prime Time* (Annenberg Oxford Communication Series, Oxford University Press).

W. Russell Neuman is Associate Professor of Political Science at Massachusetts Institute of Technology and Director of the Research Program on Communications Policy. He is currently conducting research on the impact of new communications media on politics and culture. His book, *The Paradox of Mass Politics*, will be published by Harvard University Press in 1986.

James J. Parker recently completed his thesis in sociology at the University of Colorado and is currently a postdoctoral fellow in both the Department of Sociology and the Institution for Social and Policy Studies, Yale University. He has written extensively on the relations among media organizations, media audiences, and media content. Recent papers include "Motion Picture Portrayals of Murder and Madness and Their Implications for the Mentally Ill," "The Social Control of Juvenile Delinquency Portrayals in American Motion Pictures, 1930-1955," and "Military Madmen in American Movies."

Denise H. Paz is Research Sociologist, Veterans Administration Medical Center, West Los Angeles, California. She is involved in research on social support systems of schizophrenic patients, as well as studies evaluating the effects of treatment on patients with different psychiatric diagnoses. In addition to her book with Ralph H. Turner (1986), she coauthored "Ethnicity and Reporting of Schizophrenic Symptoms" (1985) in the *Journal of Nervous and Mental Disease*.

Andrea L. Press is an Instructor at Florida Atlantic University in Boca Raton, Florida, in the Communication Department. She is completing her dissertation, entitled "Women's Changing Ideologies in Relation to Changing Media Images," in the Sociology Department at U.C. Berkeley. She has taught women's studies and sociology at U.C. Berkeley, U.C. Davis, and San Jose State University.

Melissa Rapp lives in San Francisco and is interested in American culture.

John P. Robinson is Professor of Sociology and Director of the Survey Research Center at the University of Maryland. Dr. Robinson's compilation of reference books on attitudes, *Measures of Political Attitudes* and *Measures of Social Psychological Attitudes*, integrated empirical information on measures and psychometric criteria of reliability and validity. He has also acted as research coordinator for the U.S. Surgeon General's study of television and human behavior and as a research consultant for the News Division of the British Broadcasting Corporation. He is the author of *How Americans Use Time* and *Polls Apart*.

Milton Rokeach received his Ph.D. from the University of California at Berkeley. He is the author of numerous journal and encyclopedia articles, and *The Open and Closed Mind, The Three Christs of Ypsilanti, Beliefs, Attitudes and Values*, and *The Nature of Human Values*. His most recent book, coauthored with S.J. Ball-Rokeach and J.W. Grube, is *The Great American Values Test: Influencing Behavior and Belief Through Television*. Rokeach is currently Professor of Sociology and Psychology and Director of the Unit on Human Values at Washington State University. His recent honors include the Kurt Lewin Memorial Award and an honorary degree from the University of Paris.

Karl Erik Rosengren is a professor in the Unit of Mass Communication at the University of Gothenburg. He has published several books and articles on the sociology of culture and communication.

Michael Schudson is Professor of Sociology and Communication at the University of California, San Diego. He is the author of *Discovering the News: A Social History of American Newspapers* (Basic Books, 1978) and *Advertising, the Uneasy Persuasion: Its Dubious Impact on American Society* (Basic Books, 1984). He has published numerous reviews and articles on media and the sociology of culture. In 1985 he was a fellow at the Gannett Center for Media Studies.

John L. Sewart has published numerous articles in the areas of contemporary social theory and sport sociology. He is currently on the editorial boards of the *Journal of Sport and Social Issues*, the *Social Science Journal*, and *Current Perspectives in Social Theory: A Research Annual*. His most recent work has been an analysis of professional wrestling.

Eleanor Singer is a Senior Research Scholar at the Center for the Social Sciences, Columbia University, and editor of the *Public Opinion Quarterly*. She is currently working on a study of the reporting of risks, which is also funded by the Russell Sage Foundation.

Yasemin Soysal is a doctoral candidate in sociology at Stanford University. She studies international flows of television programming and problems of development.

Ann Swidler is Assistant Professor of Sociology at Stanford University. She is author of *Organization without Authority* (1979) and coauthor of *Habits of the Heart* (1985). She does research on love in American culture and on innovation in television programming.

D. Garth Taylor is Assistant Professor of Political Science at the University of Chicago. His chapter in this book is based on the analysis in his forthcoming book, *Public Opinion and Collective Action* (University of Chicago Press, 1986). He is the author of numerous works on American racial politics and racial change in American cities, including *Paths of Neighborhood Change* (University of Chicago Press, 1984).

Ralph H. Turner is Professor of Sociology at the University of California, Los Angeles. He was recently Chair of the American Sociological Association Section on Collective Behavior and Social Movements, and was awarded the UCLA College of Letters and Sciences Faculty Prize for 1985. With Lewis Killian, he is author of *Collective Behavior* (Prentice-Hall), with a third edition now in press. Turner and Paz, with Joanne Nigg, have recently published *Waiting for Disaster: Earthquake Watch in California* (University of California Press).

Charles R. Wright is Professor of Communications and Sociology at the University of Pennsylvania, where he is a member of the Annenberg School of Communications and of the Department of Sociology in the School of Arts and Sciences. His recent publications include the third edition of *Mass Communication: A Sociological Perspective* (Random House, 1985) and an examination of national survey data on media behavior of the aged, "Social Surveys and the Use of Mass Media: The Case of the Aged" (1985). He is the author of various papers on mass communication behavior, functional theory, and mass communication, and coauthor (with Herbert H. Hyman) of *Education's Lasting Influence on Values, The Enduring Effects of Education*, and other sociological studies.